*Class Act*

# Class Act

*The Cultural and Political Life
of Ewan MacColl*

BEN HARKER

Pluto Press

LONDON • ANN ARBOR, MI

First published 2007 by Pluto Press
345 Archway Road, London N6 5AA
and 839 Greene Street, Ann Arbor, MI 48106

www.plutobooks.com

Copyright © Ben Harker 2007

The right of Ben Harker to be identified as the author of this work has been asserted
by him in accordance with the Copyright, Designs and Patents Act 1988.

British Library Cataloguing in Publication Data
A catalogue record for this book is available from the British Library

Hardback
ISBN-13   978 0 7453 2166 0
ISBN-10   0 7453 2166 6

Paperback
ISBN-13   978 0 7453 2165 3
ISBN-10   0 7453 2165 8

Library of Congress Cataloging in Publication Data applied for


10   9   8   7   6   5   4   3   2   1


This book is printed on paper suitable for recycling and made from fully managed
and sustained forest sources. Logging, pulping and manufacturing processes are
expected to conform to the environmental regulations of the country of origin.


Designed and produced for Pluto Press by
Chase Publishing Services Ltd, Fortescue, Sidmouth, EX10 9QG, England
Typeset from disk by Stanford DTP Services, Northampton, England
Printed and bound in India

*FOR EMILY*

# Contents

# List of Plates

# Acknowledgements

This book couldn't have been written without the trust and co-operation of Peggy Seeger. I'm extremely grateful to her for being so generous with her time, memories, personal papers and address book, and for enduring my intrusions with such good humour. Sincere thanks also to Jean Newlove/MacColl for her hospitality and input, and to Calum, Hamish, Kitty and Neill MacColl for all their help.

Many of Ewan MacColl's friends, comrades, acquaintances and adversaries freely shared their recollections and opinions. Thanks especially to the late Clive Barker for a memorable day in Sidcup, and to Pam Bishop, Bob Blair, Janey Buchan, Jim Carroll, Karl Dallas, John Faulkner, Mike Faulkner, Ruth Frow, Vic Gammon, Howard Goorney, Wizz Jones, Sandra Kerr, Doris Lessing, Gordon McCulloch, Pat Mackenzie, Murray Melvin, Hugh Paterson, Michael Rosen, Arthur Scargill, Joan Williams and Rosalie Williams. A special thanks to Bob Blair for all the help with audio resources, and to Fred McCormick who kindly lent me rare radio recordings. Chris Birch responded to an appeal in the *Morning Star* and helped to chase up a number of MacColl's former Communist Party comrades: I'm indebted to him. Thanks also to Graham Stevenson for sharing his encyclopaedic knowledge of the Communist Party's history and cultural policies, and to Eddie McGuire who helped with Scottish material.

I'm grateful to Vic Gammon and Alun Howkins for supporting a funding application, and to the British Academy for awarding a generous Small Grant to assist with crucial periods of research. Dr Nadine Holdsworth at Warwick University has been extremely open-handed with her expertise on Theatre Workshop and Joan Littlewood; Claire Altree of Edinburgh University helped me out with playscripts. The interest and encouragement of my former colleagues at the University of York, especially Derek Attridge, Hugh Haughton and Geoff Wall, meant more than any of them realised. I'm also very grateful to new colleagues at the University of Salford for giving me the time and space to complete the book. Thanks are also due to Veronique Baxter at David Higham Associates for all her excellent work in the early stages, and to Anne Beech, my commissioning editor at Pluto, for her confidence throughout.

This book couldn't have been written without the professionalism and commitment of countless librarians and archivists. Thanks especially to Chris Keable, David Horsfield, Val Horsfield, Valerie Moyses and Elizabeth Schlackman at Ruskin College Oxford (home of the Ewan MacColl and Peggy Seeger Archive); to Alain Kahan at the Working Class Movement Library, Salford; to Murray Melvin and Mary Ling at the Theatre Royal, Stratford East, London; and to Malcolm Taylor, Peta Webb and Elaine Bradtke at the Vaughan Williams Memorial Library in London. I'm also very grateful to staff at the Charles Parker Archive in Birmingham, the BBC Written Archives in Caversham, the Labour History Archive and Study Centre in Manchester, the National Library of Scotland, the British Library, Manchester Central Library and the J. B. Morrell Library in York. Thanks to Peter Rankin and the BBC for permission to quote material, and to Jean Newlove/MacColl for permission to quote from MacColl's plays. Thanks to Peggy Seeger and publishers EMI, Harmony and Stormking Music to quote copyrighted lyrics, and to The Estate of Ewan MacColl to quote from previously unpublished MacColl writings (© 2007, The Estate of Ewan MacColl). Unless otherwise indicated, all photographs are from the MacColl family collection; I'm especially grateful to Kitty MacColl for all her help with these. Thanks to Brian Shuel for granting permission to reproduce one of his photographs, and to Peter Outhart for sharing items from his collection.

In the course of my research for this book, many good friends in London, Manchester, Oxford, Edinburgh and beyond perhaps saw me more often than they'd have liked. Thanks to the four Leatherdales of Camberley, to Roland Birchby for always finding me a bed at Ruskin College, and to Julie Crofts, Roger Luckhurst, Cari Morningstar, Jason Smith, Kirby Swales, Emma Horn, Kate Davies, Tom Barr, Marie Crook and Douglas Field.

Special thanks to Laura Chrisman, Geoff Wall, Marie Crook and Douglas Field for reading sections of the manuscript, and for providing such constructive and illuminating criticism. Many thanks also to Janet and Kate Harker, Douglas Weygang and Judy Weygang for all their support, and to Banjo Weygang for the company and daily constitutional. Above all thanks to Emily Weygang who has aided and abetted at every single stage. Without her unstinting emotional, practical, financial and intellectual support, writing this book would have been a lonely affair.

# Prologue
## *Minstrel of Labour*

Monday 21 January 1985 was a cold, grey and drizzly day. Everton were top of League Division One and Band Aid's 'Do They Know It's Christmas?' had finally been dislodged from the top of the pop charts. The *Guardian* cost 23p and reported on a country gripped by industrial and political strife. The National Union of Mineworkers was currently in the forty-seventh week of Britain's bitterest industrial dispute since the General Strike. Almost two thousand striking miners returned to work that day; sensing victory, Prime Minister Margaret Thatcher would become increasingly bullish in the week ahead.[1] Ken Livingstone, leader of the soon to be dissolved 'loony left' Greater London Council, captured his share of column inches by urging political activists and trade unionists to occupy town halls in defiance of the government's rate-capping measures. Thirteen British women from the Greenham Common Peace Camp began appeal court proceedings against the American government's installation of Cruise Missiles on British soil.[2] And two thousand people converged at the Greater London Council's Royal Festival Hall to attend a sell-out concert celebrating Ewan MacColl's seventieth birthday.[3]

In the foyer were collection buckets and stalls with petitions, newspapers, pamphlets, books and records. The concert programme advertised holidays in the Soviet Union, the GDR, Cuba and 'beautiful Bulgaria', the latter with a concessionary rate for the over fifty-fives.[4] The audience was a motley crew, and their diversity reflected MacColl's life and career. Salfordians he hadn't seen for fifty years sat next to former colleagues from his Theatre Workshop and BBC radio days. Friends and fans from the world of folk music were in abundance. Many of those present, including concert organisers Karl Dallas and Bruce Dunnet, had been in the Communist Party with MacColl (well-schooled

1

in party discipline and punctuality, they'd scheduled the concert to start at 7.25). Some knew MacColl from his Maoist days of the 1960s, some from political campaigns such as the 1930s National Unemployed Workers' Movement, the Mass Trespass of 1932, the Aldermaston Marches, the Anti-Apartheid Movement and the opposition to war in Vietnam. There were busloads of striking miners from the Yorkshire coalfields. The most prominent celebrities were not musicians but trade unionists and politicians: Norman Willis, General Secretary of the TUC; Jack Jones, former leader of the Transport Workers' Union; Norman Buchan, currently Shadow Arts Minister in Neil Kinnock's Labour opposition; and National Mineworkers' Union leader Arthur Scargill. MacColl had a parsimonious streak and was initially concerned about hiring the Royal Festival Hall for a tribute concert. He'd given the go-ahead only when it was agreed that the evening's primary function would be to raise funds for the striking miners.

Stand-up comedian and singer-songwriter Mike Harding was MC (first choice Billy Connolly hadn't returned the organisers' calls).[5] Harding described himself as the 'Max Boyce of the Left', and scuttled on and off stage cracking jokes and introducing a roster of two-dozen folk acts. Many performers chose songs to illustrate continuity between political struggles of the past and present. Ian Campbell sang a song originally written for the 1961 CND March. Scots Communist folk singer Dick Gaughan performed an updated version of the 1920s American Union song 'Which Side Are You On?' The audience joined in for choruses. They heard traditional ballads, instrumentals, recent political songs and off-the-cuff invective.

∞

On behalf of the folk world, Norman Willis presented MacColl with an Eskimo sculpture (beneath a beaming smile, MacColl looked perplexed). Mike Harding read out a letter from Labour leader Neil Kinnock apologising for his unavoidable absence but extending birthday greetings to 'the minstrel of the working people'. Kinnock's prevarications over the miners' strike hadn't endeared him to the left, and his words were met with muted applause and a muffled boo. Miners' leader Arthur Scargill was greeted with a standing ovation. He now suspected that his strike was lost, but managed a brave face to present an old comrade with a personally engraved miner's lamp. He described first meeting

MacColl thirty years earlier at the Barnsley Young Communist League's Ballads and Blues Club – the very mention of the Young Communist League drew a cheer. He personally thanked MacColl for introducing him to radical folk music. On behalf of the striking mining communities Scargill paid tribute to MacColl's tireless fundraising work that had, Scargill said, not only raised money, but also people's consciousness. (A further £13,000 was raised that night.)[6] 'It's a pleasure and a privilege', he concluded, 'to present this special miner's lamp to someone like Ewan MacColl, who has made an outstanding contribution, not only to folk music, but to the entire working-class movement.'[7]

MacColl had grown more modest over the years and the gushing tributes made him ill at ease – 'whenever anyone got too flowery in their praises', remembers his wife and collaborator Peggy Seeger, 'his head would go down'.[8] But he felt at home in an environment where everyone was speaking his native tongue, the language of class and class struggle. MacColl had joined the Young Communist League aged fourteen in 1929, a moment when the party branded itself 'leaders of the class war in all its forms'.[9] Mass unemployment; protracted industrial dispute; barricaded communities; running battles between militant workers and the forces of the state: the 1980s seemed like a replay of the 1930s that had shaped him. He felt that recent history had vindicated his unswerving political beliefs. The resurgence of visible class struggle – at a time when many on the left were writing its obituary – had a rejuvenating effect on him.[10]

MacColl was always an assured and charismatic performer, but he was especially poised that night. His family was around him: pop-star daughter Kirsty MacColl, eight months pregnant, was in the auditorium. Eldest son Hamish came on stage and sang a song. Thirteen-year-old daughter Kitty, blushing in her best frock, performed a duet with mother Peggy. And flanked by Peggy Seeger on acoustic guitar, banjo and concertina, their two sons Neill and Calum on guitars, and a guest appearance from the communist jazz clarinettist Bruce Turner, MacColl handsomely confirmed his status as the doyen of political folk music. Bespectacled, hair immaculately parted and beard neatly trimmed, he adopted his characteristic stage posture – sitting upright on a back-to-front chair, one hand cupping his ear – and sang half a dozen songs from his repertoire. The folk material was presented with a romantic reverence that hadn't faded over the years: he introduced

'The Burning O' Auchendon' as an example of 'the high water mark of working-class creation'. He knew what the crowd wanted to hear: though he made a show of forgetting its title, he dutifully performed 'Dirty Old Town', a widely covered MacColl composition that had been helping to pay the bills for years. He gently chastised the audience for wasting valuable time clapping too much; he dedicated two new songs to the miners' wives from the Nottingham coalfield who had made the journey down to London. Tightly crafted and savagely satirical, 'The Media' and 'Daddy, What Did You Do in the Strike?' demonstrated that none of MacColl's powers as a political songwriter had deserted him. He was reluctant to say much while on stage – he said he would rather be singing – but he did manage one rhetorical flourish. 'It's no hardship', he said, 'for any artist from the ranks of the working class to devote his or her life in defence of the rights that the class have won for themselves, and all humanity.'

# 1
# *Lower Broughton*

When he reached his thirties and forties he'd form the habit of refashioning the facts of his biography. In 1945 he'd jettison his real name and start to call himself Ewan MacColl. Occasionally he'd shave a couple of years off his age. By 1950 he'd consistently claim to have be born in Auchterarder, Perthshire, the location of his mother's birth and childhood. But it was in Lower Broughton, Salford, not Scotland, that on Burns Night, 25 January 1915, the child later christened as James Henry Miller was born.

He entered the world at 4 Andrew Street, a two-up-two-down Victorian terrace where his parents rented rooms from a fellow Scot. He was named James after his mother's father and Henry after Hendry, her maiden name. Almost instantly he became 'Jimmie', which was always spelt the Scottish way. For his whole life he'd be pulled between a Scottishness he felt but could never fully claim, and a begrudging identification with what Friedrich Engels described in *The Condition of the Working Class in England* as a 'very unwholesome, dirty and ruinous locality'.[1] 'My relationship with Salford', he'd say in a television interview many years later, 'has been a love-hate one. I can't bear the place ... at the same time, everything I do, everything I've ever written, is to some extent informed by my experiences in Salford.'[2]

CŊ℘

The topography of Lower Broughton hadn't changed radically since the 1840s when Engels had conducted his conspectus of the archetypal industrial slum.[3] Jimmie's father, Will Miller, hated the place. His mother Betsy later recalled first seeing their future home through the sleet and fog from Victoria Station, Manchester. She felt sickened with fear and remembered thinking, 'this is a terrible place …. Little streets. I hated them and the dirt and squalor and smoke and filth of every kind.'[4] She never revised her opinion.

Betsy Hendry had been born in 1886, the sixth of ten girls in a family of fourteen, and grew up in the Scottish countryside with her tartan-weaver mother and a heavy-drinking, jack-of-all-trades father whose skills included weaving tweed and barbering. Family folklore always claimed that he was a likeable and easy-going drunk forever ruined by a sudden, thoroughgoing conversion to fanatical teetotalism.[5] On leaving school Betsy went into service before moving to Falkirk, Sterlingshire, where she took a job in a pawnshop. It was here she met her husband-to-be, William or Will Miller, a roguish local iron moulder with a parallel life as 'Wally MacPherson, a Fellow of Infinite Jest', a semi-professional pub and music hall singer.[6] They met when Willie pawned a gold medal won in a singing competition. He was 'shabby looking', Betsy later remembered. 'I wouldn't let you walk home with me,' she told him flirtatiously, 'only it's dark.'[7] He gave himself a makeover. The next time he showed up he was transformed, dapper in gleaming shoes and his best navy suit. Her mother had a soft spot for him, as everyone did. The young couple were married a few months later – he was twenty-four, she was twenty-two.

⋈

Throughout their son's Salford childhood, Betsy and Will's brief courtship and early marriage in Scotland was remembered as a sunny era suffused with music and optimism. Betsy would reminisce about summer evening picnics, bike-rides and singalongs in the woods with Will in fine voice and his friend Davey playing the fiddle.[8] She'd recall the affordable and pretty Bonnybridge stone cottage they rented from Will's foundry. As life became grimmer, these memories grew more luminous.[9]

Between their marriage in 1908 and Jimmie's birth in 1915 Betsy had five pregnancies – Jimmie was the only child to survive. Their firstborn child was premature and lived for two days. Two miscarriages followed. They had a son Billy, who died in his third year.[10] In 1910 most of her family left for Australia when a spot was found on a younger sister's lung. Her husband Will joined them for six months – doctors suggested that a different climate might relieve his chronic asthma. He found work on Cockatoo Island; feeling positive about the future, he began to think in terms of sending for Betsy and emigrating permanently. Billy's death forced his return and he never got back to Australia. Salford wasn't Cockatoo Island and it wasn't where either of them wanted to be, but Betsy's sister had settled there and sent upbeat reports of decent wages and cheap accommodation.[11]

They moved south reluctantly; their alienation seemed to reinforce their Scottishness. A two-volume edition of the complete works of Robert Burns was the centrepiece of their Salford front room. Like their accents, their food remained defiantly Scottish: broth and chappit tatties and mince; stovies, cock-eyed steak, cabbage and ribs.[12] Their social life revolved around other émigré Scots who also observed Scottish traditions, notably three- or four-day Hogmanay parties that MacColl later remembered as 'a feast of singing and good talk'.[13] 'They were exiles', he later wrote in his autobiography, 'and still regarded themselves as visitors rather than settlers in this new land.'[14] They sang their Scottish songs and talked endlessly of Scotland, which became for Jimmie a utopia 'more real in my mind than the place I was living in'.[15] 'I loved their stories,' he recalled; 'they were jewels embellishing my childhood with visions of a magical landscape in which my father and mother walked in a cloud of music ... For a child who had never been out of Salford it was an evocation of paradise.'[16]

CB&O

Will was saved the humiliation of failing an army medical by his skills as an iron moulder; a few months into the Great War he was employed at Hodgkinson's foundry in Pendleton, casting parts for military machinery.[17] Betsy was an endlessly resourceful woman who, like her father, could turn her hand to everything. She could deliver babies or lay out the dead. She worked in a cotton mill and took in washing. Terrified of debt, she began the charring work that would support the family for years. Between five and nine in the morning she'd clean offices in central Manchester; she'd spend the rest of the day cleaning the big houses in Broughton Park. 'If I met the ones that employed me now', she'd say forty years later, 'I'd spit on them. Dirty buggers that they were.'[18]

Shortly after Jimmie's birth the Millers rented a terrace at 37 Coburg Street. It was identical to the place they'd move from, and indistinguishable from most of the accommodation within a two-mile radius. Coburg Street had forty-eight houses and was part of a district penned in by the Irwell to the south and west, Lower Broughton Road to the east, and the tramway to the north – a grid that formed the coordinates of Jimmie's early life.[19] The house would be home to the three Millers and a long roster of lodgers and dogs for the best part of twenty years.

The front room opened on to the street and the kitchen scullery was at the back. There were two upstairs bedrooms and a paved yard and privy behind. Baths were taken in the yard with a hosepipe or in the kitchen with a tin tub – MacColl's earliest memory was watching his mother combing her waist-length auburn hair while washing in the firelight.[20] Betsy cleaned the house obsessively inside and out. She waged an annual campaign against the bed bugs that always infested the street in the summer. 'It isn't easy to live in a constant state of siege, with dirt as the enemy,' MacColl remembered.[21] She'd scour number 37's patch of pavement with a rubbing stone. The deadening anonymity induced by the amorphous slum provoked such defiant assertions of decency and dignity, and she despised 'the lazy English slatterns' who lowered the tone of the street with their filthy, smelly houses.[22] She prided herself that *her* family didn't need the service of the local knocker-up who rattled on the terrace windows to wake slumbering neighbours for work.

CﾃｮﾃｮﾃｮO

Though a socialist who espoused the virtues of egalitarianism, Will Miller was also well aware of his place within working-class Lower Broughton's complex social stratifications: he enjoyed the prestige conferred by his status as a craftsman and wouldn't tolerate the company of unskilled workers. He was a working-class intellectual who'd been radicalised during his apprenticeship, particularly by the oratory of Clydeside schoolteacher and activist John Maclean. Maclean's early teachings on the power of socialist education struck a chord in Will's undernourished but keen mind.[23] Another key influence was the syndicalist vision disseminated through the Socialist Labour Party. Based on the ideas of American socialist Daniel De Leon, a founder of the Industrial Workers of the World, and Irish revolutionary James Connolly, syndicalism argued that craft unions should be restructured into industry-wide unions capable of organising masses of workers. The ultimate goal was to control entire sections of the economy.[24] These two overlapping sets of beliefs – the importance of education and the need for one big union – were the dynamos that drove Will's political activity. '[H]e was a romantic in many respects, ... a revolutionary romantic,' said MacColl, who inherited more from Will than a singing voice.[25] Will sobbed like a child when Lenin died.[26] 'He was boycotted out of every place he worked in,' said Betsy in the early 1960s. 'He was a fighter ... he'd fight for what he thought was right. I'm a bit like that myself, but I put the bread and butter first, because you can't live on wind.'[27]

Though Betsy shared Will's political views – 'I love my own class', she'd often say, 'the working class have been kept in their place long enough' – Will's militancy was the subject of bitter quarrels where she'd berate him for not keeping his head down and mouth shut in the interests of his own family.[28] And it wasn't only strikes and blacklists that kept him from working. Will was always a sickly man whose bronchial asthma deteriorated in the sulphurous slum year on year. In 1925, when Jimmie was ten, his father took a turn for the worse. Betsy always pointed the finger at the Hodgkinson's foundry. 'That was the shop that practically killed him,' she'd say. 'It was a death trap, that place.' 'He collapsed in 1925 and he died in 1947,' she'd say, 'and out of all those years he worked three years and two months.' For most of that period his contribution to the domestic economy was the nine shillings paid through his trade union.[29]

⊰⊱

Will cut a dashing figure through Jimmie's childhood. With his shining dark hair, handsome swarthy face, belly laughter, powerful, tuneful voice and large repertoire of jokes, tales, ballads, folksongs, Rabbie Burns and Harry Lauder numbers, he was the life and soul at Hogmanay parties and would embarrass his son by singing lustily on trams. (MacColl too would later embarrass his own children by singing loudly in public places.) He took his young son on demonstrations – MacColl later recalled sitting on his father's shoulders to hear miners' leader A. J. Cook speak during the General Strike.[30] The TUC's betrayal of the miners during the strike dashed the syndicalist Will's dream of one big union (the defeat of 1984–5 miners' strike would be an equivalent turning point for his son).

When Will first arrived in Salford, he still made the odd singing appearance in clubs and at political socials; but by the mid to late 1920s, Will Miller's all-singing, all-laughing alter-ego, Wally MacPherson, a Fellow of Infinite Jest, seemed a figure from a scarcely remembered dream. There were patches of renewed health and good cheer, but he gradually assumed what MacColl later described as 'the stoop of defeat'. 'Gone was the brisk, purposeful step that I always associated with him. It had been replaced by the low saunter of the permanently unemployed.'[31]

C3&O

MacColl would later remember his childhood as a slum pastoral: he'd unflinchingly recount the unseemliness of life in Lower Broughton: domestic violence; vigilante patrols of distraught women besieging men rumoured to be paedophiles; children drowning in the Irwell; the hushed-up suicides of quiet despair. He'd also recall a childish wonder in a place where older ways and modernity existed side by side. Most deliveries to the street were still made by horse-drawn cart, and local children knew all the horses' names (the vet was ominously known only as The Man Who Kills Horses).[32] Every few weeks the street was filled with the snuffle and squeal of pigs as a local swineherd drove his animals to a nearby slaughterhouse.[33] One day local children found an incongruously exotic snake in the gutter outside Howland's greengrocer – it seemed to have smuggled itself into Lower Broughton via a consignment of bananas.[34] A couple of times a year a bewitching, long-haired songbook seller turned up on the street hawking his wares.[35] Older customs clung on. There was a May Day parade with a maypole adapted from a broom-handle and brightly coloured paper. The girls dressed up, the boys blacked up, songs were sung and pennies extracted from neighbours.[36]

Jimmie collected cigarette cards, rode in electric trams and took trips to the Victoria, a former theatre and variety show venue that smelt of 'urine, disinfectant and dust' and now functioned as a cinema.[37] Here Betsy brought him to see films including D. W. Griffiths' melodrama *Broken Blossoms* (1919). There were picnics on Kersal Moor, street charabancs to Morecombe and occasional holidays in a Blackpool guesthouse.[38] Jimmie qualified for the annual poor children's outing organised by local charities. He later recalled the hysterical excitement with which they set out from Eccles tramcar depot: 'We sang and in between songs we cheered. If a pedestrian waved at us, we cheered. If a dog barked, we cheered. If we passed another tram, we cheered.'[39]

⊙ॐ☉

Will Miller turned to God for solace in his twilight years, but in his John Maclean days he dutifully displayed 'the same antipathy to priests and parsons that some folk show to spiders and snakes'. 'As far as he was concerned', wrote MacColl, 'they were all hypocrites and part of the conspiracy to keep his class in perpetual bondage.'[40] Will took the education of his only child seriously. He found endearments difficult, but instead showered Jimmie with books purchased from a barrow in Pendleton market. The bookshelf in six-year-old Jimmie's back bedroom slowly filled with the novels of Jack London, Upton Sinclair, Frank Norris and Charles Dickens, many of which he wouldn't tackle until his teens.[41] Will assiduously warded off religion, making sure his young son possessed a copy of Darwin's *Origin of Species*.[42]

Will's commitment to secular education dictated that Jimmie should bypass the local Church of England school in favour of a non-denominational council school on nearby Grecian Street (Lower Broughton children are still taught there today). These days it has around 300 pupils; in 1920 it catered for almost three times that number, half of which were the children of East European Jews who arrived in the city between 1875 and 1914 to create the country's largest Jewish community outside London.[43] 'They were distinctly poverty stricken Jews,' MacColl recalled; '[t]heir living conditions were very little different to ours.' The only anti-Semitism he remembers came from teachers.[44]

Jimmie's first day at school was a shock: he never forgot being delivered from a cosseted infancy into what seemed an 'open-topped cage filled with shouting, yelping, screaming, threatening wild animals, who either raced past me as if I wasn't there or who pulled faces at me and taunted me with being a mammy's boy'.[45] Betsy had invested all the dashed hopes of four dead babies into her only surviving son and Jimmie had been protected from such rough children. His initial difficulties in settling at school weren't helped by the long absences forced by the weak constitution he'd inherited from Will. Jimmie stoically endured the usual run of measles, whooping cough, mumps and chickenpox, but he also suffered gastritis brought on by mysterious food allergies, and a bout of diphtheria that led to six weeks in an isolation ward – he remembered waving at his silent parents through a glass screen.[46]

He got used to school, and came to enjoy the new social horizons it opened up, but his academic career was one of resounding underachievement. The feeling of shame is a recurrent theme in his autobiography: 'Children are hopeless conformists,' he wrote; 'they soak up the ideas and opinions of the dominant group in order to increase their chances of survival.'[47] He was ashamed that his mother went cleaning and then ashamed at being disloyal in his shame.[48] He recalls the shame he felt when forced to wear an ill-fitting plum-coloured jacket cast off by one of the households in which Betsy cleaned.[49] He describes the shame brought on by his inability to make progress on the piano that the socially aspirant Betsy had bought for her musical son.[50]

School was for Jimmie a site of endless humiliation. Though most of the children were just as poor, he was especially sensitive to the class prejudice and withering contempt displayed by some of his teachers. One never-ending school year was spent under the guard of a Miss Tate. He never forgot the day she instructed the class to bring to school an apple to be sketched in the weekly drawing lesson. Betsy had no apples and sent Jimmie with an onion instead. '[Miss Tate] never let me forget it for the whole year,' he remembered. 'Little things like that can breed a tremendous sense of humiliation.'[51]

He developed a phobia of school: 'I had become thoroughly cowed, demoralised, incapable of learning anything,' he remembered.[52] At home he was a confident, clever and creative child who was always singing and writing poems: 'you could feel his thoughts in what he wrote', beamed Betsy, forty years later.[53] The schoolroom reduced him to a dullard who couldn't learn his lessons. After emphatically failing the test that filtered out cleverer pupils, the ten-year-old Jimmie was consigned to a mind-numbing elementary school education of reading, writing, woodwork, rudimentary maths and science. He would later show compassion for those who hadn't managed to jump the hoops of formal education and an uneasy mixture of envy and admiration for those who had. He also retained a deep suspicion of state education provision – three of his five children would be privately educated. 'He thought all state schools were like the one he went to,' his son Neill told me, 'where there was one Bunsen Burner for the whole school and the doctor came and took everyone's tonsils out.'[54]

Jimmie never would reconcile his private, precocious erudition with academic attainment; with the exception of one teacher, whom MacColl later described as 'the first really gentle human being to come my way', the staff at Grecian Street simply wouldn't have believed that Miller from Coburg Street was destined for anything other than a life of unskilled labour.[55] It wasn't until he joined the Young Communist League that his intellect and creativity would find a public outlet. In the meantime he idled away what remained of his schooldays with his best friend Izzy Schneider, the son of a Polish-Jewish greengrocer. They rode their bikes on Broughton Road croft and masked their nerves behind narcissistic swagger in front of the Lower Broughton girls on the Sunday night monkey parades;[56] they went to see Al Jolson's *The Singing Fool* (1928) at the Victoria Cinema and Manchester City at their new ground on Maine Road. 'What am I going to do?' he wondered, when his friends started lining up jobs in post offices and paper mills. 'I'm not much good at anything.'[57]

# 2
# *Red Haze*

Fourteen-year-old Jimmie Miller left Grecian Street Elementary School in February 1929. He was slightly built, scrawny and self-conscious about his appearance, particularly his weak chin, big ears and freckles. He was well-read and bright enough to realise how poorly educated he'd been. He was musical, had a prodigious memory for songs and was a natural mimic. Pulled between class-shame and the class-consciousness that his parents had tried to implant, he later remembered spending his early teens with a 'red haze' in front of his eyes.[1] Over the next five years the haze of anger crystallised into the revolutionary political vision that remained with him for the rest of his life.

In terms of job prospects, Jimmie couldn't have left school at a worse time. There were 1,194,000 officially registered as unemployed in Britain in 1927, but 2,500,000 by the end of 1930; in Salford almost one in three adults was out of work as the depression deepened in 1931.[2] Jimmie's brush with the types of work his father did was brief and indecisive. On leaving school he immediately joined the queues at the Albion Street Labour Exchange; two months later he was briefly employed as a labourer in a wire-drawing mill; after lay-offs there, he was moved to the company's general office as a post boy, but within a year he was back at the Labour Exchange.[3] He roamed widely looking for work: he went for jobs as a coal merchant's shoveller and as an asbestos worker in Rochdale. Early one Monday morning he trudged out to Eccles in the hope of getting an usher's job in the new Odeon Cinema – he was greeted with the sight of hundreds of unemployed workers who'd been camped out all night. He eventually found work as office boy for a trade magazine of the ailing textile industry. Three months later the publication went bust.[4]

After another spell on the dole, interspersed with casual work loading cabbages onto a truck, labouring for a slater and working as a market grafter, he secured a motor mechanic apprenticeship.[5] In his later life, MacColl's inability to change a light bulb or rewire a plug was a running joke among his friends and family, and at fourteen he proved singularly ill-suited to working with car engines. Over the years MacColl would become increasingly sensitive to the charge that he was a working-class warrior long divorced from working-class experience, and would use his flair as a raconteur to make the most of his brief foray into manual work. The narrations would become increasingly colourful. He would describe being sacked from jobs for cheeking the foreman and writing satirical poems; his final hours as a motor mechanic were later worked up into a microcosm of class struggle culminating in a punch-up between the principled young militant (Jimmie Miller) and the foreman, a spineless bosses' lackey who bullied his workmates and spent his dinner-hour preying on vulnerable women.[6]

Rather than work, it was unemployment, or at least the huge swathes of time that unemployment created, that had the most effect on Jimmie. Coburg Street was a cheerless place at this time. Will was working only sporadically. Betsy was rising at five and charring for up to eleven hours a day.[7] Cut off from the routines of home and school life, Jimmie spent as little of the day in the house as possible, retreating instead to the Peel Park reading room over the river, which was handy for his three times a week signing-on at Albion Street. Among unemployed workers studying the situations vacant column or snoozing against the radiators, Jimmie expiated for the guilt of unemployment by learning ten new words a day (never confident of pronunciation, he was wary of using them in conversation).[8] He read widely and randomly, tackling John Stuart Mill, Tom Paine, Thomas Hobbes; he later made a start on the Marxist canon, beginning with *The Communist Manifesto*, Engels' *Socialism, Utopian and Scientific*, and Lenin's *State and Revolution*. After struggling with many of these titles he rewarded himself with either American or European modernist literature – James Joyce, D. H. Lawrence, Ezra Pound, Thomas Mann – or European and Russian classics, in particular Honoré de Balzac, Alexander Pushkin, Nikolai Gogol, Anton Chekhov, Maxim Gorky and Fyodor Dostoevsky.[9] 'Books for me weren't tools', he'd later say, 'they were a refuge … unemployment in the 1930s was unbelievable, you really felt you'd

never escape ... through books I was living in many worlds simultaneously.'[10] Before long he was harbouring ambitions to become an author
himself and 'write Balzac' into his own name.[11]

ᎧᏞᏁᎧ

Like the Peel Park reading room, the Workers' Arts Club at 69
Liverpool Street was also crucial in Jimmie's intellectual and political
development. First acquired by the Salford Social-Democratic Land and
Building Society Ltd back in 1903, the rickety three-storey building
with billiard tables, a small dance floor, boxing rings and meeting
rooms was a focal point for social, political and cultural activity in
the Millers' community.[12] In the autumn of 1930 the Salford Workers'
Film Society held its inaugural meeting at the club, and pledged 'to
cater for those who are dissatisfied with the average productions of
the commercial cinema, with their shallowness and their divorce from
reality, and to offer in their stead films more closely in sympathy with
the life and thought of this age'.[13] Despite ongoing battles with the
local censors, the society flourished over the next few years, attracting
an average attendance of 450. Jimmie Miller was at the inaugural
meeting and became one of the society's regular members.[14] Here he saw
international experimental political films, such as Vsevold Pudovkin's
Storm Over Asia (1928) and Sergei Eisenstein's Battleship Potemkin
(1925), which would influence his future experiments in theatre and
radio.[15] As he later recalled: 'The opportunity of seeing films of such
stature compensated for some of the deprivation experienced by an
ill-educated adolescent who faced the prospect of trying to earn a living
in the arid desert of 1929.'[16]

Throughout Jimmie's childhood, Will Miller had been a regular at
the Workers' Arts Club; as well as occasionally singing, Will would
participate in staged Sunday night political debates where he would
hold forth on Kant, Proudhon, Marx and Engels, richly embellishing
his arguments with quotations from Burns and Shakespeare. Will's
performances were the source of much family pride: 'It was better than
going to pictures on a Sunday night,' Betsy would recall.[17] MacColl
would later describe Will and his friends as 'the last remnants of the
kind of men who were produced in the final days of the first industrial
revolution ... a brand of working-class intellectuals who were interested
in all kinds of things'.[18] Above all, MacColl remembered the debates as a

type of theatre – a compelling spectacle where serious ideas were vividly dramatised. 'For anyone with a sense of drama,' he later recalled, 'these sessions were absolutely invaluable; for a fourteen-year-old hopeful on the threshold of a fifty-year-love affair with the theatre they were unforgettable experiences.'[19]

CŁ80

Miller's previous encounters with the theatre had been forgettable enough. The groundbreaking work of the Gaiety Theatre, Manchester, which showcased the topical regionalism of Harold Brighouse and Stanley Houghton, was before his time; a school trip to see a stage melodrama had bored him rigid – compared with films or the colourful and fast-moving variety shows he'd seen with his parents at Salford Hippodrome, this was insipid stuff.[20] His introduction to radical theatre came via a man named Harrison, a cutter in a waterproof factory who lodged with the Millers in 1929 and took a shine to their bookish son.[21]

Harrison's three passions were the Communist Party, Shakespeare and opera, and he was friendly with the local Clarion Players dramatic group, a residue of the rich social and cultural life that had once clustered around Robert Blatchford's socialist *Clarion* newspaper.[22] Alerted to the musical talents of his landlady's son – Jimmie would sing elaborate parodies of Harrison's cherished opera records – Harrison introduced Jimmie to the theatre group. The Clarion Players drank coffee and rehearsed in a house with a parlour, and Jimmie was initially overawed by such surroundings. But he steeled himself and was given a part in *The Singing Jailbirds*, a play by Upton Sinclair dealing with the trial of Californian Industrial Workers of the World activists.[23] He made his theatrical debut before twenty people at a social held by the Cheetham branch of the Communist Party, and he could still remember his songs fifty years later.[24] Over the next few months he became a regular at rehearsals, appearing in the standard repertoire of the Clarion Players – a stage version of Robert Tressell's *The Ragged Trousered Philanthropists*, George Bernard Shaw's *Heartbreak House* and John Galsworthy's *Strife*.[25] It was around this time, again under Harrison's influence, that Miller was introduced to the Young Communist League, the Communist Party's youth wing.

CŁ80

The Communist Party of Great Britain had been formed back in 1920.[26] Initially it set out to penetrate and redirect the existing Labour movement, but from the mid-1920s pursued a more aggressive and independent tack. According to the analysis of the Communist International (Comintern), the international revolutionary movement was now entering a new period. The First Period covered the revolutionary years 1917–21; the Second Period was a time of necessary consolidation; the ever-deepening crisis of capitalism now gave rise to a 'Third Period' of fresh revolutionary possibility. In November 1927 Mancunian boilermaker Harry Pollitt – who would become General Secretary of the British party in August 1929 – was summoned to Moscow to receive the new line from Stalin and Bukharin.[27] The CPGB would now argue that the militancy of the British miners during the General Strike was a sign of things to come: the British working class would respond to revolutionary leadership, and the Communist Party aimed to provide it.[28] 'Class Against Class' became the unambiguous name for the left turn and the title of the party's manifesto for the May 1929 general election.

It was couched in language that spoke to one teenager from Lower Broughton who was seeking an outlet for his anger and a narrative to explain and resolve the world's injustices.[29] The party had approximately 3,500 members in the January of 1929; two years later it had more than doubled its membership.[30] Many of them were, according to the party's organisation bureau, younger, more militant and less attached to the traditions of the Labour movement than the existing membership.[31] Jimmie Miller was one of these new recruits.

Under Harrison's guidance he attended a couple of Friday night meetings, which he found initially disappointing – he'd expected something 'more exciting', even 'conspiratorial'.[32] He became a regular at a discussion group on the history of philosophy held in the West Park Street kitchen of Workers' Arts Club regular George Poole.[33] With the support of Betsy and Will, who would later follow their son into the Communist Party, he fibbed about his age – members of the YCL were supposed to be sixteen or over – and signed up with his nearest branch in Cheetham.[34] Jimmie's motivations for joining were a mixture of boredom, loneliness, anger and ideological commitment. He later described it as 'a step which was to influence my whole life'.[35]

Over the following months the Communist Party began to provide what he was looking for. It presented a new circle of potential girlfriends and a ready-made social life, the highlight of which was the one-shilling YCL gatherings at the Workers' Arts Club where the young comrades danced either to records or an amateur band. (Never much of a mover, MacColl's dance-floor manner reminded him of 'semi-paralysed invalids reaching for the nurses who were teaching them to walk'.)[36] If the party's sectarian superiority sometimes created bouts of paranoia and insecurity, it also gave a sense of belonging and the frisson of being a member of an organisation with privileged insight into the convolutions of historical change. Party members might talk in jargon, but for Jimmie at the time 'the jargon meant something to you – it was a code that you'd cracked'.[37] Communist analysis supplied a structural explanation for poverty and unemployment – the sources of his class-shame – and a revolutionary solution. Its culture of intellectual enquiry and debate provided a forum in which his hitherto secretive learning could be given an airing. And the magnitude of its ambition – 'to destroy all classes, and thus to destroy the class we were born into' – offered ample remedy for the guilty boredom of joblessness.[38] '[W]ith political commitment came peace of mind and a wonderful sense of adventure,' he remembered. 'And time, which I had borne on my shoulder like a heavy weight, was now light as a feather ... I was busy most days from early morning till late at night.'[39] With hours to fill and all the zeal of the newly converted, he was soon living the life of a full-time political activist. Numerically the Communist Party was tiny, but for a young activist these were bold and energetic years in its history.

The party's *Daily Worker* newspaper was launched when Jimmie had been a member for just a couple of months: 'The *Daily Worker* comes as a strong antidote to the poison gas of the bourgeoisie and pseudo-labour press' boasted the first issue, 'and as an instrument for enlightenment and the organisation of the proletariat for the fight for the workers' revolutionary government'.[40] Like every other member, Jimmie was expected to sell the paper on the streets. On alternate Saturdays he would do his stint at the junction of Oldham Street and Piccadilly in central Manchester.[41]

The party's one-room office on the fourth floor of 33 Ducie Street, Ancoats, became a regular haunt. It was here that the party's rash of inflammatory factory newspapers were written, typed and duplicated. With new friends like Eddie Frow, a communist engineer in his mid-twenties who would go on to co-found the Salford Working Class Movement Library, Jimmie wrote for roughly produced papers such as the *Salford Docker*, the *Crossley Motor* and *Ward and Goldstone Spark*.[42] Typical editions might draw comparisons between British unemployment and conditions in the Soviet Union – where unemployment and the length of the working day were said to be decreasing – or expose the latest chicanery of the bosses.[43] In Jimmie the work unearthed an instinct for well-crafted political satire.[44] He was always more interested in the creative side than editorial drudgery, and especially enjoyed the challenge of getting the information and terminology right – this required a contact inside the factory – and of using popular and accessible forms and tone. 'I'd write an article and maybe a song and three or four little lampoons,' he'd later recall; 'you can't write a four line squib in formal English to workers who never use formal English; you have to use exactly their terms'.[45]

Looking back on these formative and feverish years of wide-eyed political activity, MacColl recalled:

> There was scarcely a minute of the day when we weren't busy compiling, duplicating, typing, writing, printing and distributing factory newspapers, handing out leaflets, selling pamphlets, organising meetings outside factory gates, at street corners, in desolate, shoddy halls. We attended discussions, weekend schools, training classes, education classes, group meetings, branch meetings, district meetings, area meetings, conferences, congresses called by the central committee, the district committee, the secretariat, the political bureau.[46]

He also recalled the rhythms of the daily routine: the early starts, endless walking, tuppence lunches at Yates' Wine Lodge in Manchester, the small triumphs (even persuading somebody to attend a YCL social counted) and the transformed landscape of Salford and Manchester, which had never been the same since he'd read Engels' *The Condition of the Working Class in England*. The humdrum streets, once so familiar that they were almost invisible, were now seen afresh as the streets where Engels had once walked.[47] He later remembered walking home late at night, after a typical day of political legwork, 'and feeling a fantastic sense of exhilaration, and hope. And saying, "This is my world! When I grow up, I'm going to tear all this down, I'm going to make something

so beautiful and so unobtrusive that men can become human."'[48] It was
a mood he'd later capture in his song 'Dirty Old Town'.

ᏩᏂᎤ

Jimmie's conversion unleashed confidence and heightened his impatience
with the Clarion Players. They were content with performing to small
groups of the already converted; he wanted to see the revolution
in his own lifetime, and preferably before he was twenty.[49] He was
politically dissatisfied with their repertoire, which seemed mired in
a previous era and hidebound by the belief that capitalism could be
gradually transformed into socialism. Newly acquainted with the
exacting discipline of Communist Party meetings, he found fault with
the leisurely pace of rehearsals: the group were intent on tackling full-
length plays, but rarely sustained the momentum to finish anything.
Those they did complete always functioned merely as a scenic backdrop
to political meetings.[50] Tired by the timidity and mediocrity of the
Clarion Players, buoyed by political fervour, and encouraged by what
he learned of new rumblings among the small world of left theatre,
Miller parted company with the group.

His favourite item among the Clarion Players' stock of half-
rehearsed fragments was a sketch called *Still Talking,* which had
been in their repertoire since March 1928.[51] Watching the performance
reminded him of the Workers' Arts Club debates. Purpose-written
for performance at meetings, it dispensed with props and began
unexpectedly when two actors, planted among the audience, stood
up, introduced themselves as a Tory and Labour politician respectively,
and proceeded to make speeches. They were heckled from the floor
by other planted actors; confused audience members often joined the
debate. Scenes followed to illustrate political points and the production
ended when the proponents of these stale ideologies were chased
from the room; the aroused audience was exhorted to support the
revolutionary political alternative.

Jimmie Miller wasn't alone in being impressed by *Still Talking.* Tom
Thomas was a London-based communist cultural activist thirteen years
Miller's senior who was to become National Organiser for the Workers'
Theatre Movement.[52] Thomas came across the sketch at a time when
his group, the Hackney People's Players were, in his words, 'fumbling
towards the idea of an Agit-prop theatre – a theatre without a stage,

a theatre which would use music and song and cabaret, and which could improvise its own material instead of going in for full-length set pieces, a theatre in which the audience could take part'.[53] What Jimmie sensed intuitively, Thomas was able to articulate: that a production like *Still Talking* could give voice to those looking for a shift from formal and stagey Labour theatre to a more mobile form befitting the urgency of Class Against Class politics. In May 1930 Thomas wrote an article entitled 'The Theatre of Struggle' for the *Daily Worker*, urging existing left-wing theatre groups to abandon theatrical naturalism and full-length productions; he also called on every party district without a theatre group to form one, work up short, punchy material, and take it out on to the streets.[54]

With half a dozen like-minded teenagers, Jimmie followed Thomas's advice and formed a Salford branch of the Workers' Theatre Movement at some point in the middle of 1931.[55] Bob Goodman, who lived near the Millers, joined up. A clever lad, Bob was a quiet Young Communist and a promising amateur boxer who became a favourite with Betsy. From this point until 1937, when he would be killed fighting in the Spanish Civil War, Goodman and Miller were close friends.[56] Jimmy Rigby from Miles Platting also signed up, as did Alf Armitt of West Park Street, Salford, a jig-tool-maker's apprentice at the Taylor Brothers' foundry.[57] Martin Bobker was another recruit; he went on to become Manchester District Organiser of the Young Communist League.[58] Four teenage girls were also committed to the venture. Three of them – Grace Seden, Nellie Wallace, and a girl remembered only as 'Blondie', were weavers;[59] Flo Clayton and Nellie Wallace were both from communist families; miner's daughter Nellie Wallace would later marry Miller's cousin, John Logan, and remain a political activist for the rest of her life.[60]

MacColl later recalled the frustrations of early meetings, held either in the damp cellar of the Workers' Arts Club or in the Millers' kitchen. The group was young and inexperienced. No amount of political zeal, it seemed, would compensate for the lack of know-how when it came to scriptwriting or acting.[61] But they were soon affiliated to a new national movement that was in turn part of an international network of radical theatre groups.

CRXO

Under the leadership of Tom Thomas, the once moribund British Workers' Theatre Movement was resuscitated and, in November 1931, announced its revival through the first edition of a hyper-militant new monthly journal, the *Red Stage*. 'The Workers' Theatre Movement', ran page 1, 'has the task of exposing capitalism and its Labour lieutenants to the broadest masses of workers in meetings, on the streets, outside factories, and of arousing the workers' confidence in their own ability to overthrow the system that enslaves them.' It published news bulletins from the local groups: Miller's Salford group dutifully reported making good headway and pledged to sell more song-sheets 'to inspire our audiences to join lustily in the singing of our songs'.[62]

Over the next couple of years the national Workers' Theatre Movement grew into a small but significant presence on the left – sixty-odd groups appeared, although many of these could count just a handful of activists.[63] Short plays, sketches and songs were written by the groups and distributed to the other WTM branches.[64] The earnest YCLers who dominated the WTM's ranks couldn't have taken their role as the vanguard of proletarian theatre more seriously. Operating under the slogan 'A Propertyless Theatre for the Propertyless Class', they set about studying and emulating the work of their more experienced international brethren.

The Russian Blue Blouses in particular inspired awe among the British groups: named after their distinctive uniform, the Blue Blouses numbered 7,000 groups by 1927 and were credited with pioneering the 'living newspaper', a medium through which they brought topical, radical and fast-moving performances to the literate and non-literate alike.[65] By 1930 the German Communist Party (KPD) had 150 workers' theatre groups, the foremost of which was the Berlin-based Das Rote Sprachrohr or the Red Megaphone.[66] Like 'Blue Blouses', the name 'Red Megaphone' was murmured with hushed reverence by members of the British WTM.

Britain's connection to German and Soviet radical theatre was cemented through a series of congresses, tours and institutions.[67] At their worst, these exchanges highlighted the limitations of the British WTM – in 1933, for example, a delegation from the British WTM took part in the Moscow International Workers' Theatre Olympiad and came last.[68] At other moments the international dimension of the WTM created some surprising lines of communication between a dynamic

Marxist avant-garde overseas and determined cultural activists in the British provinces. German delegates attended a series of WTM events over the next couple of years.[69] Jimmie Miller himself struck up a correspondence with a Rudi Lehmann, a young communist kindred spirit from Leipzig who mailed letters and packages to 37 Coburg Street, including a script for Hanns Eisler's 1929 chorus 'Auf den Strassen zu singen' ('To be sung on the streets').[70] Lehmann also sent old copies of the *Arbeiter-Illustrierte-Zeitung* (Workers' Illustrated News), famous for its photomontage and politicised coverage of sport, cinema and music. MacColl later recalled poring over this revolutionary exotica with the aid of a well-thumbed second-hand German dictionary from Shudehill market.[71]

છ૪ૐ

Jimmie's troupe was initially known as the Manchester Workers' Theatre Movement but adopted the name 'The Red Megaphones' – partly in international solidarity, partly in wishful thinking – after line-up changes late in 1932.[72] Their early repertoire consisted of sketches supplied by the national organisation. 'Rent, Interest and Profit' – a Marxist explication of how the rent paid by tenants over the years often far exceeded the actual value of their properties – was typical fare. No script has survived, but MacColl remembered it as 'seven or eight minutes of knockabout comedy, some simplified Marxist analyses, two songs and a mass declamation'.[73] 'Meerut' was another early favourite sketch, and protested about the plight of thirty-three trade union militants awaiting trial for conspiring 'to deprive the king of the sovereignty of British India'.[74] The sketch filled in the background before acting out the communist solution to the crisis. The six speakers assembled behind four broom handles criss-crossed to represent prison bars. At the climax of the sketch, the actors pushed their hands through the broom handles to represent a reaching out to fellow workers; they cried 'SMASH THE BARS', at which point the broom handles were symbolically cast aside.[75]

Miller mercilessly drilled his troupe in preparation for the performance of 'Meerut' and it became a centrepiece in their repertoire.[76] They gave the debut at a public meeting for the League Against Imperialism on Monday 23 November 1931, held at Caxton Hall, Chapel Street, Salford. According to their own write-up, several new members were recruited for the league.[77] The troupe continued to gather experience at similar events, some of them in sizeable venues. In January 1932 they performed at the Memorial Hall, Albert Square, central Manchester, in a concert for the Manchester and Salford Workers' Film Society, with three sketches. In one, private enterprise was put on trial; 'Mammonart' critiqued the domination of culture by capitalism; 'The Death of Lenin' was an elegiac poem spoken by four voices.[78] In December 1931 and January 1932 alone they made nine similar indoor appearances. In some, such as at the League of Imperialism, they were preaching to the converted; in others they were trying to lead by example and encourage like-minded young activists to set up their own groups. They also took their message to political opponents, appearing at a Moss Side Labour Party social on 18 January 1932, where 'a small but appreciative audience' saw them present their repertoire. 'Frequent exposures of the role of the Labour leaders', they wrote in *Red Stage*, 'were received with applause.'[79]

◌֍֎

Indoor performances were all very well, but Jimmie saw them as dress rehearsals: the real business was to get the message on to the streets and buttonhole the workers in their native habitat. Remnants of older types of street performance – organ grinders, bone players, street pianists and singers – still lingered in Salford in the early 1930s, and the Workers' Theatre Movement was keen to take their place in this unruly but democratic performance space.[80] The troupe gave performances wherever people congregated. The long Saturday morning queues outside public baths provided a captive audience; 'Meerut' was performed at the Trafford Road dock gates to those gathered looking for a day's work.[81] MacColl later recalled that while hecklers, police and the Manchester rain made life difficult, most dispiriting of all was 'blank apathy … harder to take than abuse'.[82]

◌֍֎

The more politicised atmosphere of rallies and demonstrations seemed to provide a more congenial setting. The period between 1931 and 1933 – the heyday of both the National WTM and of the Salford branch – marked a flashpoint in British class conflict not seen since the General Strike. In 1930 Labour Minister of Employment J. H. Thomas had pledged to 'proceed on the basis of a process of rationalisation in industry, which must for weeks increase unemployment figures'.[83] Money was soon haemorrhaging from the Unemployment Insurance Fund, and a drastic reduction of support for the unemployed was to be the solution.[84] The Anomalies Act, passed in the summer of 1931, removed the rights of many to claim, and proved only the thin end of the wedge.[85] It was followed up that autumn with a 10 per cent benefit cut and Family Means Test, whereby the total weekly income of a family was worked out and benefit calculated accordingly. The euphemistically titled Public Assistance Committees were deployed to investigate domestic circumstances – MacColl remembered it as 'a humiliating inquisition'.[86] As a result of its enquiries 852,000 claimants lost benefits.

While these measures split the Labour Party – the cabinet resigned on 24 August 1931 and four of its key members joined forces with like-minded Tories in a National Government – they swelled the communist ranks. Formed by the young party back in 1921, the National Unemployed Workers' Movement (NUWM) provided a vehicle for resistance.[87] Under the leadership of the articulate and charismatic toolmaker Wal Hannington, membership of the NUWM more than doubled between 1928 and the end of 1930;[88] 61 per cent of the total Communist Party membership was unemployed by November 1932 and they had plenty of time on their hands.[89] Existing branches expanded and new ones were formed. The Means Test hit Jimmie's generation especially hard: wherever one parent in a household was working, unemployed sons and daughters were likely to lose their benefit, and with it any remaining illusion of financial independence. Young activists played a prominent role in the NUWM and the Salford branch was typical. Weekly general meetings were held at the Workers' Arts Club and many of Jimmie's comrades were the grassroots activists.[90] Miller was himself on the NUWM youth council.[91] His close friend Eddie Frow, who was also unemployed at the time, spoke regularly at the meetings and became the public face of the Salford NUWM.[92]

CB&O

The first of October 1931 was to prove a significant day for Jimmie Miller and his circle. The Salford branch of the NUWM had called a demonstration against the new measures – MacColl remembered publicising the protest by addressing Labour Exchange queues and chalking slogans on walls and pavements.[93] Protestors were to congregate on the croft next to the Workers' Arts Club, Liverpool Street; it was here that Miller's WTM troupe got an early taste of working at political demonstrations when they presented a sketch and a song from the makeshift coal-cart platform from which Eddie Frow and seaman Tommy Morris were to address the crowd.[94] The sketch, which hasn't survived, was probably a satirical squib about Margaret Bondfield, a Labour MP who came to symbolise the Labour Party's double-speak;[95] in the song an ideologically savvy 'WTM girl' convinces a docile and unquestioning young worker to 'Shun the forces of reaction' and 'Put [his] faith in mass class action'.[96] Though the troupe submitted an upbeat report to *Red Stage*, MacColl later remembered the performance as a nerve-wracking affair overshadowed by an ominous police presence.[97]

After the speeches, the demonstrators marched to Salford Town Hall in Bexley Square, where they planned to deliver a charter to a City Council meeting currently debating the proposed cuts.[98] The Salford novelist Walter Greenwood was an eyewitness that day, and events were recast as the pivotal moment in his debut novel *Love on the Dole* (1933).[99] Larry Meath, Greenwood's mouthpiece and hero, is clubbed to the floor by the police and later dies from his injuries. For Eddie Frow, who makes a thinly disguised appearance in Greenwood's novel as a rabble-rousing 'finely featured young man with long hair', 1 October 1931 was a memorable day in which the Leninist lesson about the forces of the state being forever at the disposal of vested interest were hard learned.[100] Frow addressed the demonstration, was singled out by the police as a ringleader, and had his nose broken when four policemen set about him. He was sentenced to five months' hard labour in Strangeways for assault.[101] As his wife Ruth told me 71 years later, 'the fine features were ruined from that day onwards. He always was crooked after that.'[102]

Nellie Wallace, who had recently returned from a spell at the Lenin school in Moscow, also remembered the day as living nightmare: '[Jimmie Miller] and I were holding a banner and were hit. Blood was on the town hall steps.'[103] The larger than expected turnout of unemployed workers and their families (maybe as many as ten thousand); the police brutality, with charging horses and flailing truncheons; the doomed resistance of underfed and unarmed demonstrators; the random arresting, trumped-up charges and repressive sentences meted out (Frow was one of four NUWM activists to get a custodial sentence) – these experiences reinforced Jimmie's recent radicalisation. He remained haunted by the events of that day. In the late 1930s he would write *The Damnable Town*, an unpublished and heavily autobiographical novel in which the Battle of Bexley Square would be one of the key sites of his fictional alter ego's political awakening.[104] Half a century later he returned to the events in his autobiography, and the undimmed red haze glowed through his prose: 'our rulers', he wrote, 'are not conscious of the fact that working people possess human dignity or indeed that they have feelings of any kind ... Don't bother trying to conceal your contempt for us,' he seethed, 'and we won't conceal our hatred of you.'[105]

CƷᏰↄ

'If only we'd had a sketch that was suitable for the occasion,' he remembered thinking after Bexley Square.[106] The experience of performing at demonstrations alerted Jimmie and his troupe to the limitations of generalised WTM scripts.[107] Rather than abstract analysis, they needed up-to-date material addressing local matters, such as the fact that the Birkenhead NUWM branch had drawn blood from the authorities and won significant concessions.[108] Sixteen-year-old Jimmie was prompted to write one of his earliest songs, only a fragment of which survives. He used the isolated Birkenhead victory to generate an optimistic message for that year's 1,500-strong national Hunger March:

> Forward unemployed, forward unemployed
> Led by the NUWM,
> We fight against the cuts again.
> From fighting Birkenhead, we've learnt our lesson well.
> We'll send the National Government
> And the Means Test all to hell.[109]

CƷᏰↄ

Though Jimmie participated in regional Hunger Marches, he was too busy with his troupe to make the trip to London that year.[110] The period between 1930 and 1932 witnessed a bitter and protracted dispute in the heartlands of the Lancashire and west Yorkshire textile industry: between 1929 and 1931, 13 million of the 19 million days lost to strike action in Britain involved textile workers.[111] Foreign competition, reduced markets and deteriorating machinery brought crisis to the industry and precipitated a new phase of conflict between mill owners and their workforce. The end result seemed inevitable: unemployment among the cotton workers rose from 14.4 per cent in 1929 to 31 per cent four years later, though textile workers put up a dogged struggle through a series of rolling strikes.[112]

The Communist Party had just 15 paid-up members working in the heartlands of the textile industry, but three of the key players in the Salford WTM – Nellie Wallace, Grace Seden and 'Blondie' – were weavers, and the troupe quickly became involved in supporting the rising militancy.[113] Inside information enabled the group to reflect workplace conditions and to target the message; new sketches were written by Jimmie and the troupe about the strike.[114] Performances were initially given in and around Salford at the Howard's Mill and the Pendleton mill of Elkanah Armitage, but the group then began to travel further afield.[115] In a pattern that anticipated the post-war Theatre Workshop years, when MacColl would insist on touring the company through working-class communities remote from even repertory theatre, the Salford Workers' Theatre Movement embarked on a hectic schedule. Nearby mill towns, such as Oldham, Rochdale or Ashton-under Lyne, were visited on weekday evenings. At the weekends the group journeyed to Wigan, Bacup, Haslingden and Bury.[116] Money was collected and, as the strikes deepened, so was food.[117] The group began to reach bigger audiences. During the depths of the strike they performed in Burnley, and MacColl remembered using megaphones to reach 'a hundred and fifty thousand strikers' awaiting the arrival of food convoys.[118] They appeared at two outdoor demonstrations in Preston's 1932 May Day event;[119] they knew they were starting to make a mark when Tom Thomas singled them out for comradely praise in the Communist Party's *International Theatre* journal.[120]

CB&O

When Jimmie wasn't either planning the revolution or acting it out, he was rambling in the Pennines. If rambling today is associated with the middle-aged middle classes, in the 1930s it was mass sport of working-class youth. The free time created by unemployment (66,000 were out of work in Sheffield during 1932) and reasonably cheap train and rail fares (Miller could get the bus to Hyde for four pence or the train to Hayfield for eight pence) made hiking a popular option, particularly in the North, where areas of outstanding beauty lay adjacent to depressed industrial cities.[121]

Most of Miller's circle went rambling, but three of them in particular formed a tight-knit group. Bob Goodman was one member; Alec Armstrong, a communist activist and slater by trade, another – MacColl later remembered him as 'like one of those tow-haired young proletarian heroes one saw depicted on Soviet posters'.[122] Joe Davies, an industrial chemist and WTM member from Lower Broughton, was the third in a group that would hike every weekend in the early 1930s.[123] Their main stamping ground was the nearby High Peak, but they also hitched to the North Yorkshire Moors, the Lake District, Snowdonia and even Glencoe.[124] MacColl always enjoyed describing these excursions, and the strenuous and competitive walking and climbing, foraging, poaching and pilfering that went with them. It was here that his lifelong love of the British countryside, and his encyclopaedic knowledge of its birds, wildlife and wildflowers, first took hold.

Like everything else in the young Miller's life, rambling was experienced politically: this was not an escape from the bump and grind of activism, but fed into it and was part of it. The beauty of nature was experienced as opposite to the social world, but this was an opposition that could be overcome by revolution: 'part of the revolutionary objective', he remembers thinking, 'was to create a world that would harmonize with that other one that you enjoyed so much'. 'If the bourgeoisie had had any sense at all they would never have allowed the working class into that kind of countryside. Because it bred a spirit of revolt.'[125]

He was not alone in connecting rambling and revolution. Armstrong saw the natural world as a type of extensive gymnasium in which he could get in tip-top physical shape. When party apparatchiks accused him of shirking real political work and spending too long in the countryside, he would reply that he was actually in training for 'the revo', and that revolutionaries had an obligation to keep fit.[126] As the slightly older and wiser Eddie Frow recalled: 'with all this unemployment, it looked like capitalism was really collapsing ... there was a lot of wishful thinking'.[127]

Though Jimmie and his friends indulged in their share of wishful thinking and dialectical abstraction, there was no mistaking that rambling was a political affair in a more concrete sense. Out of the 84,000 acres of the High Peak, just 764 were publicly accessible, with just twelve short and congested footpaths covering the entire 215 square miles of the Peak District.[128] The rest of the land was set aside for blood sports and was fiercely protected by gamekeepers and moorland patrols. For fifty years progressive voices in parliament had been trying to wring concessions from the landowning class. The first Access to the Mountain Bill was introduced back in 1888 and four more attempts were made between 1924 and 1931.[129] From the mid-1920s onwards, various groups, including the Youth Hostel Association and the Woodcraft Folk, joined the campaigns.[130]

The British Workers' Sports Federation (BWSF) began life in 1923 as an offshoot of the Clarion Cycling Club and lent its polite voice to these protests. But in the years following the General Strike, the Communist Party effectively won control and it became a more militant body committed to organising sporting events under workers' control and waging war on 'bosses' sport', which apparently both exploited workers and distracted them from their true interests in the class struggle.[131] By 1930 the BWSF was claiming a membership of 5,000. It organised sporting activities to raise funds for striking workers during the 'more looms' dispute, campaigned against high ticket prices during the 1930 FA Cup (workers refused to participate in the proposed boycotts and attended the games regardless), and promoted 'Red Sports Days'.[132]

In Manchester and Salford the BWSF's energies were channelled into ramblers' rights. The secretary of the Lancashire Federation of the BWSF was a twenty-year-old communist motor mechanic named Benny Rothman (a friend of Miller's in spite of the four-year age gap) who had previously been fined for chalking pavement slogans in central Manchester advertising the launch of the *Daily Worker*.[133] Rothman's BWSF branch organised a weekend trip to Clough Head Farm where 180 young workers spent their time rambling, singing and discussing politics. (Jimmie was there and Eddie Frow put a strain on the limited transport budget by insisting on taking along his typewriter and the complete works of Lenin.)[134] Around the same time they took a trip to

Rowarth, and were prevented from completing their hike to Bleaklow Hill by gamekeepers.[135]

In characteristically itchy-footed Class Against Class style, the BWSF, which was dominated by the YCL, grew impatient with the political dithering over access to the countryside. After the frustrations of the Rowarth camp, they decided to organise a mass trespass on Kinder Scout for Sunday 24 April 1932. The exact nature of Jimmie's input is difficult to determine, although he was sufficiently prominent to feature in a police report on the BWSF – the earliest piece of surveillance in MacColl's recently declassified MI5 file.[136] He later remembered being 'publicity officer ... and writing in long-hand laborious letters [to the press]: "We are having a mass trespass and you are welcome to come and take pictures."'[137]

The campaign was certainly managed with media awareness not typical of the Communist Party. Rothman visited the *Manchester Evening News* on 18 April and it ran the story the following day, 'Mass Trespass Over Kinder Scout'.[138] The tone of the piece was unsympathetic – the more conservative Sheffield Ramblers Federation promptly denounced the BWSF's plans – but the story carried the news of the trespass far beyond those who could have been reached by leafleting and chalking slogans.

Rothman had planned to begin the trespass by holding an open-air meeting in Hayfield village recreation ground; the police, who turned out in force on the day, instantly issued an injunction prohibiting it. Rothman foiled their plans and instead held the meeting in a disused quarry. Standing on a boulder, he proclaimed 'Our grouse is against grouse', before demanding open access to the countryside, lower fares and the lifting of the current ban on open-air singing. The size of the crowd that heard him is difficult to establish, although even the conservative press reckoned on 400.[139] (MacColl, with characteristic hyperbole, usually put the figure at 3,000, but on occasion went as high as 'eight or 9,000'.)[140] Whatever their size, the assembled group, fuelled by Rothman's rhetoric, marched en masse to the peak of Kinder where they met a small group of gamekeepers carrying cudgels.[141] A skirmish broke out in which one keeper was knocked unconscious and injured his ankle. Triumphant, the marchers then returned to Hayfield, singing songs including 'The Red Flag' and 'The Internationale', and shouting 'Down with the landlords and ruling class and up with the workers!'

and 'Down with the bobbies!' By the time they reached Hayfield the police presence had grown considerably and five 'ringleaders' were arrested.[142]

Like the trespass itself, the ensuing court case, held at Derby assizes on Wednesday 21 July, attracted widespread media coverage – for the press it became entertaining theatre in which the day's generational and class conflicts were played out. The jury comprised two brigadier-generals, three colonels, two majors, three captains and two aldermen – eleven of the twelve were country landowners.[143] The five accused were urban communists aged between nineteen and twenty-three.[144] Much was made of their political affiliations, particularly the inflammatory literature in their rucksacks, which included a copy of the *Communist Review* and a pamphlet by Lenin – 'Is that the Russian gentleman?' the judge is said to have asked.[145] All were charged with riotous assembly and assault, John Anderson with the additional offence of grievously harming the gamekeeper.[146] Rothman defended himself – full of confidence, he looked forward to presenting 'the historic and political point of view'.[147] All five got hard labour ranging from two to six months.[148]

CঃঙঃO

Music was integral to rambling culture in the 1930s. Songs like 'I'm Happy When I'm Hiking' were widely sung by rambling groups.[149] Newspapers like *The Times* bemoaned the presence in the countryside of: 'A mob of young men and women – hatless, raucous, yellow jerseyed, slung with concertinas.'[150] Even Benny Rothman had his doubts about certain 'rowdy young chaps who went out [rambling] dressed in peculiar clothes, carrying guitars'.[151] Outdoor singing was banned, and as the mass trespass revealed, the right to sing, like the right to ramble, became a politicised issue.

This was certainly true in Salford and Manchester. MacColl later recalled the group singing that went on in the trains and buses on the way to the countryside:

> you'd sit in a carriage with a lot of other YCLers ... and you'd sing songs in Russian and German and the rest of the train would be singing songs in English, but they weren't revolutionary songs, you were singing songs in German and Russian that nobody understood, including you. That's ... real sectarianism ... that's it at its final point.[152]

In less sectarian moments, Jimmie would sing in English, and it was around this time that he started to take his singing more seriously. Joe Davis apparently gave encouragement, and it was Jimmie who always led the singing on rambling excursions.[153]

Rambling provided both a new audience for his singing and an impetus for his song writing. His first song to appear in print was 'Manchester's Youth Song', published anonymously in the Workers' Theatre Movement's *Monthly Bulletin* in February 1933. Applauded by the WTM as a model 'because it deals with a particular district ...the idea of local songs is a splendid one', the particularity of the song actually borders on the comic, with its list of districts ('Workers from Salford, from Cheetham and Hulme') and references to localised industry ('waterproof factories'). The tune couldn't have been less local – if anything, the choice of the German 'Red Rockets' smacked of a sectarian fascination with the *recherché* – and the words were a lumpy mix of slogans ('Smash the oppression and boss-clad greed') and clichés ('struggle for bread'), which yoked together resistance to economic exploitation and the campaign for ramblers' rights without shedding much light on either.

'Mass Trespass 1932', the second of the three surviving songs from this period, was more focused.[154] As the title suggests, it was part of the mass trespass campaign's canny publicity drive. The demonstration was being called 'The Mass Trespass' before it even occurred, and just as Rothman's work with the media enabled the organisers' projections to become a reality (a mass of people read about it and showed up), so Jimmie's song fed into the perception that something significant was happening – it was an historical song commemorating an important event written before the event in question had actually taken place. It also keyed into a perception that the trespassers were actually recovering something that was theirs by right and had been taken from them – 'For the mass trespass is the only way there is / To gain access to the mountains once again'. He reinforced the point by using an ancient-sounding tune, lifted from the traditional Scottish song 'The Road to the Isles', which Jimmie knew from his parents' singing – the subtlety of this effect was evidently lost on contemporaries less versed in the folk tradition. Young Communist Leaguer Natt Frayman recalled: 'I heard somebody singing "The Road to the Isles" and somebody said, "Have you heard that? They've pinched Jimmie Miller's song and put new words to it." '[155] 'Everybody in the movement used to stride along singing these words of Jimmie Miller's,' Natt Frayman remembered, 'and Jimmie Miller used to stride up ahead, and he'd be off and we'd be picking it up.'[156]

It was in 1932, when he was seventeen years old, that he wrote his first significant song. 'The Manchester Rambler', also known as 'I'm a Rambler' and 'The Rambler's Song', dates from the months following the mass trespass; in spite of Jimmie's youth, it marks a departure from the leaden-footed and slogan-heavy juvenilia.[157] It's the first surviving song for which he wrote the tune, and the jaunty melody, with its waltzy swing, is the first evidence of his ability to draw upon popular forms and rhythms to create something simultaneously distinctive and familiar. The lyric is just as playful, and unlike the other earlier work, where each verse repeats the same political point, this song tacks through different settings and scenarios. It begins and ends with places and things seen while rambling, and the chorus provides an anchor, but the song gives free rein to a mischievous sense of humour. Two verses are a type of comic musical theatre describing a verbal confrontation between the rambler and a jobs-worth gamekeeper, complete with spoken lines – 'He'd the worst face that I ever saw'; a third has fun with the stock phrases, narratives and gender roles of English folksong by updating them to reflect contemporary urban experience ('I once loved a maid, a spot-welder by trade'). The song, which would be widely covered by folk artists from the late 1950s onwards, contains a defiance ('I'll walk where I will') and political line ('I may be a wage slave on Monday / But I am a free man on Sunday') in synch with the YCL culture of the early 1930s. But elsewhere the political resistance is diffused through parody, subversion, panoramic perspectives and the poetry of the writing. Whereas the other extant songs from this time were designed to be functional ephemera – throwaway culture that happened not to have been thrown away – 'The Manchester Rambler' drew upon the moment of its composition but also managed to transcend it. Not, of course, that this was something that Jimmie cared about at the time. Throughout his life he believed that the artist should 'struggle to live at the same time as himself'. By the time the song was written the rising tide of European fascism was giving him and his comrades in the Communist Party plenty of food for thought.[158]

# 3
# Welcome, Comrade

When the seventy-one-year-old Ewan MacColl came to write his autobiography, the years of his late teens and early twenties – 1933 to 1940 – proved a headache: he repeatedly interrupts his own narrative to say how difficult it is to do justice to those years. The enormity of historical events; political fervour; the rapid pace of self-education; the challenge of finding cultural forms with which to grapple with the nightmare of contemporary history; the emotions unleashed by falling in love for the first time – all conspired to strain the chronological conventions of autobiographical writing. 'The thirties', he wrote,

> is a kaleidoscope of countless coloured shapes continuously changing their relationship to one another ... politics, theatre, ideas, theories, love, friendship, rambling, climbing ... Politics was the binding force, the cement which bound everything together, but theatre – for the next twenty years was to be the medium.[1]

∽∾

Still unemployed, he was branching out from Salford and spending more time in central Manchester. The old Piccadilly reference library became a regular haunt, and so did its replacement, the mock-Roman Manchester Central Library in St Peter's Square, which opened in July 1934 and became the source of much civic pride in the depressed city.[2] Marxism might have yielded insight into the causes of mass unemployment, but it never stopped Jimmie feeling guilty about being unemployed. When he wasn't rambling, climbing or fulfilling YCL duties, he structured his life around the routine of the working day, and walked the mile and a half from Coburg Street to reach the library by nine sharp. He fell in with a group of university students, and enjoyed discussing the likes of James Joyce, T. S. Eliot and Sigmund Freud – writers and thinkers he admired, but who were considered dangerously decadent by many in the Communist Party.[3] He became interested in classical music, and a regular at the concerts given by Manchester's Hallé orchestra at the Free Trade Hall on Tuesday evenings where he could get a standing ticket for eight pence.[4] In the right company he was now confident enough to enjoy the cut and thrust of intellectual argument. The cafés of central Manchester became frequent haunts, particularly the Kardomah on Mosley Street, the cheaper Lyons café on Mosley Street, or the Imperial all-night coffee shop under the railway bridge on Oxford Road.[5]

⚬⚬⚬

In the early 1930s he'd taken an ill-fated busking adventure to London with one of Betsy's many lodgers – he was back in Coburg Street a few days later, cold, hungry, and with his tail between his legs.[6] Central Manchester, however, increasingly felt like home, and he could now often be found singing Scottish folk songs on the streets. In the spring of 1934, when Jimmie was singing outside the Manchester Paramount, his voice fell within earshot of Kenneth Adam, a BBC radio scriptwriter and journalist currently on the lookout for new acting talent.[7]

Jimmie was in the right place at the right time. The mid-1930s witnessed strong growth in regional radio, and sections of the Manchester-based North Region had become dominated by a left-wing fraternity eager to exploit the genre's artistic and political potential.[8] The mover and shaker was the region's new Programme Director Archie Harding, an Oxbridge-educated Marxist who'd been strategically redeployed from the London-based National Programme after producing two highly controversial programmes in the early 1930s.[9] Exiled in bandit country – what Harding knew of Manchester he'd learned from reading Engels – he gathered a court of like-minded souls around him: D. G. Bridson was a moustached aesthete with a social conscience who wrote Audenesque verse; communist Olive Shapley joined the team in 1934 – Harding greeted her with the words 'Welcome, comrade.'[10] The socially engaged radio favoured by Harding needed convincing performances of working-class experience, and street singer Jimmie Miller was one of many invited for audition. He could boast impeccable proletarian credentials, a strong voice and some acting experience. Jimmie made his radio debut on the North of England Home Service on the evening of 1 May 1934 in *May Day in England*, a programme exploring the history of May Day from pagan fertility ritual to modern industrial protest. Jimmie was the voice of the working class; Bridson later speculated that this 'vigorously proletarian voice … must have rattled the coffee-cups in sitting rooms all over the country'.[11] On Wednesday 18 July Jimmie was on air again in *Tunnel*, a Bridson production that celebrated the opening of the new Mersey tunnel. This time he barked out a roll call of feats of labour including inches dug, tools used, bricks laid.[12]

The new job must have been the talk of Coburg Street. Jimmie's voice was beamed off the 500-foot mast on Moorside Edge near Huddersfield and could be heard as far away as the Scottish borders. The work was sporadic, but the money was a great improvement on the weekly 9s 10d courtesy of the Labour Exchange – at the BBC Jimmie earned in the region of 4 guineas for two or three days' work, when few skilled industrial workers earned more than 2 guineas per week.[13] Though he derided most of the radio scripts – he considered *Tunnel* a 'programme of stupefying dullness'[14] – he admired Archie Harding's intellectual gravitas and eagerly listened to his new employer's back-catalogue of experimental programmes, which dispensed with reassuring narration and drew on cinematic editing techniques – jump cuts, dissolves, fading – to recreate for radio the turbulence of contemporary history. They reminded Jimmie of the Eisenstein movies he'd seen at the Workers' Film Society.[15] All broadcasting was propaganda, claimed Harding; programmes that didn't criticise the status quo supported it.[16] It was a view Jimmie shared.

C3&O

The international political scene was changing fast: Hitler was consolidating his rule over Germany; Japan's military aggression in Manchuria was clearly a sign of things to come; twice in 1933 anti-fascists disrupted Manchester meetings held by Sir Oswald Mosley's British Union of Fascists.[17] The Communist Party broadened its appeal when it moved from sectarian militancy towards more inclusive Popular Front anti-fascism, and the more tolerant new line seemed to call for a corresponding shift in cultural policies.[18] Many within the Workers' Theatre Movement argued that, while the agitprop form was tailor-made for the cartoon politics of the Class Against Class period, new times called for a corresponding reorientation towards more naturalistic, inclusive and accessible modes of theatrical expression.[19] Jimmie was frustrated with the political and artistic limitations of his Red Megaphones, but unsure how to proceed. Agitprop sketches were obviously restrictive, but they were also energetic, vivid and grounded in the working-class cultural traditions of street entertainment, variety shows and music-hall. Jimmie dismissed naturalism as bourgeois – it only reflected the world, when the point was to change it. He wanted to broaden the Red Megaphones' appeal without retreating behind the curtain of theatrical naturalism.

He read voraciously through the theatre stacks of the Manchester Central Library for inspiration, and was struck by the work of maverick Swiss theorist and stage designer Adolph Appia. Ideas that diminished the actors' role by emphasising stage atmosphere – music, movement, non-realistic lighting – were appealing to a troupe that couldn't, in the conventional sense, act at all.[20] He pored over Léon Moussinac's *The New Movement in Theatre: A Survey of Recent Developments in Theatre* (1931), which included photographs of significant contemporary international political productions, flooding Jimmie's mind with ideas he didn't know how to fulfil.[21] In the early 1930s he'd looked to Berlin and Moscow for inspiration; he now turned to New York, especially the Workers' Laboratory Theater, and their mobile unit, Shock Troupe.[22] This group represented everything he aspired to. They were bohemian and lived communally in a glamorous Lower East Side apartment.[23] They were experienced politically and thoroughly grounded theoretically. They were committed to non-naturalistic agitprop modes, but worked continually to develop artistically. They were well connected – one of their leaders had been a student of Meyerhold at the Soviet Academy of Cinema and Theatre in Moscow.[24] And they displayed a seriousness and discipline that Miller could only dream of extracting from his ragged throng. The Workers' Laboratory Theatre's days were a rigid grid of communal chores, voice and body training, discussion classes, rehearsal, self-criticism and performance.[25] It appealed both to Jimmie's revolutionary romanticism and his steely self-discipline. With the help of a Manchester Communist Party member currently working as an industrial organiser in the United States, he struck up a correspondence with his New York heroes.[26] The Red Megaphones gradually petered out over the course of 1933, but Jimmie was always thinking in terms of a relaunch. In the autumn of 1934 the remnants of the Red Megaphones regrouped, pooled their resources and paid the eight shillings a week for a dingy rehearsal studio on the first floor of 111 Grosvenor Street, off the Oxford Road in All Saints, central Manchester.[27] With a working title of 'Left Theatre', they set about preparing a new repertoire suitable for indoor performance.[28]

⊂ঙ৪৩

Joan Littlewood turned up in Manchester that summer. Like Jimmie, she was working class and a volatile mix of vulnerability and swagger. Brought up by her grandparents in south London, she was passionate about theatre, but had reached her excoriating contempt for the bourgeois theatre establishment via a different route from Jimmie. While he'd been learning about agitprop, Joan had been at the Royal Academy of Dramatic Art on a scholarship (she dropped out after three months); his radicalisation was through the YCL; hers was in Paris, where heady bohemian summers with painter friends reinforced her disaffection with bourgeois social, moral and artistic conventions. After RADA she wanted to abandon England and live in France, but Europe's political turbulence forced her back to London. At a loose end, she sought out Archie Harding, who'd previously hired her for a job on BBC radio.[29] On learning that Harding had been moved to Manchester, she decided to seek him out.

Her Long March northwards would later become part of her mythology: like Jimmie, Joan had a strong line in colourful anecdotes, and took the same liberties with her own biography she'd later take with other people's plays – borrowing scenes, changing settings, resequencing events, editing out quieter moments. According to the story, she stitched her spare skirt into a Dick Whittington-style sack, walked all day, slept in hedgerows, lived on raw potatoes, collapsed in the Midlands and eventually limped into Manchester. 'I was a bum,' she'd later say, 'but I was adopted for the first time in my life by the whole humming scene, I was adopted by the autonomous republic.'[30]

She took a room in Grosvenor Street and got radio work on *In Manchester Tonight*.[31] With her RADA training, bohemian past and Francophile tastes she was at ease among the city's glamorous radicals, and Harding's circle made her welcome. She was articulate, funny and swore outrageously. She was irreverent and well read; like Miller,

she was authentically working class, but not so spiky with it. Initially
on the run from establishment theatre, it wasn't long before she was
rubbing shoulders with Manchester's actors and directors. Desperate
for cash, she took a £2 10s per week job as assistant stage manager at
the 800-seat Manchester Repertory Theatre on the Wilmslow Road,
Rusholme.[32] That September she got a bit-part in a drawing-room
drama;[33] at Christmas she got five minutes' glory when her reworking
of the nativity play upstaged the company's adaptation of *A Christmas
Carol* – one reviewer detected 'moments of beauty in thought and
language' in her piece.[34] It was then back to *The Scarlet Pimpernel*,
farces by Ben Travers, and *The Brontës of Brontë Parsonage*.[35] One of
her favourite terms of abuse at the time was 'lousy piss kitchen', and
it was lavishly applied to the Manchester Repertory Theatre.[36]

03&0

Realising how much these teenage working-class oddballs had in
common, Archie Harding introduced Jimmie to Joan in July 1934.
She went along to Left Theatre's rehearsal shortly afterwards. 'Walking
into that gloomy studio ... sealed my fate,' she later wrote.[37] The
group's performance standards were sometimes questionable. Some
members saw theatre as a subsidiary political activity rather than a site
of creativity, and machismo often prevented male members of the group
from taking theatrical craft seriously. Compared with Manchester Rep,
it was a ramshackle affair: they had no props, no costumes and the
windows didn't open in their smelly rehearsal room. But among the
hardcore, particularly Jimmie's sidekicks Alf Armitt and 'Stooge', or
Gerard Davies, there was an intensity that appealed to Littlewood.
They knew their politics and had strong opinions about everything;
their articulate militancy chimed with her rebel instincts. They were
attuned to contemporary developments and hungry for any information
they could find. They were brainy, cranky, even bombastic, but they
took theatre seriously.

   Jimmie was obviously the leader. He had 'a way of talking to you
as if he would like to knock you down', she remembered.[38] He talked
about agitprop and naturalism, the Popular Front, the British Workers'
Theatre Movement and sister organisations in Germany and the Soviet
Union. What he didn't know, he would make up, including the claim
that he'd been to Berlin and met Bertolt Brecht.[39] 'He seemed to have

sources of information not available to the rest of us,' she noted.[40] She was a rebellious artist without a cause; he was radicalism embodied, without the training or vocabulary to give theatrical form to his many causes. 'Only the best is good enough for the workers' was his mantra, but he knew that, despite his best efforts, the Manchester Workers' Theatre Movement hadn't given them the best.[41] 'Work with the Rep theatre seemed irrelevant after that meeting', she later wrote.[42] 'Our views', MacColl wrote in his autobiography, 'coincided at almost every point. We were drunk with ideas, lightheaded with talk ... each of us jubilant at having discovered an ally.'[43] They made a gawky pair – he was freckly with big ears; she was boyish, waif-like, gap-toothed. Caught up in revolutionary zeal, their relationship deepened over the autumn of 1934. She joined the Communist Party and became Jimmie's girlfriend.

CX80

'From the very beginning of our work together,' MacColl later wrote, 'we had confidence in our ability to create a theatre which would be more dynamic, truthful and adventurous than anything the bourgeois theatre could produce.'[44] Jimmie was now running rehearsals three or four nights a week, and would even give up his Sunday rambling. He was a strict taskmaster with a disciplinarian streak – late arrivals and absences were obsessively chronicled in a pocket book. Joan worked with him whenever she could get away from the Manchester Rep.

For the second time in their uneven career, Jimmie's troupe borrowed the name of a more distinguished and dynamic company. In 1933 they had become the Red Megaphones after a Berlin agitprop troupe. Early in 1935 the American Workers' Laboratory Theater rebranded itself Theater of Action; Jimmie followed suit and his Left Theatre also became Theatre of Action.[45] The name struck just the right note of energy and urgency. A new repertoire was tested at a series of small venues in preparation for its major debut, presented early in 1935 at the Round House, Ancoats, a large venue on the edge of the Manchester University Settlement.[46] Theatre of Action evaded the cost and inconvenience of submitting its scripts to the Lord Chamberlain by constituting itself as a club. Tickets were sold in advance and receipted as membership subscriptions; as long as twenty-four hours elapsed between a new member joining and attending a performance, the system was legally watertight.

The handbill advertising its new show doubled as a manifesto. It decried the fact that 'the very class which plays the chief part in contemporary history – the class upon which the prevention of war and the defeat of reaction solely depends – is debarred from expression in the present day theatre'.[47] Theatre of Action, by contrast, pledged to perform 'plays which express the life and struggles of the workers' to mainly working-class audiences. The handbill claimed that Theatre of Action was in the throes of creative experiment, and was busy searching for the new supple forms needed to bring contemporary history on to the stage.[48] Some items in the show looked back to full-blooded agitprop. Jimmie performed three Hans Eisler songs; the sketch 'John Bull Wants You' warned about the dangers of jingoism and militarism; the mass declamation 'Free Thaelmann' called for the release of the German Communist leader imprisoned by Hitler after the Reichstag fire.

Two items broke new ground. *The Fire Sermon* by American communist poet Sol Funaroff was a Marxist rewrite of T. S. Eliot's *The Waste Land*: political transformation, not spiritual reawakening, was Funaroff's solution to the contemporary *malaise*. The poem spoke deeply to Jimmie, who was a guilty admirer of the politically conservative Eliot's verse; he passionately declaimed *The Fire Sermon*, with shifts in tempo and mood expertly underscored by the coloured spotlights Alf Armitt had assembled from biscuit tins and light bulbs stolen from Salford greyhound track.[49]

The show's centrepiece, *Newsboy*, was based on a poem written by another prominent American communist, V. J. Jerome, and showed the transformation of a newspaper vendor from an agent of big business and false consciousness into a communist class warrior.[50] It proved exactly what Theatre of Action was after.[51] Like *Meerut*, it set out a political problem (newsboy as capitalist lackey) and then enacted the solution (newsboy's transformation into class-conscious worker); in this sense, it was squarely in keeping with agitprop conventions. But it also enacted a collision between naturalistic and symbolic modes of representation, effectively dramatising the debates about political theatre currently dividing the WTM.[52] It required developments in terms of lighting, voice projection, timing, movement and overall seriousness of purpose from the cast. J. H. Miller was listed as the producer, but Littlewood's input was obvious. Jimmie later wondered what an audience of the unemployed, cotton weavers and workers from the Walls' sausage factory made of it all.[53]

The success of the poetic and balletic *Newsboy* confirmed Jimmie and Joan's self-righteousness, and they became increasingly high-handed with those unenlightened comrades pursuing the incorrect artistic line. The next Theatre of Action production was loosely based on John Hammer's *Slickers Ltd*, a tentatively experimental play widely circulated through the Workers' Theatre Movement dramatising the British Establishment's lucrative dealings with the arms industry.[54] Miller and Littlewood's version, *John Bullion: A Ballet with Words*, was less an adaptation than an act of creative spite.[55] They slashed and burned Hammer's forty-five minute play into a frenetic fifteen minutes of dazzling lighting, roaring music, stylised acting, robotic dancing and disorienting sound effects. Miller and Littlewood were delighted with their bewildering theatrical spectacle. Joan clipped the newspaper review that described them as 'the nearest thing to Meyerhold the British theatre has got'.[56]

CR80

Her parallel life at the Manchester Rep was, in contrast, a dismal round of middlebrow Brontë adaptations, but things appeared to improve early in 1935 when exiled German playwright Ernst Toller came to the theatre to stage the British premiere of his play *Draw the Fires!* (1930).[57] With its set of new songs by Hanns Eisler, this was a major coup for the provincial theatre – and especially for Littlewood's boss, Dominic Roche, who would co-direct with Toller – but the production was rehearsed in just a fortnight and tensions quickly emerged. Most of the cast were ignorant about the play's subject matter, the 1917–18 mutiny in the German Navy; they were hostile to Toller's Marxism, and unused to his style of expressionist epic theatre.[58] Littlewood suggested that Toller might draw upon the talents of Theatre of Action, and he was desperate enough to entertain the idea. Jimmie Miller, Alf Armitt, Bob Goodman, Alec Armstrong and Gerard Davies were hired on an expenses-only basis.[59] Theatre of Action rehearsals were as disciplined as Communist Party meetings; Toller and Roche's rehearsals, by comparison, were slapdash affairs.[60] Before long, Jimmie was dispensing advice to the famous revolutionary playwright and demanding subscriptions to Theatre of Action. 'Zat young man!', Toller would gasp, 'He sinks he is everybody and he is nobody!'[61]

The play opened on Monday 11 February 1935, was well reviewed, ran for a week and was extended for a second.[62] On Sunday 12 May the production transferred to the Cambridge Theatre, London, for one night. Unrehearsed for three months, it was a shambles. The actors had forgotten their lines and Assistant Stage Manager Joan Littlewood had left the prompt script in Manchester.[63] The reviews were harsh and tense relations between the bolshy amateurs and defensive cast reached breaking point.[64] This was Jimmie's first experience of working in a professional theatre, but the episode only served to reinforce his contempt: 'when we left', he said, 'we had a very clear picture of the kind of theatre we didn't want'.[65] Littlewood stuck it out for another three weeks, and then also parted company from the Manchester Rep.[66]

CʒᏰↃ

Without a job, she could no longer afford her digs. BBC work had dried up, so she moved into 37 Coburg Street. It was a difficult time. Her own grandparents were warm and easy-going people; the atmosphere at Coburg Street was cold and stiff. Will Miller was prematurely aged, wheezy with asthma and now suffered from bouts of deep depression. He made at least two attempts on his own life during this period.[67] Betsy's body was covered in painful psoriasis, making her moods volatile and her tongue even sharper than usual. Jimmie could do no wrong – 'she'd take the skin off her back for him', Will used to say – and the interloper Joan could do nothing right.[68]

The Millers were radical politically but morally conservative; Lower Broughton neighbours were gossipy, and Betsy wanted her son and Joan to do the decent thing and get married. Jimmie was receptive to the idea. He was in love and, at this point in his life, didn't want to behave in a way that might tarnish the reputation of the Communist Party.[69] Littlewood wouldn't hear of it. She was twenty years old and a free spirit.[70] Betsy became more hostile. The worse things got, the more insular the Millers seemed to become. '[Betsy] would speak of the "class enemy" with studied venom,' Littlewood recalled, 'and that meant just about everybody but Jimmie and her husband.'[71]

CʒᏰↃ

Theatre of Action was now bringing the talented young couple out of
the Grosvenor Street rehearsal room into new circles. In May 1935
their troupe hosted a weekend conference at Manchester's Grand
Hotel where, in line with Popular Front strategy, they aimed to build
a network of left-leaning theatre groups across the region's amateur
theatre scene.[72] Artists and critics attended; the keynote speaker was
Jimmie's acquaintance André van Gyseghem, a professional producer
who had worked with Meyerhold and Eisenstein in the Soviet Union,
and who would go on to become president of Unity Theatre.[73]

    This rapprochement with theatre professionals, other amateur groups
and sympathetic journalists brought new members into Theatre of
Action, and the next production increased applications still further.
Clifford Odets' *Waiting For Lefty* dramatised scenes from the 1934
New York taxi drivers' strike, and had been rapturously received by
American audiences.[74] In February 1935 it was published in *New
Theatre* magazine, and British groups were eager to stage the show.
London's Rebel Players assiduously courted Odets and his agent in an
effort to secure permission.[75] Littlewood and Miller made preliminary
enquiries but then dispensed with such time-consuming bourgeois tech-
nicalities. By August 1935 they had cast it, rehearsed it and performed
it, first at the Milton Hall on Deansgate and then in a number of
small Lancashire towns.[76] Staging the British premiere without the
author's permission was a serious violation of protocol and made it
more difficult for other British groups to perform the play. It further
widened the gap between Miller and Littlewood and what remained
of the WTM.

⊰⊱

Neither of them believed that artistic processes could be run demo-
cratically. They were in charge, and their Theatre of Action was a
benevolent dictatorship with the benevolence omitted wherever
artistically necessary. There was no secretary, treasurer or committee.
Miller and Littlewood selected the material for performance, cast
the shows and ran the rehearsals. Some of the recent recruits were
shocked by such dictatorial working methods, and infighting began.
It seems that some of the new Theatre of Action recruits who were
also Communist Party members made their grievances known to the
District Party Committee, and a meeting was called at which Miller and

Littlewood were almost expelled.[77] Under a more democratic structure, Theatre of Action was brought back into the mainstream of amateur left theatre groups, and would soon be involved in the formation of the New Theatre League – a Popular Front organisation that superseded the dissolved Workers' Theatre Movement.[78] Shocked but unrepentant, Miller and Littlewood attributed the coup to untalented and opportune middle-class intellectuals. They would have nothing further to do with Theatre of Action. 'I fondly imagined', MacColl later wrote, 'that the creation of a successful workers' theatre would be greeted with loud hurrahs by the party. The realisation that such was not the case was like a kick in the stomach.'[79]

CঙৎO

Their dignity was saved by a lucky coincidence: they were accepted as scholarship students to the prestigious Soviet Academy of Cinema and Theatre, where they were to study Marxist theory, theatre history, scriptwriting, editing and directing in a faculty that included Sergei Eisenstein, Vsevolod Meyerhold and Moscow Art Theatre's Constantin Stanislavski.[80] Jimmie applied for his first passport – he gave his height as 5'10½" (he was three inches shorter), and his occupation as 'playwright' (an intention, rather than a fact).[81] The looming journey raised the issue of marriage once more. Betsy Miller's wishes and the good reputation of the Communist Party prevailed. On 15 September 1935 Jimmie and Joan, both aged twenty, were married at Pendleton Town Hall. The newlyweds took the train to London and made for the Soviet Embassy to collect visas.[82] They were away from Manchester for just six months and never got to Moscow: 'It was like *The Cherry Orchard*,' MacColl later recalled.[83]

Jimmie had only been to London twice before, and set out in high spirits. They visited galleries, museums and took tea at the ABC café on the Strand. They loafed around in the autumn sunshine and stayed with Littlewood's grandparents for a while, then with one of her RADA friends. With brazen audacity, Littlewood hustled them accommodation at 132 Cheyne Walk, Chelsea, in the basement of a property owned by an eccentric millionairess recently converted to Christian Science. The lady was the author of a vanity-published novel expounding her new theological convictions; Littlewood agreed to write a film treatment in return for free digs.

There was a hold-up with their visas – the inscrutable bureaucrats at the Soviet Embassy were unforthcoming but predicted a long wait. Resigned to a spell in the capital, the couple talked about starting a new political theatre group and looked for BBC work to tide them over. They learned that Robin Whitworth of the Harding circle was now based in London and contacted him. Littlewood sent him a postcard offering her services: 'OUR THEATRE CATCHES FIRE LIKE A TRAIN OF GUNPOWDER' was added to the bottom, indicating that the BBC was a means to an end and that she was setting her sights higher.[84] Miller wrote too. 'Dear Whitworth', he began, brusquely dispensing with the deference expected from a twenty-year-old working-class Salfordian contacting a senior BBC producer, 'I am here in London with Littlewood trying to build a Revolutionary Theatre. Our efforts, generally speaking, are meeting with success and given a sporting chance we can make out.'[85]

The competition at the BBC was much stiffer in London; nobody knew them and the corporation wasn't hiring.[86] As the winter set in their paltry savings were running out, and they weren't eligible for the dole. Moscow seemed to recede over the horizon. Littlewood drew on old RADA contacts and fixed up temporary work teaching theatre classes in training colleges. Miller was sent off to lecture. 'I was absolutely flummoxed,' he later recalled:

> I had a broad Salford accent, very poor clothes and I'd been on the dole for years. There I was in these posh places – they seemed incredibly posh to me, where people had sinks in their rooms, I'd never seen anything so luxurious – imagine having a sink in your bedroom ! – and gave lectures on the theatre, and the great theatre that we were going to build. It was described as though it had already been built and I'd just moved away from it.[87]

They were evicted from Cheyne Walk after hosting a drunken New Year's Eve party at which 'The Internationale' was loudly sung. By late January they had moved into a borrowed flat on the north side of Wandsworth Common.[88] Without news from Moscow, they committed themselves to create the new theatre group and drew upon the most talented members of their training classes for recruits. It's a measure of their commitment and charisma that they managed to persuade a handful of youngsters to leave home for the hare-brained new venture. They rented an enormous run-down house at 113 West Side, Clapham Common, paid a month's rent deposit and a month's down, furnished the place with hire-purchase goods and set about communal living.

This was to be their version of the New York Workers' Laboratory Theater. They called themselves 'The Miller Theatre' – Miller and Littlewood were listed as 'Regisseurs' on their headed notepaper – but it was never much more than a paper exercise.[89] In Manchester they were respected and had political networks to draw on; here, apart from some of Littlewood's old RADA acquaintances, they knew no one. They had no regular income – according to BBC records, neither was hired in London at this time – and they couldn't afford to buy coal, food or to meet the payments on the furniture. Moscow was never going to happen. Years later, MacColl would claim to have uncovered what went wrong; he described how a prominent figure in left theatre, due to be in Moscow at the same time, blocked the application on hearing that Jimmie was now married:

> He'd put the kibosh on me, because he fancied me, he thought I was going to be his boyfriend when we were out there … finally somebody told us. And we were absolutely mortified, couldn't believe that anybody connected with the left wing movement could be a homosexual.[90]

Like many communists of his generation, MacColl displayed unenlightened views on homosexuality – in this respect, he was in line with the Soviet state itself, where homosexuality had been criminalised by Stalin in 1934.[91] Whatever happened to that visa application – and no record has survived – the Miller Theatre was barely a month old when the disenchanted new recruits were sneaking back to their more comfortable parental homes. Penniless, demoralised and underfed, Miller and Littlewood posted the keys through the letterbox (leaving the hire-purchase furniture inside) and made their way back to Manchester. On 1 May 1936 Jimmie was paid 5 guineas for playing 'an apprentice' and 'a worker' in the North of England Home Service remake of Bridson's *May Day*.[92] It was as though he'd never been away.

∞

They moved back to overcrowded Coburg Street for a few miserable months, and then Betsy got the chance to rent a twelve-roomed terraced house at 18 Victoria Road, Fallowfield. The four of them decamped from Lower Broughton, cleaned up the new place and Betsy advertised for lodgers seeking room and board. Joan and Jimmie got the pick of the rooms. They installed a phone, slept on a mattress on the floor, and filled their new quarters with theatre journals, newspapers, gramophone records and books stolen by Jimmie from the stalls at Hanging Ditch.[93] 'He believed he had a God given right to any book he needed,' recalled Littlewood, 'and had no scruples about plundering them.'[94]

∞૪૭

Early in 1937 they were approached by a coalition of anti-war activists from the Peace Pledge Union, the League of Nations Union, Quaker groups and the Trades Council who wanted to beef up the city's longstanding annual Peace Week.[95] Amid a city-wide upsurge in such broad-based cultural and political activism, Miller and Littlewood were paid a fee, given access to staff and facilities at the Friends' Meeting House, and invited to present a play reaffirming the message of peace and unity.[96] They chose Hans Chlumberg's anti-war drama *Miracle at Verdun* (1930), which required a large, interracial cast of around eighty. Littlewood and Miller advertised and auditioned. The production ran from Wednesday 7 July for four nights at the Lesser Free Trade Hall.[97] Ultimately, the process of staging *Miracle at Verdun* proved more significant than the worthy but dull production itself. Old contacts were re-established and new ones forged. Miller and Littlewood began to create the loose network of like-minded performers, artists, musicians and intellectuals with whom they would collaborate over the next three or four years.

∞૪૭

For the time being radio absorbed most of their attention. They lampooned the BBC and depended on it. 'There was something rarefied about the place, something unreal,' MacColl later wrote. 'Once inside those Piccadilly studios, the world outside ceased to exist.'[98] They carped about its meanness, snobbery, conservatism and the mediocrity of its output. They huffed and puffed about poor and slow payment and bitched about regular employees: 'Congratulations on the casting,' Littlewood wrote to a producer on one occasion, 'it was, quite honestly – a miracle – or perhaps that's because we have very definite views about BBC actors – and we usually find them lousy.'[99] It was no way to carve out a permanent career – both Joan and Jimmie regarded the BBC as a means to subsidise their commitment to revolutionary theatre – but a series of promotions now pushed work their way. D. G.

Bridson, who thought highly of Miller and Littlewood, was made the North Region's Features Programme Assistant.[100] Olive Shapley – with whom Jimmie and Joan would take a camping holiday to France in 1938 – moved up from Children's Hour producer to second Features Assistant.[101] This younger generation of permanent staff, who like Miller and Littlewood had entered the BBC North Region during the 1934–5 expansion, were now reaching positions of relative power from which programmes could be commissioned and the careers of promising writers and actors nurtured.[102] It was a period of eclectic, experimental and often surprisingly political programme-making.

Shapley hired both Joan and Jimmie to research and present programmes. In *Homeless People*, broadcast in September 1938, Jimmie worked opposite the young Wilfred Pickles, recording testimony on a tour of doss-houses, children's homes, Seamen's Institutes and Street Missions.[103] Shapley also encouraged Joan and Jimmie's writing, and the extra money was welcome – the going rate was 12 guineas per script, approximately double the weekly earnings of a skilled engineer. They were commissioned to co-write *Owd Nick in Lancashire*, a historical feature about the Lancashire witches broadcast in the North Region on 29 April 1937.[104] Jimmie then wrote *Westwards From Liverpool*, a feature programme broadcast on Friday 19 November. The programme was typically experimental, and blended the songs of Henry Russell with the 'real voices' of emigrants from Newcastle upon Tyne who'd moved to Canada.[105] Listed as a recommended programme in the *Manchester Evening News*, this was Jimmie's first brush with the type of wide-ranging, multimedia historical and political radio at which he would excel in later life.[106]

Such writing now brought him to the attention of producer John Pudney. Radical and sophisticated, Pudney published his poetry in the *Left Review* and mixed with W. H. Auden and Benjamin Britten.[107] He thought Jimmie a 'useful chap' and entrusted some prestigious projects to him.[108] Co-scripted by Jimmie and Margaret Lambert, *News of A Hundred Years Ago* chronicled the underground press that had shaped and nourished the Chartist movement.[109] Chartism, claimed Pudney, was 'the basis of all working class emancipation in this country', and he now set about creating a more ambitious show for the National Home Service to be broadcast to mark the charter's centenary.[110] This time Jimmie was commissioned to write short vignettes dramatising the activities of Chartists in Scotland, Wales, the Midlands and the north.[111] It proved a demanding project for a relatively inexperienced writer, and he struggled to script authentic-sounding period speech (one Welsh script editor wondered whether 'the whole episode has been written in Bloomsbury by someone who has never been to South Wales'[112]). Further problems arose when the score-composer Benjamin Britten found the rhythm to Jimmie's marching song uneven – Pudney had to step in and rewrite the piece.[113] *The Chartists March* was eventually broadcast on the National Programme on 13 May. It was a humbling experience for Jimmie, but would feature in his CV for years to come.

ᘓᔥᔥ

The flurry of BBC work temporarily created a regular income, and it was almost certainly during the spell at Victoria Road that Jimmie wrote his only novel, 'The Damnable Town'.[114] Effectively an autobiography recast as fiction, the book parades its author's hard-earned erudition; Jimmie borrows liberally from James Joyce and Lewis Grassic Gibbon's *Scots Quair* trilogy to present a portrait of the revolutionary artist as a young man. In Jimmie's novel, the sensitive, intelligent, Jimmie Miller-like teenager Martin Hoyt wants to be a writer; unlike Jimmie Miller, he initially shuns political commitment, insisting instead that 'an artist must be free'.[115] The novel presents the young man, in effect, with two choices. One is represented by Coll, a lumpen-proletarian drifter and rapist eventually escorted from the novel by police after molesting a child in a public park. The alternative to loneliness and perversity is class-consciousness and communism, as embodied by Hugh Russell, a rambler and engineer fluent in Marxist dialectics. This beacon of revolutionary rectitude rescues Martin by imparting a vision of political struggle where the artist has a central role to play:

> You must speak for your class, for the workers. As a class we are now mature but as yet no one of us has been able to express all the feelings and dream of our class; the workers are richer and deeper in experience than anybody has ever been. Here is a great task then; to be the first great artist of the twentieth century working class.[116]

Though Jimmie's book would never be published – at least one publisher rejected a manuscript considered 'sadistic in outlook' distorted by 'political bias' and with flashes of 'brilliance' – the obsessions that would structure much of his future writing are already in place.[117] The working class is in ascendancy and capable of becoming the class of the twentieth century; working-class art should be grounded in working-class experience and reinforce radical class-consciousness; careerism and aestheticism must be resisted. In writing a novel about the duties of the revolutionary writer, Jimmie was effectively giving himself a good talking-to, fortifying himself for the task ahead. The moments of heavy-handedness reveal the uncertainties he was most eager to keep under wraps: the novel's insistence that cultural work is greatly valued by the Communist Party seems to be generated by a suspicion that the opposite was true; its earnest affirmation of robust working-class masculinity – the real hero is never Martin the writer, but Hugh the tough-muscled and tough-minded industrial organiser – seems to be bound up with Jimmie's anxiety that he fell short of the sinewy worker-hero ideal.

⊗⊗⊗

His anxiety was sharpened during the Spanish Civil War, in which around 2,200 British volunteers joined the International Brigades, and 526 were killed.[118] Life in the ranks didn't appeal to Jimmie, but he knew at least a dozen of the British dead, and lost two of his closest comrades and friends in the heavy fighting at Jarama.[119] Bob Goodman and Alec Armstrong, still in their early twenties, shared Jimmie's politics, his interest in theatre, and his love of rambling and climbing. Goodman was killed in February 1937, Armstrong in June.[120]

Jimmie gave vent to some of the feelings of rage, guilt and loss in his second enduring song (the first was 'The Manchester Rambler'). 'Jamie Foyers' was a folksong Betsy used to sing lamenting a Perthshire militiaman killed in Spain during the Peninsular Wars. Recent events gave the song a new layer of associations, and Jimmie updated the text. In Jimmie's 'Jamie Foyers', the hero is a Clydeside shipyard worker, a composite of Goodman and Armstrong, who joins the International Brigade and dies fighting in Spain. Jimmie celebrates Foyers' life, dramatises his departure for Spain, and unblinkingly confronts the physical reality of his death: 'He lay owre his machine-gun wi' a bullet in his brain.' The song was a haunting requiem for fallen comrades, but closed on a note of murderous vengefulness:

He lies by the Ebro in far away Spain,
He died so that freedom and justice might reign;
Remember young Foyers and others of worth
And don't let one fascist be left on this earth.[121]

∞≫∞

The Spanish Civil War augmented Jimmie's militancy. He regarded Spain as 'the front line' where 'the bourgeoisie and proletariat stand face to face in open struggle at last, no more arguments, no more trimmings', and he raged against a British political establishment that had prevaricated and fudged as the fascist threat grew.[122] He remained extremely active within the Communist Party: he lectured on working-class history and cultural traditions to the city's YCL and party branches;[123] he and Joan participated in a series of Communist pageants in which the party paraded its own distinctive version of history's march through the streets of Manchester;[124] they provided dramatic interludes for communist-led public meetings celebrating the achievements of the Soviet Union, raising funds for the Daily Worker, and collecting cash and food for the Republican cause in Spain.[125]

∞≫∞

On 10 December 1938 an undercover police officer attended a Manchester Daily Worker fundraiser and filed a special report on 'a youth named Jimmy [sic] Miller who was the MC for the dancing and showed exceptional ability as a singer and musical organiser'.[126] Police surveillance of Communist Party activity was ongoing – they'd first come across Jimmie during the 1932 Mass Trespass campaign – and monitoring was now ratcheted up.[127] Letters from Jimmie to party comrades were intercepted.[128] When Will, Betsy, Joan and Jimmie moved from Fallowfield to a cheaper, smaller cottage at Werneth Low, near Hyde, police soon had the property under surveillance. Visits to the cottage from 'a number of young men who have the appearance of Communist Jews' were conscientiously logged.[129] Enquiries about Joan and Jimmie were made among local shopkeepers and neighbours; officers gleaned that Joan was 'highly intellectual and a keen communist' and that Jimmie had 'strong revolutionary views' and was 'a man to be watched in case of industrial unrest'.[130] The tall stories that always tripped from Jimmie's tongue inadvertently laid false leads for the constabulary: at one point they believed they were dealing with a professional balloon-rigger currently working as a rope manufacturer who'd lived in the Soviet Union.[131]

കൃ൮

The Popular Front emphasis on unity helped to reunite Manchester's fragmented left theatre scene. Late in 1938 Miller and Littlewood rehired the old Theatre of Action rehearsal room at 111 Grosvenor Street to begin rehearsals for a new group, aptly named Theatre Union.[132] More inclusive than its predecessors, talk of class struggle and revolution was subordinated to that of democracy, progress and peace. Theatre Union argued that fascism imperilled all that was best about Western civilisation, even the great art of the bourgeoisie. The company's task was to bring 'plays of social significance' to 'the widest possible public, and particularly to that section of the public which has been starved theatrically'.[133]

Theatre Union cast the net wide to draw in actors from across the local theatre scene – amateurs and professionals from groups including the Oldham Repertory Theatre, the Great Synagogue Dramatic Section and the Socialist Zionist Dramatic Society became involved.[134] This was a slicker, savvier outfit than its predecessor. Harold Lever, who would go on to serve in Harold Wilson's cabinet, acted as Business Manager.[135] Chic communist artist Barbara Niven was the doyenne of fashionable radicals at Manchester School of Art. She and her partner, the socialist realist painter Ern Brooks, lent their considerable cultural clout (they were friends with poet Hugh MacDiarmid), and offered their talents for set and costume design.[136] From the outset, the plan was to establish a permanent base in the city on behalf of 'the progressives of Manchester'.[137] Trade unions and Left Book Club groups were encouraged to take out block membership; shops and businesses were courted for sponsorship.[138]

All proceeds from the first production were to go to the Manchester Foodship for Spain, and Miller came up with the idea of launching Theatre Union with *Fuente Ovejuna* (*The Sheepwell*), a play by a contemporary of Shakespeare, Spain's Lope de Vega (1562–1635). Never performed in Britain, *Fuente Ovejuna* was a shrewd choice.[139] It was an exciting premiere with a broad appeal for serious theatregoers.[140] The play also had direct relevance to the current situation in Spain: *Fuente*

*Ovejuna* dealt with a community in rebellion against the militarism of a despotic overlord; Federico García Lorca, the Spanish poet murdered by right-wing death squads in 1936, was widely associated with the play.[141] With its mix of poetry, prose, tragedy, bawdy humour, song and dance, the play enabled co-producers Miller and Littlewood to draw on much that they'd learned to date. Jimmie added songs associated with the Republican movement and wrote some others – unable to read or write music, he sang the new pieces until the musicians learnt them.[142] Officially licensed by the Lord Chamberlain and properly open to the public, *Fuente Ovejuna* ran from 21 to 25 February 1939 at the Lesser Free Trade Hall and was widely covered in the press.[143] The *Guardian* critic heralded 'A New Manchester Movement' and congratulated Miller and Littlewood for 'their notable achievement in welding a scratch cast of amateurs and professionals into a nearly coherent company'.[144] Theatre Union quickly followed up the success with an adaptation of Joan and Jimmie's favourite novel, Jaroslav Hašek's *The Good Soldier Schweik* (1923).[145] Based on the groundbreaking 1927 Berlin production by Irwin Piscator and Bertolt Brecht, the show ran at the Lesser Free Trade Hall between 12 and 20 May 1939.[146] More new talent was recruited, including Howard Goorney, a gifted eighteen-year-old actor who would become a lifelong friend of Jimmie's.

⋈

The success of the plays gave a glimpse of what was possible. The idea of establishing a permanent, radical theatre in the city became a fixation with Miller and Littlewood. Many who met them were struck by their messianic intensity and the implausible breadth of their knowledge. Rosalie Williams was a Manchester University student dissatisfied with the University Stage Society. She ventured into the 111 Grosvenor Street rehearsal room:

> There was Joan and Jimmie, with a group of young people, doing improvisation ... They were busy looking for recruits, both artistic and political .... Jimmie was then a very ardent young communist, Joan too, and within a week I was embraced into the group and a member of the Communist Party, pressed by Jimmie, though I had no real appreciation of politics at that time.

From then on, University took second place; it was across the road every evening into classes – Stanislavski, movement, ... weight transference, relaxation, mime...Where they attained all that knowledge was astounding ... They were young and in their prime – and intellectually inspiring. ... It was a unique marriage of talents ... This basic period of training ... stayed with me through the whole of my subsequent life as an actress – and I think it stayed with every member they touched.[147]

Rosalie's experiences of Joan and Jimmie weren't unusual. Like her, many of the Theatre Union's new recruits were in their late teens; five or six years older, Miller and Littlewood were unspeakably glamorous. They now had their own small flat at 377 Oxford Road, which became a magnet for the city's activists and artists. They worked for the BBC, were gifted, outspoken and devilishly reckless about their own futures. They were demanding but stimulating teachers who were generous with talented students – rehearsals and training classes now ran every night, and Jimmie issued challenging reading lists that ranged from Marx to Aristophanes and Stanislavski. They'd already crammed a great deal of experience into their lives, and neither was shy of varnishing the basic facts for the sake of a good story.

Theatre Union was a cause; at moments, for the nucleus at least, it became almost a cult. Shoplifting from the petit bourgeoisie was sanctioned: fabrics, face paint, light bulbs, props, stationery, books – anything to assist the theatre of the future was fair game. There were obligatory trips to the Hallé on Tuesdays and twenty-mile hikes on Sundays over Bleaklow where Jimmie Miller kept them all in step by singing songs unswerving in their commitment to Comrade Stalin, the party line and the need to 'liquidate the Kulak class'.[148] There were raucous parties with songs celebrating Lenin, the Tolpuddle Martyrs and the virtues of dialectical thought.[149] The atmosphere of the months preceding the war was heady: feelings of doom-laden seriousness jostled with gay abandon. Members of Theatre Union rehearsed together, trained together, studied together and often slept together. Romances blossomed and faded. Jimmie and Joan's fertile creative and intellectual partnership soon outgrew the constraints of bourgeois monogamy. Jimmie's philandering in 1939 and 1940 was prodigious; he was 'more than ever combining his courtships with recruitment to the Communist Party', Littlewood remembered, and was 'now surrounded by a most unsuitable collection of young ladies, all carrying the Party card'.[150]

Joan would soon meet the ravishingly handsome Gerry Raffles, a Manchester University student who would join Theatre Union and become the love of her life.

C380

The Nazi–Soviet non-aggression pact signed on 23 August 1939 put British Communists in a tricky situation. Communist General Secretary Harry Pollitt had long presented his party as a beacon of anti-fascist integrity, and the Soviet Union as 'the principal guardian for maintaining peace in the world' with 'an army ready to throw its full, dynamic weight into the scales against German, Italian and Japanese fascists'.[151] Rather than throwing its military weight against Hitler, the Soviet Union had now cut a deal with him. When war was finally declared on 1 September, Harry Pollitt couldn't accept the new line – that war against Hitler was an imperialistic adventure inimical to working-class interests – and relinquished his post as General Secretary. Loyal to the core, Joan and Jimmie accepted the volte-face and were soon planning new BBC radio programmes with anti-war undertones.[152] Their names appeared on a BBC vetting list and the work dried up.[153]

In theatre they could be more explicit, and they now planned a living newspaper about 'the betrayal of the working class to Fascism and the consequent apotheosis of a second world imperialist war'.[154] The production was to cover the years from 1934 to the present day, and expose 'the real fascist nature of the National Government' and the collusion of the bourgeois media, including the 'campaign of slander' apparently waged against Stalin's show-trials.[155]

C380

*Last Edition: A Living Newspaper dealing with Events from 1934 to 1940* was premiered at the Round House in Ancoats on 14 March 1940. The young Anthony Burgess, then a student at Manchester University, saw the show:

> There was no doubt about the strength of [Littlewood's] technique and the thoroughness of its modernity. She had absorbed Brecht and Stanislavsky. A ramp thrust out from the side of the proscenium, and on it paraded workers out of *Metropolis*, some of them pressed local unemployed and their wives, many of them with their false teeth out ... She presented enormities like the 1935 Anglo-German naval agreement in lateral form, gossip spraying out

of frank but anaemic love-making between members of the ruling class. Hitler and Mussolini pranced in a ballet as good as *The Green Table*. The lightning plot was complex and oiled like machinery. Amplified gramophone records swelled in on split second cues. All the actors were amateurs, but Joan Littlewood had drilled them to the screaming limit.[156]

The show covered all the years Joan and Jimmie had known one another, and was a compendium of everything they'd learned.[157] They plundered previous shows for ideas: the newsboy device was revived; the stylised movement of *John Bullion* was developed. According to the most recent version of its frequently updated manifesto, Theatre Union was now 'intensifying [its] efforts to get at the essence of reality', and *Last Edition* was lavishly multimedia.[158] It was a ghost story: the spectres of friends killed in Spain haunted the Round House stage, silently saluting the audience. It was a visualised poem: Hugh MacDiarmid's hymn to Spain's Republic was recited.[159] It was like a movie: the sordid realpolitik of the 1938 Munich Agreement was recast as a Hollywood mobster scenario. It was musical theatre, with songs including Jimmie's new anti-war blues song 'Young Man of Our Time'.[160] It was a type of dramatised radio feature: Jimmie dominated proceedings from a side stage, providing linking narration and introducing new scenes. It concluded in classic agitprop style: capitalism was presented as the real enemy, especially 'the men who breed hatred through their press'. The peddlers of bourgeois misinformation loved the show. The *Manchester Guardian* detected 'strokes of genius'; the *Daily Express* praised 'a fine attempt in an almost new stage medium'.[161]

⊂⅋⊃

*Last Edition*'s loose form was its greatest strength; the production deliberately recreated the swift rhythm of the variety show, and individual scenes could quickly be modified to function as freestanding turns at political meetings. The company worked the show hard over the spring of 1940, adapting it to assist the *Daily Worker* fund.[162] Some scenes were toured round the Red Megaphones' old haunts – Accrington, Burnley, Bury, Huddersfield, Halifax and Oldham – and performed in Co-op Halls, clubs and market places.[163] Theatre Union took the whole production to Hyde Socialist Church for the weekend of 21 and 22 April, where a local constable's enquiries revealed that the 'thinly veiled communist propaganda' was much appreciated by 'the younger generation'.[164] By early May *Last Edition* was back for a second run in Manchester, this time at the more central Milton Hall on Deansgate.

The Ancoats shows in March had coincided with the so-called phoney war, a period of blackouts, boredom and relative military inactivity. By May the war was dangerously close. Hitler's forces were sweeping through Denmark and Norway.[165] The police were jumpy and visited the homes of some recent Theatre Union recruits, warning parents of the undesirable company their children were keeping.[166] On the second night of the new run, police raided the show. Joan and Jimmie were arrested, escorted to Stanley Street Police Station and charged with the technicality of contravening the 1843 Theatres Act by giving an unlicensed public performance. They were summoned to appear at Manchester City Police Court on 31 May 1940.[167] 'When the dreaded day arrived I put on my ... only suit,' remembered Littlewood, 'gave my hair an extra brushing and breathed deeply. Walk tall, I said to myself, and sailed into the courtroom with Jimmie Miller like a star at a photo call.'[168] They were found guilty as charged. Jimmie was fined £1, Joan was bound over, and Theatre Union was thrown into temporary disarray as nervous members resigned.[169] It was a suitably dramatic finale to a tumultuous decade.

# 4
# *Browned Off*

Between July and October 1940, 460,000 British men were called-up into the armed services and twenty-five-year-old Jimmie Miller was one of them.[1] He said goodbye to Theatre Union with a speech that contrasted the brutalities of militarism with the beauty of art; he told them to steel themselves for the ordeals ahead, and offered reassurance that the company would be reunited as soon as possible. After issuing a final round of reading lists, Jimmie reported to the King's Regiment at Wathgill near Richmond in North Yorkshire. On 24 July 1940 he was formally conscripted into the army.

He became Private 3779986 and received a haircut, a pint mug, a mess tin, a pair of boots and a uniform. His living quarters were an ill-ventilated wooden hut furnished with twenty mattresses and a pile of sour blankets. He was to wash and shave at a nearby cold tap, relieve himself in an evil-smelling latrine, and take meals with 2,000 other fresh recruits in a huge mess tent.[2] For the six weeks of his basic training, this would be home. He'd left Manchester burning with visions. 'He'd hardly been in the army twenty-four hours before the mood changed,' recalled Joan Littlewood. 'His letters were so utterly dejected that we all had to hitch-hike up to Richmond ... on the Sunday to cheer him up.'[3] The trip became a regular event for Theatre Union loyalists, who'd courier food parcels prepared by Betsy.

He immediately hated life in the ranks, and not only because the Communist Party denounced the war. Jimmie's civilian social world now comprised working-class radicals and intellectuals, university students, theatre enthusiasts, BBC employees; the King's Regiment had a reputation for drawing tough recruits from Liverpool and Manchester. He recoiled from the foul-mouthed brutishness of army life – the type

of cap he was forced to wear was commonly known as a 'cunt cap';
recruits lewdly referred to their sexual triumphs as 'meat injections'.
He'd never been keen on taking instruction, and the early morning
parade ground drillings were torture to him. Military life magnified
the rigid class hierarchies he'd spent his life rebelling against: he was
confronted with an aristocracy of public school-educated commissioned
officers, lower ranks of unskilled and unemployed workers, and a
bourgeoisie of middle rankers. He found the rhetoric about 'a war for
democracy' laughable when it came from the class that administered
the British Empire. He hated the food, the dirt, the lack of privacy, the
mind-numbing boredom and the incessant medical inspections. Bitter,
miserable and feeling vulnerable, he wore a fixed smile and kept his
head down.

CRGO

MI5 notified the King's Regiment of Private Miller's communist
tendencies, and investigations were made 'to see whether he is trying
to carry on propaganda'.[4] His Lieutenant Colonel filed a report
describing Jimmie as a model recruit of 'much greater intelligence
than the ordinary soldier', but 'cheerful and willing', indeed 'almost
ingratiating'. Jimmie, it was noted, had produced a number of songs
and sketches for the Regimental Concert Party, one of which 'was a
favourite with the men'.[5] The text to Jimmie's 'Browned Off' was duly
circulated and scrutinised by the top brass at the Northern Command
HQ in York:

> O, I was browned off, browned off, browned off as can be;
> Browned off, browned off, an easy mark, that's me.
> But when the war is over and again I'm free,
> There'll be no more trips around the world for me.[6]

'I am inclined to think', wrote one Major,

> that in all probability it was rather subtle propaganda, the theme being
> generally disparaging to life as a private soldier, and enlarging upon the
> fact that the discipline and alleged discomforts, to which he is subjected,
> although nominally in the cause for democracy, were really for the benefit
> of some supposedly superior class.[7]

His lyrics had never been taken so seriously. Private Miller was placed
under Special Observation.[8]

C3 EO

With the interminable ordeal of basic training over, Jimmie was granted a weekend's leave and went home to perform propaganda of a less subtle kind. On 29 September Joan, Jimmie and other members of Theatre Union shared a stage with Harry Pollitt at the Free Trade Hall where excerpts from *Last Edition* were presented to raise funds for the embattled *Daily Worker* (the newspaper would be banned the following January). Jimmie's presence was noted by undercover police officers, now keeping an even closer eye on the activities of the city's communists.[9] He enjoyed Betsy's cooking at Oak Cottage, Hyde – Joan and Jimmie had given up their Oxford Road flat shortly before he was called up – and attended rehearsals for Theatre Union's new production, Aristophanes' *Lysistrata*. A classical play about ordinary citizens resisting war was considered nicely in step with the Communist Party's current line.[10]

Jimmie dragged himself back to the army where, awaiting posting, he divided his time between clerical duties in Richmond and North Shields, Tyneside.[11] Ten days later he was home again for another appearance at the Free Trade Hall, this time celebrating the achievements of the Soviet Union. Police noted that he was now dressed in civilian clothes; their enquiries revealed he was on 'extended "sick leave"'.[12] He secured a further fortnight's leave between 29 October and 11 November – why so much leave was granted is unclear from his military records – but he finally returned to his regiment on 12 November.[13] The following day he took and failed a medical (records are imprecise on the details).[14] Demoted from the 11th Service Battalion (with whom he'd have seen active service in Italy, Greece and Burma) to the 10th Battalion (assigned to Home Defence), he spent another fortnight on administrative duties at the Regimental Headquarters in Liverpool, before being transferred to the Railway Training Centre, Derby, where he clocked in on 11 December.[15] The nature of his new duties is unclear, but by the end of the week he'd parted company from life in the ranks. On 18 December 1940 he was officially declared a deserter.[16]

He made straight for his parents' cottage. 'What do you think of it, mother?' Betsy remembered him asking. 'You please yourself, son,' she replied. 'If you want out, get out. Out you get.' She'd never liked the idea of him doing manual work, and she certainly felt no obligations to the British Army. 'He was mine,' she'd later say, 'and he was welcome to everything I got … They would have shot him if they'd got him.'[17] He stayed a couple of nights; when the Military Police appeared the family gave nothing away. Their visit was followed up by police. 'Enquiries and observations have since been continued,' reported the Hyde Borough Constabulary two and a half years later, 'but no information can be obtained as to his whereabouts.'[18]

∞∂∞

In the week following Jimmie's desertion the streets and skyline of Manchester were smashed by the Luftwaffe: 363 Mancunians were killed as the city centre was engulfed in a fire-ball fuelled by blazing cotton warehouses.[19] Private Miller was nobody's priority, and he quietly made the journey from Hyde across to Urmston, a suburb to the south-west of the city. He headed for 5 Manor Avenue, an imposing three-storey Victorian house owned by the Williamses, well-heeled liberal schoolteachers who were spending the war in the United States. The family home had been left in the hands of their daughter Rosalie, an active member of Theatre Union, a close friend of Joan's, and Jimmie's current girlfriend; 5 Manor Avenue was to be Jimmie's home for most of the war.

'We didn't question the rights or wrongs of it,' Rosalie Williams told me in the front room of that same house seventy years later, 'we just knew he must be preserved as the writer of the new theatre of the people.' She added, 'we were really amoral or immoral, single-minded'.[20] Clothes, books and food parcels sent by her parents were collectivised and shared with Jimmie and whichever Theatre Union members were currently staying – 5 Manor Avenue became the company's unofficial wartime headquarters. Some Theatre Union loyalists undertook shoplifting sprees for extra food and equipment. Rosalie pooled the cash she earned at her Town Hall clerical job; Joan, who regularly stayed in the house, had been reinstated at the BBC and contributed whatever she could.[21]

'Theatre Union is part of a worldwide movement to create a people's art,' claimed the most recent manifesto.[22] Political persecution had only compounded the company's self-righteous resolve. Rehearsals were held wherever possible – in the crypt of All Saints Church, in the Communist Party offices on Rusholme Road, in a centre for Jewish refugees – and continued for as long as possible. Relieved to be back among his comrades, Jimmie worked from behind the scenes at Urmston doctoring scripts, writing songs and music, working with actors who visited. Not until most of Theatre Union's membership had been called up did the company cease their work, and even then the main players kept in touch by letter. Planning the future relaunch made the present more tolerable.

○ॐ○

Since the formation of Theatre Union two years before, the pressure of producing shows had kept Jimmie from his desk. The company cherished him as the dramatist of the future, but he was yet to write a full-length play. He now had a room in which to work, no political commitments and endless time on his hands. While Joan was networking to lay the foundations for their future theatre, Jimmie's job was to write the plays they'd perform.

He worked on *Hell is What You Make It*, a political morality play that recast heaven as a Soviet-style utopia, hell as a fascist dictatorship, and earth as a precarious midpoint where capitalism still prevailed. The main joke was that earth and hell were indistinguishable: 'The greatest torment in hell', claimed one character, 'is to deny man the fruits of his labour. Put an end to that and you put an end to hell.'[23] He hammered out a draft of *Rogues' Gallery*, a comedy about a struggling theatre group who embark on a life of crime to raise funds for their radical work.[24] He started a third 'genre experiment', *Blitz Song*, an update of Aeschylus' *Agamemnon* where the feelings of jealousy and resentment generated by his and Joan's unorthodox combination of creative partnership and sexual independence were exorcised.[25] George Bernard Shaw would later accurately describe it as 'powerful but depressing'; Jimmie would himself dismiss it as 'overblown and melodramatic'.[26] *Blitz Song* would never be staged; *Hell is What You Make It* would be performed in 1950 by London's Unity Theatre after an earlier premiere in Prague; a heavily revised version of *Rogues' Gallery* would be produced by Theatre Workshop in 1949. He'd produce better work in the future, but these Urmston years provided a solid apprenticeship in the playwright's craft.

○ॐ○

When he wasn't writing, he was reading or listening to the wireless. If the weather was good he could safely sit in the secluded garden and reflect on the impulsive course of action that had brought him to this point. Throughout his life he'd use the language of politics both to express and camouflage more personal feelings. Those who hurt him would often be dismissed as bourgeois, or revisionists, or middle-class intellectuals. He couldn't tell his mother he loved her, but would freely praise her as 'a fine representative of the finest class in society' for whom the revolution would be a thoroughly deserved 'personal compensation' for previous suffering.[27] Jimmie's desertion was not primarily ideologically motivated, but he now explained it to himself in political terms. This was an imperialistic war. Jimmie Miller had opted out.

Life became more difficult for his conscience in June 1941 when Hitler defied the Nazi–Soviet pact and invaded the Soviet Union, transforming an imperialist dogfight into a worthy crusade to defeat fascism and defend the revolution. Harry Pollitt, who'd been removed from his post as General Secretary for refusing to implement the doublespeak of the Nazi–Soviet pact, was now reinstated. 'Red Joan Littlewood' was commissioned to work on BBC programmes celebrating the military heroics of Stalin and his army.[28] Communists in the armed forces suddenly appeared less untrustworthy.[29] Communist deserters, if anyone thought of them at all, seemed thoroughly inconsequential – they could be dealt with later. Rosalie, Joan and Jimmie now pinned a battle-chart to the wall and chronicled Stalin's progress. They became vociferous advocates of the opening of a Second Front to alleviate the massive military pressure being endured by the Soviet Union. Loyal to the new line as he'd been to the others, Jimmie was stripped of even the semblance of ideological justification. He was now a deserter from a war that imperilled the very existence of the workers' state.

 C380

It's possible that Jimmie broke up his long Urmston house arrest with a visit to central London, where Joan Littlewood lived for a spell. A trip to Scotland would loom large in rumours of Jimmie's war for years to come; one character in a later play describes a wartime life 'on the trot, kipping in air-raid shelters ... dodging the MPs and the busies', and it's tempting to speculate that Jimmie was reworking his own experiences.[30] In later life he'd never talk openly about his war – he'd change the subject, become vague or tell stories of active service in the

Pacific, or of a military career blocked by anti-communist hysteria.[31]
Mystery will always shroud these years, but if he left Urmston at all,
it wasn't for long and he was careful to leave no trail behind him.

CRBO

Reliable wartime sightings were rare, but he made one final and surprising
public appearance before a couple of thousand readers in the pages of
*Our Time*, a 1940s cultural journal loosely aligned to the Communist
Party.[32] Published in July 1943, James Miller's article 'Capitalism,
Writing and the War' yields an intriguing glimpse of Jimmie suspended
in limbo and eagerly waiting for the next phase of life to begin.[33] The
article casts a critical eye over British literature of the previous twenty-
five years: the modernist writers who had seduced him in his youth are
now sternly rejected as symptoms of 'the ever-quickening decay of an
outworn civilisation';[34] the promising Marxist orientations of 1930s
writers of 'the Auden–Spender–Isherwood group' had, he claims, been
restricted by their bourgeois backgrounds.[35] Looking to the present, he
detects a 'tremendous revolution pregnant, indeed already being born'
in the current war (safe in Urmston, he hoped that the war should be
brought to a 'vigorous prosecution').[36] The post-war future would
liberate the new world from the old and would, he predicted, belong to
writers who combined proletarian pedigree with a Marxist perspective.
His article was in fact a job specification describing a post he intended
to apply for. Successful proletarian Marxist applicants would shape 'a
new, vigorous, realistic and ultimately optimistic literature' in a post-
war Britain 'where true culture may flourish at last'.[37]

# 5

# A Richer, Fuller Life

In May 1945 thirty-year-old Jimmie resurfaced. He was a deserter from the British Army and if caught he'd be imprisoned, court-martialled and possibly sent abroad to fulfil military duties. He knew he couldn't make himself permanently invisible to the State – he had no ration book, and if he ever needed medical treatment, took paid employment, or resumed his communist activities, the authorities were likely to catch up with him.[1] Sporting a freshly grown auburn beard and a new name, Ewan MacColl, he took his chances.

'Ewan MacColl' was simultaneously an alias and a pseudonym.[2] With three full-length plays under his belt, Jimmie now saw his future as a writer. The romantic connections he'd always felt to Scotland had been subtly reinforced by his experience of the British Army, and he would come to feel more Scottish over the next five years. In his wartime literary experiments he'd enjoyed writing in the Scots spoken by his parents, and he was increasingly drawn to the literature of the current Scottish literary renaissance, especially the work of nationalist and Marxist polymath poet Hugh MacDiarmid whom he'd met through Theatre Union's Barbara Niven in the late 1930s.[3] Jimmie greatly admired MacDiarmid's early poetry, and shared MacDiarmid's conviction that the Scots language was a vital medium for modern literary creation. Jimmie also avidly read novelist Lewis Grassic Gibbon, whose panoramic and richly idiomatic *Scots Quair* trilogy (1934) would obsess him for years.[4] These two literary heroes had collaborated on *The Scottish Scene* (1934), and it was almost certainly in their satirical compendium of poems, essays and stories that Jimmie first came across his new name. 'There is no one today in any way approaching the stature of the great Gaelic poets,' Gibbon wrote in one essay, 'Alasdair MacMhaighistir Alasdair and Duncan Ban MacIntyre – or even Alexander MacDonald or Ewan MacColl.'[5]

Gibbon says no more, but Evan or Ewan MacColl was the anglicised name of nineteenth-century Gaelic poet Eóghan MacColla of Lochfyneside (1808–98). An enigmatic figure and accomplished songwriter on the Clydeside ceilidh circuit, MacColla was an incorrigible ladies' man who drew literary inspiration from his amorous exploits.[6] When he adopted his new name, Jimmie Miller had no idea how much he had in common with the other Ewan MacColl. He probably hadn't read MacColla's work, which hadn't been translated from the Gaelic since 1836.[7] Rather than profound literary affiliation, it was a question of the name sounding sonorously Scottish and carrying appropriate political and literary overtones: W. D. MacColl was a notorious nationalist and Gaelic revivalist; 'Ewan' was the name of two characters in Grassic Gibbon's trilogy (one was brutalised by army life and shot for desertion, the other a fervent young communist). There was a fashion in Scottish letters for assuming the names of literary and genealogical forebears: Hugh MacDiarmid's real name was Christopher Grieve, Lewis Grassic Gibbon's was James Leslie Mitchell. By taking a new name, Jimmie was not only attempting to spoil the scent for the Military Police. This was also an act of cultural reorientation: he was inserting himself into a vibrant and diverse literary movement that spoke to his political radicalism, latent Scottishness and literary ambition.

೦೩೮೦

The nucleus of Theatre Union hurried back to Manchester that spring. Littlewood was now inseparable from Gerry Raffles, a former Manchester University student nine years her junior who'd spent the war down Pendleton Pit.[8] Jimmie's former girlfriend Rosalie Williams was the third founder member.[9] Howard Goorney, who deftly extricated himself from his Belgian barracks, was the fourth.[10] Ewan MacColl was the fifth.

Throughout the war, Littlewood had been manoeuvring to secure funding for the relaunch. She'd struck a deal with John Trevelyan, the Director of Education for Westmorland, who'd agreed that the new ensemble should be installed in Kendal where they would run training classes, support local amateur groups, and fund their own productions via the Council for the Encouragement of Music and Arts (CEMA).[11] Suitable premises were found, but arrangements fell through at the eleventh hour.[12] Exactly what happened is unclear: Littlewood's politics might have been a factor (she'd been blacklisted by CEMA the year before);[13] it's also possible that the plans were foiled when CEMA was subsumed by the new Arts Council, which favoured metropolitan professionals over provincial grassroots initiatives.[14] Either way, it was an omen. For ten years the company would doggedly apply for funds without success, and Littlewood's bitterness could still be felt fifty years later. 'The Arts council wouldn't touch us,' she hissed in a 1994 television interview. 'They hated my guts ... They'd have pissed on my grave, they would, they're still there. Don't mention them ... Someone ought to write a book about those unspeakable people.'[15]

What the group lacked in institutional credibility they compensated for in self-belief and bloody mindedness. Goorney surrendered his army gratuities, Raffles handed over compensation money from a pit accident, Littlewood and Williams gave what they could. MacColl had nothing to offer except his genius, but with £400 in the kitty (worth around £11,500 today) they went to Kendal anyway.[16] 'If we'd known what lay in store for us we might have stayed home,' Littlewood wrote later.[17]

Full of youthful idealism, post-war optimism and summer sun they took digs, rented rehearsal space above the town's Conservative Club and set about building up the company. They ran auditions and recruited new talent. David Scase was headhunted by Littlewood; he jettisoned a promising BBC career to join this theatre group without a theatre.[18] Pearl Turner and Ruth Brands were persuaded to throw in their lot (teenager Lillian Booth came too, but was soon retrieved by an irate mother).[19] Kristin Lind was an exotic Swede who regularly flabbergasted Mancunians with her nude sunbathing on the roof of the Central Library – she signed up and dragooned her friend William Davidson, an aircraft designer who would prove indispensable for his set-designing skills.[20]

Theatre Workshop was to be the name. Once again, it was borrowed from the American scene – *Theater Workshop* was a late 1930s radical magazine.[21] The new manifesto, smudgy with Ewan MacColl's fingerprints and designed to resemble an election handbill, was the most bombastic to date. The great theatres of the past, it claimed, those of fifth-century Athens, the Elizabethans, the Commedia dell'arte and Molière, 'derived their inspiration, their language, their art from the common people'. The bourgeoisie, now a class in decline, had lost touch with the movement of history and filled the radical public forum of theatre with rubbish. The contemporary British working class displayed impeccable judgement in staying away from this 'high class circus' of 'performing seals'. The task in hand was simultaneously one of excavation and innovation. Theatre Workshop set out to develop 'the heroic line of Aeschylus, Shakespeare and Lope de Vega' with 'a theatre arising out of the needs of the most important and vital sections of society – miners, engineers, weavers and fishermen'.[22]

This brusque diagnosis was fleshed out in articles written over the following year. Members of Theatre Workshop were to live communally, work co-operatively and be paid a standard wage. Most of the company would not only act but also work on costumes, décor, lighting, secretarial duties. Training would be ongoing and would cover voice-work, movement, dance, theatre history and politics. The company was to be eclectic in its approaches and alert to international developments – the names of Erwin Piscator, Constantin Stanislavski, Yevgeny Vakhtangov, Adolph Appia, Rudolf Laban were frequently cited. Cutting-edge sound technology would be used: Theatre Workshop sought to bring theatre into the age of the motion picture. They envisaged a role for themselves in post-war Britain's cultural renewal, and pledged to take theatre to places that didn't feature on theatre's map. 'We believe that the return of the young people of Britain to their homes will bring about a great change in values,' they explained on one promotional flier, 'the young men and women who have fought for civilization will want a richer, fuller life for themselves and their children.'[23]

In July the company celebrated the Labour Party electoral landslide; MacColl was encouraged that the Communist Party had doubled its parliamentary representation with the election of a second MP.[24] They busily booked halls for their launching tour and worked up two new shows. MacColl wrote *Johnny Noble*, an hour-long ballad opera that drew on wartime radio features made by Joan Littlewood and Olive Shapley.[25] Through a conventional love plot, the play gauged the impact of depression and war upon a north-east fishing community. MacColl framed accessible naturalistic acting with a self-conscious theatricality: two singing narrators would comment on events through the folksongs he'd rewritten. Sound and light rather than representational sets would create atmosphere: there would be over 200 lighting changes.[26] The play was politically emphatic: travel enables Johnny Noble to see his community's suffering in terms of broader economic and political structures; he concludes that the war was won through huge working-class sacrifice, that society must change, and that change will only come from the efforts of those who stand to benefit.[27] *Johnny Noble* was to be performed alongside *The Flying Doctor*, MacColl's free adaptation of *Le Médecin malgré lui*, a short, partly improvised Molière farce written in the Commedia dell'arte style.[28] MacColl worked with the Molière structure, was assisted by notes made by the Commedia dell'arte player Domenico Biancolelli, but mostly drew on his own considerable knowledge of Marx Brothers movies.[29] Perfect for Theatre Workshop, *The Flying Doctor* was a raunchy comedy that lampooned the old, materialistic and slow-witted, and celebrated youth, optimism and unbridled sexuality. The two shows were rehearsed in shifts while costumes were stitched and sets built in Kendal. On 13 August 1945, the self-styled saviours of British theatre were ready to face the public. Their campaign began at the Girls' High School, Kendal.

ೞೲ

Over the next five weeks they played thirty-two evenings, plus matinees, in eight north-west venues. They played schools (Kendal, Penrith), community halls (Grange over Sands, Workington, Windermere, Wigan, Staveley) and the Kirby Stephen Masonic Hall.[30] Reviews ranged from the baffled to the euphoric. Good write-ups in the *Wigan Examiner*, *Lake District Herald* and *Westmoreland Gazette* were never likely to bring instant fame, but they enabled the group to assemble strong publicity material that said 'The workshop idea will triumph' and 'the company is highly trained and immensely versatile'.[31]

And the good reviews were necessary to lift flagging morale. The company had no transport and relied on trains, buses and the goodwill of friends. The halls they played often weren't designed for theatre and the short runs meant endless rigging and derigging. Training classes were ongoing; Producer Littlewood and Art Director MacColl insisted that the next show should be rehearsed during the first run. So with the help of Dr Luis Meana, a Manchester University academic who had worked with Federico García Lorca's La Barraca travelling troupe, the company were rehearsing their next show, Lorca's tragic-comic miniature masterpiece, *The Love of Don Perlimplín and Belisa in the Garden*, between performances.[32]

The tour schedule reflected the company's pioneering zeal, but it was always unlikely that small places like Grange over Sands could support a five-night run of experimental drama. Often there were more people on the stage than in the audience, and the company was losing money hand over fist. Lorca's surrealist-influenced meditation on sex did nothing to boost box office takings, and as winter set in the situation became still grimmer. In Leeds, Theatre Workshop shared digs with a variety show donkey; the Dewsbury Empire smelt strongly of circus animals; in a moment of optimism, they booked the Jubilee Theatre, Blackpool, but cancelled the run after failing to sell a single ticket.[33] MacColl later recalled members of the tiny Blackburn audience bringing their hot water bottles along.[34] 'The names of those places', he said:

> Are like scars on the memory: Staveley, Windermere, Kirkby Stephen, Keswick, Grange over Sands ... I remember so clearly the feeling of embarrassment, which overcame me every night, at the thought of disturbing the slumbers of those nice old ladies, who had been lured out of their boarding houses at the thought of being cheered by a performance of *Merrie England* or *The Bohemian Girl*.[35]

csℬℴ

Theatre Workshop's idealistic founding principles were thoroughly tested in late May 1946 when Gerry Raffles secured the company a week-long booking at the 12,000-berth Filey camp in Billy Butlin's rapidly expanding empire of mass-produced holidays.[36] In terms of repertoire, Theatre Workshop took no prisoners; they performed the full spread of current productions – Lorca, Molière and MacColl's *Johnny Noble* – on an entertainment roster that also featured magicians, all-in wrestling, bingo and Old-Time dancing. The company's centrepiece was MacColl's new play. Written in the wake of the mass slaughter at Hiroshima and Nagasaki, *Uranium 235* told the story of atomic science from Ancient Greece to the modern bomb. Its central idea was that science is as good or bad as the uses to which it is put, either a force for civilisation or an agent of death and destruction. As well as cautioning against anti-scientific irrationalism and public apathy, the play critiqued those modes of mass culture – the press, cinema, popular music, sport – which fostered social and political disengagement. Eleven episodes, fifty-seven characters, scores of costume changes, planted audience interruptions, blues songs, jitterbugging, puppeteering, ballet, film pastiche, agitprop, voiceover and old fashioned sermonising – the dizzying spectacle by turns entertained and harangued the Butlin's audience. It anticipated criticism by turning its own difficulty into a theme: those who dismissed it as esoteric were showing the very indifference to scientific thought that the play was warning against.[37] For MacColl the Butlin's experience was a vindication: the audience recognised that *Uranium 235* was a fast-moving variety show and their response was refreshingly impolite – baddies were booed, bores were heckled and actors planted to interrupt the action were tutted and shushed.[38] 'Of all the bizarre and unexpected things you come across in this phantasmagoria of a place,' wrote a *News Chronicle* reporter, 'there is nothing quite so surprising as the brilliant band of young strolling players who have been packing the Camp Theatre this week':

> They specialise in dramatic dialectics, but you will be glad to hear that there is nothing of the raffish roguery or lushgush of our Bloomsbury Exquisites about them.
>
> Just like the Molière team, Theatre Workshop carries its own playwright around, young Ewan McColl [sic] (a Scot with a Lancashire accent) who ... has a flaming red beard and a tendency to lapse into lecturing, but the play he is putting on here, *Uranium 235*, is undoubtedly a theatrical event of the first importance.[39]

ⵣ

The Arts Council declined from assisting Theatre Workshop, but it sometimes seemed that other gods were smiling. Colonel James Pennyman was a Cleveland Tory aristocrat who resided in his ancestral hall at Ormesby village, near Middlesbrough. In the 1920s he'd caused a minor scandal by marrying Ruth King, an art school graduate with left-wing views and a passion for the performing arts: Morris dancing, local orchestras and amateur dramatic clubs all flourished under her watchful eye. The couple believed that privilege brought responsibilities, and worthy causes such as unemployed miners or refugee Basque children were assisted.[40] In February 1946 Ruth Pennyman saw Theatre Workshop perform at the Newcastle People's Theatre. Intrigued, she went to a second show, after which the bemused company were chauffeured out to Ormesby and dined handsomely. By early June Theatre Workshop had become the Pennymans' most recent concern.[41]

The Ormesby East Wing, with its courtyard, refectory, kitchen, bedrooms, workshops and stables was hosed down and made available for a peppercorn rent.[42] After life on the road, it was a haven of tranquillity from which the next move could be plotted.[43] Depleted funds were restored by an ongoing series of training classes; students were recruited from local amateur dramatic societies, Workers' Educational Association groups and youth clubs.[44] The company was always on the lookout for talent, and the courses doubled as lengthy auditions: John Bury, who eventually became head of design at the National Theatre, was recruited in this way, as was Tyneside singer Isla Gledhill, who as Isla Cameron would cut records with MacColl in later years.[45]

MacColl thoroughly enjoyed having a new audience for his talents, and the sensation of living on borrowed time brought a manic edge to his usual intensity. He gave dazzling, unscripted lectures about German and Soviet agitprop and radical American theatre. 'His rhetoric would flow in a turbulent stream with quotations flying in the air like paper darts,' recalled Littlewood. 'It was heady stuff.'[46] He would hold forth about his work as a playwright, and as an actor – he was now playing the singing narrator in *Johnny Noble* and the lead in the Lorca. Days at Ormesby often ended with open fires and impromptu MacColl concerts in which he'd sing widely from his repertoire. According to hostess Ruth Pennyman, Ormesby's bearded bard was also 'easily and frequently amorous': 'At the weekend schools', she remembers, 'girls would emerge from his bedroom looking flushed, excited and in some disarray.'[47] 'He worked through women, all through the whole company, one by one,' adds Rosalie Williams, who sometimes bore the brunt of MacColl's jealous tantrums. 'He used everybody, and inspired devotion from everybody,' she remembers. 'He was a master of emotional blackmail. He hurt a lot of people on the way. And I don't think that worried him very much. He was hurt as well, but not everybody loved him and a few people in the end came to resent him deeply.'[48]

CᴙℬↃ

Littlewood's lover Gerry Raffles increasingly took on the company's thankless promotional spadework. Limited as an actor, he now spent most of his time writing letters, making phone calls, speaking to the press, cajoling potential backers, securing bookings, networking with other theatre groups and trying to balance the books. He was referred to as Theatre Workshop's 'business manager', two words that barely featured in MacColl's vocabulary. He and Raffles were increasingly at loggerheads. Raffles resented MacColl's previous marriage to Littlewood and their enduring creative rapport; MacColl resented Raffles' indispensability to Theatre Workshop in general and to Joan Littlewood in particular. MacColl typically expressed his feelings in the terms of class: Raffles was a bourgeois who'd been to Manchester Grammar School; sometimes an intellectual bully, MacColl wasn't above pulling rank and undermining Raffles in public.[49] Raffles made jokes about the size of MacColl's ego, his meanness with money, and the frequency of his sexual entanglements. 'It was a war that never stopped,' recalled Howard Goorney.[50]

⊂ℬ⊃

Flat-footed actors were the bane of Littlewood's life and were often compared to 'turds on blankets'. The answer to the problem now appeared in the form of Jean Newlove, a gifted dancer in her early twenties who'd been discovered and employed by exiled German choreographer and movement-theorist Rudolph Laban four years earlier. Littlewood had first been in touch with Laban when Theatre Union members were sent along to classes run by his new Manchester Dance Circle during the war.[51] Laban was keen on Littlewood's ideas about balletic theatre and now offered assistance to her company.[52] Jean Newlove was released to run weekend classes at Ormesby Hall.[53] As MacColl recalls:

> She turned out to be a magnificent teacher, serious but good-natured, full of ideas and quick to recognise the unique character of Theatre Workshop. Under her tutelage, the dormant capabilities of the actors in the group underwent a complete transformation and it wasn't long before our part-time tutor fell under the spell of the theatre and joined us.[54]

As he goes on to say, MacColl fell under her spell as soon as she set foot in Ormesby. 'You're good,' he told her after the first class. 'You're just like Joan.'[55] The aptly named Newlove was eight years his junior, and MacColl courted her assiduously over the coming months. She hadn't imagined falling for a stocky and bearded thirty-one-year-old playwright, but his blandishments gradually did their work. 'He was writing at that time,' she recalled:

> and he'd read what he'd written to me. It sounded marvellous. And he wrote me wonderful letters. But what I really loved was his singing. He sang so beautifully. He was also very supportive of my work.[56]

Littlewood was pleased too, and not only because there was a sharp improvement in MacColl's behaviour. She liked Newlove, and was delighted when the talented dancer and choreographer decided to join the company permanently. In giddier moments Littlewood referred to Newlove, MacColl and herself as the 'trinity' of Theatre Workshop.[57]

CRUX

The company now formed an imaginary business, 'Pioneer Theatres', to provide a gloss of professionalism to public relations, and established a board of four directors to lend cultural clout.[58] James Ford was a headmaster from Merseyside, Freddie Piffard was Head of BBC Variety. The other directors were prominent figures in the Scottish cultural renaissance. The kilt-wearing William MacLellan was a patriotic publisher keen on MacColl's writing.[59] Hugh MacDiarmid was the fourth, and his enthusiasm for MacColl and Theatre Workshop was boundless. He was delighted to learn that a tour of Scotland had been arranged for the autumn of 1946 and trumpeted the company's importance in his journal, *The Voice of Scotland*:

> Amateurism has been the curse of all the arts in Scotland; a real fight to get rid of it is long overdue. Theatre Workshop are the people to wage it. We believe they will and that the effect of their tour will be to blast a monstrous accumulation of rubbish out of the way of creative effort in Scotland.[60]

CRUX

The company headed north in an ancient GPO van custom-fitted with the shell of an abandoned furniture wagon. 'It rarely broke down more than two or three times a day,' MacColl recalled.[61] He was in high spirits to be visiting the country he increasingly regarded as his intellectual and political homeland, and sang Border Ballads all the way up the A1.[62]

⊂Ჽ✑

They played good venues in Scotland – *Johnny Noble*, *The Flying Doctor* and *Uranium 235* ran for a week at the Little Theatre, Edinburgh, followed by a fortnight at the Queen's Theatre, Glasgow.[63] Compared with their English shows, they attracted plenty of press coverage, some of which was critical – the company's arrogant promotional material set some reviewers on their mettle – but most was enthusiastic.[64] MacColl was described as 'the Picasso of drama' and his *Uranium 235* as a 'moving and beautiful modern morality' play.[65]

⊂Ჽ✑

Excused from heavy acting duties to work on his writing, MacColl's new Scottish identity underwent a baptism in whisky on the tour. He attended 'flytings' – twelve-hour booze-fuddled rows about politics, literature and music that were often resolved with punch-ups. He caroused with the young-bloods of the literary renaissance, larger-than-life characters like poet Sydney Goodsir Smith whose work had appeared in the movement's key anthologies.[66] He imbibed some of Scottish Nationalism's mythology, including stories of Douglas Young, the Nationalist poet and professor who had been imprisoned for opposing the Second World War (Young argued that an allied defeat might be good for Scotland, as Hitler would leave the Scots to their own affairs).[67] In this zealous company MacColl frequently refashioned his biography. Newspaper write-ups, based on interviews with the group, now referred to MacColl as 'a Glasgow dramatist'; over the next eighteen months he straightened out his story and adopted as his birthplace Auchterarder in Perthshire, the town where Betsy was born.[68] He was anxious that Hugh MacDiarmid might discover that Ewan MacColl, the man he was calling 'the most important living Scottish playwright', actually originated from Lancashire.[69]

⊂Ჽ✑

After Scotland the company headed down to London for a week-long run at the Park Theatre, Hanwell followed by a one-night performance at the St Pancras Assembly Hall.[70] The idea was to take their talents into the heartland of the Arts Council.[71] With characteristic chutzpah, Littlewood invited prominent Labour MPs to attend the show, believing that if the architects of the New Jerusalem liked Theatre Workshop, pettifogging Arts Council officials would soon come to their senses and supply funding. The strategy wasn't successful, though MPs including Nye Bevan and Tom Driberg showed up and the company got a free lunch at the House of Commons.[72]

જ૭૪૦

Back in Ormesby, they rehearsed the new show. *Operation Olive Branch*, MacColl's new adaptation of Aristophanes' *Lysistrata*, was due to open in Middlesbrough early in 1947.[73] Theatre Union's wartime version had suited the Communist Party anti-war line; the play now took on a new topicality as Aristophanes' Greece was drawn into the force-field of post-war power politics, and Britain promoted a reactionary Greek monarchy to resist the communist threat. More immediately, the new text expressed personal tensions within MacColl. He added a nationalistic Scottish deserter who argued that the war meant nothing to him – his people had always been cruelly oppressed by the ruling class for whom he was now expected to fight. It was a potent mix of confession and desperate justification, which Littlewood recognised as 'an expression of his own isolation'.[74] MacColl insisted on playing the part himself. After giving his speech, the Scottish deserter was to be stabbed to death. In a strong casting decision, Littlewood gave the assailant's part to Gerry Raffles, whose acting had seldom been so convincing.

જ૭૪૦

On 16 December 1946 Ewan and Jean had a break from rehearsals and caught the bus from Ormesby village to Middlesbrough to see a Marx Brothers film. While they were gone two plainclothes policemen turned up at Ormesby Hall asking for James Miller. A nervous Colonel Pennyman escorted them to the East Wing. 'I felt like running to the village to warn Jimmie,' Littlewood recalled, 'but I hesitated and it was too late.'[75] Jean Newlove remembers: 'We were walking back down the long drive to Ormesby Hall and we saw two police outriders ... They had come for Ewan.'[76] MacColl was arrested, taken to Middlesbrough Police station and charged with deserting from his

regiment. The following day he was transferred to detention barracks
at Northallerton. He was then moved a third time to Parkhall Camp,
Oswestry on the Welsh border, where he spent a wretched Christmas
and New Year.[77]

⊂Жᴏᴄᴑ

That January, Will Miller became dangerously ill. His chronic asthma
and bronchitis had been deteriorating since before the war, and MacColl
had been called back to Oak Cottage on a number of occasions. Betsy
now telegrammed for her son; a haggard and disorientated MacColl
was granted compassionate leave to visit his father's bedside. 'He
seemed to have shrunk, to have become a youth again,' MacColl later
wrote of his father.[78] Will died shortly after MacColl's return, and was
cremated at Stockport crematorium four days later. There were just
three people at the ceremony – Betsy, MacColl and Joan Littlewood.

MacColl returned to Oswestry. Shaken by his humiliating arrest and
now stunned by his father's death, he had few resources to cope with the
casual brutality meted out to deserters.[79] He was in a desperate state,
and his battalion commander made no bones of the fact that he was
facing a spell in the glasshouse followed by a tour of duty overseas.[80]

⊂Жᴏᴄᴑ

The company was in agitated shock: MacColl was a dominant force
in Theatre Workshop and none of the newer recruits, including Jean
Newlove, knew he'd deserted. Even among progressive circles, desertion
carried a stigma. Rumours circulated that one of MacColl's many
enemies had tipped off the police.[81] Not for the first time, it fell to
Littlewood to calm the chaos, and her priority was to keep Theatre
Workshop afloat. They were financially dependent on the new show
going ahead, but MacColl's absence left a gaping hole. Parts were
quickly reassigned, scenes re-rehearsed and the show went ahead as
planned at St John's Hall, Middlesbrough on 6 January 1947. Tom
Driberg, the flamboyantly homosexual Labour MP and distinguished
journalist, was in the audience – he'd met the company in London and
had taken an optimistic shine to the heterosexual Raffles. In his Sunday
column for Reynolds News, he lavished praise on Theatre Workshop
and sounded the first note in the campaign for MacColl's release:

Only a week or so before the opening, Ewan MacColl, adaptor of the play, author of several others, and a key member of the group, has been arrested for alleged desertion from the army.

He is now awaiting trial. I must not, of course, make any comment that might prejudice the trial, but I hope – and am sure – that the court will take into account the fact that, since his Army Service ended, his considerable talents have been used creatively.[82]

∞

Theatre Workshop sailed out of Hull at the end of January 1947 for a two-month tour of occupied West Germany under the auspices of the Combined Services Entertainment Unit.[83] All were appalled by the bombed-out devastation they witnessed; some felt they were compromising themselves as 'part of the army of occupation, reaping the rewards of victory'.[84] On one occasion, Jewish members of the group were subject to anti-Semitic abuse by drunken British officers.[85] Those eight weeks in the freezing devastation of occupied Germany cured many Theatre Workshop members of their love affair with experimental theatre. Over half who took the tour would leave the company that spring.[86]

∞

Littlewood stayed at home to work for her estranged husband's release. His court martial was scheduled for Monday 17 February 1947 and the campaign would involve two main strategies. To emphasise MacColl's significance as an artist – which she hoped would inspire leniency – Littlewood petitioned those who'd praised his work in the past. Hugh MacDiarmid and William MacLellan were both involved; prominent playwrights including George Bernard Shaw and James Bridie were approached for testimonies; public figures such as Tom Driberg, Harold Lever and John Trevelyan helped out.[87] She also planned an appeal claiming MacColl was temperamentally incompatible with life in the ranks (of the 335,000 discharged from the armed services during the war for medical reasons, 118,000 cases were released on psychiatric grounds).[88] With the help of left-wing MP Arthur Blenkinsop, funds were raised to prepare a psychiatric profile of MacColl.[89]

∞

He reached his lowest point the week before the court martial. 'Ewan is contemplating suicide and I don't blame him frankly', Littlewood wrote to her right-hand-man Howard Goorney in Germany. 'We have made pretty much of a mess of our lives … They have the power to break him and me through him.'[90] The following day, the psychiatrist's report was submitted and MacColl's court martial was cancelled on medical grounds. MacColl, it was claimed, suffered from a form of epilepsy and the case was now placed in the hands of his Commanding Officer.[91] The worst outcome would be a period of detention, and it was possible that MacColl could now be fully discharged on medical grounds. 'God I hope we are altogether [sic] again soon,' Littlewood wrote to Goorney on hearing the news. 'What work we will do with Ewan free … What a company we will be!'[92]

CЗ୫О

Exactly what happened next is difficult to reconstruct from MacColl's army records, but on 26 February he was moved to Northfield Military Hospital in Birmingham.[93] It isn't clear whether this was part of a detention, or whether MacColl was simply receiving treatment, though Littlewood reported to Goorney that 'he has been put in the "violent ward" which has guards and [he] is locked up'.[94] Jean Newlove visited him there: 'He said that some of the wardens … were cruel. There was one man who suffered from euphoria, smiling all the time, and they'd slap him and say "now smile." They'd punch him and he'd smile.'[95]

MacColl spent eleven weeks in the hospital. He would never discuss his arrest or incarceration, any more than his desertion, though all these experiences would cast deep shadows over his writing in the years to come. It's possible that he used some of his acting skills to secure a medical discharge from Northfield: he never suffered from epilepsy before or after the arrest; he knew that discharge on psychiatric grounds was his best bet; his army records imply that there was some scepticism around the diagnosis – it was ordered that MacColl should 'suffer the same forfeitures and deductions from pay as if he had been convicted of desertion'.[96] It's also possible that 'epilepsy' was mutually convenient shorthand tacitly agreed between the army and MacColl, neither being of any real use to the other.[97] At Easter-time, 10 April 1947, he was granted 'terminal leave' and released. 'He has carried out his duties to the best of his ability,' claimed his statement of services. He immediately sent Jean Newlove a telegram that read 'Christ has risen.'[98] On 4 June he was formally discharged from the army, and deemed 'permanently unfit for any form of military service'.[99]

∞

The events of early 1947 heightened tensions within Theatre Workshop. Raffles thought Littlewood should be in Germany with her actors rather than in England campaigning for her ex-husband, and the resentment he felt towards MacColl was vividly registered in letters home from Germany. 'The only element which will militate against us becoming a popular theatre is Jimmie,' he wrote to Littlewood. 'I come more and more to the conclusion that his overall influence is directly opposed to the sort of theatre that you and most of us want.'[100] According to Raffles' diagnosis, MacColl's writing was part of the problem: 'Jimmie's work is no longer sublimated here. There is a lot of criticism of the way he insults the audience.'[101] Raffles wanted a leaner and more economical company: 'If you concentrated your efforts on a few people', he wrote to Littlewood, 'got rid of everybody who showed no promise, we'd crash the big time much sooner.'[102]

Whether or not these feelings were widely held within the company, they were certainly shared by the Pennymans of Ormesby Hall. MacColl was never somebody to receive patronage graciously. His brusque manner and sexual morality antagonised the couple, and the confirmation that MacColl was also a deserter reinforced the Colonel's antipathy. It was made clear to Littlewood that the company was welcome to stay at Ormesby, but that MacColl wasn't.[103] From late April, Theatre Workshop was homeless again.

∞

In June 1947 they congregated in Felixstowe to begin a tour of seaside theatres. Audiences were small – the company had no star names to tempt the holidaymakers – and the repertoire of Aristophanes, Molière and *Johnny Noble* wasn't typical end-of-the-pier fare. They took guesthouse digs, lived off fish and chips and persuaded sunbathers to buy tickets. MacColl was delighted to meet the ailing Chico Marx who was playing out his career with a never-ending tour.[104]

They went back to Manchester for a six-week residency at the Central Library's 300-seat basement theatre, and received some welcome publicity when *From Kendal to Berlin*, a radio feature programme written by Littlewood about the company, was broadcast on the North of England Home Service at the beginning of their residency.[105] Old friends, family and sympathetic journalists turned out to see them. MacColl was never more than a solidly competent actor, but the 'sincerity and depth' of his performance as the deserter in *Operation Olive Branch* was singled out for praise by the critics.[106] That October they returned to London for a fortnight run at the Rudolph Steiner Theatre – critics and audiences stayed away in such numbers that the show had to be cancelled. In December a disastrous five-night run at the Dolphin Theatre, Brighton plunged their dire finances to new depths.[107]

○ჳ৪○

The company was in trouble and Gerry Raffles increasingly embodied their instinct for survival. He now took on the task of trying to find permanent premises, and to secure Theatre Workshop's future in a climate increasingly hostile to progressive, experimental culture.[108] He knew that public funding was now primarily targeted at highbrow and metropolitan endeavours (Covent Garden Opera received £68,000 while theatre as a whole got £65,000, £10,000 of which went to the Old Vic).[109] And he realised that Theatre Workshop would go under before their merits were recognised by the powers-that-be.

As John Bury recalled, 'Gerry's contribution was absolutely enormous. He had the worst job of the lot of us.'[110] Littlewood remembered 'how many trade union leaders, theatre owners, eccentric millionaires and theatre speculators showed him the door' while he was trying to get the company a base.[111] He tried to secure Theatre Workshop a permanent residency at Manchester Library Theatre, but the campaign went nowhere.[112] He spent months preparing a scheme to convert the Grosvenor Square Presbyterian Church and School in central Manchester into a theatre, but plans collapsed over licence problems.[113] Next was a utopian project to convert the dilapidated David Lewis Theatre, Liverpool, into a drama school, theatre and engine of cultural regeneration. The indefatigable Raffles collected signatures, massaged egos, buttered up local worthies and wheeled and dealed to secure financial backing. MacColl pooh-poohed the scheme. He didn't concern himself with the petty details of incomings, expenditures and bottom lines, but regarded himself as Theatre Workshop's writer and political conscience. The scheme fell through and the animosity deepened.[114]

CS80

The company was temporarily disbanded in January 1948; with his papers now in order, MacColl went cap in hand to the BBC for the first time since 1940. The highbrow Third Programme had been launched in September 1946, and he submitted two of his plays for consideration. They were rejected out of hand: the Head of Drama found them politically biased and irritatingly experimental.[115]

He had better luck at the North of England Home Service in Manchester, where he resumed his part-time acting and presenting work that February.[116] No longer a 'rough voice' – his accent now ranged from working-class Salford to Lowland Scots to BBC English depending on the company – over the next two years he appeared in around eighty different programmes, the vast majority for Children's Hour. To a generation of northern children, MacColl was one of the teatime voices who spoke and sometimes sang in programmes like 'Biggles Flies North', 'Bunkie and Belinda', 'The Mouse Who Wanted the Moon' (MacColl played the Captain of the Mousehold Brigade) and 'The Improvident Squirrel'.[117] Though it was fashionable among progressive theatre circles to deride BBC work, MacColl now quietly enjoyed it. One producer from the period recalls the gusto with which MacColl played his parts and sang his songs. At its best, Children's Hour was a reasonably lucrative playtime, and MacColl gave free reign to the quirky and mischievous side of his personality that the communist dramatist usually kept under wraps.[118]

CS80

Theatre Workshop moved into the first of its communal Manchester houses that spring; 13 Wilmslow Road was a large property in the suburb of Withington. Rented from an Indian restaurant proprietor and Theatre Workshop supporter, the place was now furnished with the props of old and current productions – MacColl needed the stepladder used in *The Flying Doctor* to reach a bed assembled from the remains of another show's set. The company planted vegetables in the garden, took rehearsal premises in a nearby Jewish Community Centre, and set about preparing the next production.

Commercially speaking, Gerry Raffles argued, the worst thing they could do was to stage one of MacColl's plays. True, MacColl was a young playwright earmarked for big things: *Uranium 235* had recently been published and Hugh MacDiarmid's foreword proclaimed MacColl as 'by far the most important and promising young dramatist writing in English, or any dialect of English, at the present time'.[119] It was also true that publishers Allen & Unwin were now considering a single edition of all his plays, and that many luminaries had supported his campaign the previous spring.[120] Even so, Raffles insisted, MacColl's work was difficult to stage, often opaque, always ideologically driven and never likely to pull the crowds. His latest, *The Other Animals*, was the most ambitious to date and had already been rejected by the BBC Third Programme. Raffles was in favour of staging a money-spinner like Stanley Houghton's *Hindle Wakes*, but was overruled. MacColl had ardent followers in the company: the poetry of his new piece appealed to some of the actors; the choreographic possibilities excited Jean Newlove; Littlewood always liked a challenge. Rehearsals began on *The Other Animals*.[121]

Theatrically the play looked back to 1920s Expressionism – extreme psychological states are evoked through a combination of Gustav Mahler's music, stark lighting and carefully choreographed movement. Set in a Kafkaesque nowhere zone, *The Other Animals* deals with a crisis in political conscience. Hanau is a revolutionary imprisoned by powerful counterrevolutionary forces; to save his own life he must broadcast a renunciation of his political beliefs. At the moment when he almost succumbs, he experiences a hallucinatory pageant of political martyrs from the Paris Commune, the Chartist movement and the Spanish Civil War. Fortified by the vision of his forebears, he holds his nerve and is executed.

Just as MacColl had previously insisted on playing the deserter in *Operation Olive Branch*, he now took the part of Hanau. Littlewood, who had to rein in some over-enthusiastic acting, joked that he was 'exposing his self-mutilated ego' in this new sublimated autobiography.[122] The bearded Hanau is called 'the Professor' by his tormentors – MacColl had been nicknamed the Professor at Oswestry.[123] One of Hanau's co-prisoners has euphoria – here MacColl was recycling his experience of military hospital. But the differences between autobiographical fact and fiction are more revealing than the similarities.

MacColl's imprisonment was the consequence of his desertion, which was in turn a confused and desperate act of self-preservation. *The Other Animals* is a parable of suffering, temptation and incorruptible revolutionary integrity. In writing the play, MacColl was drawing on chaotic and confused wartime experiences, synthesising them with visions of revolutionary fortitude, and creating a narrative that was epic and instructive. He was exorcising the past by recasting it as art, and striving to heal his ego by reclaiming the ideal from which he felt he'd fallen short.

CRSO

*The Other Animals* opened on 5 July at the Library Theatre, and the cast was almost upstaged by a member of the audience. Anuerin Bevan, Prime Minister Attlee's Minister for Health and Housing, was in the city for a premiere of his own – the National Health Service opened its doors the same day as MacColl's new play. According to the *Daily Telegraph*, Bevan enjoyed this 'unusual hybrid of acting, ballet, symbolism and soliloquy'.[124] The *Manchester Guardian* found some of MacColl's writing heavy-going, but detected in Littlewood's production 'an air of conviction rare in experimental theatre'. 'She and Ewan MacColl,' the critic went on, 'deserve great credit for their ability to play so complicated an instrument.'[125]

It had been a rocky year for Theatre Workshop – at moments they'd had to requisition the piggy banks of fresh-faced recruits to pay their debtors – but the successful performance refocused their vision.[126] MacColl now took out his first Equity card and the Wilmslow Road house became a blur of activity as the company trained, rehearsed, made and repaired sets and costumes.[127] In early September 1948 they met in Paris from where they took the train across Germany to Czechoslovakia for their second overseas tour.

CRSO

Over a five-week period they visited sixteen Czech towns on a tour conceived by Tom Driberg, set up by Gerry Raffles and co-ordinated by Umeni Lidu (Art for the People), an institution closely connected to the Czech Co-operative and Trade Union movement.[128] In places audiences were hostile to the British group – Chamberlain's betrayal of the Czech people hadn't been forgotten.[129] *The Other Animals* provoked fierce debate. Like MacColl's Hanau, many prominent Czech communists had died for their beliefs during the Nazi occupation, and some found MacColl's parable of revolutionary martyrdom naïve.

Disagreements arose, but the level of intellectual and political engagement was refreshing. Theatre Workshop visited prominent figures in Czech theatre and swapped stories. Newspaper reviews were sympathetic to the company's philosophy. Flattering comparisons were made with the Commedia dell'arte; lines of communication were established with like-minded artists and intellectuals.[130] 'I have found great interest here in the Scots literary renaissance,' MacColl wrote to Hugh MacDiarmid towards the end of the tour, 'and feel that something should be done to make permanent contact with artists of the Eastern democracies.'[131] His wartime play *Hell is What You Make It* was passed around and would be staged at the Realistic Theatre, Prague the following year.[132]

The company slept in palatial hotels recently vacated by senior Nazis. Amid desperate food shortages, they were regally wined and dined. They sampled the famous Pilsen lager, visited the Skoda works and took a brief holiday in the Tatra Mountains. The tour ended with a question-and-answer session at the miners' hall in Ostrava, where they discussed peace and solidarity and together sang 'The Internationale'. MacColl performed 'The Collier's Rant', a Tyneside pit song. The audience clapped and stamped their feet in time.[133]

cs80

Theatre Workshop took the train from Ostrava up through the Polish Corridor, and then sailed from Odreport for Sweden.[134] Czechoslovakian hospitality had been offered in spite of real hardship; the lavish welcome enjoyed in Sweden amply reflected the country's affluence. Manchester had never seemed so far away. The long-undernourished company continued to put on weight and stayed in sumptuous residencies. They played sixteen shows to full houses in the finest theatres. Their performance at the 1,200 capacity Royal Opera House in Stockholm was attended by the Swedish Prime Minister and greeted with a standing ovation. Reviews were the best they had ever received – Littlewood was so proud of them that forty-five years later she reprinted them in her autobiography.[135] In November the company stuffed their luggage with foods still rationed at home and sailed back to Britain.

After Christmas they moved into a second communal Manchester house, this time at 151 Bury Old Road on the city's north side.

ೞ೮

Desperate for money, they hit on a new earning-scheme: they noted a gap in the market for high-quality theatre productions in schools and nominated Howard Goorney to secure bookings – 'because I had worked in an accounts office and could add up', he explained.[136] Charging between £15 and £20 a time (around £350 today), he sometimes also managed to negotiate free school dinners for the cast. *Twelfth Night* was toured in the spring of 1949; *As You Like It* would be added later in the year.[137]

In July they were back at the Library Theatre to premiere *Rogues' Gallery*, a reworking of the play MacColl had written during the war about an impecunious theatre company who turn to crime.[138] The new version included some sharp satire on topsy-turvy post-war morality – MacColl's gangsters learn the Brechtian lesson that conventional business is more lucrative than crime – but the play was above all an occasion for Theatre Workshop in-jokes. It was a hastily rehearsed flop. 'This is not Theatre Workshop's line of country,' wrote the *Manchester Guardian*. 'The actors were uncertain whether to stylise or play straight, they gave us all shades from self effacing gloom to some embarrassing over acting.'[139]

ೞ೮

Jean Newlove and MacColl lived together in the communal house, and their relationship continued to develop. The trauma of MacColl's arrest had brought them closer, and they now decided to marry. (Littlewood and MacColl had been quietly divorced by mutual consent in 1948.) Jean's conventionally minded parents were initially frosty – she was their only daughter and they'd always envisaged a church wedding. Her mentor Rudolf Laban, on the other hand, heartily approved the match. He liked MacColl, with whom he shared an offbeat sense of humour (MacColl would be the life and soul of Laban's seventieth birthday party the following year).[140] They admired one another's work, and often discussed collaborating on a book developing Laban's theories of bodily movement to encompass voice and vocal projection.[141] On the day of the ceremony, Laban joked that if he were forty years younger

he'd be at the altar with Jean himself. The thirty-four-year-old Ewan
MacColl and twenty-six-year-old Jean Newlove made their vows
at Manchester Register Office on Friday 13 April 1949. It was an
inauspicious date but a happy, low-key affair (marriage was regarded
as suspiciously bourgeois by many in Theatre Workshop, and little fuss
was made of weddings). After a celebratory lunch, Jean went back to
the rehearsal room and MacColl to his desk.

C3‍80

It was not only MacColl's love affair with Jean Newlove that
was consolidated at this time: 1949 saw his passion for Scotland
consummated when Theatre Workshop gate-crashed the prestigious
Edinburgh's International Festival of the Arts. In its third year, the
official festival's line-up was typically glittering. Visitors could choose
between the premiere of T. S. Eliot's *The Cocktail Party*, Tyrone
Guthrie's acclaimed production of David Lindsay's *The Three Estates*,
the Dusseldorf Theatre's *Faust*, or leading orchestras from London,
Paris and Geneva.[142] Undaunted, the ragged Theatre Workshop booked
themselves into the city's Epworth Hall between 22 August and 10
September. They presented *The Proposal, Don Perlimplín, The Flying
Doctor* and *The Other Animals*, and became a magnet around which
excluded Scottish musicians, poets and painters clustered. Hugh
MacDiarmid applauded their brand of cultural guerrilla warfare – he
dismissed the official event as a 'a monstrous welter' of 'terrible duffery'
where 'sworn enemies of everything that is truly Scottish and truly
creative' conspired 'to put an end to the ... Scottish Renaissance'.[143]

    As in 1946 the company scooped some excellent notices. The
influential *Theatre Newsletter* singled out Theatre Workshop as one
of the outstanding unofficial acts;[144] the *Glasgow Herald* found *The
Other Animals* 'exhilarating and mentally exciting'; the company was
featured as a photo-spread in *The Scotsman*;[145] the cultural journal *Con
Brio* breezily discussed them alongside Guthrie and Eliot, arguing that
MacColl was 'the one really outstanding Scottish dramatist' around.
'I sent Sean O'Casey *Uranium 235* when it was published recently,'
wrote drama critic Winifred Bannister:

> and this is what he said about it: 'A fine documentary play, dealing fearlessly
> and poetically with the crucial problems of our day ... Marlowe is in
> the wings. A most important contribution to Scottish theatre. Why is it

being ignored? ... When you see Ewan MacColl, give him my most sincere admiration.'[146]

CɜƏↃ

MacColl was fast becoming a prominent figure in the Scottish Renaissance. The contrast between English indifference and Scottish enthusiasm for Theatre Workshop convinced him that their future now lay north of the border. Through his festival drinking buddy – the poet, translator and folklorist Hamish Henderson – MacColl heard a rumour that new town East Kilbride had money available for initiatives in the arts, and possibly premises for a resident theatre group.[147] He was enthusiastic about the prospect. He implored Henderson to find out all he could and to press Theatre Workshop's case. 'We are mad keen to settle in Scotland, anxious to play a role in developing the Scots revolutionary movement,' he wrote to Henderson early in 1950. He imagined Theatre Workshop bringing its 'strong ideological line and ... carefully planned artistic programme' to 'the heart of a working class area'. They could, MacColl argued, enrich the cultural life of the community and train actors up to the larger task of building the Scots National Theatre. All that East Kilbride municipal authority had to do was put up some money and provide a building:

> In exchange for a hall with seating accommodation we would be prepared to provide a stage, lighting and sound equipment, curtains, repertoire and a trained group of artists and technicians with an international repertoire. This is a bargain by any standards – don't you agree?[148]

Henderson did agree, but by the time he received the letter he was travelling abroad. Whether or not he'd have been able to help Theatre Workshop isn't certain, but the run of events is typical of their luck at the time. After the festival the company returned to Manchester, but Scotland loomed ever larger in MacColl's mind.

# 6
# Towards a People's Culture

When the lease expired on Bury Old Road in the spring of 1950, most of the company moved into 177A Oxford Road, a crumbling three-storey building big enough for living, rehearsing and equipment storage. Jean was now expecting her first child and the MacColls decided to take a break from communal life; unable to find an affordable place of their own, they decamped to Betsy's cottage at Werneth Low. Their son, born on 15 July, was named Hamish after MacColl's new friend Hamish Henderson. Betsy helped out with the baby and Littlewood was the natural, if atheistic, Godmother. In the autumn Theatre Workshop regrouped and rehearsals began once more.

The company was now caught in a vicious circle. Raffles' ongoing efforts to secure a permanent base were yielding no results, and MacColl's overtures to East Kilbride had fared no better. Arts Council funding was not forthcoming. The company was not sufficiently well known to fill decent commercial theatres and lost money whenever they tried. Their last tour, when they'd presented Littlewood's adaptation of *Alice in Wonderland* to bemused pantomime-goers, had been financially disastrous. But if empty auditoriums and mice-infested dressing rooms eroded everyone else's morale, nothing seemed to dampen MacColl's dream of bringing radical theatre to the masses. Over the next two years it would be his ambitious visions, rather than Raffles' measured realism, that guided the company. Theatre Workshop would now return to the idealism of 1945 and tour 'those areas of Britain which are outside the current theatre circuits', attempting to create theatre 'arising out of the needs of the most important and vital sections of society – miners, engineers, weavers and fishermen'.[1]

The company bought another ex-GPO van and booked tours of between fifteen and thirty dates in a different town or village each night. Industrial areas were now targeted: in November 1950 they played seventeen dates in seventeen days in South Wales mining villages; the following year they played a total of seventy one-night-stands in three tours, two in South Wales and one in the North-East of England; early in 1952 they went back to the North-East for a further nineteen performances over a three-week period.[2] As in 1945, every performance involved rigging and derigging village halls, town halls, miners' welfare clubs, Mechanics' Institutes – even a Wearside 'Mental Asylum' on one occasion.[3] Unless a friendly trade union branch helped out, company members were responsible for ticket sales, and hawked their wares round houses, pubs, chip-shops and pit canteens; if they were lucky, they persuaded local shopkeepers to act as booking agents.[4] Digs had to be arranged. In the Welsh valleys they slept in miners' homes – Littlewood stayed in one pit-cottage where the landlady shared her bed with two gentlemen and explained the unconventional arrangement as her 'pension'.[5] As ever, training exercises and rehearsals were ongoing.[6] The exhausting routine took its toll on the company's health – MacColl recalled one compassionate valley GP treating them all with antibiotics and vitamin injections.[7]

The repertoire mixed old and new material. *Johnny Noble*, *The Flying Doctor* and *Uranium 235* were played up and down the valleys – the latter enjoyed a new topicality when, early in 1950, American attempts to create a hydrogen bomb hit the headlines.[8] The best of the school productions were brushed up for the road, including *Henry IV*, now featuring future *Steptoe and Son* television star Harry Corbett as Hal, who'd thrown in his secure job at Chorlton-cum-Hardy rep to work with Littlewood.[9]

MacColl's new play, *Landscape with Chimneys*, opened at Cwmaman on 8 January 1951 before touring South Wales and the North-East.[10] Drawing heavily on MacColl's memories of Lower Broughton and Coburg Street, this atmospheric blend of song, dance, agitprop and documentary revisited the 1946 Squatters' Movement in which 45,000 homeless British citizens commandeered disused military camps, ex-government blocks of flats and luxury Kensington apartments.[11] Like a latter-day Johnny Noble, Hughie Graham – the character is revived from the pages of MacColl's unpublished novel – returns from six years in the army full of post-war optimism. But instead of peace he finds intimations of future conflict – fighting in Malaya, the Marshall plan, rearmament – and sheds his military number only to become number 930 on the housing list. Defiant, he occupies a disused parsonage where his wife gives birth to their first child. Stirred to solidarity by the family's plight, local residents unite to prevent eviction. MacColl was sounding a warning: if the struggling Labour government didn't create a new Britain, the people were capable of building it for themselves. This militant mood for radical social reconstruction was quietly echoed by the final verse of the play's signature tune, MacColl's jazzy 'Dirty Old Town':[12]

> I'm going to make a good sharp axe,
> Shining steel, tempered in the fire,
> We'll chop you down like an old dead tree.
> Dirty old town, dirty old town.

At a time when the Communist Party's popularity was beginning to recede from its wartime height – both of the party's MPs failed to hold their seats in the election of February 1950, bringing to a permanent end communist parliamentary representation in Britain – MacColl's faith in the radical instincts of the British working class remained.[13] It wasn't a view of the workers shared by the script censors at the Lord Chamberlain's office. 'A pretentious, bad play about the poor,' noted their report on *Landscape with Chimneys*, 'a brutal libel on the inhabitants of slums [which is] being inflicted on miners all over South Wales.'[14]

ⱷ℈℧

These were thoroughly disorienting years for the company: sandwiched between *Landscape with Chimneys'* seventeen-date premiere tour of South Wales – Colbren, Resolven, Cwmavon, Ystradgynlais – and a twenty-two-night tour of the North-East – Aycliffe, Ferry Hill, Easington Colliery, Spennymoor – they sailed back to Scandinavia, playing *Uranium 235* to full houses in plush Norwegian and Swedish theatres, and sleeping in butler-manned apartments. In Britain they were touring places where theatre critics seldom ventured; Scandinavian critics compared Littlewood to Kurt Jooss, Erwin Piscator and Ernst Toller.[15] 'As an artist she is worth the entire Old Vic,' gushed one critic.

'Her name should be written in letters of fire until the blinkers are burned off the eyes of the English theatre public.'[16]

ଔ୫ଈ

On 12 February 1951 MacColl took a break from the road to sing on a BBC Third Programme, 'Traditional Ballads'.[17] It wasn't an unusual booking, except that while recording at Broadcasting House, London, MacColl met Texan folklorist Alan Lomax, also working on the programme.[18] MacColl would recall the meeting as 'an event which was to produce a major upheaval in my life'.[19]

The two men knew of one another by reputation, and immediately hit it off. The ebullient Lomax was six days younger than MacColl and had been every bit as precocious in terms of radical cultural activism.[20] A Harvard graduate and son of distinguished folklorist John Avery Lomax, by the time Alan Lomax was thirty he'd published influential song collections, recorded musicians including Leadbelly, Jelly Roll Morton, Woody Guthrie and Muddy Waters, established himself as an academic, archivist, singer, musician, and begun to enjoy a significant cultural profile as an impresario, promoter, journalist and broadcaster.[21] Lomax's work wasn't confined to the United States: his wartime radio programme *The Martins and the Coys* brought the likes of Woody Guthrie, Burl Ives and Pete Seeger to listeners on the BBC Home Service, where they caught MacColl's attention;[22] song compilations such as *The People's Song Book* (1948) made the music of the American labour movement available to British activists and musicians (MacColl had used the 1920s strike anthem 'Which Side Are You On?' in *Landscape with Chimneys*).[23] In 1950 Lomax's name appeared in *Red Channels*, a McCarthyite publication listing subversives.[24] Knowing which way the wind was blowing, Lomax accepted an offer from Columbia Records to oversee a colossal thirty-LP project exploring the folk traditions of faraway places. After a brief sojourn in Europe, he based himself in London.[25]

He was as passionate about folk culture as MacColl was about theatre, and spoke the same language of creating a dynamic, radical popular culture grounded in everyday speech and experience. Lomax's boundless enthusiasm was a catalyst that helped to convert MacColl's considerable expertise in folk music into an abiding fixation. A born hustler, Lomax hadn't been in town long before he was making his own programmes for the BBC and enjoying the free run of the facilities.[26] On 21 February 1951, just nine days after first meeting MacColl, he booked a studio to gather material for the Columbia LP set, *A World Library of Folk and Primitive Music*. It was MacColl's first recording session. Lomax was after authenticity and MacColl gave him the voice of the people, croaking and rasping like a man twice his age. 'When he first took to folk-singing', Littlewood recalled, 'Jimmie had abandoned his own good baritone for the cracked voice of some old farm labourer and in time evolved an authentic, original style, quite synthetic, but much admired.'[27] Lomax used two of his MacColl recordings on the English LP of the Columbia series.[28] 'Fourpence a Day' chronicled hard times in the Teesdale lead-mining community and had been collected by MacColl and Littlewood for a Children's Hour programme the year before – for MacColl it was typical of folksong in expressing 'the dreams, the aspirations and the every-day thoughts of large groups of people'.[29] 'The Four Loom Weaver' was a soulful, embittered Lancashire song well known in the region.[30] As far as Lomax was concerned, MacColl also qualified as an honorary Scot: two more MacColl performances, including his version of the gory border ballad 'The Dowie Dens of Yarrow', appeared on the Scotland record of the Columbia series.[31]

ᛉ

MacColl's Scottish cultural nationalism flourished unabated. With James Bridie and Compton Mackenzie, he now sat on the advisory board of The Dunedin Society, an organisation dedicated to promoting Scottish arts, headed up by Hugh MacDiarmid and publisher William MacLellan.[32] At one time his two cultural heroes had been novelist Lewis Grassic Gibbon and Hugh MacDiarmid; he was now numbered with them, by MacDiarmid at least. 'As far as the Scottish Renaissance Movement is concerned,' wrote the poet in October 1952, 'Communist writers head every department of literature. Lewis Grassic Gibbon in the novel, Ewan MacColl in drama, myself perhaps in poetry.'[33] MacDiarmid was becoming something of a mentor for MacColl – they discussed collaborating on a truly Scottish adaptation of *Macbeth*, and MacDiarmid advised MacColl on possible new projects.[34] MacColl appreciated the attention from Scotland's foremost poet, and reciprocated. In February 1951 he wrote and presented 'The Poetry of Hugh MacDiarmid' for the BBC Third Programme, choosing and discussing eleven poems.[35]

⊂ঽৎ৩

Like MacDiarmid, MacColl now dreamed of an independent Scottish Workers' Republic. He needed no persuading that Scotland was ultimately Theatre Workshop's destined home, but his conviction was further reinforced by the company's highly successful late summer visit to the 1951 Edinburgh People's Festival. Centred on Oddfellows Hall and organised primarily by communists, the festival committee had been inspired by the cultural guerrilla tactics employed by Theatre Workshop's Edinburgh trip two years earlier: running parallel to the cosmopolitan Edinburgh International Festival of Music and Drama, the People's Festival now offered a rival week-long programme designed to be affordable, accessible, culturally grounded and politically provocative.[36] Glasgow Unity Theatre, Hugh MacDiarmid, Hamish Henderson, poet Helen Cruickshank, Tom Driberg and filmmaker Ralph Bond were all involved.

MacColl was in the thick of things. He participated in the festival's opening one-day conference, 'Towards a People's Culture', reciting a freshly written Scots poem sending up the insipid Englishness of the official festival.[37] Theatre Workshop's production of his play *Uranium 235* was one of the festival's highlights; MacColl's public lecture 'Towards a People's Theatre' restated some familiar claims: the bourgeoisie was a class in decline whose theatrical art reflected their moribund state; theatre's future lay with the working class, who alone could reconnect the art form to the vital movement of history.[38] And he lent his voice to the Friday night folk music concert organised by Hamish Henderson to showcase some of the Scottish talent recently recorded by Alan Lomax for his Columbia series. Billed in the *Daily Worker* as a concert of 'authentic folk singers', the line-up included Jessie Murray, a singer and fishwife from Banffshire, street singer and casual labourer Jimmy MacBeath, and ballad-singing farmer John Strachan.[39] The music itself was distinguished enough – exotic-sounding to most – but in the politicised context of a festival exploring questions about class, nation and cultural traditions it was powerfully resonant. An initially sceptical *Daily Worker* reporter was not alone in concluding 'the popular folk tradition in Scotland is far from being dead or dying'.[40]

For MacColl it was further confirmation that the people's music was alive, well and profoundly relevant to a better future.

ᏒᏴᎤ

In 1952 Theatre Workshop came closest to making a national breakthrough when, not for the first time, the well-connected and charming Theatre Workshop ambassador Tom Driberg pulled some strings. Sam Wanamaker, eminent American actor and producer, and Michael Redgrave, currently at the height of his fame as a classical actor, called round at the company's Manchester rehearsal room. The surroundings were a long way from the Aldwych or Old Vic (Redgrave remembered a 'cold, bare basement'); but moved by the combination of talent and poverty, both luminaries offered support.[41] Redgrave put up some cash, Wanamaker provided eye-catching blurb – 'The Most Exciting Theatre I Have Ever Seen' – and Theatre Workshop were 'presented' performing MacColl's *Uranium 235* at the sympathetic Embassy Theatre, Swiss Cottage, London in May.[42] 'There is no knowing what they may not achieve in the years to come,' wrote Redgrave in the publicity leaflet. 'Let us support them now.'[43]

They trooped down to London. George Cukor, Lawrence Olivier and Vivien Leigh turned out for the opening night, but the critics were divided.[44] The *Daily Mirror* took issue with *Uranium 235*'s strident political tone; the *Daily Mail* registered the 'violent vitality' of the acting; Harold Hobson preferred the idea behind the company to the production itself.[45] The show was certainly a talking point in fashionable metropolitan theatre circles – it wasn't so often that communist activists turned up outside Swiss Cottage theatres to sell the *Daily Worker* – but Littlewood's brand of balletic political theatre was ultimately perceived as worthily eccentric rather than the next big thing.[46] 'We'd no best clothes, no small talk,' Littlewood recalled. 'We sounded more like North country comedians than smart actors.... The public who came couldn't make head or tail of us.'[47]

The production then transferred to Brighton, where MacColl moonlighted on singing engagements, including a well-received late night folksong concert at Brighton Jazz Club.[48] After Brighton they returned to London, appearing at the Comedy Theatre for their West End debut. Here their run coincided with a heatwave: ticket sales were disastrous and they came away £1,000 in debt. Littlewood sent

SOS letters to friends and supporters seeking donations for food. 'If you know anybody rich that any of our characters can seduce, let me know,' she wrote in one letter.[49] They were entering an endgame. With no communal house – the Oxford Road lease had expired – they took up an offer from Tom Driberg and camped in the grounds of his run-down Tudor mansion in Bradwell Juxta Mare, Essex. They slept in tents, swam in the sea and ate whatever John Blanshard could shoot. To raise funds, Harry Corbett subcontracted work from local farmers and drew up a work roster. Between shifts, they rehearsed MacColl's new play *The Travellers* for the 1952 Edinburgh People's Festival.[50] Without success in London, Littlewood was also wondering whether they were destined for life north of the border.[51]

ೞ೮

Written sporadically during 1972, MacColl's *The Travellers* took as its theme Cold War politics and, in particular, the American presence in Europe.[52] Stylistically he jettisoned the open structures and mixed media of *Uranium 235* and *Landscape With Chimneys* in favour of a dour socialist realism, now the official artistic mode of the Soviet bloc.[53] There were no songs, dances, nor bearing of the device, but a realistic train journey through Europe on which the various travellers are all involved in the building of an American military installation. The journey symbolised Europe's headlong rush towards a Third World War, and all the Americans are straightforwardly villainous. The hero is George Mehring, a seasoned revolutionary whose mission is to persuade his fellow travellers to take responsibility for the direction of history and stop the train. Though killed in the course of his efforts, he's successful in his assignment: the disillusioned are re-engaged in political action and the westward rush of the train is halted. Agitprop style, the play instructs its audience in the appropriate course of anti-American action.

MacColl had never rejoined the Communist Party since the war. In 1945 it was unsafe to do so – communist activity was likely to bring him to the unwanted attention of the authorities; throughout the endless touring of the late 1940s he'd been remote from party life. Events like the Edinburgh People's Festival now brought him back into contact with party activists and he renewed his card (his reapplication was intercepted by MI5, who duly resumed their surveillance).[54] He didn't agree with everything the party now stood for – especially the parliamentary road to socialism advocated in the most recent manifesto – but liked the fact that cultural questions were being taken more seriously (a Cultural Committee had been established in 1947). He agreed with party analysis that the penetration of American culture was another strategy in America's pursuit of post-war economic and political domination, and that indigenous British (especially Scottish) cultural traditions were being swamped by 'the synthetic imperialist culture of the States'.[55]

*The Travellers* was a measure of his reintegration; in form and content it toed the party line with a discipline not seen since *Last Edition*. America is presented as the primary aggressor in Korea;[56] as in the *Daily Worker*, there's a conspicuous silence about Stalin's recent 'revolutionary justice' of purges and show-trials in Yugoslavia, and about ongoing Cold War realpolitik in Eastern Europe.[57] While the brutal history of Stalin's state terror is obscured behind dialectical abstraction – peace as 'the sheer unimpeded movement of history' – MacColl makes no bones about equating contemporary US hegemony with fascism.[58] The play points out – not implausibly – that many former Nazis were re-employed in the higher echelons of the new West Germany; it goes further, arguing that fascism and American hegemony are part of a political continuum. 'It was merely a change of leadership,' claims former Nazi Eckert, 'the war goes on and I go on.'[59]

For the past seven years the *Daily Worker* had consistently overlooked Theatre Workshop's eclectic innovation – the lapsed communist Littlewood saw little difference between the philistinism of the left and the right – but MacColl's new play was feted by the communist newspaper.[60] *The Travellers* was previewed, reviewed and defended; the correspondent in Edinburgh wrote a long retrospective piece on the company;[61] the *Daily Worker* even suggested that MacColl should be awarded a Nobel Peace Prize.[62] The play was good for MacColl's reputation behind the Iron Curtain:[63] *The Travellers* was serialised in *Soviet Art* and scheduled for performances in Warsaw and Stalingrad in 1955, and in East Germany the following year.[64] But it proved damaging to the Edinburgh People's Festival: the dominant tone of 1952 event was a shrill anti-Americanism, and MacColl's play caused disquiet among some of the fifty affiliated moderate organisations now backing the festival.[65] By the following January the Edinburgh People's Festival had become an item on the Scottish TUC and Labour Party's list of proscribed organisations, which made it extremely difficult to secure future funding.[66] MacColl was unrepentant about his contribution to difficulties.[67] 'It was inevitable', he wrote in the *Daily Worker*, 'that a successful attempt to create a popular workers' culture should meet opposition from reactionary circles.'[68] The scaled-down 1953 festival would be the last.

⊂ঌ৪৩

After the festival, the company took the plunge and headed for Glasgow, where they now resolved to find permanent premises and settle for good. They moved into a subsiding and cockroach-infested communal house at 12 Belmont Street. Bedrooms were assigned; the usual roster of duty cooks was drawn up; Raffles acquired a wine-importer's licence, and there was much late-night carousing and singing of revolutionary songs. MacColl was often away doing radio work in London; Jean ran dance classes in the large kitchen; the two-year-old Hamish had a colourful array of Theatre Workshop baby-sitters – when the snow came, Godmother Littlewood taught him to make snow pies.[69]

Theatre Workshop's van was now too unreliable for serious touring, and the company survived by performing *Twelfth Night* in schools.[70] A new production of Molière's last play, *Le Malade Imaginaire*, opened at Glasgow's Jewish Institute that December to strong notices.[71] 'The going is very difficult at the moment,' MacColl reported to Communist Party Cultural Commissar Sam Aaronovitch, 'as premises are rarer than honest Americans.'[72] Company members wandered the streets looking for suitable buildings.[73] In vain, Raffles haggled over disused cinemas and derelict churches.

There were no viable options in Glasgow and Raffles now heard, via a theatrical agent, that if the company could raise six weeks' rent of £250 (worth around £5,000 today), they could take on the Theatre Royal and Palace of Varieties, Angel Lane, Stratford-atte-Bow, East London, a venue previously visited on the company's ill-fated *Alice in Wonderland* tour two years before.[74] Like Littlewood, most of the company were now exhausted, demoralised and desperate to settle somewhere; MacColl was indignantly opposed to the plan. London was the heart of darkness as far as he was concerned, the capital of the nation's diseased theatre industry. A move to London would, he argued, inevitably shift emphasis from creating a following among a working-class audience to titillating London theatregoers and critics. And hadn't they failed to make an impression every time they performed in the capital? For MacColl, the answer remained the same: a more fully developed political agenda, more rigorous training, and an ongoing commitment to building a working-class audience, preferably in Scotland.[75] The debate went back and forward, sometimes acrimoniously, during long evenings at Belmont Street.[76] MacColl's vision of taking theatre to the workers had prevailed in the previous crisis of 1950; Raffles' pragmatism won the day now. In January 1953 Theatre Workshop decamped to Angel Lane, Stratford East, London.

C3&O

The Victorian theatre awaiting them was filthy, damp, badly lit, the drains were blocked, the paint was peeling, the roof leaked, there was no hot water, the cantankerous boiler seldom worked. Nobody could afford digs, so they squatted in the theatre; gas rings and camp beds were installed in dressing rooms. Posters were printed in the theatre basement and pasted at tube stations in the small hours. On top of the usual routine, company members were now also painting, repairing and cleaning their theatre. They opened in mid-February with *Twelfth Night*. The theatre's recent clientele were used to saucy variety shows with titles like *Strip, Strip Hooray!*, and seemed to misconstrue the title of *Twelfth Night*. 'I think they thought it was a bedroom farce or something,' recalled Theatre Workshop actor George Cooper. 'I was playing Malvolio with this enormous hat on, and as soon as I got on the stage there were cries of "Big Head, Big Head". They threw toffees on the stage, they threw pennies, they really had a ball.'[77]

With no choice but to persevere, they staged revamped versions of the old repertoire in fortnight runs – *The Imaginary Invalid*, *Landscape with Chimneys* (now called *Paradise Street*), *Operation Olive Branch* (now with the original title of *Lysistrata*) and *The Travellers*. The older shows were interspersed with hastily rehearsed new productions – Stanley Houghton's *Hindle Wakes*, Sean O'Casey's *Juno and the Paycock*, Ben Jonson's *The Alchemist*.[78]

MacColl and Jean made the move down to London with the company – Hamish stayed with Jean's parents while they found somewhere to live – and that Easter the family moved into a rented flat at 109

Rodenhurst Road in Clapham Park.[79] Jean would remain central to Theatre Workshop as movement coach and choreographer for the next decade, training a new generation of actors, and leaving an indelible mark on the company's distinctive aesthetic. Increasingly absorbed in music and radio work, her husband quickly became a more peripheral figure. That year he worked with the company on his own plays and adaptations, acting in *Paradise Street, Lysistrata* and *The Travellers*, but took part in only one new production, the Christmas *Treasure Island* (he was listed in the programme as 'Ewan McColl' [sic]).[80] 'Almost from the moment we occupied Theatre Royal,' he wrote in his autobiography, 'my relationship with the rest of the company was subtly altered. More and more I felt like a stranger, and an unwelcome stranger at that. It was an uncomfortable state of affairs.'[81] From now on, the divided life that MacColl had been leading since meeting Alan Lomax would become increasingly pronounced.

❁

When he moved to London, MacColl was already a minor recording artist, and the opportunity to cut his first solo record had come from an unlikely quarter. Based in a grand, redbrick building in affluent Regent's Park, the English Folk Dance and Song Society had existed in various incarnations since the turn of the century. Its patron saint was Cecil Sharp (1859–1924), a minor composer who'd avidly collected songs from the English folk and tidied them up for concert-platform performance in the hope of stimulating a patriotic musical renewal. The EFDSS was frequently dismissed by MacColl as an assemblage of 'silver haired ladies of both sexes', but early in 1952 it had proposed subsidising two Ewan MacColl discs for the specialist folk market.[82] MacColl was happy to entertain the suggestion, even from an organisation patronised by Princess Margaret.

The society put up the money and HMV issued two 10-inch 78 rpm records of the unaccompanied MacColl singing four songs.[83] Glowing reviews in the society's in-house publications congratulated MacColl for combining authenticity and artistry, but the recording session couldn't have been further removed from the chaotic communality of Theatre Workshop.[84] 'It was lonely sitting in the centre of that enormous studio at HMV with only the microphone for company,' MacColl later wrote. 'I didn't know anyone in the place and nobody spoke to me except to tell me where to sit. The technicians, looking like hospital orderlies in their white coats, did nothing to reduce the tension and formality of the occasion.'[85]

CR80

MacColl found life much more convivial across town in the bustling and smoky Paddington basement office of the Workers' Music Association. Dominated by communists, the WMA had been founded in the Popular Front years to co-ordinate workers' musical activity, and boasted a distinguished roster of nominal vice-presidents including Paul Robeson, Benjamin Britten, Humphrey Lyttelton, Pete Seeger, A. L. Lloyd and, from 1954, MacColl himself. They supported choirs, orchestras, brass bands, and ran instrument classes and residential summer schools.[86] They printed sheet music – 'The Internationale' arranged by association president Alan Bush was one of their biggest sellers; in 1939 the WMA had established the Topic Record Club, which survives today as Britain's oldest independent record label. Light-hearted political songs like 'The Man that Waters the Workers' Beer'; balalaika arrangements of 'Soviet Land'; choral arrangements of political songs performed by the Topic Singers (nicknamed the 'Red Singing Men of Battersea') – all found a place in the Topic catalogue.

By 1952 the company were aware of a growing market for folk music and MacColl, who had plenty of contacts in and around the WMA, started to record for them.[87] Between 1952 and 1956 he would cut nineteen 10-inch 78 rpm 'singles' on the Topic label, initially in small pressings of a couple of hundred discs. Recording facilities were mobile – Topic didn't yet have its own studio – and many of the recordings were made in MacColl's flat with Jean, or even Hamish, at the dials of the cumbersome Ferrograph machine.[88] Al Jeffrey played basic guitar accompaniments on some tracks and tenor banjo on others; accomplished session guitarist Brian Daly provided more elaborate backing for the 1954 recordings.[89] Through these emphatically low-fi offerings, MacColl became tiny Topic's recording star and the bard of the communist left.

The recordings covered the spectrum of MacColl's repertoire from 'Dirty Old Town' to 'The Sheffield Apprentice', but his 'Ballad of Stalin', written and recorded in 1952 and rushed out shortly after Stalin's death in 1953, proved one of his most popular.[90] On Stalin's death the *Daily Worker* mourned 'the greatest working-class leader, genius and creative thinker that the world has ever known'; MacColl's new record joined the elegiac chorus (the tune was recycled from a song he'd recently written about railway magnate George Hudson, and Al Jeffrey supplied jaunty banjo licks).[91] Power struggles, show-trials, 'revolutionary justice', gulags – all were air-brushed from the picture. MacColl presented Stalin as a colossal landscape gardener who rerouted canals, planted trees and improved the Russian weather. 'A mighty man' with 'a mighty plan', Stalin had 'made the workers' state the best the world has ever seen'.[92]

CB&O

Embedded in metropolitan leftist circles, it was a matter of time before MacColl met journalist, singer, folklorist, translator, broadcaster and fellow working-class communist A. L. or 'Bert' Lloyd. In a fashion, their paths had already converged more than once: in the late 1930s, Littlewood and Jimmie Miller had pored over Lloyd's translation of García Lorca's book, *Lament for the Death of a Bull Fighter* (1937);[93] after the war, Lloyd's unpublished translation of Lorca's play *Blood Wedding* fell into Littlewood's hands and was earmarked for staging; Lloyd's signature appears on Theatre Workshop's 1948 bid to take on the David Lewis Theatre, Liverpool.[94] But it was the catalytic Alan Lomax who finally introduced MacColl and Lloyd while the latter was collecting material for his anthology of industrial folksong, *Come All Ye Bold Miners: Ballads and Songs of the Coalfields* (1952).[95]

MacColl was instantly fascinated by the idea of a book recovering submerged workers' culture. 'I didn't know there were so many miners' songs,' he later recalled, 'I thought maybe there were half a dozen extant. Bert told me he'd got hundreds. I thought – this is the kind of exaggeration *I'm* prone to.'[96] MacColl gave him the songs he knew, three of which went into the collection.[97] Lloyd's book was principally designed to preserve the residues of a vanishing coalfield culture, 'barely kept alive in the mouth of a solitary singer here and there'.[98] He signed off, however, with a new note, which angled the book towards the future: 'If this humble collection can encourage one miner to make up one ballad out of his working life, it will have achieved its aim.'[99] Revival of industrial song culture, as well as preservation, was in his mind.

ⳍℬⳎ

Impecunious, fired-up about folk music, and inspired by Alan Lomax's go-getting manner – which always seemed to result in the most attractive commissions – MacColl now became more forceful in hawking his wares to the BBC: 'There is a growing audience for folk music,' he wrote to one producer, 'and I'm sure ... I could turn out some really good programmes, given the opportunity.'[100] Alongside humdrum assignments undertaken to pay the bills, MacColl now worked on a series of broadcasts that developed and disseminated the ideas forming in his head.[101]

As a keen reader of communist and classics professor George Thomson, MacColl believed that all music, poetry and dancing ultimately originated in what Thomson called 'the rhythmical movement of human bodies engaged in collective labour'.[102] MacColl's *Come All Ye Good People: A Programme About Ballads* argued that traditional ballads were 'the product of communal effort' and thus embodied a collective rather than individualistic perspective.[103] And if, as Thomson claimed, all songs originated in work, it followed that songs created to assist work (like sea shanties) and industrial folksongs about work had a very special status in the folksong canon, remaining somehow in touch with the source of song itself. A creature of industrialisation, MacColl was already defining his ideas against what he saw as earlier folklorists' construction of folk music as a rosy, reassuring window on to a vanished rural past.[104] MacColl's radio programme *St Cecilia and the Shovel* took issue with the ways in which earlier song collectors and concert platform singers had sanitised and depoliticised songs of labour.[105] In tandem with Lloyd, he was rapidly arriving at a different definition of folksong. It was an ongoing, deeply rooted workers' culture 'in the idiom of popular speech'; it recorded 'very exactly the conditions in which people lived in certain periods in history'; it functioned as an archive preserving the feelings arising from working people's experiences.[106] Special Branch were soon tuning in to his broadcasts expecting 'as much Communist propaganda as can suitably be inserted'.[107]

ⳍℬⳎ

These programmes adopted the tones of the seminar room and the Communist Party Cultural Committee meeting. MacColl's next project was deliberately populist and wide-ranging in scope, and aimed to disseminate his new ideas to the widest possible audience. Scripted and co-ordinated by MacColl and produced by Manchester-based Denis Mitchell, *Ballads and Blues* was a series of six programmes broadcast on the National Home Service in the spring of 1953 and repeated on the Light Programme that June.[108] MacColl always harboured big plans for the series, which he launched with a polemical article in the *Radio Times*.[109] 'There are', he wrote in an early public use of the term, 'many indications that we are on the eve of a great folk-song revival.' The task of creating a wide audience for folksong was, he noted, easier in the United States where the familiar folk forms of the blues had provided the basis of jazz and much popular music; *Ballads and Blues* aimed to illustrate that Britain had folk forms related to the blues in tone and theme. The implication was that Britain's folk tradition could provide the foundation for an equivalent revival of nationally rooted musical creativity.

No expense was spared from the BBC in terms of the musicians placed at MacColl's disposal: communist Humphrey Lyttelton was the most significant figure in British jazz; Guyanese calypso singer Cy Grant was hired alongside Theatre Workshop's Tyneside singer Isla Cameron; A. L. Lloyd and Irish piper Seumus Ennis appeared; Alan Lomax made larger-than-life contributions to two programmes and brought in American authenticity in the shape of Kentucky singer Jean Ritchie and touring bluesman Big Bill Broonzy. Each programme explored how different musical traditions had engaged with common themes such as crime, the city, seafaring, railways, work or soldiering. Shared genealogies were shown to link very different songs – one programme traced the well-known 'St James' Infirmary Blues' back to a British ballad. MacColl's main point was to celebrate the diverse creativity of working people: folk music was presented as a musical vulgate transcending national and cultural boundaries. Though some of the audience found the music 'dreary and depressing' and the narration 'terribly boring', at least one listener took from it exactly what MacColl hoped.[110] 'I think these programme make one realise that folk singing is not, as some people would have it, a dying art, but is indeed very much alive,' s/he wrote on her BBC feedback questionnaire. 'The words and accompaniment alter to suit the times, but the old, old points and morals are still there.'[111]

ભૃુદ્ધ

In September 1953 MacColl returned to Scotland for the third Edinburgh People's Festival. He travelled and socialised with Theatre Workshop, who were presenting two plays, but he was now preoccupied with music.[112] Throughout the year he'd been working on *Scotland Sings*, a WMA anthology of one hundred folksongs that was due to receive its Scottish launch at a solo folk concert entitled 'Songs of the People' on Sunday 13 September 1953.[113]

Now thirty-eight, he sat up on the Oddfellows Hall stage on a back-to-front chair and worked through his programme. He was a charismatic performer who'd always felt at home before an audience. Experience as a playwright and scriptwriter had taught him about plotting and pace – the apparently improvised set was actually planned around thematic patterns and shifts in tempo. His skills as a broadcaster and presenter were put to good use: carefully crafted and informative song introductions were presented with an apparent artlessness, creating an impression of effortless erudition. His repertoire was vast, ranging from long ballads like 'Lord Randal' through Jacobite songs, snatches of street chants, saucy Bothy Ballads, and his own requiem for those killed in Spain, 'Jamie Foyers'. His pitching was faultless, his voice disciplined through years of training exercises. He could vary volume and sing in a range of styles and accents. His acting skills weren't wasted: there was an understated theatricality to his performances – he seemed to move through different personae as the set unfolded. It was a compelling performance and ran to three hours, including several encores. 'As a folk singer (and collector)', wrote the *Jazz Journal*, 'he must rank with the world's best, an opinion held by all who have seen him in person.'[114]

ભૃુદ્ધ

The MacColl family was now settled in a roomy, rented flat at 11 Park Hill Rise in suburban East Croydon. Betsy moved in with them, played with Hamish and pottered in the large garden. Old Theatre Union friends Barbara Niven – now a full-time fundraiser for the *Daily Worker* – and her partner, the social realist painter Ern Brooks, took the flat upstairs. It was a stimulating, sociable time. They went to Theatre Workshop parties and rowdy all-night affairs at Lomax's St John's Wood flat. Jean was an excellent cook and the family were hospitable people (MacColl enjoyed good wine and food, even before he could really afford to). Visiting musicians spent the night. Big Bill Broonzy, who always drank brandy with his breakfast, was a regular guest;[115] Alan Lomax was around; Hugh MacDiarmid came to stay, and steadily polished off whatever drink was available. Whenever tradesmen came to the house, MacColl would attempt to recruit them to the Communist Party. On Sundays the family sometimes visited the Lloyds at Greenwich. Hamish and Bert's daughter would play together while their fathers talked about the workers' music.

Always animated in one another's company, Lloyd and MacColl agreed that trade unions were crucial in providing an institutional grounding for a British revival in radical music-making, and began to lobby. Sometimes with Alan Lomax, they sang at labour movement meetings around London, appearing at the National Union of Railwaymen headquarters on Euston Road and the National Amalgamated Engineers Union, where MacColl renewed his acquaintance with Wal Hannington, formerly leader of the NUWM.[116] And as fellow communists, Lloyd and MacColl were intent on diffusing the workers' music through the workers' party. They shared the stage at a concert celebrating the life and work of militant American songster Joe Hill; they sang together at the 1953 conference of the National Cultural Committee; at various socials, picnics, puppet shows, Eastern European embassies and events supporting the People's Democracies, Ewan MacColl and A. L. Lloyd provided the entertainment.[117] A singing Marxist double act, they soon cut the first of many records, *The Singing Sailor*, a 1955 album of sea-songs for Topic.[118]

cs&o

Unlike Lloyd, MacColl never found a niche for himself in the cultural committees of the Communist Party – he disliked meetings and was seldom diplomatic with those who disagreed with him. He did, however, become loosely involved in the World Federation of Democratic Youth Festivals. Held every two years in major Eastern Bloc cities, these noisy and colourful cultural and sporting exchanges aimed to promote peace and to resist the polarised politics of the Cold War.[119] In 1953 MacColl was invited to sing at the fourth festival at Bucharest, and found the anti-American tone and celebration of progressive anti-imperialistic national cultural traditions to his liking.[120] Invited to join the planning committee for the following festival, he attended preparatory cultural congresses in Hungary in January 1954 and Vienna that December.[121] The following summer he flew to Warsaw and joined the 30,000 delegates from 114 countries for the fifth festival. This time he had one foot in his old life, one in his new.[122]

He sang at various concerts while Theatre Workshop performed *You're Only Young Once*, a ballad opera hastily written by MacColl to illustrate the festival's message of peace and international friendship.[123] His play dramatised how young working-class lives were transformed by the prospect of a trip to Warsaw: a promising but ill-disciplined young boxer improves his footwork by joining his girlfriend's Warsaw-bound dance team; a snarling and narcissistic teddy boy is transformed into a happy and well-adjusted worker by the thought of playing ping-pong in Warsaw (the relevant song ran 'I'll bet that you're a menace / When you're playing table tennis').[124] The music was carefully composed – members of Humphrey Lyttelton's band provided the soundtrack and young English folksinger Shirley Collins took a large singing part. Jean Newlove provided characteristically inventive choreography; dispirited by the poor quality of the British dance teams in Bucharest two years earlier, she'd now assembled and drilled her own team, who took awards in the 1955 festival competitions and animated MacColl's new play.[125] But *You're Only Young Once* was further evidence, if any was needed, that theatrical craft was no longer foremost in MacColl's mind.

C8&0

Previously his songs had been subordinate to a larger cause or work – useful for a demonstration, a street-theatre sketch, a radio programme, a play – but he now started to see writing songs as 'an activity just as important as writing plays ... and one which could, and must, play a role in the folk revival we were trying to bring about'.[126] He always disliked the term 'songwriter', and not only because he never learned to read or write music. MacColl thought of his activity in terms of labour: songs were made, constructed, produced, sometimes 'cobbled' together from fragments.[127]

Some of his new songs were adaptations of older folksongs, a strategy he'd been using since at least the 1932 Mass Trespass but which now took on a conscious rationale in terms of connecting longstanding song traditions to contemporary realities.[128] 'The Dove' was an anti-military song that inflected an older Anglo-American folksong with a new message of peace; 'Fare Thee Well, Westminster' borrowed the tune of 'Prince Rupert's March' to lampoon the unstoppable Tories during the 1955 election campaign. Some of the songs from the period – 'For Peace and Lasting Friendship', 'Ballad of the New Poland', 'It's Only Propaganda' – remain buried in the pages of *Sing*, a magazine that consolidated the cultural assumptions of the young revival's political flank.[129] Other MacColl compositions would seep into the future. 'The Ballad of Tim Evans' vividly reconstructed the final hours of a man wrongly convicted of murder, and would later be performed by the young Bob Dylan;[130] 'The Ballad of the Carpenter' recast Christ as revolutionary leader and would appeal to the rebel sensibilities of American protest singer Phil Ochs.[131]

C3&O

MacColl was not only an established solo performer and the singing partner of A. L. Lloyd, but also a member of 'Ballads and Blues', a loose coalition of like-minded jazz and folk musicians that emerged from the 1953 radio series.[132] The fluid line-up variously included MacColl, Lloyd, Isla Cameron, West Indian guitarist Fitzroy Coleman, jazz clarinettist Bruce Turner, concertina player Alf Edwards, and musicians borrowed from the jazz bands of Humphrey Lyttelton and Ken Colyer. Early appearances included guest slots at Humphrey Lyttelton shows, Sunday night Theatre Workshop benefits at Stratford East, and a financially disastrous Scottish tour in February 1954.[133] The ensemble's finest hour came on Monday 5 July 1954, when the Ballads and Blues gave a sell-out benefit concert for *Daily Worker* at the South Bank's newly built Royal Festival Hall. (MacColl's seventieth birthday party would be held in the same venue thirty years later.)

There could no mistaking whose vision was shaping the event. MacColl gave a promotional interview with the *Daily Worker* and wrote a plug in the Young Communist League journal.[134] His concert programme notes described music that was 'unadulterated, in the authentic traditional style'.[135] He was the no-nonsense MC for the evening, ticking off those – including 'Lloydy' – slow to appear on-stage when announced.[136] Jean Newlove was involved, and presented her troupe of East End girls to the Royal Festival Hall audience (MacColl thought of them as a 'proletarian dance ensemble' like those he'd seen in Bulgaria).[137] And as a performer, MacColl's forceful presence dominated proceedings. Singing alone he performed long Scottish ballads, songs about transportation, pit disasters, and his newly penned panegyric to Vietnamese revolutionary hero Ho Chi Minh. He and Bert Lloyd delivered rousing sea shanties; MacColl later joined Ken Colyer's Jazzmen to perform American convict song 'Another Man Done Gone,' complete with a spiralling clarinet solo by the *Daily Worker*'s occasional jazz correspondent, Bruce Turner.[138] It was a memorable evening and enthusiastic reviewers on the left congratulated the team for successfully occupying one of London's key cultural sites; the in-joke was that the Royal Festival Hall would be a good place to hold the revolution.[139]

ᚳ₰ᚩ

'The Colyer Skiffle Group' played half a dozen songs that night. Trumpet player Ken Colyer had long admired American folk music, particularly Woody Guthrie and Leadbelly, and took to 'skiffling' this material, with guitars, washboard and upright bass during interludes in his full band's performances.[140] The formula offered by skiffle – raw, rhythmic, exuding authenticity – became a hit at Colyer's shows and beyond. Skiffle managed to combine all the exotic glamour of American culture with a visceral, DIY, anti-commercial ethos, and quickly caught on with the nascent folk scene, which had always insisted there were two Americas – one of big business, Hollywood, comic books and cultural imperialism, the other of Joe Hill, Leadbelly, Woody Guthrie, and the cultural resourcefulness of the regular working man.[141] By 1954 the new skiffle sound could be heard in London pubs, including the Perseverance on the Tottenham Court Road and the Princess Louise in High Holborn;[142] within two years skiffle fans could find sessions seven nights a week at the Skiffle Cellar on Soho's Greek Street, the Gyre and Gimble behind Charing Cross Station and newer coffee shops like The Partisan on Carlisle Street and The Troubadour at Earls' Court.[143] MacColl and Bert Lloyd sometimes dropped in, and cast a curious eye over proceedings.[144]

Before long they could listen to the new music without leaving the house: the Lonnie Donegan Skiffle Group's raucous rendition of Leadbelly's 'Rock Island Line' reached number eight in the charts in January 1956. A rash of commercial releases followed, weekly BBC radio's *Saturday Skiffle Club* drew audiences of two and a half million, and skiffle was transformed from a Soho subculture into a two-year-long national craze of music-making.[145] Jazz purists hooted with derision at the 'neighing ... jukebox hillbilly' Donegan, who was vulgarising noble music he didn't understand, but MacColl, Lomax and Lloyd were more paternal than puritanical.[146] This wasn't exactly the revival they'd envisaged – American culture was supposed to be resisted rather than spread – but MacColl still regarded the outburst of DIY music-making as 'a unique and extraordinary awakening' in which British youth was rightly rejecting crooners Tony Bennett and Dean Martin for more proletarian heroes like Guthrie and Leadbelly.[147] 'I have the greatest confidence in the world,' Alan Lomax wrote of the skifflers, 'that their mastery of instruments will increase, that they will get tired after a while of their monotonous two-beat imitation of Negro rhythm and that, in looking around, they will discover the song-tradition of Great Britain.'[148]

# 7
# Croydon, Soho, Moscow, Paris

Early in 1956 Alan Lomax and Ewan MacColl decided to form a new ensemble. A sincere desire to steer skiffle towards more British musical authenticity vied with more personal ambitions. If anyone was entitled to feel proprietorial about the skifflers' standard repertoire of Leadbelly and Woody Guthrie songs, it was Lomax, who'd played such a prominent role in shaping those careers; both Lomax and MacColl were freelance cultural activists whose incomes fluctuated alarmingly. MacColl had already made one pitch towards the skiffle market by recording Merle Travis's Kentucky coalfield anthem 'Sixteen Tons' during Lonnie Donegan's chart success;[1] Lomax would soon follow with his own solo recordings.[2] The new band was a more decisive step in the same direction.

They were to be called 'Alan Lomax and the Ramblers', and were joined by Sussex singer Shirley Collins, whom Lomax had first met at one of MacColl's parties.[3] Guitarists Fitzroy Coleman and Brian Daly were hired, as were jazzmen Bruce Turner and Chris Barber's bassist, Jim Bray. Nigerian Nat Atkin was to provide percussion; A. L. Lloyd, Alf Edwards and harmonica player John Cole were to appear on an informal basis. With three guitarists (including Lomax), four singers (including MacColl and Lloyd), and top session musicians and jazzmen, the line-up already read like a who's who of mid-1950s London musicians. But Lomax still wanted a five-string banjo player. Always a sharp reader of cultural trends, he understood that skiffle was a festival of Americana and that, among a scene of American impersonators, authenticity had a special value. His first choice was twenty-one-year-old Peggy Seeger.

114

০৪৪১

Seeger represented an impeccable combination of highbrow panache, left-liberal politics and real connection to the sources of skiffle. Her mother, Ruth Crawford, was a distinguished avant-garde composer and the first woman to win a Guggenheim Scholarship to Europe; her father, Charles Seeger, was a pioneering academic musicologist of good New England, Yankee Puritan stock.[4] From the 1930s the Seegers had worked with the Lomaxes as American folk music's most prominent disseminators, activists and experts. Leadbelly, Woody Guthrie and singing labour organiser Aunt Molly Jackson were memorable figures from Peggy's childhood;[5] the family's African-American housemaid, Elizabeth 'Libba' Cotten, was a singer, much-imitated guitar-player, and the source of the song 'Freight Train'.[6] By the time Peggy was eleven, she was helping to transcribe field recordings from the Library of Congress archive: 'the music came right into us, we osmosed it,' she remembered. 'Even now, I can close my eyes when a tune's played and see it written on that staff line, including the sharps and flats.'[7] And by the time she went to Radcliffe College, Cambridge, Massachusetts, her folk-singing half-brother Pete Seeger – Charles's son from his first marriage – was a household name with folk group The Weavers.[8] Though initially hesitant to embark on a career in music, her future seemed mapped out. Saturated by traditional songs, intuitively musical, well-connected, articulate, attractive, college-educated, she was poised to take a prominent role in the American wing of the popular folk music revival currently beginning to stir. But in 1953 her fifty-two-year-old mother died; the sudden bereavement added family tragedy to the already traumatic McCarthy years in which the patrician and publicly radical Seegers were vulnerable. The Weavers were ruined by the blacklist and Pete, in refusing to testify before the House of Un-American Activities Committee, faced a lengthy legal battle and the possibility of a substantial prison sentence.[9] Charles Seeger lost his passport and job.[10] By September 1955 the money for Peggy's education had run out. The twenty-year-old bought a new banjo, took a leave of absence from college and a boat to Europe. The plan was to visit relatives in Holland, see Europe and learn Russian. She was staying in a Danish youth hostel when Lomax finally tracked her down. He explained that he was looking for a North American banjo-player. Would she be interested in appearing in a Granada Television

programme, *Dark of the Moon*, he asked? She arrived at Waterloo
Station in March 1956.

☙

Lomax envisaged his folk group as a British equivalent to The Weavers.
He hustled up record company interest from Decca, but The Ramblers'
single and seven-inch EP made no splash in Britain (their only album
seems to have been quietly sidelined for German-only release).[11] Aware
of the power of television, Lomax also used his Granada connections,
negotiating a series to showcase the band's talents.[12] Broadcast over
the summer of 1956, the programmes were excruciatingly hokey
affairs.[13] The straw-bales in the folksy set created a rheumy allergic
reaction in Peggy Seeger; Lomax came across as gushingly earnest,
inviting viewers to 'lean back in those easy chairs, grab tight hold
of your beermugs and your teacups, because tonight we're rambling
round the world!'[14] Any allusion to the music's political context was
excised, including a reference to the Highland clearances.[15] Far from
resisting skiffle's American emphasis, The Ramblers now added to it:
even MacColl lapsed into fashionable impersonations of American
speech.[16] Overstaffed and bulging with egos, The Ramblers always
managed to be less than the sum of its parts. 'We didn't deserve to
succeed,' Seeger later recalled. 'And we didn't.'[17]

☙

But if The Ramblers didn't make a mark, it did bring MacColl and
Seeger together; from their first meeting in Lomax's Chelsea flat on
25 March 1956 they spent countless hours in one another's company.
She was soon recording programmes on American Folk Songs for the
BBC, and accompanying MacColl on his BBC singing commissions.[18]
Their musical rapport was instant. MacColl, who couldn't read music
or play an instrument, was currently dependent on session musicians
like Fitzroy Coleman, Brian Daly and Al Jeffrey – all more at home
in musical idioms other than folk. Peggy Seeger was a folk musician
through and through, and keen to develop her skills on the basis of
instrumental styles learned from the American tradition.[19] Her five-
string banjo sounded exotic in mid-1950s Britain, and she was also a
guitarist, autoharp player and singer. She'd come at the right time: the
market for recorded folk music was expanding.[20] With A. L. Lloyd (a

friend of Peggy's father) in a position of influence at Topic, and MacColl
a sometime member of the WMA executive committee, there was plenty
of work. Peggy Seeger joined fellow-American Ramblin' Jack Elliott
on Topic's roster;[21] her strident and powerfully rhythmic banjo would
soon become part of MacColl's recorded sound.[22] She was a regular
visitor at the MacColl family home at Park Hill Rise where she and
MacColl rehearsed and recorded.[23]

C3ED

Indirectly, Peggy had encountered MacColl once before when a
college friend had played her Alan Lomax's *World Library of Folk
and Primitive Music, Volume 3: England*, enthusing about the singing
of a Ewan MacColl.[24] It made little impression on her: she didn't care
for the cracked, unaccompanied voice singing about 'The Four Loom
Weaver'. But in the flesh the forty-one-year-old MacColl (who told her
he was thirty-nine) was an imposing figure who combined professorial
intellectual authority, a radical edge and a forceful reputation.

He was charismatic and convivial, a well-connected *bon vivant* who
socialised with the London literati including roaring boy Brendan
Behan.[25] MacColl was always the centre of attention at parties – one
acquaintance from the period recalls him boasting that he'd re-read
the entire *oeuvre* of Dostoevsky in the past six weeks.[26] He was part
of the increasingly prestigious Theatre Workshop, and proudly took
Peggy Seeger along to Stratford East to see a production of Marlowe's
*Edward II*. They sat in a row with Littlewood and Jean Newlove. 'Joan
dismissed me with a glance,' Seeger recalled. 'She was full of vinegar for
folk music – she thought it had ruined Ewan.'[27] MacColl was enjoying
additional celebrity that year, playing the street singer in the British
premiere of Bertolt Brecht's *The Threepenny Opera*. Directed by Sam
Wanamaker, the play opened at the Royal Court in February 1956,
before transferring to the Aldwych in March and playing out at the
Comedy Theatre in June.[28] In letters to Hamish Henderson MacColl
dutifully reviled the West End as a 'cesspool', but he showered Peggy
Seeger with complimentary tickets.[29]

'Ewan took any chance he could to sit next to me, to put his hand
on my shoulder,' she remembers. 'He was the kind of fella who, two
weeks after he met me…says "I'm going to make love to you, just tell
me when." This was nowhere in my galaxy of approaches.' 'I was very

flattered by his attentions, I'd never met anyone like him before.'[30]
They became lovers that spring. 'Remember all the happy times we
have known,' he wrote to her in a letter two years later:

> Walking and talking and kissing our way through London, sitting on
> benches in Golden Square, in railway carriages going to Manchester ... You
> calling on me in my dressing room at the Aldwych and Comedy Theatres,
> walking through Berwick Street Market with my arm round you while
> you fed me cherries, recording together ... making love in all the places
> we ever made love in.[31]

ೞ಄ಌ

These were chaotic months in MacColl's life. His existence was split
between family life in Croydon – socialising with old friends like Bert
Lloyd, Barbara Niven and Ern Brooks, playing with the seven-year-old
Hamish, whom he adored, pottering in the garden – and the fast-living
bohemianism of Soho and his affair with a woman twenty years his
junior. 'I was forty, married with a young son,' he later wrote. 'I seemed
to be living in a world where frustration, exhilaration and guilt were
my constant companions.'[32] Passionate, clandestine and guilt-ridden,
the love affair with Peggy was oppressively intense, and MacColl could
be jealous and overbearing. At moments she rebelled against the weight
of its inevitability. 'I was hard times for him for the first three or
four years,' she recalled. 'I just couldn't adapt to the fact that he was
married, and I left and came back, left and came back, went with other
fellas and came back.' Once MacColl hit her. 'I was being beastly,
I was being a twenty-two-year-old and this poor forty-two-year-old
didn't know what to do, so he whacked me and then burst out crying.
It never happened again.'[33] The whole situation was unbearable, and
drove Peggy back to the United States at the end of 1956.

ೞ಄ಌ

She divided her time between California and a six-week singing
residency at the Gate of Horn in Chicago, a club run by Bob Dylan's
future manager, Albert Grossman.[34] 'This drastic "solution" to our
problem', recalled MacColl, 'left me even more wretched than I had
been before and things didn't improve with the passing of time.'[35]
They spoke on the phone and exchanged letters. Love-sickness was

the inspiration for what would become MacColl's best-known song, written in early 1957.

According to MacColl's retelling of the story, he was at home in Croydon drinking scotch and feeling melancholic when Peggy called from Los Angeles.[36] She asked whether he knew a short love song suitable for her concert that evening. He didn't, but in the course of the call came up with a three-verse, twelve-line lyric and hummed a melody to match. The song that would later settle into 'The First Time Ever I Saw Your Face' chronicled seeing, kissing and 'lying' with a lover for the first time. A résumé of their relationship, it describes the 'dark and empty skies' of one life being transformed by the lover's arrival on the scene.[37] Peggy took the song down and performed it that evening. It was an untypical MacColl song in its confessional introspection. A long way from the folk idiom, 'The First Time Ever' would later attract pop stars, soul singers and advertising companies. He saw the song as a gift to Peggy; it mapped the contours of his emotional life, but he would never sing it again. It quickly passed into her repertoire. 'Scores of other singers have recorded it,' MacColl wrote later, 'but only Peggy's singing matches the feelings that gave rise to it.'[38]

⊰⊱

Paradoxically, MacColl's reputation as a playwright was burgeoning now his mind was on other things. He received sporadic royalties from behind the Iron Curtain – in 1954 MI5 heard that a large cheque had arrived from Moscow; their informer noted that 'members of Theatre Workshop were inebriated for an entire evening celebrating'.[39] MacColl's early Cold War Aristophanes adaptation, *Operation Olive Branch*, was enjoying a revival at Sydney's Attic Theatre.[40] His new adaptation of Jaroslav Hašek's *The Good Soldier Schweik* caught the novel's subversive humour, was premiered at Stratford East in 1954, and scooped Theatre Workshop's first West End Transfer in March 1956. The production attracted the London literati (if not the theatregoing public), drew praise from Harold Hobson, and was later staged at the Third International Theatre Festival of 1956.[41]

The 1955 revival of his play *The Other Animals* had flopped at Stratford East, costing the company £1,000, but Theatre Workshop was keen for MacColl to write a new play for the company to present at the 1957 World Festival of Democratic Youth in Moscow.[42] With his recording schedule thrown into disarray by Peggy Seeger's departure, he now began work on *So Long at the Fair*, a loosely structured piece about life in military prison interspersed with songs. Once again MacColl returned to the shattering events of 1947: the play explored how military institutions, prisons and even conventional models of masculinity oppress the soldiers. Four years later, the play would be successfully staged at the Maxim Gorki Theatre in East Berlin, but the lovesick MacColl felt harassed by the deadline and couldn't get the script into shape in time for Moscow.[43]

Instead Theatre Workshop took *Macbeth* there – Littlewood reasoned that a study in tyranny would have obvious relevance in the Soviet Union the year after Khrushchev's denunciation of Stalinist atrocities. MacColl was asked to play the lead, but dithered and eventually announced he was too busy with other projects. At this point it was obvious that his future career lay outside theatre. He was more critical than ever of Gerry Raffles' top-down managerial style – one former company member recalled that nothing more significant than toilet paper allocations was now discussed in Theatre Workshop company meetings.[44] But MacColl always found it difficult to acknowledge that the comparative security Raffles provided had indeed created a context in which talents could flourish.[45]

Theatre Workshop now owned their Stratford premises and received modest but welcome grants from the Arts Council and local authorities.[46] Productions like *Richard II* and *Arden of Faversham* had consolidated the company's reputation for quality ensemble acting and innovative direction; appearances at the Paris Festivals of 1955 and 1956 now brought them to the attention of an international audience; even the disastrous 1955 British premiere of Brecht's *Mother Courage*, in which Littlewood unceremoniously ejected from rehearsals the young German assistant whom Brecht had dispatched to help out, seemed to add to the company's notoriety for fierce independence.[47] The company now stood on the edge of its golden years. There would be the agenda-setting and headline-grabbing West End transfers of Brendan Behan's *The Hostage* (1959), Shelagh Delaney's *A Taste of Honey* (1959), Stephen Lewis's *Sparrers Can't Sing* (1961) and the company's own *Oh! What A Lovely War* (1963). Theatre Workshop would become famous for its genre-blurring innovation, improvisation and as a stable of British acting talent – Brian Murphy, Victor Spinetti, Richard Harris, Murray Melvin and Barbara Windsor were all Littlewood protégés. Littlewood would become a household name as an iconoclastic producer and dependably outspoken celebrity artiste whose colourful language famously offended the Kray twins. MacColl would be a strong influence behind that story, but wouldn't play a direct role. That summer he amicably travelled to Moscow with the company, socialising with new members including the young Richard Harris. In Moscow, Littlewood was busy with *Macbeth*, Jean Newlove with the folk dance ensemble that had won awards in Warsaw in 1955, and MacColl with his music.[48]

ભુજ

Like the Warsaw festival of 1955, Moscow 1957 was a significant occasion for showcasing Britain's burgeoning musical subcultures. The new Soviet administration was receptive to music from the West: fifteen prominent jazz musicians made the trip, prompting the *Melody Maker* headline 'Soviet takes to Jazz'.[49] Young Scottish promoter and communist Malcolm Nixon was head of the British Youth Festival Committee and ensured that skiffle was well represented. Skifflers shared the bill with Bulgarian goatskin bagpipe players, the Shanghai Opera Company, the Symphony Orchestra of the Soviet Union and the Bolshoi ballet;[50] John Hasted's Skiffle and Folksong Group even played at a reception in the Kremlin, where Khrushchev approved the music. Members of the *Sing* fraternity later wrote an ironic 'Talking Blues' about Khrushchev's musical revisionism:

> Well Britain sent – God bless my soul –
> Skiffle, jazz and rock 'n' roll
> Says Comrade Shepilov, 'Man alive!
> I don't dig this bourgeois jive'
> But N. K. Khrushchev, he's the man
> Wants more skiffle in the five-year plan.[51]

MacColl was involved in the more scholarly side of the festival, helping to co-ordinate a panel of guest speakers for a series of folklore seminars organised by the Soviet Academy of Sciences. He also worked alongside Malcolm Nixon to present his 'Ballads and Blues' folk ensemble, which now included Shirley Collins, guitarist Steve Benbow and Peggy Seeger, who had returned to London in late June 1957 en route to Moscow, and resumed her tumultuous affair with MacColl.[52]

Wherever music and politics were concerned, MacColl was an exacting taskmaster. This was his first visit to the Soviet Union, and the festival marked the fortieth anniversary of the October Revolution, for MacColl 'the first time in history the working-people could straighten their backs and knees and look towards the horizon'.[53] He was proud of the ensemble, but especially proud of Seeger's abilities. He brought her into one meeting of luminaries – writers, artists, party officials – to sing the militant American protest music from her repertoire. 'I had things like "Which Side Are You On?" ... and a number of very telling songs ... like "Girl of Constant Sorrow,"' she remembered. 'Ewan wanted to show me off and he wanted them to see that Americans were more than the Cold War.' Misjudging the political intricacies of a situation in which she was supposed to illustrate the fighting culture of the American working class, she sang a couple of gospel songs. MacColl was incandescent with rage. 'I embarrassed him horrifically,' she said. 'Ewan came up in a fury at the end of it and said, "this is the end, I don't want to see you anymore".'[54] After the festival they headed off in different directions. Seeger defied stiff warnings from the American State Department and joined a group of young American musicians on a tour of China (she'd continue her four months of travelling with a visit to Eastern Europe; passport and visa complications would follow in due course). MacColl and Newlove returned to London. Within a month, MacColl and Seeger were exchanging letters of reconciliation. He apologised for his ill-tempered behaviour, writing 'it is no secret to you that I can on occasion be domineering, jealous, childish'.[55] He advised her what to sing at her concerts and mailed her copies of his songs: 'don't sing too many hymns! As museum pieces they are alright, but at the moment, people need to believe in themselves rather than in God.'[56] She reported on her travels behind the Iron Curtain. 'I am enormously impressed by your receptiveness and your ability to communicate your impressions,' he wrote in response.[57]

C26ED

MacColl had rejoined the Communist Party in 1952 at a time when 'The American Threat to British Culture' had galvanised cultural policy in a fashion that excited him. The early days of the Cold War were like the Class Against Class period of his youth projected on to an international scale: on one side was the decadent bourgeoisie of America, with its corrosive imperialistic culture; on the other, the progressive cultures of the international proletariat, with the Soviet Union in the vanguard. He was heartened that national folk music had become significant in cultural policy – for a while in the mid-1950s, MacColl was invited to advise members of the Young Communist League National Committee (including the young Arthur Scargill) on establishing a network of DIY music clubs along the lines of the Ballads and Blues radio programmes and concerts.[58] For MacColl this was the correct cultural line: the Communist Party should be helping to stimulate culture grounded in working-class experience and speech; it should unearth and disseminate the hidden history of Britain's politically radical industrial folk culture. This was the way to tap into the radical past, reinforce national class-consciousness and give definition to a cultural formation capable of resisting the American threat.

But the Communist Party's appetite for the cultural Cold War waned in the mid-1950s as Stalin's adversarial attitude to the United States gave way to a policy of peaceful co-existence, codified as the party's official position in the 1957 version of *The British Road to Socialism*. Conferences on the corrupting ideologies of American culture dried up; in 1955 Sam Aaronovitch was moved from his post on the cultural frontline.[59] Then 1956 was a famously traumatic year for the party faithful: Khrushchev's 'secret speech' to the Twentieth Congress denounced the cult of personality that had enabled Stalin's reign of terror;[60] the autumn witnessed a popular uprising against despotism in Hungary, ruthlessly crushed by Soviet troops.[61] MacColl would take a hard line on these convulsions during his turn to Maoism in the 1960s. He was quickly clear that the Communist Party that emerged from the wreckage of 1956 was not to his taste.

Ailing General Secretary Harry Pollitt, whose Manchester background, working-class warmth and instinctive socialism MacColl admired, was replaced by the conscientious but comparatively colourless John Gollan – some joked that the Communist Party had replaced the cult of personality with the cult of impersonality.[62] MacColl had long been suspicious of the emphasis on the parliamentary road to socialism adopted by the Communist Party in 1951; he preferred 'For Soviet Britain', the party's revolutionary programme, which made no bones about the fact that the 'capitalist class will never allow itself to be gradually expropriated by successive Acts of Parliament'.[63] In his developing analysis, the post-1956 Communist Party was entrenching creeping revisionism. Communism was turning away from the authentic revolutionary tradition both nationally and internationally. It was also turning away from the folk tradition, and for MacColl folk music was not an optional extra but the key component in a progressive workers' music culture. He watched in consternation as initiatives like the Ballads and Blues clubs slid down the cultural agenda and the party adopted a more conciliatory approach to America and the emerging consumer and credit culture of post-war Britain.[64] He dutifully appeared at Young Communist League cultural festivals in November 1957 and May 1958, but became increasingly remote from the party. Some time in the near future – almost certainly in the early 1960s – he would allow his membership to lapse.[65]

CBEO

Back in 1954 MacColl had edited a slim songbook, *The Shuttle and Cage: Industrial Folk Ballads*, for the Workers' Music Association. During Peggy Seeger's first visit in 1956, a selection of the songs was recorded for a tie-in disc. The twelve-track, ten-inch record was issued by Topic during Peggy's post-Moscow travels of late 1957; by January 1958 it was one of Topic's bestselling titles.[66]

In appearance, the *Shuttle and Cage* resembled the earlier songbook: the cover showed Ern Brooks' socialist realist painting of a muscular proletarian wiping his hands prior to enjoying the fruits of homemade culture. The sleeve-notes recycled MacColl's original preface. These songs were not about nightingales, sunshine or flowers, he explained, but 'work, poverty, hunger and exploitation'. They weren't part of the culture industry – 'made with an eye to the quick sale, or to catch the song-plugger's ear'; instead this was the culture of the industrial working class, created to 'relieve the intolerable daily grind'. For MacColl, the songs comprised part of a hidden history, a rich formation of radical culture embodying working-class cultural resourcefulness. Uncovering that history, MacColl claimed, still awaited the type of 'comprehensive survey' that only the trade union movement could provide. *Shuttle and Cage* was a mere intimation of what was possible.

The record sampled the musical cultures of British industry: two of the songs were about weaving, five about mining, five transport. *Shuttle and Cage* reflected the regional diversity of British industrial songs, representing Scotland, Wales and the North of England. Some songs were drawn from published collections such as Lloyd's *Come All Ye Bold Miners* (1952); five songs had been collected by MacColl directly from the industrial folk in Teesdale, Oldham and Sheffield, a process aided by a questionnaire circulated in loco sheds. Three of the songs were MacColl compositions – here he sought to draw upon and add to the culture of industrial song.

Artistically, the record was a success. The elaborate theories and rules about preserving and transmitting traditional musical authenticity later devised by MacColl and Seeger would often box in their talents and inventiveness. By contrast, these early recordings chart voyages of musical exploration. The speed with which this record was rehearsed and recorded is caught on the vinyl as freshness; the tunes are strong and the songs range from defiance to comedy. MacColl deploys his acting talents to create various accents and personae; Seeger's instrumentation on guitar and more full-bloodied banjo settings give the songs an uncanny charge: they sound simultaneously of the past and of the present, unfamiliar and familiar. Peggy Seeger's name appears only on the record label, where she's described as MacColl's accompanist, but this is unmistakably a collaborative work. The first MacColl and Seeger title to be issued in Britain, *Shuttle and Cage* consolidated a musical rapport and successfully blended seriousness of political purpose with artistic lightness of touch.[67]

∽∾

'Those who hoped that skiffle would, in time, help to pave the way for something better, may have been right,' observed the *Melody Maker* in January 1958.[68] Through the previous year the outlines of the British folk revival anticipated by Alan Lomax had begun to form. Skiffle sputtered out almost as quickly as it had appeared, enjoying one last spasm during the wet Easter weekend of the Bury St Edmunds' National Skiffle Contest – even the *Jazz Journal* now conceded that the skiffle craze had created thousands of young guitarists who were 'better off groping for those three lost chords than sitting at home twiddling their knobs'.[69] Books were published to guide lapsed skifflers towards British traditions of music-making;[70] Lomax, who would return to America in June 1958, was back on the BBC Home Service with an eight-programme survey of the British Isles' music traditions;[71] the

English Folk Dance and Song Society ran an 'Experimental Folk Music Festival' in October 1957. Reg Hall, who would later play a significant role in British folk music, described the festival's atmosphere as 'a cross between a mortuary and an approved school. Every attempt to liven up the proceedings,' he complained, 'was crushed ruthlessly.'[72]

CRBO

Back from Moscow, the Ballads and Blues ensemble was formally relaunched. Malcolm Nixon and MacColl were the key figures and, despite the common ground of Scottish roots and communism, made an unlikely pair. The homosexual Nixon was in his early thirties and wore his communism lightly; a busy, dapper man with an entrepreneurial streak, Nixon's work for the World Youth Festivals had taught him about accounting, promotion and the techniques in ego massage appropriate for managing an unruly roster of temperamental artists. He set up the Malcolm Nixon Agency; he and MacColl pooled their talents and scheduled a series of Ballads and Blues concerts for October and November 1957. Nixon provided the acumen and organisational skills, MacColl the political and cultural gravitas. They had big plans for the project. Unsuccessful attempts were made to persuade the BBC to commission a parallel new radio series of *Ballads and Blues*;[73] Nixon placed adverts in the music press and distributed promotional leaflets through the remaining skiffle cellars, record shops and youth clubs.[74]

MacColl was always drawn to the genre of the manifesto – it was a way of defining objectives from the outset. He spelt out the goals of Ballads and Blues in that promotional leaflet. They aimed to 'give British audiences the opportunity of hearing folk music and folk musicians of their own country', 'provide an informed audience for folk singers from overseas', 'provide a platform for young singers, musicians and songwriters who are experimenting in traditional forms' and 'give expression to folk elements in traditional jazz'. Held at the Theatre Royal, Stratford East and eclectically billed as 'Folk Music* Jazz* Work Songs* Skiffle', the shows were to draw on the talents of a pool of musicians including former Ramblers Alan Lomax, Fitzroy Coleman and Nat Atkins, jazzmen Jim Bray and Bruce Turner, visiting Americans Guy Carawan and Ralph Rinzler, and a range of musicians from the former Ballads and Blues radio and concert series including Harvey Webb, Margaret Barry, Seumus Ennis and Sligo fiddler Michael

Gorman.[75] MacColl was the MC, and the evenings were based on the titles of the earlier radio series.

The concerts ran smoothly, but Stratford East was a long way from the vibrancy of Soho. The theatre auditorium was too big and seldom full. Nixon started to look around for a venue closer to central London, and settled on the 250-capacity upstairs room of the Princess Louise, a long, narrow Victorian pub on High Holborn already on the map of central London's skiffle scene. It was an assured move. The folk scene now had magazines and a record company, but had yet to discover a performance setting where the required sociability could be combined with appropriate attentiveness to the music. A new leaflet advertised 'The Hootenanny, A Completely Informal Evening of Folk Music, Ballads, Work Songs and Instrumentation' with hosts including MacColl, Fitzroy Coleman, Ralph Rinzler and Isla Cameron; all mention of skiffle and the prescriptive formulae of themed shows were dropped for the relaunch of 24 November 1957.[76] The Ballads and Blues Club's move into the upstairs room of a pub played a significant part in inventing the institution of the British folk club.[77]

The evenings now really caught on and the press was soon aware of the subcultural rumblings. The *Manchester Guardian* commissioned an article by *Sing*'s Eric Winter in which he described the pub room 'overflowing with refugees from the skiffle craze ... indistinguishable in dress or appearance from a Tommy Steele fan club, drinking in and applauding large instalments of the Child Ballad collection'. 'Folk song is no longer the exclusive province of cycling parsons and genteel schoolmistresses,' he concluded.[78]

In the first few months at High Holborn the young audience heard musicians including Irish Republican raconteur, writer and singer Dominic Behan – brother of the more famous playwright Brendan – virtuoso piper Seumus Ennis, calypso singer Fitzroy Coleman, seventy-two-year-old Norfolk farm-worker and folk singer Harry Cox, A. L. Lloyd and MacColl. The two or three guests would sit on the small stage and sing songs. Others would be invited to perform from the floor. Songsheets were issued, choruses sung at ear-splitting volume. 'Regular hoots are being run,' MacColl wrote to Peggy Seeger as she travelled through Poland that December. 'We tell stories, talk about songs, sing and generally raise merry hell.'[79]

There was all skiffle's energy, but a new self-consciousness about shaping culturally grounded, alternative music: those present felt the frisson of being there at the beginning of a new movement. By January 1958 a midweek overspill Ballads and Blues evening was set up to accommodate the multiplying audience and the available performing talent.[80] Teenage office worker Pat Mackenzie was a typical devotee, a music fan whose eye had been caught by the Ballads and Blues' *Melody Maker* listing. 'It was just a revelation,' she remembered. 'I'd never heard anything like it ... Ewan at the time was singing a lot of industrial songs from *Shuttle and Cage* ... To me it was like English blues, songs about working people, their lives and work and love ... it was mind boggling.'[81]

There was a great emphasis on inclusion, on breaking down barriers between audience and performer, on making culture something people did rather than passively consumed. 'There are generally about thirty bods with guitars,' MacColl reported to Peggy Seeger, 'and, when they remember, performers shout out the chords sequences and everyone joins in.'[82] Nixon was an advocate of this raucous participatory element, and was keener on the American word Hootenanny than his partner.[83] MacColl, however, continued to regard the club as a site of resistance to American cultural imperialism. He was torn, as he often would be, between inclusive democratic impulses and an insistence that if folk music was going to stimulate a radical musical movement capable of challenging polished pop, then standards had to be maintained. At the Ballads and Blues events MacColl acquired a reputation for his charm, wit and warmth, but also for ruthlessness when it came to cutting out performers he didn't rate. He and Nixon frequently disagreed over which guests were invited; on occasions MacColl would pointedly forget to call Nixon's singers to the stage.[84] MacColl was especially uneasy with the lingering American impersonators and the earnest cosmopolitanism that encouraged some singers to sing in languages they could barely speak. By March 1958 he was trying to impose a new Ballads and Blues rule that performers restrict themselves to music from their respective national traditions – English people should sing English songs, Scots should sing Scottish songs (MacColl could sing both), only Americans should sing American songs.[85] 'We must work and work for a greater purity of approach in our singing,' he would write to Peggy Seeger later that year. 'I have come to the conclusion that we cannot afford to be tolerant ... the slightest concession on matters of taste will provide seeds which will germinate into monsters.'[86] Relations with Nixon grew worse.

◦ॐ◦

In later life MacColl maintained that he was blacklisted by the BBC through the mid-1950s. 'I was banned', he said in one 1972 interview, 'for taking a militant line over the question of working class music':

> And also for taking a patriotic line for a change. History had put us in the situation where we ... were the ones fighting for British music, for British identity. But as the BBC bosses were so bloody scared of the whole idea of a British identity, they were scared shitless that the State Department would sit on them. They had to be adjuncts to the American machine.[87]

The 2006 declassification of MacColl's MI5 file lends weight to his claims. In September 1953 MacColl's name appeared alongside those of R. D. Smith (radio producer husband of novelist Olivia Manning), A. L. Lloyd and Elsa [sic] Cameron on a list of Communists 'prominently associated with the BBC'.[88] The same month, a memo was added to MacColl's BBC employee file warning potential programme makers that any proposals to commission work from MacColl needed to be rubber-stamped at a senior level.[89] MacColl was exaggerating in saying that he was banned outright, but right to detect new levels of vigilance in employing him, especially when it came to writing scripts.[90] This all changed in 1957 when he embarked on his first major collaboration with Charles Parker.

◦ॐ◦

Apart from the scale of their vision, BBC radio producer Charles Parker and MacColl had little in common. A conscientious Christian churchman active in parish affairs, Parker spoke in an Oxbridge drawl and habitually wore a bowtie. Four years MacColl's junior, he'd distinguished himself as a Royal Navy submarine Lieutenant during the war before taking the historical tripos at Queen's College, Cambridge.[91] Politically to the right, Parker later joked that he'd been 'brought up to believe that everywhere north of Winchester was an industrial wilderness of wife-beaters and insanitary slums'.[92] After Cambridge he worked for the BBC North American Service, and first met MacColl while producing a programme on experimental theatre.[93]

Promoted to Senior Features Producer for the BBC Midland Region in 1954, Parker was forever embattled at the BBC, and considered himself 'surrounded by Philistines and men of no or little imagination'.[94] 'He cares, really cares about his work,' MacColl wrote to Peggy Seeger in 1958, 'but he hasn't got a clue how to fight his bosses or to sidetrack the establishment. His method is to barge into their offices and talk to them about folksong and life and the responsibility of the artist ... they think he's a nut. They think anybody's a nut who gets worked up about work.'[95]

Parker was ambitious for radio. His time in America had exposed him to significant radio broadcasting, especially Millard Lampell and Earl Robinson's cantata *Lonesome Train*, a CBS programme that used the final railroad journey of the assassinated Abraham Lincoln to frame questions about democracy in America.[96] Parker was struck by the sophisticated mix of narration, folk music and oral testimony; he saw this and surrounding programmes as models for equivalent developments in Britain.[97] He was equally alert to the contemporary British documentary film innovations of the so-called 'Free Cinema' movement of Lindsay Anderson, Karel Reisz and Tony Richardson currently in full swing at the National Film Theatre. Parker was impressed by these clear-eyed chronicles of British social and cultural life and by the films' use of music: contemporary rock and roll, skiffle and traditional jazz provided the soundtrack – some of MacColl's erstwhile collaborators from the Chris Barber band were central to the way Free Cinema sounded.[98] He was also taken with Denis Mitchell's parallel pioneering work on radio and screen, in particular the use of interviews with working people and the quality of MacColl's musical input.[99] For Parker, there was no mistaking that MacColl's breadth of expertise across music, radio and drama made him a valuable ally in any effort to shake up radio documentary. Parker wrote to MacColl on 12 July 1957 about a project 'absolutely up your street'. 'The conception', he wrote, 'is going to hinge rather on whether or not you can participate.'[100] How Parker persuaded his superiors to hire MacColl isn't clear, but MacColl was paid 100 guineas in advance (approximately £1,750 today), and employed on a freelance basis to gather material, write a script and compose, arrange and perform the music for Parker's new commission, a 'contemporary railway epic'.[101]

ও৪৪৩

In 1957 the name of fifty-six-year-old Stockport train driver John Axon hit the headlines. The steam brake valve on his loaded freight train had failed on the morning shift of 9 February, filling his cab with scalding steam. Rather than jump free, Axon clung to the side of his train – he hoped to regain control once the gradient eased off and to warn a nearby signalman that the train was running free. His engine reached speeds of 55 miles per hour before crashing into a second train at Chapel-en-le-Frith, north Derbyshire. Both Axon and John Creamer, the guard of the second train, were killed.[102] Axon was posthumously awarded the George Cross for bravery that May; in July his widow Gladys Axon made the journey to Buckingham Palace to collect the medal on her late husband's behalf.[103]

The story of heroic self-sacrifice caught Parker's imagination, and within six months of the accident he'd secured Gladys Axon's consent to make a radio programme based around Axon's final journey.[104] As in the *Lonesome Train*, the journey provided a dramatic structure through which broader questions could be explored. From the outset Parker saw the project as an opportunity to fulfil longstanding ambitions.[105] 'I shall hope to be breaking new ground in terms of radio technique,' he wrote in one letter, 'to achieve a blend of musical ballad, dramatic reconstruction and background material.'[106]

The portable EMI Midget tape recorder, which had come on stream in the early 1950s, made it technically possible to collect 'actuality' (recordings made on location) of a quality sufficient for broadcasting.[107] In the past, the machines had primarily been used for gathering raw material to inform the process of scriptwriting; influenced by the likes of Denis Mitchell, Parker was keen that, if possible, a small amount of interviews and industrial noise should play a direct part in the broadcast programme.[108] In October and November 1957, Parker and MacColl equipped themselves with one of the machines, booked rooms in a Stockport pub and made research trips to the locations of Axon's working life and death. Initially impeded by the Ministry of Defence and Civil Aviation – currently conducting its inquiry into the recent accident – MacColl and Parker rode and recorded on the footplates of steam engines, visited the station where Axon's train was assembled, and took their tape machine into the Edgeley loco shed where Axon had worked.[109] They were interested in the accident, but also the culture of

Axon's world, what Parker called 'the intangible complex of attitudes
– pride in the job, relationship to a locomotive and railway tradition
– in short, of all that goes to making up The Railwayman'.[110] They
recorded Axon's workmates, family and widow, gathering twenty hours
of material in total.

MacColl returned to Croydon and set about writing the script. He
spooled through the eighty fifteen-minute tapes over and over again,
transcribing the sections he wanted, organising them by theme and
pasting them into a large hardback notebook. Enthused by the sheer
scale of the project, he resorted to his old obsessive playwriting habits.
Stationed at his desk from mid-morning to the small hours, he pored
over the actuality, drank jugs of coffee, chain-smoked and typed out
the script taking shape in his mind.

Parker had always planned to dispense with formal voiceover
narration in favour of ballad-style songs sung by MacColl; in essence,
Parker's idea was to use real voices and sounds to add authenticity to
a musical radio play.[111] Confronted with the quality of the material
running through the machines, MacColl's mind returned to the
cinematic experiments of Eisenstein and Vertov.[112] He wrote instead
a multilayered montage of edited actuality intercut with song and
orchestral effects – a highly complex synthesis of recorded speech,
sound, music and song. Music displaced dramatised reconstruction,
and became increasingly sophisticated as it did so, ranging across
folk, jazz and blues styles. The musically illiterate MacColl was soon
out of his depth. 'I've got to have your help for the more-involved
arrangements,' he wrote to Peggy Seeger, now travelling in Poland,
that December. 'I've been planning all along on the assumption that
you and Ralph Rinzler would play an important part in hammering
the musicians into shape.'[113]

She came back from her Eastern odyssey in January 1958, moved
in to Bert Lloyd's house in Greenwich, and resumed her professional
and personal relationship with MacColl.[114] (The Lloyds strongly
disapproved of the affair.) Seeger refined and scored out MacColl's
music – song accompaniments, music to be played behind the actuality,
passages to link actuality sequences – and offered suggestions about
the script. They assembled a music team: singers Isla Cameron, Fitzroy
Coleman and A. L. Lloyd; strings from Jim Bray, Brian Daly and fiddler
Bob Clark; Alf Edwards' concertina, John Cole's harmonica, Bruce

Turner's clarinet, session drummer Billy Loch and a thumping brass
section of Terry Brown on trumpet and Bob Mickleburgh on trombone.
Under the eye of the twenty-two-year-old Seeger, they rehearsed for
two-and-a-half days, before recording at BBC Maida Vale Studios on
27 January 1958.[115] With scissors and razor blade, spools and slivers
of tape, Parker retreated to an editing cubicle to segue actuality and
recorded music into a sixty-minute programme.[116] Broadcast of the
finished programme was postponed, possibly because John Axon's
death was so recent. *The Ballad of John Axon* eventually went out on
the BBC Home Service at ten o'clock on the evening of Wednesday 2
July 1958.[117]

෬෮

For MacColl, the new project had provided an opportunity to explore
his abiding obsessions on a vast canvas – like *Shuttle and Cage, The
Ballad of John Axon* is best seen as the site of an ongoing argument
about class, politics and culture. Suffused with MacColl's abiding faith
in the wisdom, decency and resourcefulness of the working class, the
programme documented Axon's epic heroism, and strove to add to the
tapestry of British culture a figure to match epic industrial American
heroes John Henry and Casey Jones.[118] It was a fable of socialism in
that Axon had put collective interests above individual ones (in later
accounts MacColl would spice up John Axon's story, introducing 'an
entire trainload of schoolchildren' saved by the heroic train-driver).[119]
The programme gave airtime to working-class voices, which MacColl
considered to be 'charged with the special kind of vitality that derives
from involvement with a work process'.[120]

He went further, sensing in the workers' speech 'the same kinds of
symbols and verbal nuances as those which inform the ballads and
folksongs of our tradition' – immersed in ballads himself, he heard
in the speech of Axon's friends and family an ongoing oral culture,
a residue of the popular linguistic creativity from which folksong
had emerged.[121] In the course of making the programme, MacColl
and Parker began to see their role as shaping this contemporary raw
material of balladry (the workers' speech) into a modern 'radio ballad':
they saw themselves fusing the spontaneous creativity of working-class
speech, time-honoured story-telling traditions and modern technology
to create a mid-twentieth-century ballad for the mass media.[122]

The objective was to document working-class experience *and* turn it into art, to show culture arising from workers' lives. MacColl wrote individual songs based around the exact words and phrases uttered by Axon's community; he saw the whole radio ballad as emerging from the community's speech and experiences. He was demonstrating that the linguistic and cultural resourcefulness of the people represented a culture in waiting, an outline of the grounded, progressive radical culture that the left should be building. *The Ballad of John Axon* was both a highly accomplished cultural artefact and a manifestation of MacColl's own cultural policy.

⋄⃝⋄

*The Ballad of John Axon* was hotly controversial. There was some unease about making the programme so soon after Axon's death, though not with Gladys Axon, who publicly endorsed the broadcast.[123] Some of Axon's colleagues took issue with the fact that MacColl had included a calypso song recounting the experiences of a West Indian railway worker. Concerned about mounting racial tension in Britain, MacColl had written the song to emphasise the railwaymen's traditions of solidarity and tolerance, but some of the actual workers proved less tolerant than he hoped, and complained about the song.[124] Some critics objected to the banjo-dominated music, plausibly pointing out that the score's American flavour conflicted with Parker's stated intention of resisting Americanisation.[125] One member of the BBC feedback panel made the point more bluntly: 'John Axon deserved something better than this pseudo-American Annie-Get-Your-Gun-Calypso Nonsense.'[126]

At the same time, there was ringing consensus that the programme marked a significant moment in British radio broadcasting. Parker's painstaking efforts in hyping the programme, which extended to co-ordinating a series of pre-broadcast playbacks for forty-five cherry-picked journalists, paid dividends in terms of column inches.[127] Distinguished *Sunday Times* radio writer Robert Robinson considered it 'as remarkable piece of radio as I have ever listened to'; the *Daily Worker* applauded MacColl's 'excitingly fresh' broadcast; Paul Ferris of the *Sunday Observer* claimed that *The Ballad of John Axon* had fundamentally reconfigured the reference points within which future radio features would operate.[128] Long-term MacColl advocate Tom Driberg used his

*New Statesman and Nation* column to claim that 'a generation from now – I would even say centuries from now – listeners will surely still be moved by the recording of *The Ballad of John Axon*'.[129]

The upbeat reception matched Parker's own estimation of what they'd achieved. He tried to follow Denis Mitchell's lead and turn the radio programme into a documentary film; despite attracting the enthusiastic interest of legendary film editor Stewart McAllister – former collaborator with Humphrey Jennings, now second in command at British Transport Films – *John Axon* the film failed to get off the ground.[130] Undeterred, Parker fired off letters to everybody with influence whom he thought might be interested – complimentary copies of the programme landed on the doormats of jazzman Johnny Dankworth, actor Charles Laughton and Norman Corwin, producer of *The Lonesome Train*.[131] Flushed with the success, he also wrote to his boss Laurence Gilliam, Head of BBC Features. The programme, he pointed out, was potentially 'the powder train to new and exciting forms of radio and television'. 'All depends on Ewan MacColl', he wrote, 'whose finger is, I believe, on the true pulse of this emerging music and who commands the technique to give it effective musico/dramatic utterance.' MacColl, Parker suggested, should be placed on the BBC payroll for twelve months and commissioned to work full time on a further five programmes; such a bold appointment would 'write a new page in the history of Broadcasting'.[132] The BBC didn't share Parker's enthusiasm for MacColl, but did choose the programme as their entry for the prestigious international documentary award, the Italia Prize.[133] Ever the perfectionist, Parker proposed re-recording the entire musical score, but was overruled.[134] Unsuccessful in 1958, the Radio Ballad team would take the Italia Prize two years later with the third radio ballad, *Singing the Fishing*.

◌�◌

A loose and baggy coalition beset by controversies and quarrels, the folk revival continued to make ground. The political wing, centred on the Workers' Music Association, the London Youth Choir and *Sing* magazine, now included communists, former communists (including supporters of the non-aligned 'New Left' journal *Universities and Left Review*), and young activists radicalised by Suez. The Campaign for Nuclear Disarmament, formally constituted in February 1958, helped to focus the scene.[135] With skiffle still in the air, music-making became prominent in the annual mass marches to Berkshire's Aldermaston's Atomic Weapons Research Establishment. The reunited MacColl and Seeger joined the 4,000 protestors for the first march over the damp Easter weekend of 1958; an updated version of the African-American spiritual 'Down by the Riverside' broke the proposed silence and vied with the sounds of traditional jazz and John Bruner's protest song 'The H-Bomb's Thunder'.[136] Like the Mass Trespass campaign twenty-five years earlier, CND provided both subject matter and ample singing opportunities.[137]

Events run by MacColl for the Ballads and Blues Association were the natural home for those on the folk scene drawn to an anti-commercialism, cultural authenticity and left politics.[138] Once again, the Ballads and Blues team sought to drum up interest from the mass media. Charles Parker made recordings of sessions early in 1958 (Nixon acted as agent for most of the artists).[139] Eventually broadcast on BBC Midland Home Service twelve months later, those programmes capture all the energy and fervour of the early revival.[140] 'This is a critical audience that has a short way with the false and meretricious while demanding that the music be popular, the performance direct and uncontrived,' wrote Parker for the *Radio Times* plug.[141] With characteristic enthusiasm, he argued that the hootenannies represented a 'development in popular music which could be as important as the emergence of New Orleans jazz'.[142]

CO&BO

MacColl and Seeger continued their productive collaboration and compulsive affair through the first five months of 1958. Peggy worked on *John Axon*, became a regular at the Ballads and Blues Hootenannies, and rehearsed, recorded and performed with MacColl. More than ever, she cast a spell over the wannabe Americans who thronged Soho; her banjo lessons at the Workers' Music Association were unusually well attended. Blues guitarist Wizz Jones went along. 'We all sat around ogling her,' he remembered. 'We didn't really want to play the banjo at all.'[143] She enjoyed the company of the colourful characters on the scene – like her, many were in their twenties, musically gifted and restlessly bohemian. MacColl was jittery and frequently jealous.

ᬍᬍ

Work for Peggy Seeger was plentiful, but she was now without a visa. Relations with the American Embassy hadn't been helped by her forbidden trip to China or her recent travels behind the Iron Curtain. Britain's Home Office Aliens Department – just a few doors down from her regular haunt, the Princess Louise – finally caught up with her that spring. She was deported on 17 May:

> I went to France via Dover but made the mistake of trying to return too early. I was kept overnight in the marine cells and put on the boat back to France. The French authorities shoved me over the border into Belgium. The Belgians bequeathed me forcibly to the Dutch who discreetly shoved me back into Belgium a week later. The Belgians made a deal with the French and there I was, back in France again.[144]

Of no fixed abode, she stayed with friends in Paris, fetched her mail from American Express, and mixed with itinerant musicians drawn to Paris's cheap living and lucrative busking. Friends and former colleagues at the BBC continued to request her services as a musician and arranger, but the Ministry of Labour proved intractable over renewing the permit.[145]

MacColl was plunged into a state of distraction. He wrote her long, tortured letters chastising her for living in undesirable districts, encouraging her to write songs and to practise her guitar. He complained that without her he was dull, morose. Whenever he could, he headed off to Paris, Cherbourg or Boulogne to spend time with her; that July he went with Hugh MacDiarmid to a cultural congress in Bulgaria, and called to see Peggy en route.[146] His depression would lift during each meeting, then descend within hours of returning to Croydon. Even dinner with Paul Robeson, who was in Britain that summer, didn't lift his spirits for long. At moments he now rapturously envisaged a life with Peggy. 'We are going to record, to write songs, musical documentaries, books; we are going to walk on mountains, camp far away from anybody, sing together, lie in each other's arms, have kids and walk hand in hand through life.'[147] He'd then be tortured by guilt over Jean and Hamish. 'I wonder if I will ever be wholly good for anyone,' he wrote in one letter to Peggy. 'I wonder whether I'll ever be able to enter another person's life without bringing them pain.'[148] It was a miserable summer for everyone. Jean knew of the affair and insisted that MacColl make a decision. She remembers: 'He kept going over at weekends, and I said this isn't on. You're upsetting Hamish and I can't take this, either it's got to be one or the other. And this went on for many months.'[149]

○8○

MacColl's mind was currently elsewhere, but the revival continued to build. Despite parting company with the Princess Louise pub – and steadily working through a long list of unsuitable premises from Paddington Green to the Tottenham Court Road to Woburn Place – the Ballads and Blues launched a new series of Sunday night 'Hootenannies' in October 1958. True to the original manifesto, these combined performances by folk veterans (MacColl, A. L. Lloyd and Isla Cameron), American folk musicians (Ramblin' Jack Elliot and Ralph Rinzler), and rare appearances by so-called 'traditional' singers including Sam Larner, billed as 'the magnificent field singer from Yarmouth'.[150] If the point of such visits was to alert the young London audience to the exotically unfamiliar riches of English folk music, then the singing of the octogenarian Larner had the desired effect on one seventeen-year-old ex-skiffler. Martin Carthy would later trace the origins of his unrivalled career in English folk music back to that night. Hearing the former fisherman sing from his repertoire 'turned my conception of music upside down', recalled Carthy:

> It's something for which I will always thank Ewan MacColl. [Larner] was astonishing.... Ewan was an egotistical sod but that night he completely submerged his identity and sacrificed himself to an evening of Sam Larner and making Sam Larner available and loved by this audience.[151]

○8○

MacColl's home-life continued to deteriorate. He was in love with both Jean and Peggy: confused, guilt-ridden and unable to make his mind up, he talked optimistically with Jean about reconciliation;[152] with Peggy he planned a bright future.[153] It would take months before the situation was anywhere near settled and, given MacColl's anguish and divided affections, it's unsurprising that events are remembered very differently by those involved. Before Christmas 1958 he and Jean were talking in terms of a fresh start and a second child;[154] Jean conceived early in the new year of 1959. On 24 January 1959 Peggy Seeger – now seven months pregnant with MacColl's child – saw through a last-ditch strategy that she, MacColl and a friendly lawyer had discussed over the previous months.[155] To get back to Britain and MacColl, in Paris Peggy Seeger married the laid-back Glaswegian folk singer Alex Campbell, who'd agreed to help her out of an impossible fix. For years rumours would circulate that Campbell was actually in love with Seeger and took the ceremony seriously, a story that can be traced back to the reminiscences of Campbell himself. Seeger insists that it has no basis in fact.[156] 'We should have paid him something,' she recalled. 'I offered him money later and he turned it down.... Alex did it out of sheer goodness of heart. He did it light-heartedly. He was not in love with me. He never made any advances.'[157]

Marriage to a British subject finally freed Seeger to re-enter Britain. She and MacColl now rented a small first-floor flat at 55 Godstone Road, Purley and set up house together. Their first child, Neill, was born that March. The transition from life with Jean to life with Peggy would be slow and painful: Hamish missed his father terribly; the disapproving Betsy, who had stayed with Jean, eventually moved into Godstone Road. MacColl divided his time between his old and new families. That October, when Jean gave birth to her baby Kirsty, he temporarily took on the flat upstairs in order to offer support, but the ten-year marriage to Jean was now over. From here on MacColl would be a weekend father to Hamish and Kirsty, visiting on Sundays for family meals and trips out.

ෆ৪৩

Considering the upheaval, emotional trauma and young baby, it's a wonder that MacColl and Seeger got any work done at all, but the 1950s were played out in a flurry of creativity in which their partnership was further consolidated. They were undisputed headline acts at the Ballads and Blues Club, now relocated to the 250-capacity Anthony Asquith Room of the ACTT trade union headquarters in Soho Square.[158] Radical politics were to the fore;[159] it was sometimes tricky squaring the Ballads and Blues' anti-commercial ethos with connection to Nixon's increasingly lucrative agency and promotional business;[160] some on the folk scene cracked jokes about the amount of American music that could be heard at a club with well-known hostilities to American culture.[161] Many who would take leading roles in the revival over the decades to follow first saw MacColl and Seeger there, including John

Faulkner and thirteen-year-old Vic Gammon: 'I don't know what my parents thought I was doing in Soho on a Saturday evening,' academic and musician Gammon remembered, 'but I was really listening to Ewan and Peggy and the other people who would turn up. I was very impressed. [MacColl] was larger than life and the material he was doing I thought was fascinating. Still do.'[162] Attendance at the club dipped noticeably during their first lengthy overseas tour to Canada that autumn.[163]

MacColl's songwriting was unusually prolific. As well as the songs purpose-written for radio, he was producing material across a range of themes and styles: 'Rosalie' was a calypso love song exploring a West Indian immigrant's perspective on the city; 'Wonder Boy' was a theatrical and pungently defamatory account of Prime Minister Harold Macmillan's rise to power and premiership.[164] Seeger had also been writing songs: written in France, her 'Ballad of Springhill' about the Nova Scotia pit disaster of October 1958 would later be covered by artists including Martin Carthy and U2; the Brechtian 'Jimmy Wilson' was a rebarbative protest against liberal complacency and racism that linked events in contemporary Alabama to Apartheid South Africa and the Notting Hill race riots in Britain – it remained a standard in Seeger and MacColl's live sets for three decades.[165] They were now a songwriting partnership, commenting on one another's work, offering suggestions about phrasing, melody lines, singing and accompaniment styles.

They cut significant records for the British and American markets. MacColl continued to embroider his questionable Scottishness, now implying a wholly invented Glasgow childhood for his collaboration record with Irishman Dominic Behan, *Streets of Song: Childhood Memories of City Streets from Glasgow, Salford and Dublin*.[166] There was little need to make such bids for Scottish authenticity: pre-Seeger records like *Scots Folk Songs* and *Scots Street Songs* had amply established his credentials as an interpreter of Scottish music.[167] Accompanied by Seeger, his *Songs of Robert Burns* bore out the sleeve-notes' claim that the Burns-like MacColl – with his radical instincts, controversial turn from literature to song, bardic persona – was ideally suited to do justice to the poet's music.[168] Listening to these early recordings from the perspective of a later purism, Seeger would flagellate herself for deviations from authenticity (obtrusive accompaniments, playing too fast, unconvincing imitation of Scots accent).[169] But like *Shuttle and Cage*, these records were timely acts of radical cultural archaeology. They urgently and energetically drew upon swathes of forgotten popular music – ballads, children's chants, eighteenth-century street songs, nineteenth-century songs about boxing matches and card games, soldiers' songs from both world wars – and animated it for a contemporary audience.[170]

જ્ઞરો

The critical success of *John Axon* raised MacColl and Seeger's profiles at the BBC. Seeger was now in demand as a singer, musician and arranger; MacColl's name was erased from the blacklist. They worked together on two ambitious D. G. Bridson Home Service productions that summer, one a historical feature about General Wolfe, the other a ballad opera – complete with Russ Henderson's Trinidad Steel Band and MacColl in the role of a young Scottish skiffler – that called for racial and cultural understanding in the aftermath of the Notting Hill riots.[171]

જ્ઞરો

The main event through 1959 was the follow-up radio ballad. From the outset, expectations were high. Parker searched for a suitable subject, making fruitless visits to folk singers in rural Norfolk, an electric ceramics plant in the Potteries, foundries in the Black Country and Birmingham.[172] After a push from his boss at Midland Regional Programmes, he settled on one of the day's big news stories, the building of the first sixty-seven-mile section of the M1, or the 'London–Yorkshire Motorway'.[173] The road would formally open in November 1959, and the contractors had nineteen months to build it. Parker made reconnaissance trips to the construction sites in October and November 1958. In December he and MacColl started recording material.

Broadcast eleven months later, and three days after the motorway's official opening, *Song of a Road*, would parallel the building of the motorway in terms of economic pressure, conflicting interest and bad feeling.[174] From their base at Dunstable, Bedfordshire (now Junction 11) MacColl and Parker drove around in Parker's Morris Minor, collecting 120 fifteen-minute tapes of material over twenty-five days.[175] They picked their way through the four thousand workers on the project, carrying the Midget recorder across the yawning mud track, gathering material in plant headquarters, offices, the cabs of bulldozers, in pubs, dormitories and canteens. According to MacColl's memory, their on-site movements were monitored by a Public Relations Officer representing the contractors; guile was necessary to evade the constant scrutiny of a company determined that its industrial relations should be presented in a positive light.[176]

The material they recorded ran the spectrum of Britain's class structure. They interviewed road designer Sir Owen Williams, farmers whose land had been compulsory-purchased, the middle strata of managers, surveyors, contracting engineers, and labourers who'd been on the night shift for fourteen months.[177] Williams and the civil engineers talked authoritatively about the job in hand; the testimonies of the workers yielded a vivid glimpse of a submerged population of economic exiles from India, the West Indies, Eastern Europe, Ireland and the economic blackspots of Britain, all living and working in desperate conditions. Parker would later recall: 'One of the most harrowing experiences of my life was spending a night at a hostel accommodating some two or three hundred of these men ... some of whom had spent twelve hours at work with only a snack to sustain them.'[178] One man compared conditions in his dormitory to a concentration camp;[179] Seeger, Parker and MacColl were all later haunted by the memory of one Irish teenager who broke down when describing his ten-hour shifts cutting concrete.[180] 'He talked hysterically of his feelings,' Parker would later write, 'and this seemed to me such a naked expression of a human agony that I switched the tape recorder off in embarrassment.'[181]

The best section of the programme sampled the stories they did manage to record. There was a sound montage in which a medley of workers' voices listed where they were from;[182] another sequence mischievously juxtaposed Sir Owen Williams's homily on job satisfaction with the workers' stories of protracted unemployment, rough sleeping, heavy drinking and the impossible dream of ever owning a house.[183] MacColl's best compositions crystallised the testimony into song, notably 'The Exile Song', performed by piper and singer Francis McPeake.

The overall programme pulled in different directions. As with *John Axon*, documentary objectives competed with mythic visions: Parker had gone into the project with a notion of road-building as a heroic and epic project, and he was determined to communicate humanity's epic battle with nature even though his ideas were shared by few who built the road. There was also the pressure of the programme's educational remit – to communicate to the public about a national feat of civil engineering – which MacColl resented. It was as if, he would later grumble, 'our intention was to create a programme which would inform the listener how to build his or her own motorway'.[184]

The reviews weren't bad, but there was a feeling that an opportunity had been squandered.[185] MacColl would later describe the programme as a 'thoroughly confusing – and at times boring' hybrid of radio ballad and feature programme.[186] He blamed BBC political pressure, the contractor's Public Relations Officer, civil engineers and managers for speaking in a colourless style, Parker's compliance in capitulating to BBC directives, and even Parker's interference in the selection of the actuality.[187] Parker was no less tetchy about the programme. He wrote a hot-headed letter to one unsympathetic critic who'd accurately argued that 'bits and pieces of individual lives were lost inside the total concrete-mixer' (Parker received a dressing-down by his boss for his trouble).[188] He was ratty with the *Radio Times* art editor for producing an illustration that diminished 'the awesome size and powers of Civil Engineering Machinery' – and by implication, his programme – to the status of a 'dinky toy'.[189] But as he often would, he ended up blaming himself. In a later article, his mind returned to that Irish teenager in the hostel. 'I indeed had much to learn myself,' he wrote. 'A radio ballad can only be about people, not about processes, and I have since discovered that it is the responsibility of the artist to face the reality of the subject he is tackling, no matter how harrowing it may be.'[190] Though *Song of a Road* hadn't been a success, MacColl, Seeger and Parker remained convinced that the radio ballad formula was capable of great things. Within a fortnight of the broadcast, they were planning the next programme.

# 8

# The Bard of Beckenham

Financed by a philanthropic Scot and opened in 1891, New York's Carnegie Hall remains a key venue in American cultural life. Its early years witnessed barnstorming performances from Mark Twain and Jack London, writers who'd lit Jimmie Miller's boyhood imagination. MacColl's comedy hero Groucho Marx had trodden the famous boards; in 1955 Pete Seeger's band The Weavers took to the stage for a McCarthy-defying union concert that quickly came to symbolise the beginning of the post-war American folk revival.[1] On Saturday 3 December 1960 Pete Seeger returned to the venue, this time in the capacity of MC, and introduced to an audience of 1,200 New Yorkers the forty-five-year-old MacColl and twenty-five-year-old Peggy Seeger.

The concert was the climax of a fifteen-month period in which the couple had made three separate trips to North America. In the US, both had names to live up to, and the lustre of each enhanced the other. Peggy Seeger belonged to American folk music's blue-blooded family – Bob Dylan would later enviously describe Peggy's musician brother Mike Seeger as 'the supreme archetype' of the folksinger with music in 'his genes'.[2] Peggy's recording career was already matching up to the Seeger DNA, and her work had appeared on the Folkways label that all the young singers, including Dylan, aspired to.[3]

MacColl was a more enigmatic proposition – he'd never set foot in America, and his stateside reputation rested on the hefty back-catalogue of records cut for the American market since the mid-1950s. These recordings of Scottish and English ballads, shanties and songs were esoteric chronicles of American folk music's back-story. Like the man himself, the discs blended scholarly seriousness and artistic fluency. They bridged the gap between the folklore seminar room and the concert hall, and promised to reward those who took music seriously. Young folk aficionados like Dylan pored over them.[4]

MacColl was already well known among the small fraternity of intellectuals who dominated the leftist milieu of the American folk scene. There was Alan Lomax and Peggy's father, Charles; record producer Kenneth Goldstein (with whom MacColl and A. L. Lloyd had recorded the *English and Scottish Popular Ballads*);[5] Moe Asch, who presided over the Folkways label; and irascible hard-line Communist activist Irwin Silber, founder editor of *Sing Out!* magazine.

MacColl and Seeger were hot property among the impresarios, agents and promoters who managed the business end of the American revival. Paul Endicott, who had previously set up tours for Pete Seeger, organised MacColl and Seeger's first Canadian visit in 1959.[6] Harold Leventhal had staged The Weavers' comeback; Manny Greenhill would go on to manage Joan Baez – both played prominent roles in overseeing and promoting MacColl and Seeger's careers in the United States. Albert Grossman had booked Peggy for his Gate of Horn club back in 1957;[7] in the summer of 1960 he organised the American folk scene's central event, the Newport Folk Festival, and made sure MacColl and Seeger were on the bill. They shared stages with John Lee Hooker, Odetta and Jesse Fuller; a few weeks later they played the six-day Berkeley festival alongside bluesman Lightnin' Hopkins.[8] MacColl, with his comb-tracked hair, neatly trimmed beard and preferred concert outfit – pressed brown or blue trousers, clean shirt and woollen cardigan – seemed every bit as exotic in the beatnik ambience of the American folk scene as Peggy Seeger had in Soho.

The Carnegie Hall show was a fitting finale for a whirlwind series of tours in which they'd played the main stages of the burgeoning American revival. That night the audience enjoyed the concert formula that Seeger and MacColl would use throughout their shared career.[9] MacColl adopted his characteristic on-stage posture – sitting up straight on a back-to-front chair, elbows resting on the chair back, occasionally cupping one ear with the palm of his hand to bring his voice closer and block out surrounding noise. Peggy sat a few feet to his left, instruments beside her. From a pool of light in the shadowed stage, they worked through twenty-six songs, alternating between sets of two or three songs each; on some songs they joined in for one another's choruses, some they sang together. She performed American folk songs and ballads, most of British and Irish origin, punctuated by her own titles and a set of banjo tunes; MacColl sang mainly Scottish and English folksongs, some unaccompanied, some with Seeger's accompaniments on guitar, banjo or autoharp. Songs were prefaced with introductions that sketched in the historical context and drew out the political undertones. MacColl's introductions typically ranged from Burns' politics, the class tensions expressed by a particular ballad, or the survival of folksong into the industrial age: the underlying theme was that folk music represented a record of working-class experience and feeling. He sang a small selection of his own songs, though the emphasis was consistently angled towards the creations of anonymous forebears.

The on-stage atmosphere was calm, serious, highly contrived and apparently natural: MacColl knew enough about theatre to realise that, in large auditoriums, intimacy was an illusion that had to be created. The concert was a carefully co-ordinated musical and political journey. Distinguished *New York Times* music writer Robert Shelton singled out the 'mastery of mood, scene and voice control' and considered the 'doughty, bearded baritone' MacColl a 'virtuoso performer' whose 'sense of tradition and ... theatre were so beautifully integrated throughout that thrilling moments cascaded after each other'. Though critical of aspects of Seeger's singing, Shelton described the show as 'one of the most substantial and enjoyable folk concerts New York has had in several seasons'.[10] MacColl and Seeger cut out the write-up for their records.

CISO

Back in Purley, MacColl and Seeger were eager to exorcise *Song of a Road*'s demons and get the sequel radio ballad under way. 'I want this programme to be a great one,' MacColl wrote to Parker on New Year's Day 1960, 'so let's start properly and plan down to the last detail.'[11] Within ten days they were out in the field recording new material; over the following twenty months they produced two further programmes, the first of which took the Italia Prize that had eluded them in 1958.

Both programmes revisited primal scenes of British documentary – first the fishing communities of filmmaker John Grierson's *Drifters* (1929), then the pit communities of *Coal Face* (1935); it was as though the team needed to enter into creative dialogue with earlier traditions and measure the scope of their achievement. Both new radio ballads grew out of MacColl's own current work in documentary film – one from a programme on fishing communities for Tyne Tees television, the other from the National Coal Board's Film Unit, where MacColl often provided music and voiceover narration for the *Mining Review* newsreel.[12] Strikingly similar in terms of structure, style and themes, both synthesised the familiar radio ballad components – creatively edited interviews, recorded sound effects, music and song – to chart lives in key British industries. After the confusions of *Song of a Road*, MacColl was emphatic that 'the effects on human beings of a type of work or technological advance', rather than abstracted industrial processes, should be the primary focus.[13]

಄ఄಃ

Relations with the BBC were typically fraught. MacColl was now insisting that Peggy Seeger was integral to the team and should be formally recognised in the research budget;[14] *Song of a Road* had taken eleven days to rehearse and record with sound engineers working sixteen-hour days; Parker was told that such arrangements were beyond the pale, and was chastised for overspending on research.[15] He complained about miserly budgets, poor equipment and restrictions on studio time.[16] He believed that more should be spent, not less, and argued that the programmes would be greatly improved if the musicians could also tag along on research trips – this would, he argued, enhance empathy and sharpen performances.[17] He was caught between habitual perfectionism, visions of the radio ballads as a new art form, and his more plodding day-to-day responsibilities as a BBC employee. At moments he managed to reconcile utopianism and pragmatism; at others he griped about the 'philistine banality' of life at the BBC and dreamed of working independently.[18]

If little had gone right with *Song of a Road*, the programme that became *Singing the Fishing* seemed charmed from the outset. Programme structure had been a problem in the past; here it was dictated by material. *Singing the Fishing* was to be a one-hour mini-trilogy exploring the three phases of the herring industry from the late nineteenth-century era of sail fishing boats, through the Edwardian steam drifter boom, to the mechanisation of fishing in the post-1945 period. The programme had two geographical centres, one in the declined East Anglian ports, the other in and around the Moray Firth in north-east Scotland. Throughout January and February 1960 MacColl, Parker and Seeger recorded extensively in both locations. MacColl and Parker took a voyage on *The Honeydew* diesel-drifter (Peggy stayed ashore as the fishermen thought it bad luck to have a woman aboard); they managed to ingratiate themselves with the fishermen of the Closed Brethren religious sect in Gardenstown, Aberdeenshire; they recorded the frenetic bidding at Ullapool fish market and tracked down and interviewed Ronnie Balls, a retired steam-drifter captain from Great Yarmouth whose lyrical Norfolk burr was made for radio.

The star of the show was always going to be Sam Larner, an eighty-two-year-old fisherman born and still based in Winterton, Norfolk. Larner had first gone to sea as a twelve-year-old cabin boy, and his life spanned the story they were telling. He was a natural raconteur with a ribald sense of humour and a filthy cackle. His speech was punctuated with bursts of song – he was what the folk revival came to term a 'traditional' singer, a living link with an oral tradition who had learned old ballads, work songs and music-hall ditties from his father and fellow fishermen. A flamboyant performer, Larner was already known to the folk scene from his eightieth birthday appearance at the Hootenanny. MacColl, Parker and Seeger spent days in Larner's Winterton cottage recording the fisherman. Larner was working class, mistrustful of authority and proud of his folk culture. Larner made Parker feel inhibited and repressed; MacColl thoroughly enjoyed his company.[19]

One recurrent problem with the first two radio ballads was that the songs had often seemed alien to the recorded speech – too American in the case of *The Ballad of John Axon*, too lyrical for the grinding work in *Song of a Road*. Larner's singing instantly created a link between subject matter and surrounding narrative: as the title *Singing the Fishing* implied, music was part of the story. It felt right that the new songs about Larner's experiences should match up with the kinds of songs the fisherman knew. This suited MacColl, who was most at home writing in the conventions of folksong. For the lyric to 'Shoals of Herring', a first-person song narrating Larner's early seafaring experiences, MacColl listened carefully to recordings of the fisherman's speech, concentrating on his breathing, tone and phrasing. He borrowed and adapted a tune from the traditional English ballad, 'The Famous Flower of Serving Men'.[20] He then tried out the carefully simulated authenticity by singing the song to Larner. The fisherman responded to the uncanny experience of hearing his own words sung in a familiar tune by claiming to have known the song all his life. A highly accomplished folk pastiche, 'Shoals of Herring' would become one of MacColl's most popular pieces.

While 'the tradition' was central to the way that Singing the Fishing sounded, it wasn't allowed to dictate all the musical effects. Over the next few years MacColl and Seeger would become identified with a narrow purist mode in which artistic endeavour had to be justified in terms of fidelity to 'the tradition'; here they used what they could to create the dramatic effects they were after. Jazz clarinet and saxophone player Bruce Turner thoroughly enjoyed the licence he was given: one scene used a melancholic alto saxophone sequence to create depression-era period atmosphere; another intercut recorded actuality with swelling discordant effects to dramatise a storm.[21]

Parker, unwilling to make the cost-cutting compromises requested by his seniors, booked a Birmingham studio for a fortnight. On the first day the full ensemble of six musicians, seven singers and an additional six-piece choir listened to MacColl and Seeger improvise the musical score against the completed tape of sound effects and actuality. By the end of the first week, they knew their parts.[22] For the first time in the radio ballads, the music was recorded as the actuality ran: the voices and sounds of the fishing communities were cued into the studio headphones, and the musicians played off them.[23] The result was a more integrated soundtrack, in which studio technicians became collaborators, and musicians responded to the nuances of the actuality.

Parker, who had already spent six weeks editing and assembling tape to match MacColl's paper script, now retreated once again to balance actuality and music. MacColl was full of admiration for Parker's creative production: watching Parker cut tape was, he once said, to witness real artistry, 'like watching a painter in the throes'.[24] Parker's mood now swung from jubilation to despair. One day he had a strut in his stride, proclaiming 'Singing the Fishing is magnificent';[25] a week later he was pitched into depression when listening to the programme. It was no better than The Ballad of John Axon;[26] there were 'deep fissures in the structure'; his own production was worthless. 'As a work of art', he grimly concluded, 'it doesn't get off the ground.'[27] The original assessment was closer to the mark. First broadcast on the Home Service on 16 August 1960 and repeated on the highbrow

Third Programme that November, audience feedback was enthusiastic, and so was the press assessment.[28] The BBC remained uneasy about lavish expenditure, but entered the programme for the 1960 Italian Press Association Award for Radio Documentary.[29]

The nomination for these radio Oscars brought to the fore a problem that had been sidelined during the heat of creativity. On the early broadcasts, the radio ballads were always billed as 'by Ewan MacColl and Charles Parker', even though Parker's creative input was largely centred on his role as producer of MacColl's scripts, and Seeger's contribution was extensive. She was sometimes registered as music director; sometimes she was altogether omitted from BBC publicity material. The situation arose through a combination of old-fashioned chauvinism, the twenty-five-year-old Seeger's reticence about pushing herself forward, and probably some strategic considerations: the BBC, who were already querying the fees Parker was demanding for Seeger, were aware that officially promoting her to co-author could only further inflate the budget.[30] Even so, Parker was uncomfortable with the anomaly: twelve months earlier he had filed a request that Seeger should be listed as 'co-author and composer of the final work'.[31] Nothing came of it. According to MacColl, the question resurfaced at the time of the Prix Italia nomination, but Parker had already submitted a copy of the programme, complete with a presentation pack listing credits.[32] For now, the creative energy and collectivist ambience made the business of correct accreditation seem distastefully bourgeois – Seeger stayed at home with the baby while Parker and MacColl travelled to Trieste to collect the award. In later years, when the ownership and authorship of the radio ballads became bitterly contested, MacColl would chastise himself for dropping the matter too easily.[33]

CB&O

They rode high into the next programme, which was under way before *Singing the Fishing* was broadcast. For *The Big Hewer*, MacColl, Parker and Seeger visited pit communities in County Durham, South Wales and the Midlands. MacColl's colleagues at the National Coal Board Film Unit helped with contacts; in the Welsh valleys they sought out miners and families MacColl had first met during the gruelling Theatre Workshop tours a decade before; Gateshead cabinet-maker Louis Killen, a MacColl protégé from the London Hootenannies and now a regular singer on the radio ballads team, provided a foothold in the North-East.[34] They went down pits and visited miners' homes; they sought out miners in pit canteens, welfare clubs and pubs. MacColl was pleased to note that many drank from tankards engraved with quotations from Marx and William Morris.[35]

Peggy Seeger found the experience 'an eye opener, just wonderful'. 'If anything has taught me what working people do, it was the radio ballads,' she recalled. 'I was the only woman there and they treated me with respect and welcome ... It was the first time I had been in the camaraderie of men who weren't trying to get into my knickers ... These things are life changing.'[36] It had an equally powerful effect on Parker, whose interview technique up until this point often involved more talking than listening.[37] Parker confessed to being shocked by the miners' powers of expression.[38] With MacColl in one ear, and articulate railwaymen, labourers and miners in the other, Parker's preconceptions were soon under pressure. Few emerged from MacColl's company with their political beliefs unscathed, and Parker was no exception. As he would later admit, these experiences turned his political beliefs upside down: 'This little machine', he would joke, pointing to an EMI Midget tape recorder, 'has taught me socialism.'[39] MacColl watched these educational encounters with the air of one who'd seen it all before. He insisted in finding nothing surprising in articulate miners. 'After all', he wrote in his autobiography, 'I had been brought up among people who talked about important things like politics and revolution ... I had been fairly familiar with miners and their families since the days of my childhood.'[40]

Individual sections of *The Big Hewer* were pitch-perfect. One segued three miners reminiscing about their first day at work with MacColl's song 'Schooldays End': the song's nostalgic lyricism neatly framed the miners' contributions. Another sequence wrapped Brian Daly's skittering bluesy guitar arpeggios around a montage of testimony dealing with working conditions and the prevalence of pneumoconiosis.[41] But despite the poise of these quieter moments, overstatement was the dominant effect.

*The Big Hewer* took as its title a common piece of coalfield mythology: wherever MacColl, Parker and Seeger went, they heard about the Big Hewer, a semi-legendary miner known by different names in each place who performed superhuman feats at the coalface. In

interviews about the programme MacColl was quick to point out that
this common folklore figure emerged from a particular history – life in
pit communities had generated a superhuman archetype to help cope
with the potentially dehumanising effects of pit-bound lives.[42] But not
for the first time, MacColl's critical faculties were overruled by his
fraught creativity. The unease of a working-class intellectual who'd
escaped from manual labour, and now made his living singing songs
and writing radio programmes, imbued the programme. Rather than
familiarity with pit communities, the programme suggested anxious
distance; rather than getting to the bottom of the coalfield folklore,
*The Big Hewer* simply reproduced it, and the myth came to function as
a ready-made narrative form to express MacColl's romantic views of
manual labour. Broadcast on 18 August 1961, the programme managed
to combine unblinking realism and wide-eyed wonder. The political
acumen and poetic cadences of the miners' words only magnified the
problem. One critic accurately compared the contrast between the
miners' words and MacColl's 'big gestured' ballads as 'similar to that
between a real working man, and a civic statue to the dignity of labour
in the socialist realist style'.[43]

CRBO

Set back from a quiet, privet-lined South London suburban road, 35
Stanley Avenue, Beckenham, Kent is a large, three-storey Victorian
house. The property is split into two flats – one on the ground floor
and a maisonette above – and has a swing-in gravel drive and a third-
of-an-acre garden behind. MacColl and Seeger pooled their resources,
took out a mortgage and bought the upstairs flat in the summer of
1961. Formerly owned by a Coal Board doctor, the property cost
£4,800 (roughly £75,000 in today's money). MacColl would live there
for the rest of his life.

Beckenham had been a salubrious retirement location for moneyed
eighteenth-century merchants and later the home of children's author
Enid Blyton. Quintessentially suburban – famous for its tennis club
– the one-street town hadn't witnessed an outbreak of radical politics
since Jack Cade's Kentish rebellion of 1450. 'It was ... a very snobbish
area, like I'd been brought up in,' remembered Peggy. 'I didn't want
to live there.'[44] Though she'd have preferred a more urban set-up,
the forty-six-year-old MacColl was insistent on the quiet, suburban

life. Ten miles to central London was close enough, and Beckenham was handy for Jean, Hamish and Kirsty in nearby Croydon. The flat was roomy, light and good value for money. After the cramped living in Purley, and the emotional trauma of recent years, it represented spaciousness, comfort and security. It could accommodate all of them, including Betsy, who was given the biggest bedroom. The property was in good repair, which appealed to MacColl and Seeger, neither of whom had any flair for practical tasks.

The garden closest to the house belonged to the downstairs flat; the plot for the upstairs flat lay behind. The former owner of their flat had fashioned garden walkways and borders from huge rubber belts discarded from pits in the Kent coalfield. MacColl and Seeger wanted a lawn for the children to play on. In the late summer and early autumn they went at the garden with gusto. 'He had a feeling for the garden that I didn't understand,' Peggy remembered. 'This was the first piece of land he'd ever owned.'[45] Together they dragged out the rubber belts by hand and dug up a protruding rusty motorbike; rubbish was cleared from around the trunks of the apple trees. They put in a lawn and planted vegetables, soft fruit, flowers. MacColl would walk down the garden every morning with a cigarette and a cup of tea. It became a sanctuary for him.

CB80

'We are now witnessing', wrote Seeger and MacColl in 1961, 'an intensive bout of popular music-making, the likes of which has not been seen in these islands since Elizabethan times.'[46] At the start of the 1960s they were involved in numerous projects that helped to shape the revival, and which further established their status as two of its leading figures.

The first of many publishing collaborations, *The Singing Island* was designed as an instruction manual for the 'new generation of young singers ... discovering their national music'.[47] The book anthologised ninety-six songs, many from Seeger and MacColl's own repertoires, including hoary Child Ballads about incestuous and murderous noblefolk, tales of impotent old men cuckolded by young wives, and a nineteenth-century broadsheet about a Dublin butcher's apprentice turned pirate. There were children's chants and rhymes, drinking songs, songs recycled from the *Shuttle and Cage*, and a sprinkling of MacColl compositions. Some of the material had been culled directly from the folk, notably Sam Larner, who supplied a dozen songs. Others came from folk even closer to MacColl: twelve songs were lifted from his mother's repertoire, fifteen from his father's. *'The Singing Island* is what we have been waiting for,' enthused the *English Dance and Song* magazine; 'it is perhaps the richest treasure house of British folksong to be published since Cecil Sharp.'[48]

There are few forms of music in which cutting a record with a seventy-six-year-old mother could augment a reputation, but the folk scene was all about authenticity, and Betsy Miller was living proof of MacColl's. Recorded by Peggy on a primitive Ferrograph machine and issued in 1962 as *A Garland of Scots Folksong: Betsy Miller and Ewan MacColl*, the LP presented a sample of the family's folk culture.[49] MacColl and Betsy sang as a duet the Child Ballad 'Lord Randal' – MacColl took the part of the eponymous hero who eats eel soup poisoned by his grasping sweetheart, Betsy was his distraught mother. They lovingly crooned 'A Wee Drappie O't', a drinking song that had been popular back in the Coburg Street Hogmanay parties of the 1920s. Betsy steadily worked her way through the pleasantly lubricious seventeenth-century song 'The Spinning Wheel'. Her sometimes quavering voice and deadpan delivery contrasted with MacColl's rotund baritone and more theatrical style; the critics applauded a disc that so conclusively established MacColl's 'undisputed traditional roots' and represented 'a perfect blending of traditional and revival'.[50]

Other records from the early 1960s were equally concerned with uncovering and recirculating traditional song. Cut for the American market, *The Best of Ewan MacColl: British Folk Music for the Connoisseur* subverted the greatest hits genre by including only traditional songs. A reverential tone was creeping into MacColl's attitude to 'the tradition'; in the liner-notes he spoke of a childhood where traditional songs were absorbed and became 'a private language for communicating with those elusive, often mutually opposed, personalities which inhabit you'.[51] He recorded more unaccompanied big ballads and an LP showcasing nineteenth-century songs originating from the 'bothies' – living quarters of male farmworkers in the north-east of Scotland – prefaced with a scholarly sleeve-note essay on the economics of Scottish agriculture.[52]

Two further releases found MacColl again in the role of performing cultural archaeologist, digging deep into the substrata of previous popular culture and bringing into view vanished artefacts. He now regularly haunted the stacks of the British Library, where he spent days leafing through 'black letter' broadside ballads that had flourished as street literature in the seventeenth and eighteenth centuries. Here he exhumed the earthy and satirical popular pieces for two volumes of *Broadside Ballads, London (1600–1700)*.[53] He was forever searching for antecedents to his own vernacular and politically charged creativity, and found them in the most unlikely places. The eighteenth-century Scottish Jacobites shared MacColl's nationalism and distaste for the bourgeoisie, but these feudalists and royalists were unlikely candidates for his political sympathies. Nonetheless, the doomed movement had inspired fierce loyalties, a binding mythology and a crop of songs suffused with a profound yearning for political and social change. *Songs of Two Rebellions: The Jacobite Wars of 1715 and 1745* was possibly the finest collaboration with Seeger to date.[54]

∞∞

Resisting the 'plasticization of popular culture', 'recovering the folk idiom', 'relearning the methods of folk creation': you couldn't spend long with MacColl in the early 1960s without hearing these phrases. MacColl had a diagrammatic view of the cultural field. There was high culture, the preserve of a privileged elite. There was the culture industry churning out its plastic products; the development and intensification of this industry through the twentieth century meant that 'one class could actually control the musical taste of the other class' with increasing efficiency.[55] An elaborate means of bourgeois social control, the products of the culture industry – whether Eddie Cochran or bingo halls – induced amnesia, suspending the working class in a perpetual present and severing them from their own homegrown popular culture, such as the artistically and politically nourishing 'music of the people' that they'd created or adapted for themselves.[56]

Rediscovering and developing vernacular cultural traditions from the past was therefore essential to creating a more vibrant and democratic culture for the future. MacColl considered the folk scene a key site in this resistance. Cultural archaeology was important, but not enough in itself: cultural traditions had to be brought into meaningful dialogue with current realities, as in the radio ballads. 'A tradition which cannot make terms with contemporary life is a dead thing,' claimed MacColl in 1961; 'it belongs to the museums and to the library shelves for the specialists to study.'[57] The challenge was to create music 'which honour[s] the tradition without emerging as a pastiche or romantic antiquarianism', in the words of Charles Parker.[58] Hungarian folklorist and composer Béla Bartók, who'd collected indigenous folk music and drawn upon it extensively for his compositions, was frequently cited as a worthy model.[59] MacColl and Seeger likewise saw their own song-writing as deliberate attempts to synthesise forms inherited from the past with contemporary concerns;[60] as the title suggested, their two volumes of The New Briton Gazette presented their work as a type of modern-day balladry.[61]

They were increasingly identified as heading up a movement of likeminded young British songwriters, and were asked by Folkways to edit a compilation record of new talent. Some of the artists they selected had already appeared in an earlier MacColl and Seeger book, Songs for the Sixties, which approvingly numbered a 'steadily-growing army of young creators' including Glasgow's Matt McGinn, Newcastle's Johnny Handle and Liverpudlian Stan Kelly.[62] MacColl was heartened by this 'small army of people who feel that there is something unique and beautiful in their traditional songs'. Their enemy was easily identified: 'It's inevitable', wrote MacColl continuing the military imagery, that 'the folksong revival should produce a legion of smooth operators, five and ten per centers, top twentiers, goons, gimmickers, gagmen, third rate comics.'[63] Denmark Street, London's Tin-Pan Alley (from where The Singing Island was published), was identified as the headquarters of the commercialism marshalled against the revival.[64]

෨৪ৎ

The club scene boomed in the early 1960s. There was now a thriving scene north of the border, centred on the Howff in Edinburgh High Street.[65] The Spinners had their club in Liverpool, which had been going since 1958; The Watersons' club in Hull had started at the same time.[66] Clubs in Bradford, Manchester, Glasgow, Grimsby and Newcastle were all on the map as the decade turned. By the beginning of 1962 there were at least seventy folk clubs in Britain; three years later the figure was nearer 300.[67] In a typical week in March 1962, there were twenty-seven folk club nights and concerts in and around central London alone; many of the venues, such as The Troubadour at Earl's Court or the Partisan on Carlisle Street, Soho, dated from the skiffle craze; others, like the Folk and Blues Night at the Roundhouse, Wardour Street or the 'Folknite' at the Albany, Camden Town reflected newer growth.[68] To service demand, the national music weekly *Melody Maker* introduced a folk column, written by *Sing* journalists Eric Winter and Karl Dallas, from May 1960.

The scene soon had its supergroups: 'Which is the Best Folk Group, The Spinners or The Ian Campbell Folk Group?', debated the *Melody Maker* in 1963.[69] It had its institutions, notably Colletts record shop at 70 New Oxford Street, which doubled as a meeting place, unofficial information bureau and sometime hostel for many of the folk pilgrims finding their way into London.[70] Before long folk had its first TV stars. Glaswegians Robin Hall and Jimmie MacGregor made the breakthrough before eight million viewers on the BBC's flagship teatime news programme *Tonight* in the January of 1960.[71] With regional accents and boy-next-door manner they became a popular hit. MacColl was alarmed to see his protégé and occasional guitarist MacGregor – who had been first converted to folk music during the Ballads and Blues Scottish tour of 1954 – on a show in which folksong became 'quaint' and 'sapped of vigour'.[72] The *Radio Times* TV listings would soon give him further cause for concern (MacColl put to one side his own small-screen appearances on *The Ramblers*). When the Saturday night music show *Easybeat* introduced folk music in 1960, viewing figures reached four million.[73] Folk variety type shows with names like *Barndance*, *Hullabaloo* and *The Hoot'nanny Show* were regular fixtures on British TV through the first half of the 1960s, creating plenty of work for artists including The Spinners, The Ian Campbell Folk Group, The Clancy Brothers, and Robin Hall and Jimmie MacGregor.[74]

CʒՖↃ

'The only notes that some people care about', blustered MacColl in 1961, 'are banknotes.'[75] As folk music slipped inexorably from the cultural margins to the mainstream, relations between Malcolm Nixon and MacColl passed breaking point. Nixon was now an established London agent and impresario, managing a long roster of artists and

staging concerts for visiting Americans like Josh White and bluesman
Jesse Fuller.[76] The Ballads and Blues club was small beer in comparison,
and Nixon's enthusiasm for it fluctuated. With MacColl and Seeger
away on tour for much of 1960, the club was mothballed. The final
split came that autumn when, a few weeks before MacColl and Seeger
were due to leave for a further twenty-date tour of America, Nixon
announced that he'd capitulated to popular demand and scheduled a
new-look Ballads and Blues season.[77] According to Seeger's memory, the
bone of contention was that he'd appropriated the 'Ballads and Blues'
brand name without consulting MacColl, though the most surprising
thing about the Nixon–MacColl alliance is that it lasted so long.[78] At
the end of his short tether, MacColl announced that he was to start a
new club the following year.[79] To vent his contempt for Nixon – now
the embodiment of commercial opportunism engulfing the revival
– MacColl wrote a scurrilous squib. MacColl would perform 'No
Agents Need Apply' on-stage, mimicking Nixon's manner and accent
with exuberant theatricality. Nixon was lambasted for dragging 'the
tradition' up and down Denmark Street, for turning promising young
artists into performing poodles. 'Today, tonight or anytime, you never
will repent,' went the chorus, 'If you join the happy family that pays
me ten per cent.'[80]

CXEO

In 1957 MacColl had needed the organisational and promotional skills
of Nixon; in 1961 he and Seeger sought the assistance of another
enterprising Scottish communist. Whereas Nixon was camp and
flamboyant, Bruce Dunnet was a self-styled man's man – gruff and
morally conservative, his persona was straight-talking and working
class. A couple of years younger than MacColl, Dunnet had manifold
commercial considerations on the London music scene: he was a well-
connected promoter and manager; he ran the club Folksong Unlimited;
he'd played a hand in the breakthrough of Robin Hall and Jimmie
MacGregor; in the future he'd famously pass up the opportunity to
manage the Rolling Stones (he saw no future in long-haired London
college boys playing the blues).[81]

    These commercial activities ran alongside Dunnet's hard-line
communism and appreciation of 'real' folk music's political relevance.
He liked and admired MacColl, and the feeling was mutual. MacColl

was never much of an organiser, and the opening of the new club was dogged by a string of blunders: Dunnet stepped in to straighten things out. 'It belongs to the singers – call it the Singers' Club,' he remembers advising MacColl.[82] Over the next twenty-five years Dunnet would function as one of the Singers' Club's principal backstage figures – promoter, organiser, accountant, bouncer, glass-collector.[83]

∝≈∾

The new club opened back in the 250-seat Anthony Asquith room of the ACTT premises, 2 Soho Square, on Sunday 25 June 1961 at 8 pm prompt (entrance was 4s 6d, or £3.40 in today's prices). The *Melody Maker* listing described the guests – MacColl, Seeger, A. L. Lloyd and Dominic Behan – as 'The Old Firm': the launch was deliberately, if ironically, presented as a restoration to power of those figures who'd been around since the beginning in the Princess Louise days.[84] The format was consistent with that earlier period – MacColl was MC, there were floor singers, each of the guests sang for half an hour.

The purpose of the Singers' Club was spelt out in a manifesto-style statement written by MacColl and published in both *Melody Maker* and *Sing* magazine that summer. In paternalistic tones, MacColl outlined the club's desire 'to rescue a large number of young people, all of whom have the right instincts' from 'influences that are doing their best to debase the meaning of folk song'. 'Traditional singers' also needed protection, in their case 'from the ravages of the commercial machine'. The folksong revival should respect traditional material and be regrounded in its 'traditional basis'. Good singers needed a stage. Performance standards should be maintained. The folk revival might be under threat, argued MacColl, 'but it's not too late to retrieve the position'. The Singers' Club was to function as a bulwark against encroaching commodification.[85]

∝≈∾

'At the hundreds of concerts and hootenannies where I have sung or acted as chairman', wrote MacColl that year in the sleeve-notes to an LP, 'I have made a point on insisting on the rule that singers do not sing anything but the songs of their own native tradition.'[86] This rule or 'policy' had been around since at least 1958, and was one of the many issues upon which MacColl and Nixon disagreed. The 'policy' was now instituted as a club rule, and was central to the Singers' Club's high-minded brand of cultural nationalism. Though the club's leading lights were able to joke about their prescriptive edict, this didn't detract from the ultimate seriousness with which it was taken.[87] During the club's second month, MacColl, Lloyd and Charles Parker unsuccessfully lobbied the English Folk Dance and Song Society to recommend implementing an equivalent policy for all folk club events under its sphere of influence.[88]

The policy was in part a residue of the anti-American cultural thrust of the early 1950s Communist Party in which MacColl had felt at home. American culture, ran that argument, was privileged by the economic power behind it; the promotion of national cultural traditions was therefore a mode of resistance to American imperialism. MacColl was interested, as he always would be, in the creation of a democratic and politically charged popular culture in touch with what had come before and close to the idiom and the textures of working-class life. 'If we subject ourselves consciously or unconsciously to too much acculturation', he warned in one interview, 'we'll finish with no folk culture at all. We'll finish with a kind of cosmopolitan, half-baked music which doesn't satisfy the emotions of anybody.'[89]

The policy was purposefully provocative and inevitably divisive. The paradox behind the British folk revival's attitude to American culture was widely recognised. Certain types of American music – particularly the work of Woody Guthrie, Leadbelly, Big Bill Broonzy – had in the second half of the 1950s kick-started a movement that often defined itself in opposition to 'commercialism', and particularly the American and Americanised manifestations of commercialism that dominated the pop charts at the time – artists such as Perry Como, Johnnie Ray, Frank Sinatra and Tony Bennett. The policy was, for MacColl, a way of declaring that phase over. 'The vanguard of the popular folksong revival in Britain today', he wrote in 1961, 'is largely made up of ex-skifflers; they are by far the most devoted, and the best informed, people in the whole movement and they have become rather intolerant of British singers who use American material.'[90] It was obvious that non-Americans who persisted in singing American material wouldn't be welcome to do so at the Singers' Club.

The club was run for and by MacColl's like-minded vanguardists. Its booking policy reflected the purism it espoused, and after a moderately successful summer, attendance picked up in the final months of 1961.[91] As MacColl had pledged, the Singers' Club coaxed to the stage the singing folk. In the course of 1962 there were appearances by a visiting family of music-making Venezuelans, the Scottish ballad singer Jeannie Robertson, Scottish shepherd Willie Scott, and four appearances from the Stewarts of Blairgowrie, a family of musical Scottish travellers with whom MacColl and Seeger would work extensively over the years.[92]

Alongside these guests and the residents – MacColl, Seeger, Lloyd, Dominic Behan – appeared younger singers, and the club was especially keen to encourage those with repertoires grounded in particular regions. On one hand, the policy played a significant role in stimulating exactly the type of cultural recovery that MacColl was after. An artist like Louis Killen, one of MacColl's favourites at this time, was a case in point. Working class, intellectually curious, increasingly committed to performing the music of his native Tyneside, Killen appeared on a number of occasions in the club's early days (his own club, Folk Songs and Ballads in Newcastle, followed the Singers' Club in adopting a British material-only policy shortly afterwards).[93] In 1962 Killen cut for Topic records *Northumbrian Garland* and *Colliers' Rant*, an influential brace of EPs that connected regional songs with instrumental traditions in a way that freshened up both.[94] Martin Carthy also saw merit in the Singers' Club diktat: 'It did get people off their backsides and make them look in other places and life became more interesting as a consequence.'[95] MacColl and Seeger generously encouraged those who were on the right lines: young singers in search of material were given a free hand with the books, broadside collections, records and tapes in the ever-expanding Beckenham music library.[96]

But though strategically effective, the policy was impaled on glaring contradictions that many were quick to point out. Hadn't music always been wonderfully oblivious to national boundaries? If one accepted that musical traditions had been lost and needed recovering for political reasons, then why were nation and region important at all? Why not take what you needed from wherever you could find it (as MacColl, Parker and Seeger did in the radio ballads)? And why did being from the right place and having the right accent entitle someone to perform music when they might be from a social class, gender or religion that actually had nothing to do with that music? Why should Peggy Seeger, for example, be entitled to sing 'Freight Train', a song collected from her family's African-American housemaid, when a vast social, economic gulf – in which all the complexities of American racial history intervened – separated the Seegers from that housemaid's world? And weren't Seeger and MacColl themselves above all a fusion act who brought instruments associated with American folk music (banjo, steel-string acoustic guitar, autoharp) into creative tension with British traditions of unaccompanied singing? And didn't MacColl's carefully managed personae neatly illustrate the complex relationship between individual, national and cultural identities? English and Scottish threads were closely enmeshed in the MacColl mix: the earthy man of the people with a nasal Salford twang; the contemporary Rabbie Burns; the BBC broadcaster in eloquent command of the Queen's English (what family referred to as his 'restaurant voice'). The Singers' Club policy now took a line on questions of cultural identity that seemed staggeringly simplistic. With his dubious Scottishness, MacColl in particular was on thin ice.

The situation wasn't helped by the increasingly high-handed manner in which MacColl and Seeger carried themselves. 'Many find them "cold" and single-minded on initial encounters,' observed their friend Irwin Silber in his preface to their songbook.[97] 'We had very little tolerance for anybody who didn't do things exactly the way we did,' Seeger told me in 2004, 'and you can quote me on that. I regret that now ... because I think we missed out.'[98] Embattled and full of self-righteous indignation, MacColl seldom visited other London clubs, and yet was accused of presenting the Singers' Club as 'the only genuine folk club in London'.[99] Resentment built. In December 1961 he was criticised in a *Sing* magazine editorial for being arrogant, aloof and 'sitting on his throne'.[100] 'The general impression of him was that he was an ogre, dominated everything, told you how it was, laid down the law all the time,' recalled London contemporary Wizz Jones. 'It was standard to knock Ewan all the time, everybody knocked him, you know, "bloody Ewan MacColl, that's not even his real name".'[101]

From the free-and-easy folk scene flourishing outside, the Singers' Club was easily ridiculed for its contradictory purism. From the inside, it was a vibrant and stimulating cultural centre. If you accepted the principles, which many did, it was a warm, friendly place with beer, excellent music, plenty of on-stage banter and the added frisson of being in-the-know. In October 1961 it moved to the upstairs room of

The Plough pub, opposite the British Museum.[102] By December 1962 it had relocated to the Pindar of Wakefield near King's Cross, and was opening both Saturday and Sunday nights to create additional performing opportunities for new singers.[103] Nobody who visited could be in any doubt that it was primarily MacColl and Seeger's club, and it soon became the institutional bedrock of their careers: they notched up nineteen performances in the first year and thirty-four the second.[104] They took their appearances at the Singers' Club as seriously as anywhere, and devised an elaborate card index system to ensure they weren't repeating material too often.[105]

◌৪০

In 1961 the Friends of Pete Seeger support group was formed in New York to raise funds towards the popular singer's snowballing legal bill. (Seeger had been found guilty of Contempt of Congress in March and released on bail; his lawyers were now working on an appeal.)[106] MacColl, Peggy Seeger and the Singers' Club residents set up a British wing.[107] Paul Robeson was the nominal president; MacColl, as the hands-on chairman, worked through his address book to secure the backing of prominent figures. Benjamin Britten, Doris Lessing, Humphrey Lyttelton and Sean O'Casey were all signed up.[108] To get things under way, MacColl, Seeger, Bert Lloyd and Dominic Behan gave a benefit concert at the St Pancras Town Hall (now Camden Town Hall) that June.[109] The British campaign was a success: Pete Seeger would tour Britain that autumn and play the Royal Albert Hall on 16 November; the following year he would win the appeal and clear his name, but MacColl would pay a price for his own involvement.

With a mortgage, an eighteen-month-old baby and a longstanding penchant for stimulating work that paid small fees, he and Peggy Seeger had committed themselves to a lucrative ten-week, forty-date tour of North America for October to December 1961. Worth £7,000 (£100,000 in today's money) before travel and subsistence expenses, the tour was a lifeline of revenue.[110] It hadn't been easy to get US visas back in 1959 and 1960 – there'd been tortuous negotiations with agents, lawyers and finally the intervention of the American Civil Liberties Union.[111] But when MacColl applied for a visa this time, the State Department categorically declined. He and Peggy went down to the American Embassy to press his case. 'They presented him with a dossier that was about six inches high,' she explained. 'We actually compared our dossiers. Mine was about two inches high.'[112] MacColl's file bulged with thirty years' worth of intercepted letters, transcripts of tapped phone conversations, newspaper cuttings, passport and visa applications, and letters between MI5 and police inspectors in Salford, Manchester, London. Public identification with Pete Seeger's campaign seems to have finally tipped the weighty evidence against him, and it left them in a tight corner.[113] Cancelling the tour was out of the question.[114] MacColl stayed at home with Betsy and baby Neill while Peggy went alone. He wrote every day; she replied with news. Some concerts in the Midwest had been picketed by right wingers brandishing placards vilifying 'Red Peggy Seeger'; the song 'First Time Ever I Saw Your Face' was proving especially popular with audiences.[115] She got some good reviews, but it was a lonely and difficult tour.[116] MacColl was the main draw in the US: 'I'd walk past the box office after the sound rehearsal,' she remembered, 'and people would be returning their tickets by droves when they discovered that Ewan wasn't there.'[117]

CX80

Ralph Bond was a Marxist filmmaker, on old CP comrade of MacColl's, and a prominent activist in the Association of Cinematograph, Television and Allied Technicians union (ACTT). On behalf of his union, he moved a motion at the Trade Union Congress in September 1960 stating: 'We want all people to have the chance to enjoy the beauty and riches of life in all its forms. Too much that is good is being cheapened and vulgarized by the purveyors of mass entertainment.' Delegates voted through Resolution 42, and a 'Centre 42' pressure group was duly launched, whose leading lights included Bond, TV scriptwriter John McGrath, playwright Arnold Wesker, Theatre Workshop actor Clive Barker and novelist Doris Lessing.[118] Their manifesto, *Centre 42: First Stage in a Cultural Revolution*, was reminiscent of Theatre Workshop's brand of cultural warfare: they were setting out to 'destroy the mystique and snobbery associated with the arts'.[119] 'We have lost our popular culture somewhere along the road,' wrote Clive Barker in one report. The prime culprit was 'American-derived but anonymously cosmopolitan culture', which had debased 'classical and folk art in the name of entertainment'.[120]

Centre 42 ended in battered egos, bad blood and monstrous debts, but it momentarily helped to create a rapprochement between the resources of organised labour and MacColl's type of cultural activity. The arguments associated with him – that vernacular folk culture represented a repository of working-class memory and resistance – enjoyed a flare of publicity during Centre 42's moment in the sun. MacColl was featured in a full-page article in *The Times*, and commissioned by the National Union of Tailoring and Garment Workers (NUTGW) to write and record a union theme song. Piped through factory public address systems and issued free as a novelty cardboard record, MacColl's 'Come on Gal' implored young garment workers to join the union.[121]

Centre 42's most eye-catching event was a series of six one-week festivals held through the autumn of 1962. Trades councils from Wellingborough, Nottingham, Leicester, Birmingham, Bristol, Hayes and Harlington hosted the cultural road-show; events ranged from poetry readings with Adrian Mitchell, Christopher Logue and Laurie Lee, the National Youth theatre's production of *Hamlet*, dances with a sixteen-piece jazz band, and screenings of British new-wave films.[122] Charles Parker was prominent, producing an amateur theatre production of Earl Robinson's *The Lonesome Train* and also *The Maker and the Tool*, a hugely ambitious multimedia documentary play that drew on radio ballad style techniques to celebrate local labour traditions.[123] MacColl and Lloyd functioned as semi-official musical consultants, and oversaw the formal folksong concerts that opened each festival.

Personnel changed from town to town, but the overall line-up included many of the main figures of the early revival. Lloyd, MacColl, Seeger, Alf Edwards and Dominic Behan represented the Singers' Club; Louis Killen, his fellow Tyneside singer Bob Davenport and the Ian Campbell Group were among the younger talent.[124] MacColl tried to keep the politics in the foreground: one of the festival organisers ticked him off for succumbing 'to the lure of nostalgia for the old days of a black and white fight, the goodies verses the baddies ... in an attempt to rouse the audience'.[125]

Folk-singing guerrillas, many recruited and drilled by MacColl's right-hand man Bruce Dunnet, were dispatched to nearby pubs, clubs and bingo halls. Reintroducing the people's music to the people was frequently a bruising experience: according to festival organiser Clive

Barker, the folksingers were ejected from most of the venues they infiltrated.[126] In Nottingham eighteen-year-old singer Anne Briggs was sent to perform at the Raleigh bicycle factory canteen.[127] The workers didn't know what to make of the bare-footed young woman singing 'Let No Man Steal Away Your Thyme' during their tea break, and gave her short shrift.[128] Roy Bailey had better luck in Leicester. 'We went round, on the whole, the post-war council estates... We just used to go into pubs.' 'I remember my first blooding with Centre 42,' he said:

> Cyril Tawney, the wonderful Belle Stewart, Ray Fisher and myself went into a pub called The Rocket.... [The pub regulars] were not the slightest bit interested in what we were going to do; they're playing their games, this is their pub, this is what they do on a Friday night... I decided, in order to be really impressive, I suppose, and a bit of an upstart, to sing 'The Four Loom Weaver' unaccompanied.... And the place shut up! They actually listened. We went from strength to strength and we had a great night... And that convinced me that there was something in this revivalist thing. People are interested in these songs.[129]

Though stalwarts of the formal concerts, MacColl and Seeger remained apart from these cultural incursions. 'Ewan and I didn't like pub singing. We weren't good at it,' Peggy Seeger later told me. 'I didn't have a strong enough voice ... The songs that we had were not appropriate for pub singing. We weren't good time singers. I envied people who could do it.'[130]

⊂ঙ৳⊃

'As communists we have a special interest in [the folk revival]', wrote A. L. Lloyd in 1962, 'seeing it as a valuable popular weapon with which to combat the brain-softening commercial culture that the masters think fit for the masses.'[131] Folksong wasn't central to the Communist Party's cultural policy in the way that MacColl would have liked, but some of its prominent members shared his view that the correct way forward for British popular culture was through the folk music of the past. Journalist Karl Dallas, academic George Thomson and his musician wife Katherine Thomson – who had worked with MacColl and Lloyd on *Singing the Fishing* – were all still in the Communist Party and felt that the trade union movement should be properly lobbied to implement resolution 42, and that folk culture should be emphasised.[132]

Lloyd was quick to point out that the international communist movement was currently promoting the collection of workers' songs – a 900-page tome of Czech material was published in 1958.[133] Lloyd wondered whether the time was right for a long-overdue British equivalent, and wrote a proposal for the Labour movement and TUC, which he sent to MacColl. The themes were familiar from their joint 1950s work: unbeknown to bourgeois folklorists, folk creativity had 'passed almost entirely into the scope of the industrial working class'; 'hidden riches' needed 'bringing to light'. Lloyd proposed that the TUC and Labour Party should put up £5,000 (£75,000 today) and employ for eighteen months two specialists (presumably Lloyd and MacColl) to produce an anthology of working-class cultural traditions. This could, argued Lloyd, represent 'a great step toward the vital job of stimulating specifically working-class culture'. The Labour Party and TUC offered encouraging noises, but no cash.[134]

CS80

MacColl was unsurprised. Trying to persuade the Communist Party to recognise the fundamental importance of folk culture was like banging one's head against a wall. As for the Labour Party and the TUC – mealy-mouthed philistinism was what he expected. Entrenched in Beckenham and the Singers' Club, he was increasingly a one-man party: he recognised that systematic song collecting would be easier with the resources of the labour movement, but it wasn't dependent upon them. The main thing was to get the work done. It was still possible, he insisted, to find working-class men and women who carried in their heads scores or even hundreds of songs, some of which were one, two, three hundred years old or more. These songs were for MacColl a resource from the past greatly endangered in the present; they also represented the faint outlines of a different workers' culture of the future. Their collection was paramount.[135]

MacColl and Seeger weren't alone in their commitment to song collecting – some of the figures associated with *Ethnic* magazine had been collecting back in the 1950s, and the field became busier as the 1960s got under way. But with his ideological agenda, access to BBC facilities, and close association with the habitual song collectors Alan Lomax and Peter Kennedy, MacColl had been long aware of the job in hand. In 1955 he'd visited the cottage of seventy-year-old Norfolk farm labourer Harry Cox, and recorded a selection from the singer's substantial repertoire of old songs, ballads, ditties and fragments.[136] From then on, MacColl had his nose to the ground. He and Seeger acquired their own reel-to-reel machine, and visited singers whenever possible. Tapes were labelled, indexed and shelved in the Beckenham workroom. If a singer's material was used for a book or record, payment was paid – up to £2 (about £30 today) for a long song. It became MacColl and Seeger's policy not to copyright traditional material, and if copyright had to be assigned, it went to the singer.[137]

CRBD

The TUC might be reticent about putting up money to disseminate the music of the people, but with their reputations, MacColl and Seeger had other avenues open. Record companies were keen to hear from them, and in 1961 Moe Asch's Folkways label issued *Now Is the Time For Fishing*, an LP edited by MacColl and Seeger that presented the songs and speech of Sam Larner.[138]

Like Sam Larner, Jack Elliott was exactly the type of figure MacColl might have invented had he not existed in the flesh. Broad-shouldered, handsome, irrefutably working class, politically militant, Jack Elliott was a singing collier from Birtley, County Durham whom MacColl had met while recording *The Big Hewer*. Song and storytelling remained part of everyday life for Jack Elliott, his wife Emily and their extended family. MacColl and Seeger recorded nine hours of material in the Elliotts' kitchen, including a rare version of an old ballad.[139] These recordings formed the basis of another Folkways LP, *The Elliotts of Birtley: A Musical Portrait of a Durham Mining Family*.[140] The family were embraced by the folk revival, and embraced it in turn. Surrounded by neighbours who preferred Cliff Richard and Elvis Presley, the Elliotts were heartened that friendly strangers were suddenly interested in their music. 'We didn't know we were folksingers,' recalled Jack Elliott's songwriting friend Jock Purdon, 'till Mr. Lloyd came along and told us we were.'[141] The family soon started their own folk club at The Three Tuns pub in the village. MacColl and Seeger were occasional visitors, while the Elliotts returned the favour, appearing at the Singers' Club.[142] Like Lloyd, MacColl was encouraged that the revival was breathing new life into endangered musical traditions.[143]

 C380

Produced on a fraction of previous budgets, and dealing with subjects remote from MacColl's natural artistic territory, the next two radio ballads were the weakest in the series. *On the Edge* scrutinised the phenomenon of the contemporary British teenager.[144] Though MacColl and Seeger coaxed richly revealing testimony from the forty-six teenagers interviewed – MacColl was especially taken with Dot Dobby, a seventeen-year-old Salford factory worker with a poetic turn of phrase – he was out of his depth when it came to writing songs close to their pop cultural reference points.[145] Broadcast on the eve of Beatlemania, *On the Edge* was cast in a folk music idiom remote from the lives depicted – one teenager was forthright in the opinion that only 'beatniks' and 'girls who wear really long skirts, no make up' would bother with music other than pop.[146] MacColl loathed contemporary pop music so much that he couldn't bear to listen to it, and certainly didn't know enough to parody it. Parker was unapologetically hard-line in defending the muddled programme, claiming to hear in teenage speech the ancient music of the folk tradition. 'They do not talk in that mid-Atlantic Americanese of pop,' he wrote. 'Their language is still akin to the language of the traditional ballads.'[147] Traditional folksong was, he argued, therefore uniquely placed to frame recorded speech, including that of teenagers.[148] For Parker the programme was a deliberate challenge to the phoney pop idiom; *On the Edge* had, he claimed, 'thrown down a musical gauntlet to the pop song idiom so absolutely associated with the teenager'.[149] MacColl wasn't so strident, and later conceded that 'the songs were a failure insofar as they were not organically related to the actuality'.[150] Peggy Seeger put the point more bluntly: 'I was definitely not up to doing any mimicry of pop music ... We should have gotten in some advisers.'[151]

C380

*The Body Blow* grew out of work for a Polio Research Council film and was based on extensive interviews with five polio sufferers.[152] One polio victim movingly but matter-of-factly described being taken ill for the first time during her annual summer holiday. Her words were clenched between a MacColl folk pastiche:

It was in the season of the year when the small birds they did fly
When the flowers are blooming fresh and gay, the sun burns in the sky
I spied a fair young woman by the margin of the sea
A-taking of the pleasant air with her young babe at her knee.
...
Drunk and drowsy with the sun she lay there half asleep
While undetected at her side the enemy did creep
Death did stand at her right hand and did no mercy show
But to this young woman cruelly dealt a body blow.[153]

The jarring song was typical of the programme, and diminished the understated dignity of the testimony. At the beginning of the radio ballad series, MacColl and Parker had argued that the ballad form, with its complex narrative structures and proximity to the rhythms of vernacular speech, remained relevant in the age of the mass media. *On the Edge* and *The Body Blow* found them in unflinching purist mode, making a fetish of the folk music of the past: the assumption now seemed to be that the archaic syntax and phraseology of many folksongs had a timeless relevance that transcended time and place. Rather than a means to transform and reground contemporary culture, folksong was in danger of becoming a sanctuary from it.

ை

MacColl was, however, a contradictory character whose artistic instincts had long rebelled against rules, whether imposed by commercialism, communism or Ewan MacColl himself. For the next radio ballad he resorted to the more pragmatic and eclectic approach of his theatre days, using what he could to achieve the results he wanted. Broadcast on 3 July 1963, *The Fight Game* was the most effective and critically acclaimed radio ballad since *Singing the Fishing*.[154]

With its rituals, theatricality, brutal commercialism and class dynamics, boxing seemed the ideal subject for a radio ballad. To make the programme Parker, MacColl and Peggy Seeger – now heavily pregnant with their second child – interviewed boxing promoters, managers and trainers; they visited back-street gyms, sat in on fights and recorded the sounds of the crowds; they spoke to boxers' wives, girlfriends and fighters including punch-drunk veterans, British heavyweight champion Henry Cooper, and articulate Glaswegian bantamweight, Peter Keenan.

The songs MacColl wrote were racy and ranged indiscriminately across genres. Unlike the work for *On the Edge* and the *Body Blow*, these songs revelled in the cadences and idioms of everyday speech. He wrote a music hall-style song detailing the Partick childhood of Peter Keenan; he wrote rhythmic songs to simulate the gym rhythms of skipping, punch-bag training and the speedball. Folksong models were used, but rather than purporting to be the real or authentic expression of the spoken material, the songs were used contrapuntally and satirically – they were like musical cartoons that magnified and lampooned the myths and clichés of boxing.[155] The songs' quality was matched by the instrumental score. Despite ongoing wrangles with the BBC over recording costs, Seeger drew memorable performances from the orchestra, especially the appropriately bombastic brass section.[156]

The previous two programmes didn't seem to know what they were saying: this one was unflinching in its political diagnosis – MacColl never lost sight of boxing's bottom line, and presented the sport as pugilistic prostitution trading in the bodies of working-class men. At the same time, he managed to get inside the boxer's dream of earning in the ring status that wasn't available in a class-ridden society. As ever, he and Seeger worked obsessively on the project. Whatever the stage of the production – interviewing, transcribing tape, writing the music, rehearsing and recording – sixteen-hour days weren't unusual. The money was good, but unspectacular. MacColl received just over £350 (about £5,000 today) for the ten long weeks he spent on the project; Seeger got slightly less.[157]

෪෨

22 December 1962 was a typical Saturday for MacColl and Seeger. MacColl would have spent the day in Croydon with Jean, twelve-year-old Hamish and three-year-old Kirsty. He often took Hamish out for a few hours – maybe they went to the pictures, or Christmas shopping. 'He'd sing at the top of his voice walking down the street,' Hamish remembered.[158] Betsy, Neill and Peggy would be at Stanley Avenue getting ready for Christmas – Peggy would be shopping, cooking, cleaning, attending to correspondence and trying to find an hour to practise. That evening she and MacColl drove the ten miles

from Beckenham to the Singers' Club, now running two nights a week at the Pindar of Wakefield, King's Cross. They crossed the Thames, which had been frozen for weeks in the worst winter on record. They might have sung in the car; they might have discussed which songs to perform that night; or they might have cast their minds ahead. On New Year's Eve they were taking the train up to Manchester to host Granada TV's live New Year's Eve Party, where they'd mix into the required festive bonhomie a few political songs. It was a lucrative booking, but they were always more at home at the Singers' Club.[159]

They were looking forward to this evening. MacColl was the MC, and they were sharing the stage with Joe Heaney, a forty-three-year-old Irishman known for his fine singing and repertoire of roughly 600 songs in Gaelic and English. When he wasn't singing in Camden pubs like The Bedford, Heaney lived in digs and worked on building sites.[160] With his piercing eyes, craggy face and shock of hair, he had a powerful presence, not unlike that of his countryman Samuel Beckett. He fascinated MacColl. This was a working man who took great pride in his singing and saw himself as an artist. 'He and Ewan had an excellent relationship on stage,' remembered Peggy. They 'just enjoyed each other's singing to the full'.[161]

As usual in the early 1960s, the pub's upstairs room was full to its 150 capacity by eight o'clock, and doorman Bruce Dunnet was keeping things in order. The three artists eventually took to the floor for the first half and traded songs. Heaney sang unaccompanied, some songs in English, some in Gaelic. 'The songs in Gaelic were his favourites', recalled Seeger, 'and he would sink into them as into the arms of a lover.'[162] Seeger's sets provided instrumental colour – she performed arrangements of American folksongs with banjo, guitar and autoharp. MacColl, like Heaney, sang unaccompanied. He did 'A Wee Drappie O't', the drinking song he'd recorded with Betsy. He entertained the audience with the ribald 'She was a Rum One'. He did 'McKaffery', his old favourite about an insubordinate soldier sentenced to hanging. And he sang three ballads, two in Scots, one in English, the longest running to over twenty verses.[163]

Twenty-one-year-old Bob Dylan was in London to work on a BBC television play, and he was in the clubroom that night. He and Joe Heaney would cross paths again at the 1965 Newport Folk Festival, when Dylan would famously shatter the acoustic tranquillity of the

American folk revival with his blisteringly noisy new electric direction. (Pete Seeger would reportedly attempt to cut the electricity cable with an axe; an apoplectic Alan Lomax would have a fist-fight with Dylan's manager.)[164] Dylan thought the English a buttoned-down bunch. 'They could do the twist', he noticed, 'by moving only one leg.'[165] The atmosphere of the Singers' Club induced a fit of the giggles, but he'd been determined to visit the sanctum where Seeger and MacColl – whose music he admired – held court. Proceeded by a small but gathering reputation, he pulled himself together and was asked to sing.[166]

His performance is captured in a now-famous photograph. The image shows a chubby-faced Dylan sporting a black cap and a sheepskin jacket. Behind him sits Bert Lloyd, wearing his usual grin. To Lloyd's left is MacColl, hands in his lap, eyes closed, a tranquil expression on his face: he could be engrossed, asleep, or pretending to be asleep. Dylan is singing one of the two songs he performed, possibly 'The Ballad of Hollis Brown', a protest song about an impoverished farmer who murders his family before shooting himself.[167] According to the Singers' Club ground-rules, Dylan was on the right lines with such a song – it was political, written in a traditional idiom and performed in a style that previous American folksingers would have recognised. But according to the memory of the late Anthea Joseph, who was with Dylan that night, MacColl and Seeger didn't enjoy being upstaged at their own club and responded haughtily to the performance.[168] Whatever was said – and memories differ – Dylan continued to hold MacColl in high esteem, and singled him out for praise in an interview two years later.[169] The feeling wasn't mutual. For MacColl, the trajectory of Dylan's career – away from traditional songs, political causes and acoustic instruments towards chart success and electricity – would increasingly come to symbolise the dangers that threatened the folk revival.

೫೫೦

MacColl and Seeger spent a great deal of the early 1960s tracking down and recording Britain's travelling people. Rapid changes in post-war society were further marginalising these already beleaguered communities. 'The horse has been usurped by the automobile', wrote MacColl:

Mass-produced kitchen ware has made their skill with iron and tin superfluous; the invention and development of plastics has put them out of business as basket-makers; machines are more and more taking over from human beings in fields and orchards. At the same time, regional, county and borough authorities have introduced legislative acts which have ... combined to make the lot of Travellers more and more intolerable.[170]

Working with travellers convinced MacColl and Seeger that this largely illiterate submerged population had become 'the real custodians of English and Scots traditional song'; folksong for them was what it should be for all of us – a shared and valued cultural resource integral to collective identity.[171] The plight of the alienated but resilient travellers seemed tailor-made for the radio ballad form.

*The Travelling People* would be the most assured and politically pointed programme to date. It was common knowledge among the team that this would probably be the last of the radio ballads, and the proximity of the axe focused everybody's mind.[172] According to Parker, travellers from all points between Scotland, Dorset and Kent proved 'the richest source of songs and stories ever tapped for any of the radio ballads'.[173] Through the late summer of 1963 MacColl, Seeger and sometimes Parker recorded at horse-fairs and in the homes of settled travellers; gypsy shanty dwellings in the New Forest reminded Parker of Johannesburg slums.[174] They recorded the songs and stories of Queen Caroline Hughes, a sixty-three-year-old gypsy matriarch living on rank wasteland beside the Wareham bypass in Dorset. MacColl and Seeger taped the invective of outraged residents, and Smethwick schoolchildren chanting about gypsies.[175]

Two main problems had consistently dogged the previous radio ballad scripts: MacColl's tendency to romanticise the working class, and a folk purism that imposed his preferred music on to material to which it had little relevance. None was a problem here. MacColl's script was charged with a carefully measured rage. And as with *Singing the Fishing*, folk modes were embedded in the subject matter; three travellers – Belle Stewart of Blairgowrie and Jane and Elizabeth Stewart of Fetterangus – were recruited into the singing team. Through the autumn of 1963 MacColl was back at his desk in Beckenham with the recorded actuality running through his headphones. He wanted the programme to end with the voice of a senior Birmingham councillor who regarded travellers as 'the maggots of society'. In the programme's dying moments, the councillor would propose his final solution: 'Doesn't the time arise in one's mind,' he asked, 'when one has to say: Alright, one has to exterminate the impossibles?' For the first time in any of the radio ballads, the interviewer's voice would be left on the tape. 'Exterminate?' gasps Parker, 'That's a terrible word. You can't really mean that?' 'Why not?' replied the unabashed councillor.

For weeks on end MacColl's workroom was a fug of cigarette smoke. He wrote an ironic song, 'The Gypsy is a Gentleman' that satirised nostalgic stereotypes of gypsies and challenged society's reassuring distinction between 'real' Romanies and fraudulent tinkers. He produced and polished a further seven songs, each assimilating, adapting and framing the programme's voices.[176] He felt that the central recitative song should be created around the words of Minty Smith, a traveller woman who'd raised thirteen children with her knife-grinder husband.[177] MacColl kept rewinding her voice, recorded earlier that summer in a Kent fruit field:

> I was expecting one of my children, you know, one of my babies, and my son ran for the midwife. In the time he was going after the midwife, the policeman came along. 'Come on,' he said. 'Get a move on. Shift on. Don't want you here on my beat.' So my husband says, 'Look sir, let me stay. My wife is going to have a baby.' 'No, it doesn't matter about that,' he says, 'you get off.' They made my husband move and my baby was born going along while my husband stayed on the road.

MacColl fashioned a chorus from the words of the policeman:

> You'd better get born in someplace else
> So move along, get along!
> Move along, get along!
> Go! Move! Shift![178]

He then wrote a first verse that summarised Minty Smith's experience, opening with the lines, 'Born in the middle of the afternoon / In a horse drawn wagon on the old A5.' He added verses based on other travellers' testimony. The melody for the verse tune was sombre with an understated lyricism; this deliberately clashed with the staccato style of the spoken chorus, 'Go! Move! Shift!'

Thoroughly absorbed in the material, and at the height of his songwriting powers, MacColl worked himself into a frenzy that autumn. By the time the team entered the studio in late November, he was in the grip of flu and on the point of nervous exhaustion. Wracked by a hacking bronchial cough, he collapsed in the studio, but wouldn't rest until the recording was completed.[179] Parker wanted the programme broadcast quickly, preferably at Christmas, as it had 'such obvious "No Room at the Inn" associations'. It eventually went out the following Easter.[180]

By then the radio ballads were all over. At the end of the *Travelling People* recording session, the BBC provided £6 for a post-production party and, as expected, pulled the plug.[181] Rumours would circulate for years about behind-the-scenes political motivations, but the economic case against the programmes was easily made. Documentary films were created on far smaller budgets.[182] The singers and musicians alone for *The Travelling People* cost over £400 (about £5,500 today); each programme was assigned a budget of approximately £1,500 (£21,000), which was frequently exceeded.[183] Individual radio ballads often left in their wake a series of wrangles about budgets, fees for MacColl and Seeger, rehearsal time, and the strain that the team's perfectionism placed on limited recording facilities. Parker had tried to keep his superiors happy by making a pair of cheaper local radio ballads without MacColl and Seeger, but the perception remained that the costly programmes served only a dwindling niche audience on the Home Service.[184] Parker was well aware that his way of working seemed 'most extravagant' by usual BBC standards.[185] As MacColl was quick to point out, all-in wrestling on the TV and radio disc-jockey pop music programmes commanded far large audiences for a fraction of the cost.[186]

They would never get to make the radio ballad now forming in MacColl's mind – a modern-day *Ulysses* based around the experiences of an Irish merchant seaman encountered in a Mile End pub.[187] But the last seven years had, at least, provided a forum for him to demonstrate and develop his own distinctive cultural policy. He'd been instrumental in fashioning a genre of radio theatre by synthesising longstanding music-making traditions and the mass media; he'd given airtime to working-class voices and shown them to be articulate and often poetic; he'd created cultural forms from those voices and the lives they expressed. In part the programmes had created a space for MacColl to indulge his fantasy of everyday life and folk-style song being reconciled once more; at moments they were hopelessly entangled in his romance of the working man; Parker's convoluted theorising often bore little resemblance to the programmes they actually made.[188]

Even so, bolstered by Seeger's increasingly assured musical direction, Parker's highly skilled production and a body of MacColl songs that would take on their own lives in the years to come, the radio ballads were always destined to transcend their time, place and ephemeral medium. *Singing the Fishing* was broadcast in eighty-six countries; for years the radio ballads would reappear in BBC radio schedules; some were adapted for television in the early 1970s; six were eventually released as LPs in the latter half of the 1960s.[189] Topic Records would have issued them sooner, but the BBC wouldn't do business with a company with murky origins in the communist movement.[190] By 1999 that all seemed ancient history, and the surprisingly resilient Topic Records put out the entire series on eight CDs. By then MacColl had been dead for a decade, but he would have felt vindicated that work in which he'd invested so much creative energy in the 1950s and 1960s – not to mention bitterness in the 1970s and 1980s – was now commonly recognised as a landmark in post-war British culture.[191]

# 9
# *Let a Hundred Flowers Blossom*

Betsy Miller lived in the upstairs room at Stanley Avenue with a mynah bird who shared her strong Scottish accent. She carried her Communist Party card in her purse, and survived on her preferred diet – tea, buttered bread and the occasional bottle of stout. Since 1959 she'd provided invaluable back-up childcare; in 1963 Peggy Seeger gave birth to a second son, Calum, and seventy-seven-year-old Betsy was clearly too frail to cope with both boys alone. Twenty-year-old folksinger Sandra Kerr was hired, the first in a long line of live-in nannies exposed to the watchful eye and sharp tongue of the superseded Betsy. The agreed terms and conditions were, however, untypical. Sandra would provide additional childcare – especially when Peggy and Ewan were on tour – and see to odd domestic chores. In return she would get board and lodging, £3 a week (about £45 today), and one-to-one musical tuition from her employers.

MacColl and Seeger had a high opinion of their new nanny's artistic potential. Sandra was intuitively musical, sang well and had found her way through skiffle to the British tradition. She was articulate, passionate about the music of the people, and political (she would join the Young Communist League a few months after moving in). MacColl liked her solid working-class East End credentials. Since her first appearance at the Singers' Club, she'd been one of those many young enthusiasts who enjoyed free access to the MacColl/Seeger library. Her promotion to resident folk-music apprentice would have far reaching repercussions over the decade to follow.

ᘓ৪ᘓ

'With the BBC decision to stop the Radio Ballads,' observed the *Melody Maker* in January 1964, 'the formidable talent and energy of Ewan MacColl and Peggy Seeger will be freed to attack from yet another quarter.'[1] With the childcare problem alleviated, they stepped up the relentless touring schedule that would continue for much of their working lives. MacColl still couldn't get a visa to the United States – a new application was turned down in 1964 – but the British folk scene now boasted a grassroots network of around 300 clubs in pubs, hotels and social clubs. MacColl and Seeger felt most at home in these volunteer-run institutions; club bookings formed the foundations of their working lives. Excluding appearances at the Singers' Club, they took on around 25 club bookings per year in the very early 1960s, 43 in 1964, and up to a peak of 85 by 1969. In the course of the 1960s, MacColl and Seeger played to something like 50,000 people in around 500 folk club concerts.[2]

Peggy was always in charge of arranging the club tours (bigger concerts and media work were left to their agent, Felix de Wolfe). Their club fee was £30 at the beginning of the 1960s and £35 ten years later (between £300 and £400 in today's money), plus petrol and accommodation. 'We quartered the country like a hawk quarters a field,' Seeger recalled.[3] A typical day on the road began with a leisurely breakfast over the *Guardian* followed by hours in the car – they drove a series of second-hand cars distances of 40,000 miles per year.[4] 'I was a good driver and had all the accidents, which I was never allowed to forget,' says Seeger. MacColl had learnt to drive during his brief spell as a car mechanic in the 1930s, and had never taken a test. He drove fast and erratically. 'It's astounding that he didn't kill us,' she recalls.[5]

Wherever possible they avoided the new motorways, preferring to be off the beaten track. They would sing, talk, or sit in silence – neither liked background music. The tours were long, gruelling and involved weeks away from home, but the daytimes were usually surprisingly tranquil. Often they'd have a big pub lunch – they were early enthusiasts of *The Good Beer Guide*. If they were staying in a hotel near the folk club, they'd have a rest in the afternoon before limbering up with pre-concert vocal exercises. If not, they'd go for a walk or sit in the car with the *Guardian* crossword. Getting an early evening meal was difficult in 1960s Britain, and they ate a lot of curry, and fish and chips; sometimes they used their portable stove and cooked fry-ups on the

car's backseat. At around seven they made their way to the venue and
carried the guitar, banjo, autoharp, dulcimer, concertina and mobile
record stall up to the club room. 'I'd walk into these clubs virtually like
a general walking into a battle zone,' Peggy remembers: 'I'd rearrange
the whole room. Sometimes they'd have the performance space in the
most ridiculous place ... I think I was probably a little bit unpleasant
at times.'[6]

Their tour in late autumn 1964 is fairly typical of these years. They
played a cluster of dates within a hundred miles of home in early
November – Colchester, St Albans, Sussex University – returning to
Beckenham after each. On 18 November an audience of five hundred
heard them at the Surbiton Assembly Rooms.[7] The following day they
flew to Belfast for a concert; the night after that they appeared at
Dublin's 1,100-seat Stephen's Green Cinema, where the show was
opened by Luke Kelly, later The Dubliners' charismatic front-man. The
raucous Dublin crowd needed some disciplining. 'Is there a psychologist
in the house?' MacColl growled into his microphone. 'He'd make a
bundle here.'[8] They returned to England and rounded off the tour
with eight concerts in the more orderly folk clubs in East Anglia,
Lincolnshire, the Midlands and London.

Their fee was expensive for smaller clubs; they tried to give audiences
their money's worth, frequently staying on-stage for over two hours.
The performances were underpinned by a seriousness that divided
audiences: some found them compellingly professional, some arrogant.
As in Dublin, audiences who talked through a performance were
chastised. Those who expected the showbiz ritual of an encore were
often disappointed. Singing along with choruses was encouraged, but
out-of-tune participation was off-limits: MacColl and Seeger would
conduct an impromptu chorus rehearsal to put things right.[9] After the
show they chatted to the audience and sold records. Often they spent
the night in the homes of club organisers and sat up late talking: 'We
stayed in the houses of miners, textile workers, fascinating people,'
Seeger remembers.[10] Sometimes they were harassed by overbearing
hosts, kept awake by protruding bed-springs, itchy sheets, barking
dogs and screaming children. Some mornings they lingered over
breakfast and talked of future meetings, on others they were keen to
get on their way.

1. Betsy Miller
The photograph was taken in the 1960s

2. Will Miller

3. Jimmie Miller as a young boy

4. Jimmie and Betsy in the early 1920s

5. Jimmie Miller in 1937

6. Joan Littlewood in 1934

7. Theatre Workshop at Kendal in 1945
Howard Goorney is second from the left at the back; David Scase is on his left;
Joan Littlewood is third from the left on the front row; Gerry Raffles sits to her
left. MacColl is on the far right.

8. Ewan MacColl, Kristin Lind and Howard Goorney
Enjoying a Marx Brothers moment at Kendal, 1945.

9. Joan Littlewood and Ewan MacColl
Theatre Workshop's overseas tour, 1948.

10. Joan Littlewood
Publicity photograph,
early 1950s.

11. Ewan MacColl
Publicity photograph,
early 1950s.

12. Ewan MacColl's 1954 anthology of industrial
folk-ballads
The tie-in record was released three years later.

13. Peggy Seeger, Ewan MacColl and Fitzroy Coleman
Performing at the Ballads and Blues Club at the Princess Louise, High Holborn, 1957/8.

4. MacColl in Moscow, 1957    15. Betsy and Ewan on holiday, 1960

5. Seeger and MacColl
ublicity shot, early 1960s.
hotograph by Russell Jarvis.

17. Relaxing at home in Beckenham,
early 1960s

18. Bob Dylan takes the floor at the Singers' Club, 22 December 1962.
A.L. Lloyd sits behind. MacColl is to Dylan's left. Photograph by Brian Shuel.

19. Performing at the Singers' Club, late 1960s

20. MacColl at the Singers' Club, 1968

21. MacColl and Seeger
On-stage in Havana, Cuba, 1967.

22. Ewan and Kitty MacColl, 1973

23. Promotional handbill for a Peggy Seeger
and Ewan MacColl concert
Newcastle University Theatre, 1974.

24. MacColl on the hills, 1970s

25. Ewan and Kirsty MacColl, late 1980s

**26. MacColl's last tour**
East Berlin, February 1988.

ᲒᲜᏏᏏ

MacColl liked the underground cultural energy of folk clubs; after the first of their two 1964 British folk club tours he reported being 'greatly impressed with the standard of both singers and audiences'.[11] He was less impressed by the mid-1960s American folk-boom in which a number of folk-scene artists enjoyed mainstream pop success: Bob Dylan's records were now outselling those of seasoned crooners like Tony Bennett and Andy Williams;[12] superstar folk trio Peter, Paul and Mary were touring Britain (where they spoke familiarly of 'Ewan and Peggy');[13] pop stars including Ringo Starr and Mick Jagger were invited to make predictions about the likelihood of an equivalent British folk-boom.[14] For MacColl, pop music remained a bourgeois cultural imposition, a retreat from the musical complexity and grounded realism of the music 'created by the people or adapted by them from other kinds of music'.[15] Those who bought into pop were selling their birthright for a mess of pottage, and the folk-boom represented the commodification of folk music by Tin Pan Alley. The products served up were, he insisted, slick, stripped of all complexity, gutted of politics and created 'a false idea of what folk music is'.[16] It was time, he warned, for American folk musicians to decide 'whether their objective is to "improve" pop music or to extend the tradition'; it was a mistake 'to imagine that both objectives are identical'.[17] He hoped that the hyped folk-boom would 'end as quickly as possible', and he did what he could to help it on its way.[18]

ᲒᲜᏏᏏ

The oozing, feel-good 'togetherness' of the American folk scene appalled MacColl (it reminded him of the Nuremburg Rallies), and he detected in the gushing prose of the folk press another manifestation of the same phenomenon.[19] 'The folk magazines', he wrote in the foremost American folk magazine *Sing Out!*:

> seem to compete with each other in the hunt for superlatives with which to describe Bobby and Phil and Tom and Peter and Buffy ... *Sing Out!*, which should have acquired dignity with age, is not exempt from criticism in this matter. It has, on occasion, published reviews ... which would not have been out of place in fanzines published by the Brownies.[20]

MacColl believed that rigorous music journalism had a role to play in the struggle for a more nourishing popular music, a view shared by communist journalist Karl Dallas, always keen to bring MacColl's acerbic tones to the pages of his *Melody Maker* folk column. 'Folk music has reached its 1905,' Dallas wrote in 1963. 'But it's got a very long way to go before it reaches 1917.'[21] Later that year Dallas launched his own magazine, *Folk Music*, which aimed to play a small part in the ongoing musical revolution. Dallas went to see MacColl, who gladly lent assistance.[22]

ೞ೮೧

MacColl used the new forum to issue brickbats and settle old scores. Peggy's legal husband, Alex Campbell, was a likeable and accomplished performer who made no secret of regarding folksinging as a branch of the entertainment industry. He wasn't intimidated by MacColl, and there was no love lost between them. 'I deplore the bigots on the scene who cry that one shouldn't sing American or French songs,' Campbell wrote in the first issue of *Folk Music*, with MacColl obviously in mind. 'I hope that the years to come will see a wiping away of the pompous humbug that seems to permeate the revival at the moment.'[23] MacColl retaliated with libellous invective – 'If [Alex Campbell] is ever driven to play Patience he'll have a hell of a time preventing himself from cheating.' He followed through with all the condescension he could summon – 'we played a leading part in creating the [folk] scene ... Campbell was a schoolboy at the time'.[24]

MacColl also invented a pseudonymous alter ego, Jack Speedwell (a pun on the name Jonathan Swift), to lampoon individuals and trends he considered dangerous to the revival. Less a *nom de plume* than a fully formed literary creation, Speedwell was bumbling and avuncular, a philistine and prude with a large vocabulary and a tiny mind. His columns endorsed all that MacColl despised; Speedwell's purple prose encomiums were calculated to render ridiculous whatever they praised. Speedwell disliked songs about politics or sex: 'no more songs about bombs and racial intolerance', he implored in one column, 'no more of those beastly and malicious attacks on the best of all possible representatives of the best of all possible governments'.[25] He celebrated folk magazines for conscientiously protecting the reader from 'the awful malaise of cerebration'.[26] 'I love, for instance, after a hard day of the office,' he wrote in one column:

to take refuge in my basement playroom where, surrounded by my discs and my folk mag files I can, like Marcel Proust, conjure up remembrances of things past … Proust was able, merely by sniffing the faint odours of a duchess' old hat, to recapture the past; I achieve similar results by leafing through copies of the folk mags. They are so delightfully simple, every word breathes a kind of innocent wonder as if their writer had been startled by the discovery that words can be strung together to form sentences.[27]

When invited to comment on Ewan MacColl, Speedwell had no hesitation: MacColl's influence on the revival was 'disastrous'. 'His preoccupation with the working class has inhibited the development of folk music,' wrote Speedwell, and 'made the revival a minority movement like jazz or chamber music, when it could have been a form of mass entertainment as important as rhythm and blues.'[28]

CʒՑ

The highly competitive MacColl harboured irrational animosity for Bob Dylan, whose critically acclaimed British tours of 1964 and 1965 established a vocal fan-base ranging from schoolgirls to university professors. Though his familiarity with Dylan's work was clearly slight, MacColl sternly took issue with this 'youth of mediocre talent' whose success appeared to symbolise the convergence of the folk scene and the culture industry. 'Only a non-critical audience,' Ewan MacColl wrote with Speedwellesque pomposity, 'could have fallen for such tenth rate drivel.'[29] It worried MacColl that 'we're going to have lots of copies of Dylan – one foot in folk and one in pop'.[30] MacColl attacked Dylan on two fronts simultaneously. In a carefully orchestrated row in the pages of *Melody Maker*, MacColl dismissed Dylan as 'the perfect symbol of the anti-artist in our society' whose songs had 'no more passion in them than Mrs Dale's Diary'.[31] Meanwhile, in the pages of *Folk Music*, Jack Speedwell gave his views on 'Bobby's recordings':

> For a long time, I must confess, I found them disappointing, and the more I played them the more banal they sounded. I tried comparing them with some of our traditional songs and ballads and found them wanting. I compared them with the works of Valery, Rilke, Lorca, Blake, Donne, Skelton and others, but, alas that didn't work either.
>
> In a great blaze of inspiration I leapt to my bookcase and took down one of my most treasured possessions: the well-thumbed volume of the works of the great McGonigal. It was then I *knew* that in Bobby we had a genius of almost equal stature.[32]

Speedwell's true identity was a carefully guarded secret, though among friends MacColl was open in his admiration for the column. 'He read them out to us,' Sandra Kerr remembers, 'and obviously enjoyed his own writing enormously.'[33] The satire proved less of a pleasure for Karl Dallas, who was widely rumoured to be Jack Speedwell's creator. 'It caused a great deal of embarrassment to me,' he remembers. '[MacColl] attacked all of my friends. Some of them took it very personally.'[34]

CℬℬↃ

The motivations behind MacColl and Seeger's major mid-1960s project, 'The Critics Group', are complex and overlapping, although certain facts are clear. MacColl's unwavering ideological agenda – that folk music was workers' culture to be protected from the bourgeoisie and safeguarded for 'the day when workers came into their own' – hardened in the climate of the folk-boom.[35] The purist and political wing of the revival debated the dangers of commercialism, questions of club policy and how clubs were run. Beckenham became a focal point for such discussions.[36] Informal conferences were held, bringing together Singers' Club regulars and like-minded folk activists whom MacColl and Seeger had met on their British club tours.[37] 'Twenty, thirty, forty people would descend on Stanley Avenue,' Peggy Seeger remembers. 'We'd have three shifts of spaghetti lunch for everyone. It was chaos. But we'd talk about where the revival was going.'[38]

Many younger singers were persuaded by the MacColl/Seeger analysis that the performance of folk music was a serious matter demanding respectful analysis and careful development. Back in 1961 journalist Eric Winter had publicly criticised MacColl for not being a team player where the revival was concerned;[39] others now suggested that MacColl might form a study group to disseminate his expertise to a wider number of people.[40] MacColl and Seeger agreed in principle, and had been giving occasional workshops and lectures since the early 1960s.[41] Their initial reluctance to start a study group stemmed primarily from uncertainty about the form it should take. Sandra Kerr's stay at Stanley Avenue eased the situation: her tuition functioned as an experiment in how to teach skills relevant to folk performance. Towards the end of 1963 a small group began to assemble on a regular basis at Stanley Avenue.

From the outset, public relations weren't the group's strongest suit. There was confusion about how one joined, and some who expected

to be included felt put out when they weren't asked.[42] The entrance
criteria were also unclear. Creating better singers was always central to
the group's stated remit, and yet some who passed through the group
could barely carry a tune – a contradiction that inevitably raised the
eyebrows of MacColl's many adversaries. MacColl and Seeger looked
for recruits with a commitment to traditional music and an enquiring
mind; MacColl, who was forever sensitive to the charge that the folk
scene was a middle-class affair, favoured those from working-class
backgrounds. 'I had a love of the music,' member Jim Carroll told
me, 'but he certainly took it into consideration that I was a left-wing
worker. My father had been in Spain [in the International Brigade].
He jumped at that.'[43]

The precise nature of MacColl and Seeger's relationship with the
group was also ill-defined. In public, MacColl would describe the
venture as a 'mutual aid group', and yet there was no doubt about
who was in charge.[44] 'Ewan was the guru,' Sandra Kerr told me.[45] While
MacColl talked of 'the group', those who attended always talked,
more accurately, of 'classes'. The problem was made worse by the
decision to call themselves the 'Critics Group'. Supplied by Charles
Parker, the name served further to arouse the suspicions of those who
regarded MacColl and Seeger as arrogant.[46] Parker intended 'Critics
Group' to suggest rigorous and democratic self-scrutiny, with overtones
of Marxist traditions in auto-criticism. It only fuelled rumours that
MacColl's new group was a bunch of know-alls who spent their time
passing judgement on others.

CB℘

The stalwarts who congregated in the Beckenham workroom on one,
two or three evenings a week in 1964 were mainly in their early twenties.
They were typically from working-class backgrounds, had been caught
up in the skiffle craze, and had subsequently renounced American-based
music in favour of British or Irish traditions. Left-wing credentials
weren't compulsory, although right-wingers were unlikely to seek out
MacColl's company. Some of the Critics had been to grammar school,
almost none to university. There were schoolteachers and trainee social
workers; others worked at trades. Early members included Sandra Kerr
and her husband-to-be, John Faulkner, a young electrician's mate and
Singers' Club regular who greatly admired MacColl. 'I found Ewan

very magnetic,' Faulkner recalled. 'I wanted to be close to this talent.'[47]
Glaswegian socialist Gordon McCulloch was another skilful performer
who appeared regularly at the Singers' Club and, like Faulkner, had
been invited to sing on the radio ballads. Irishman Luke Kelly was
also attracted by MacColl's aura. Born in 1940 to a working-class
Dublin family, Kelly was converted to communism and folk music in
Birmingham, where he'd taken night classes run by Marxist classics
professor George Thomson. '[MacColl] was a sort of cult figure,' Kelly
would later say. 'If you didn't know him very well, you tended to be
afraid of him because of his reputation. But when I finally got to know
the man I found him very generous with his time, with his songs.'[48]
Frankie Armstrong from Workington in Cumbria was one of the few
women in the group. The forty-five-year-old Charles Parker cut a
conspicuous figure among the youthful circle, but was eager to continue
working with MacColl. Parker had a high opinion of MacColl's genius,
and an eye forever fixed on posterity: wherever possible, he taped those
evenings in the crowded Beckenham workroom.[49]

cs&>

It wasn't a question of MacColl imposing longstanding views on those
he referred to as 'the new young singers'; the Critics Group created an
impetus to develop ideas, some of which were aired in magazine articles
and radio broadcasts. MacColl's key preoccupation at this time was
that folksong had once been 'an integral and important part of everyday
life' in Britain. 'The traditional patterns of oral culture were shattered
by the industrial revolution,' he stated; 'long established modes of
expression were disrupted; and the mass circulation of newspapers,
films, radio and television have disrupted them even further.'[50] 'The
tradition' – both a body of songs created or adapted by the people *and*
a manner of singing those songs – had become 'run down', 'decayed'
or even 'moribund'.[51] Surviving folksingers like Sam Larner, Harry
Cox and Jeannie Robertson had carried the songs through tumultuous
cultural change, and were worthy of great respect. Their performances
provided an intriguing glimpse of the music's former grandeur, but also
inevitably reflected the tradition's eroded state.[52]

The challenge was to revitalise and 'recreate a tradition ... complete
enough to reflect the constantly changing twentieth-century scene'.[53]
As so often, the direction forward was through the past. MacColl

wanted to know what the tradition was like at its height (he was vague
on precisely when this was) and to work towards its reconstruction.
Much could be learned, he argued, from song-carriers like Cox and
Larner, even if their singing styles were fragments of a broken whole,
and he advocated the serious analysis of source recordings. It was
MacColl's belief that 'folk singing is distinguished from other kinds
of singing by certain stylistic features', many of which transcended
geographical, cultural and linguistic boundaries.[54] So in terms of singing
style, MacColl said, Norfolk's Harry Cox had more in common with
folk singers from Spain and Syria, or even an Azerbaijan muezzin,
than with a British pop artist.[55] Music from faraway traditions was
thus a useful stylistic model in the re-creation of the British tradition.[56]
(MacColl didn't say how this strategy squared with the Singers' Club
policy of honouring the specificity of national musical traditions.) He
talked enthusiastically of oral traditions in Romania and Bulgaria, in
which young ballad singers were apprenticed for seven years, and where
journeyman bards could produce Homeric-style improvisations around
traditional forms. These traditions, he argued, gave an indication of
how the British tradition was in the past, and what it might become
again in the future; the ultimate objective was that the Critics Group
should overcome the historical and cultural force of modernity, industrialisation and mass literacy, and somehow recover these bardic skills.[57]
'Our job is to try and extend ourselves both vocally and intellectually,'
MacColl told the Critics Group in the spring of 1964, 'so that we can
transform the best of the music of the past, or rather make it speak
for our time too.'[58] As ever, he thought on a grand scale. He wanted to
see the people's music returned to the people in the form of 'a genuine
movement of popular art', and he regarded the Critics Group as central
to the task in hand.[59] 'Although we're interested in you personally, we
are infinitely more interested in you as teachers,' he told the group. He
hoped they would study under him before setting up classes in their
own areas. 'When we've done this, when we have a dozen classes, it
may be in a year's time, functioning all over Great Britain, then we can
begin to say we're moving.'[60]

୯୫ଥ୦

The Critics Group was always a mix of grand designs and more
grounded performance training. MacColl had little talent for producing

realistic plans or cool-headed historical analysis – he tended to start from his own beliefs and select the facts that best backed him up – but his credentials as a magnetising performer were indisputable. He set about teaching the group everything he knew, and got things under way with a reading list comprising ninety-three books on folksong, fifteen picaresque novels, sixty plays and twenty collections of poetry. He rounded off the list with critical works from Engels, Christopher Caudwell and George Thomson.[61] 'It was a mind-boggling list,' recalled Frankie Armstrong. 'Ewan, in his exaggerated fashion, assured us that we could not consider ourselves serious, educated people if we hadn't read every book on the list.'[62]

He drew extensively on his theatre training, and taught them the relaxation exercises he and Littlewood had used in the days of Theatre Union. (MacColl always maintained that there was no need for physical manifestations of on-stage nerves – serious actors or singers should train themselves to identify and eliminate tension.) He taught them the vocal exercises that Theatre Workshop had learned from Australian voice coach Nelson Illingworth. He made them think about how to prepare the mind and voice immediately prior to a performance, and how to create the appropriate impression when walking on and off stage.

The teachings of dance guru Rudolf Laban had been central to Theatre Workshop's balletic aesthetic. Laban categorised the body's physical movement into a series of 'efforts' – thrusting, slashing, flicking, pressing, floating, dabbing, gliding and so on – and tabulated the different ways in which these 'efforts' might be carried out (direct or indirect, quick or slow, weak or strong). Theatre Workshop had used Laban's work to make actors think about how they moved, and to help them develop the flexibility necessary to represent a character at the level of physical movement. For MacColl, voice was an extension of the body – he believed that, with a little adaptation, Laban's system also provided a concise vocabulary for analysing vocal effects.[63] Members of the Critics Group would listen to recordings of traditional singers and identify the efforts being used; they would then attempt to imitate the sounds, using Laban's grid to help them. 'It was a wonderful shorthand,' says Sandra Kerr, who now teaches folk music at Newcastle University. 'It's immediate, it's graphic – I still use it all the time with my singers, especially choirs.'[64]

MacColl always maintained that there was far more to performing a folksong than learning the words and tune. Vocal technique was important; so was emotional and intellectual identification with the material. When singing a traditional ballad, he told the Critics Group:

I find it necessary to close my eyes and shut the audience out, and to identify, either with some character in the song, or with the kind of person I think may have originally sung the song, or even may have created the song. This means that you have to equip yourself with a fair amount of the data about the period in which the song was created ... say this song was perhaps written in 1736, written by a ploughman in Dorset. What was it like? I wonder what it felt for a bloke like that to create a song like this, and all the other people who contributed to the song later. All the other men and women who polished it over generations ... suddenly you find yourself filled with an extraordinary sense of compassion and respect for all those people who went before. And suddenly you find yourself in the tradition – you're with them. And at that moment you also disappear in a strange way, and the song really takes over ... the audience comes with you.[65]

MacColl believed that for singers and actors alike the best performances were animated by such moments, and he challenged group members to forge equivalent identification with their repertoires. The writings of acting theorist Constantin Stanislavski – also used extensively during Theatre Union and Theatre Workshop – were now adapted and presented to the Critics Group. During meetings MacColl might set up role-play exercises to encourage a singer to develop a clear image of the character whose viewpoint was being expressed in a song – here he drew extensively on 'Imagination', the fourth chapter of Stanislavski's manual *An Actor Prepares*.[66] When a singer was having trouble with a particular song, MacColl might devise an acting exercise to free up the performance.[67] On one occasion MacColl criticised a singer for performing a bawdy song without relish for the narrative: to inject some zest, he made the singer imagine he was performing before a drunken music-hall audience, a part played raucously by the rest of the group.[68] Where possible, he encouraged them to activate personal experiences and feelings in performance, what Stanislavski called 'emotion memory'.[69] 'It was challenging,' remembers Sandra Kerr. 'It demanded a lot of emotional input, very personal stuff.'[70] Like Joan Littlewood, MacColl had a ruthless streak. He never held back if he thought a singer had more than they were giving him. He'd flatter, mimic, goad, bully and snarl – whatever he thought was necessary to release a moving performance.

CঙB০

It was MacColl's belief that the folk revival suffered from its cosy, non-critical atmosphere – whenever performers at the Singers' Club asked him what he'd thought of their performance, he always told them directly, and made enemies in the process.[71] The centrepiece of Critics Group meetings was, naturally, 'the criticisms'. With the exception of MacColl and Seeger, who were exempt from the process (something Peggy now regrets), all members were periodically required to give a thirty- or forty-minute performance, and received detailed critical feedback from the rest of the group.[72] Every aspect of the performance was scrutinised – stage manner, song introductions, singing style, instrumental accompaniment. They were often painful encounters – Gordon McCulloch described it as a formulaic 'trial by ordeal';[73] Luke Kelly was among the first to leave the Critics Group.[74] The 'criticisms' always concluded with MacColl's analysis, in which he'd criticise the criticisms offered so far, before offering his own. He'd say things like, 'Really, what disturbs me about this evening is that so few of you have been so completely non-critical'; his own verdict was usually the most forthright. 'It was only in the last song', MacColl said during one feedback session on Charles Parker's performance, 'where he finally broke through to produce a voice like a normal human being.'[75] 'For me it was a disappointing performance,' he'd say on another occasion. 'It lacked presence. I was unmoved. I was not entertained. I was given no facts I didn't know before … I can't even remember the songs anymore.'[76] 'He had the ability to make you feel like a small heap of shit,' says Sandra Kerr, 'but when the energy was positive it was an extraordinary inspiration … He was generous when other people gave great performances, never jealous of it, he loved it.'[77] His summing-up criticism would often segue into long, off-the-cuff lectures in which he'd settle back in his leather chair and talk about Greek theatre, Marxist aesthetics, anthropology, the origins of language, cathedral design, the radio ballads, punctuating his lecture with snatches of song.[78] They were impressive performances of erudition. 'He had an immensely forceful personality with an emphatic way of speaking which gave him an air of great authority,' recalls Frankie Armstrong.[79] Jim Carroll still recalls how the lectures made him feel: 'you'd walk a foot above the pavement for the rest of the week. You would end up buzzing. It was special.'[80]

ⓒ੪ੴ

One of MacColl's ideas was that the Critics Group should run a network of folk clubs where their ethos could prevail. Though the reality never matched the empire of strongholds stretching through MacColl's mind, new clubs were established at the Lamb and Flag on Garrick Street and later in Stratford East and Croydon.[81] Just as importantly, the Critics Group's youthful energy freshened up the Singers' Club, which had experienced some difficulties after a miserable homeless spell in the winter of 1963.[82]

Pub refurbishments and unco-operative landlords ensured that roving around central London premises would always be part of the club's story, but in early 1964 they settled at the Royal Hotel, Woburn Place for their relaunch.[83] They were now to be sponsored by the London Co-operative Society (where MacColl had some contacts). The Singers' Club brand of historically rooted popular culture fitted the Society's educational remit, and for years to come the Co-op Education Department would provide administrative assistance and a small subsidy.[84] Stabilised by the new sponsorship money and revitalised by the roster of Critics Group talent, the Singers' Club reached the height of its influence during the mid-1960s.

For five shillings (£3.30 today) per week, Singers' Club audiences in 1965 and 1966 got to hear MacColl and Seeger, now at their musical best, around thirty-five times per year.[85] They also heard established revival singers, such as Enoch Kent, Bob Davenport, Anne Briggs, The Watersons and Martin Carthy. 'Traditional' singer Joe Heaney was a resident; Donegal's Paddy Tunney, a fine, lyrical singer who'd served seven years for his nationalist activities in the 1940s, also appeared a couple of times. New acts like flamboyant three-part harmony outfit The Young Tradition took the stage alongside the Critics Group singers, and the programme wasn't restricted to British and Irish acts. Clarence Ashley was a banjoist-cum-tobacco farmer from Tennessee who'd worked in prominent bluegrass outfits in the 1940s – he appeared on 1 May 1966.[86] Seventy-year-old African-American blues guitar legend,

Reverend Gary Davis, was booked for 30 July 1966; sitar player Ravi Shankar had appeared a fortnight earlier.[87]

The club took itself seriously as working towards 'the revival of a healthy folk culture' and discussion events were organised to explore pressing questions.[88] One such event, held at the John Snow pub on 27 May 1966, ended in predictable acrimony when singer Bob Davenport expressed the opinion that the revival's version of folk music was a middle-class affair.[89] It wasn't a view that MacColl could tolerate, and he would later quote statistics that established beyond doubt that the majority of the Singers' Club audience were manual workers aged twenty-four or under.[90] 'He always said that they were 90 per cent workers', remembers Singers' Club volunteer Pat Mackenzie, 'but they weren't and that was wishful thinking.'[91] Christy Moore, who performed at the Union Tavern in July 1968, has fond memories of the club's untypical clientele and cultish atmosphere:

> The capacity was maybe 150, and there was a small raised stage. This was not a folk club audience, but an assorted gathering of radicals and intellectuals and anarchists and banjo pickers and singers and rebels come to pay homage at the shrine of McColl [sic] and quite rightly so, too.... I'll never forget McColl [sic] for recognising my nervousness and giving me a few words of comfort and a dram or two of whiskey to settle me down.... The audience were a strange lot, and took their lead in all things from the Buddha of Ballads. If McColl [sic] liked it, they went wild, and if McColl [sic] was not impressed, neither were the minions. I had a great night and nearly got off with a Trotskyist.[92]

෴

MacColl's creative habits had been formed in his theatre days: even as a songwriter, his best work seldom emerged from emotion recollected in tranquillity, but when he had a deadline to meet. After writing his last play *So Long at the Fair* (1957), he'd channelled all his creative energy into the radio ballads; with the demise of the series he missed the creative surges unleashed by the big productions. Tour dates, Singers' Club appearances and Critics Group meetings were all very well, but never enough. More than he'd ever admit, it disturbed him that friends from his former life thought he was wasting his time singing in pubs; he was especially raw about the anti-folk diatribes of Hugh MacDiarmid, who now publicly lampooned MacCollite 'left-wing advocates of regression to the simple outpourings of illiterates and backward peasants'.[93] He also felt aggrieved by the recent success of Theatre Workshop, the new toast of the West End and Broadway with their most successful show to date, *Oh! What A Lovely War* (1963). With its mix of catchy period tunes, sassy dances and savage irony, the revue-style smash-hit had consolidated Littlewood's reputation as the most original and iconoclastic producer of her generation. MacColl didn't detect much irony in *Oh! What A Lovely War*, only political compromise. He regarded the show as a bastard offspring of early political productions like *Last Edition* (Littlewood admitted the influence).[94] The mention of *Oh! What A Lovely War* always set his heart pounding. 'You couldn't get near the Theatre Royal for Bentleys and Mercedes,' he'd say sourly. 'It was at this point we could say farewell to the dream of creating a working-class theatre.'[95]

೫೦

He took on various projects, including advisory work on *Landmarks* (1964), a radio ballad-influenced six-part documentary series broadcast on the BBC Midland Home Service.[96] MacColl's signature tune, 'The Ballad of Accounting', owed more to the songs of Brecht and Eisler than to British folk tradition, but became a centrepiece of MacColl/Seeger concerts through the 1960s and 1970s. He wrote the score for BBC producer Philip Donnellan's television film *The Irishmen: An Impression of Exile* (1965); MacColl's updated versions of Irish folksongs were the strongest element in this radio ballad-style television documentary.[97] He wrote and presented *The Song Carriers*, a fourteen-part radio series produced by Charles Parker that paraded the talents of Peggy Seeger and the Critics Group to illustrate MacColl's increasingly unorthodox theories of folk music.[98] MacColl assumed the tone of a disappointed schoolmaster to chastise revival singers whom he thought had lost their way. 'During the last couple of years ... he has developed a number of irritating vocal idiosyncrasies,' he observed of his former protégé Louis Killen. 'If he can rid himself of these annoying habits he could still be a force to be reckoned with.'[99] The BBC didn't share Charles Parker's view that MacColl's ideas were 'dynamite' and deserving of a national audience on the Third Programme: they consigned the programme to regional release in Parker's BBC Midlands patch.[100]

MacColl also wrote his first full-length play in seven years, *Ours the Fruit* (1964). Commissioned by the new sponsors of the Singers'

Club, the play plotted the story of the co-operative movement from its eighteenth-century origins to the present day global Co-operative Commonwealth (MacColl explained that in 1964 the Co-op numbered 850 retail stores and 13,000,000 members in Britain alone).[101] Staged as a one-off Sunday afternoon show at Theatre Royal, Drury Lane to mark International Co-operative Day, the script played to MacColl's strengths as a writer.[102] There were strong, funny songs, knockabout pantomime-style set-pieces, sound-effects borrowed from radio, and a clear political line. It was a community show: amateur drama groups and choirs from Hainault, Romford and Barking were involved. Peggy arranged and directed the music. For an orchestra MacColl reconvened the old radio ballad team including Alf Edwards and Bruce Turner; for solo singers he used Critics including Luke Kelly, Gordon McCulloch and John Faulkner. A hastily rehearsed affair, *Ours the Fruit* was never likely to grab the headlines, but the *Daily Worker* dutifully sent along a reporter who praised the show for 'a polish many professionals would envy'.[103] The under-stimulated forty-nine-year-old MacColl thoroughly enjoyed the adrenalin rush brought on by shaping the show. It seems to have stirred up some of the old desires about bringing radical theatre to the people. He again rued the decline of Theatre Workshop from political pioneers to West End jesters, and allowed himself to envisage a new and better group who wouldn't lose their way.[104]

∞

Within a year he had the Critics Group in greasepaint. A tension between reluctant realism and grand plans would be a feature of the years to follow, but for the time being he kept his feet on the ground and worked from the facts: here was a group of talented young performers whose apprenticeships already involved extensive acting techniques; they needed as much exposure as possible; nothing matched acting experience for learning about audiences.[105] Didn't folk clubs need to widen their horizons and become cultural centres? The integration of theatre, he argued, 'might be investigated with great advantage to the revival'.[106]

He started to investigate. Officially at least, MacColl's creative ventures now had to be justified in terms of tradition. Traditional mumming plays, sometimes called guising or pace-egging plays, were suitably ancient in provenance to provide promising material for his new outfit. He noted that the plays originated with the birth of drama in primitive seasonal rituals, and that variants of the basic plot structure, in which a hero (usually St George) is killed and resurrected, recurred throughout Western drama. 'Their structure is such', wrote MacColl, 'that they can easily be adapted to the contemporary scene without any reduction of their traditional message.' Updating them was 'a process sanctioned by history'.[107] Why the same leeway wasn't usually permitted with folksong was left unclear, but MacColl recognised that these traditionally short, non-naturalistic musical pieces were within the artistic reach of an amateur group. Punctuated by song and music, they were ideally suited to folk club performance.[108] He'd soon written his own pace-egging play.

He recast St George as a leather-clad biker, originally played by a young butcher, Ted Culver ('I need no seaside punch-ups to enhance my fame,' Culver sang, 'For I am known to one and all – St. George is my name').[109] MacColl revelled in the word-play opportunities created by characters with names like Double Talk and Captain Slashall, and by the clear-cut distinctions between good and evil – villainous characters were dressed to resemble representatives of the American military-industrial complex and Harold Wilson's cabinet. MacColl and Seeger wrote a couple of new songs, the Critics Group was put through their paces at Beckenham, and the show was performed at the Singers' Club in May 1965, then repeated over the summer.[110] Buoyed by the positive reception, the Critics spent accumulated weekly subs on a van, and toured folk clubs between Southampton and Stoke on Trent that October.[111] MacColl was proud of them. For years he'd griped about the execrable standards of music in British theatre, and he was encouraged by the ease with which the group made the transition from singing to acting. 'It's a testament to the training he'd given us', says Sandra Kerr:

> We could take direction. We had always been fed these stories of Theatre Workshop, the Commedia dell'arte, how every actor should be able to sing, dance, act, juggle and play an instrument ... We had heard all about that, and seen what we were aiming for.[112]

⋘⋙

The next show formed in MacColl's mind before the first was fully under way. Paucity of ambition had never been one of his faults: deprived of an outlet for his restless creativity and excited by the talent at his disposal, he thought big. Once again, he wanted the show to have some grounding in Britain's folk customs. He found in the medieval Festival of Fools a suitable precedent: orgiastic excess and anti-establishment views fitted nicely with the mid-1960s zeitgeist. He traced the genealogy of the pagan midwinter festival, in which the powers-that-be granted temporary licence to carnivalesque indulgence, back to the Babylonian Sacaea and Roman Saturnalia; he followed it forward to the accounts of outraged Puritans and its outlawing in the mid-seventeenth century. He took what he needed. It had been common for revellers to crown a King of Jest, Lord of Misrule or Abbott of Unreason as a symbolic figurehead.[113] His idea was to use these traditions as a dramatic frame through which contemporary events could be focused. *Last Edition* functioned as a model. As then, his script would be based on reports culled from the press. 'The mass-media should assist us in our understanding of society,' noted one *Festival of Fools* programme, 'but often they only confuse us. Perhaps by turning the world upside down … we can see the world clearly.'[114]

Theatre Workshop, MacColl maintained, had made the mistake of doing business with the establishment. He wanted his new venture to be part of the 1960s folk scene's underground energy: like folk clubs, the show would happen in the pub. The Co-op was tapped for funds, the 250-seat Singers' Club room at New Merlin's Cave, Margery Street, near King's Cross was hired, and two additional stages and lighting rigs were built. (Here too *Last Edition* provided the blueprint.) With a sheath of newspaper cuttings collected by Critics Group members, MacColl retreated to his workroom and wrote the script, resuming the old pattern of twenty-hour days, meals at his desk, coffee jugs and an endless chain of Senior Service cigarettes.

Rehearsals began in November 1965. Peggy was in charge of printing scripts, co-ordinating transport and the complex logistics of arranging rehearsals: she issued brusque and frequent newsletters keeping the twenty-strong cast abreast of arrangements.[115] Parallel rehearsal sessions were held four or five times a week in Stanley Avenue and New Merlin's Cave; John Faulkner remembers the 'military fashion' in which the cast was drilled.[116] MacColl expected total commitment: sometimes oblivious to family lives and day jobs, he made phone calls late at night to impart news of script changes.[117] As the production grew closer, additional members of the Singers' Club audience were recruited to help with publicity and front-of-house work. In the best tradition of pantomime, MacColl wanted twelve performances between Boxing Night and 9 January. The press release hailed the show as 'the most important event in the Folk Music revival since rural music took root on the city'. The *Festival of Fools*, it boasted, would 'return to the people an old form of folk theatre sparked with new directions and new meanings for contemporary society'.[118]

Around 2,500 folk-revivalists, radicals and in-the-know theatregoers huddled into New Merlin's Cave over those twelve nights. The room was cluttered with stages, sound equipment, lighting rigs, musical instruments and beer glasses. The show was slick, sharp and funny. It opened with the whole cast taking to the three stages for a raucous rendition of a traditional wassail, or festive drinking songs (these moments made the *Festival of Fools* seem less a contemporary revue than pre-industrial England's nightmare of future history). Narrator Brian Pearson then sketched in the etymology of the term 'wassail' and glossed the festival's historical origins. Amid folk music and choreographed tomfoolery, the revellers elected schoolteacher Jim O'Connor for mock-coronation as Lord of Misrule (a threadbare dressing gown, colander and lavatory ball-cock substituted for gown, crown and sceptre). The show then cut to its main-matter, a series of sketches and songs covering the events of 1965, each played out in response to a news item relayed via Charles Parker's sound-deck.[119]

Vietnam dominated the headlines that year. Regular US bombardment of North Vietnam had begun in January;[120] the first assignment of US Marines was dispatched to Vietnam in March; by the *Festival of Fools*, American military presence had reached 200,000.[121] One song, written by an American Critic Group member currently based in London and resisting the draft, equated President Lyndon Johnson with Hitler. The point was rammed home with a song and scene about the Saigon public execution of a twenty-year-old suspected of collaboration with the Vietcong.[122]

The show was global in scope, but also reflected events closer to home. Back in March MacColl had read in the *Guardian* that capitalism was literally radicalising its own gravediggers: 'The Gravediggers' Song' was performed to honour the hundred workers from three Dublin cemeteries who'd downed tools over working conditions.[123] Harold

Wilson was the butt of many jokes: the fools lustily performed a song by Peggy Seeger that made sport of Wilson's claim to be the only British Prime Minister who cleaned his own shoes.[124] There were in-jokes about folk scene enemies, and 1930s-style spoofs of degenerate aristocrats. To maintain its traditional aspect, the show was punctuated by snatches of ancient weatherlore quarried from old almanacs, but the combination of topical songs, non-naturalistic lighting and blaring sound-effects created an overriding impression of cutting-edge political theatre. It concluded in classic agitprop style: one by one MacColl had the cast step out of their characters and introduce themselves according to their jobs. They were not professional actors, they told the audience, but house painters, schoolteachers, electricians, office workers and butchers. The narrator explained that it was not for the cast to create a tidy ending: the story they were telling was unfinished. (History, MacColl was saying, was made by people, though not in circumstances of their own choosing.) The future was in everyone's hands: 'The old year was a mess; the new one ... well, we can at least greet it with hope, using the words of those who have lived and died believing there is always room for hope.' The cast trooped off singing their wassail and the audience went down to the bar and street where they argued vociferously about the show's various provocations.[125] The controversies pleased MacColl. 'Theatre, when it is dealing with social issues,' he claimed, 'should hurt; you should leave the theatre feeling furious.'[126] Considering the last-minute rush, limited resources and inexperienced personnel, the *Festival of Fools* of 1965–6 was a solid success, and would serve as the template for subsequent New Merlin's Cave festivals in the early weeks of 1968, 1969, 1971 and 1972. The speed with which the company had been transformed from enthusiastic folksingers into a polished and highly efficient musical troupe further fed MacColl's still half-formed desire for a more ambitious theatrical venture.

⊂ॐ৩

The war in Vietnam not only loomed large in the *Festival of Fools* shows, but also in MacColl and Seeger's music. In July 1966 MacColl called for the folk revival's musical differences to be subordinated to political unity around Vietnam, and Karl Dallas and Gordon McCulloch constituted The Folksingers' Committee for Peace.[127] That

September the committee issued a press release for the immediate end of the American bombing and the withdrawal of all foreign troops. Signed by over sixty prominent folk-scene figures including singer Julie Felix and enigmatic guitar-hero Bert Jansch, the statement became the masthead for a range of activities that also drew on the talents of the Incredible String Band and Sandy Denny.[128] MacColl, Seeger and the more politically minded of the Critics Group appeared at a host of concerts and special club nights through 1966 and 1967: wherever possible MacColl distanced himself from fashionably nebulous anti-war sentiments and instead emphasised explicit support for the National Liberation in Vietnam, which he increasingly regarded as 'the vanguard to resist and destroy imperialism'.[129]

Back in 1954 he'd put his songwriting talents at the service of Vietnamese revolutionary hero in the 'Ballad of Ho Chi Minh'.[130] With its chant-like refrain of 'Ho, Ho, Ho Chi Minh', the song enjoyed a new lease of life on anti-Vietnam war demonstrations of the late 1960s including the explosive march on the American Embassy in London's Grosvenor Square in October 1968.[131] His outrage at America's brutality also found expression in a number of new songs, some of which were used in future Festival of Fools. He updated 'Yankee Doodle' with reference to carpet bombing and Agent Orange ('Yankee Doodle's got a plan / It's called "defoliation"; / Tried it out in Vietnam / To civilise the nation').[132] One of his big songs of the 1960s, 'Disc of Sun,' juxtaposed images of Vietnam's devastation with a pained howl of disbelief: it was performed in the 1967/8 Festival of Fools, recorded in 1968, became a standard at concerts, and was later issued on a record to raise funds for medical equipment in North Vietnam.[133] Some of MacColl's songs also enjoyed a currency in Vietnam itself. With the help of a Vietnamese newspaper with London staff sympathetic to the Liberation Front, a number of MacColl and Seeger compositions were translated and broadcast on The Voice of Vietnam radio station.[134] MacColl's 'Ballad of Ho Chi Minh' even reached the ears of Uncle Ho himself. Shortly before his death in 1969, Ho Chi Minh cabled MacColl a message of thanks.[135]

 C₃&O

Seeger and MacColl's celebrity in the fervent 1960s was a strange affair. On the one hand they were identified with the terminally unhip and relentlessly self-destructive purist sectarianism of the British folk revival; on the other their longstanding integrity and commitment to radical causes, not to mention Peggy's undimmed glamour, bestowed on them considerable radical chic. Prominent counter-culture figures such as Frank Zappa and Phil Ochs were among their fans, and MacColl always enjoyed describing how he'd met Mick Jagger at a 1968 music industry award ceremony and quizzed the *enfant terrible* about the political meaning of the counter-culture *tour de force*, 'Sympathy for the Devil'.[136] The names of Ewan MacColl and Peggy Seeger were at the fore whenever political music was discussed. In August 1967 Havana's Centro de la Cancion Protesta (Centre of Protest Song) organised a two-week festival, and they were invited as guests.

They never missed an opportunity to advance the development of the Critics Group, and additional invitations were secured for John Faulkner, Sandra Kerr, Terry Yarnell and Brian Pearson. Festival director Estelo Bravo was put at their disposal as translator, and took them to hear Castro's interminable speeches in the pounding Havana summer heat. They were introduced to Castro's ministers, including brother Raul, and Latin American poets, singers and musicians. They performed at conferences, concerts, in coffee co-operatives and leather workshops. If the language barrier muffled the impact of MacColl and Seeger's lyric-driven music, it didn't get in the way of MacColl's enthusiasm for the literacy programmes and healthcare provision created by the seven-year-old revolution. Always a man who appreciated fine smoking materials, he especially enjoyed the visit to a cigar factory.

ᘓᏸᎧ

'We actors are so accustomed to embroider facts with details drawn from our own imaginations,' wrote Constantin Stanislavski in MacColl's favourite theatre manual, 'that the habit is carried over into ordinary life.'[137] It was often carried into MacColl's, who always had a fine line in self-dramatisation. He regarded embellishment as part of the oral tradition, and the exotic Cuban trip furnished him with plenty of material. Within a few years he was claiming to have met Malcolm X (assassinated in 1965) on his 1967 trip to Havana and he would frequently adopt and adapt stories told to him by others.[138] When Sandra Kerr and John Faulkner returned from their extended stay in Cuba, for example, they told him two anecdotes. They'd met a young soldier full of tall tales about his time with Fidel, Che Guevara and the other *compañeros* in the Sierra Maestra; the soldier had reassured them that the proximity of mountains was also the key to revolution in Britain. Fidel had later visited the collectivised farm where they were staying, and Sandra had sung for him. MacColl enjoyed the stories, and within weeks was telling an amalgamated version, now with Ewan MacColl as the protagonist. The highlight of his Cuba trip, he would say, was when Fidel had dispatched his jeep to fetch MacColl from his Havana hotel in the dead of night. He and Fidel smoked and chatted together. Fidel had joked that however difficult things were for the British Left, as long as there were mountains, there was hope.[139]

 headings

The creative energy that animated his self-dramatisation also found expression in more new songs. In 1968 he wrote two about the Cuban Revolution: 'The Ballad of the Big Cigars' imagined the glowing tip of Fidel's Larrañaga cigar as the lodestar for fellow revolutionaries in Guatemala, Venezuela and Colombia; 'The Compañeros' took a boyish glee in the plucky revolution and recreated its derring-do in five jaunty verses.[140] Peggy also hit songwriting form in the late 1960s with 'Song of Choice' (later covered by Dick Gaughan), the haunting 'Song of Myself' (which recounted her own radicalisation), and a rousing elegy for Che Guevara.[141] The Critics Group was now also writing songs, including 'Grey October', the song about the 1966 Aberfan tragedy that Sandra Kerr had sung to Fidel Castro. MacColl proposed that they start a song magazine: Peggy duly launched the pocket-sized *New City Songster* in the autumn of 1968. The first editorial pledged to circulate new topical songs, including those dealing with 'burning issues, too burning perhaps for most "folk" magazines to handle'.[142] Published more or less annually, the magazine was distributed primarily through the folk club network and reached a peak circulation of 4,000 in the early 1970s.[143] The twenty-one volumes published over the next eighteen years provided a forum for their songs, plus those of writers they admired, including Graeme Miles from Teesside, Ed Pickford and Jock Purdon from County Durham, MacColl's eldest son Hamish (who showed early signs of his father's songwriting talents), and the Australian-based Eric Bogle.

ᘔᕒᘒᕐ

MacColl's mid-life theatrical renaissance was caught up in a parallel resurgence of revolutionary Marxist-Leninism. Sometime in the early 1960s he'd quietly allowed his Communist Party card to lapse, but remained too loyal to issue a public renunciation, and many assumed he was still a paid-up member.[144] This changed in the mid-1960s, when he came into contact with a circle of like-minded London firebrands who discerned the outlines of a new revolutionary bloc forming under the rising star of Chairman Mao's China.

Stealthily in the late 1950s, and then more confidently in the 1960s, the Chinese Communist Party had begun to challenge the Soviet Union as the nerve centre of Marxist insurrection.[145] MacColl now regarded Khrushchev as an opportune revisionist whose arguments about achieving socialism via parliamentary means betrayed a depressing ignorance of basic Marxist tenets; by 1964 MacColl was pleased to note that Chairman Mao was giving public speeches with titles like 'On Khrushchev's Phoney Communism and its Historical Lessons for the World'.[146] Mao spoke MacColl's language on cultural questions, imploring artists to master 'the people's language' spoken by 'the masses of workers, peasants and soldiers';[147] he also appeared to share MacColl's enthusiasm for those revolutionary national liberation struggles in Cuba, Algeria, Vietnam and Latin America that the strategically minded Soviet Union seemed intent on ignoring. And while Khrushchev was mollifying America with diplomatic visits and talk of Cold War stalemate and peaceful co-existence, the Chinese Communist Party detected in America's savage foreign policy the crazed thrashings of an empire in decline.[148] Mao thumbed his nose at American imperialism, dismissing its representatives as 'paper tigers, dead tigers' and even 'bean-curd tigers'.[149] 'Political power', wrote Mao, 'grows out of the barrel of a gun.'[150]

If such ultra-left rhetoric functioned as a smokescreen to conceal China's own grubby realpolitik in India and Tibet, it played well with sections of the British Left, both the disenchanted Stalinist old-guard like MacColl who considered that the Soviet Union had gone soft, and also a younger generation discovering in the writings of Marx and Mao intimations of the realm of freedom. MacColl had many associates, and he now talked politics with the movers and shakers of Britain's Maoism, including the gifted hyper-militant trade unionist

Reg Birch (former member of the National Executive Committee of the Communist Party, soon to be expelled from the party), Texan novelist and BBC script-editor William Ash (so unruly the CP never permitted him to join), public intellectual and filmmaker Felix Greene, and MacColl's old friend Professor George Thomson, now one of the leading lights in a tiny pro-Maoist Sinophilic organisation called the China Policy Study Group.[151]

MacColl started his own Beckenham political reading group to run alongside the Critics sessions: Mao's writings were discussed until the small hours.[152] MacColl and Seeger became readers of the *Peking Review*, a publication that offered cut-out-and-keep photographs of the great leader and articles with titles like 'Closely Follow Chairman Mao to Still Greater Victories!' and 'Chairman Mao's Military Thinking is the Magic Weapon in Defeating the Enemy!'[153] (MacColl cancelled the subscription in 1970 shortly after the Shanghai Revolutionary Mass Criticism Group criticised the 'reactionary bourgeois' Stanislavski.)[154] MacColl was courted by London's Chinese Legation, and became an occasional visitor at their social and cultural events (there was talk of a Critics Group trip to China).

In 1966 he threw in his lot with *The Marxist*, a journal edited by John Faulkner's brother Mike and bankrolled by a consortium of Maoist London businessmen rumoured to have trading links with China. (Rival Maoist factions, eager to present *themselves* as the legitimate heirs to Marxist-Leninism, were quick to smell a rat.)[155] Though MacColl would later claim to have edited the magazine, his input to *The Marxist* was actually slight; by far the most important contribution was the name Ewan MacColl itself, which appeared in a list of editorial board members from the first issue, published in November–December 1966.[156] Long associated with the Communist Party, MacColl's public involvement conferred gravitas on a tiny splinter journal openly critical of the official line. *The Marxist* wasn't destined to reorient the British Left (as anticipated, those editorial members who were still members of the Communist Party were promptly expelled; the publication soon collapsed beneath the weight of intra-Maoist factionalism). Nevertheless, MacColl's willingness to be identified with a journal openly critical of his political *alma mater* marked a significant leftward shift. He was unrepentant when the Communist Party, alarmed by the public defection of the famous radio balladeer, dispatched a party

official round to Stanley Avenue.[157] MacColl wouldn't be persuaded
to rejoin. Neither would he sign up to Reg Birch's newly launched
breakaway Maoist micro-party, the Communist Party of Britain
(Marxist-Leninist), or indeed to any of the other new Marxist groups
that courted him in the 1960s.[158] He now preferred to work instead as
a freelance Marxist-Leninist cultural activist, and would judge causes
and organisations on their merits.

CʒƁꙄ

In 1966 MacColl and Seeger cut their last record for Topic and started
to record on the Argo label.[159] Recently bought out by the Decca
corporation, Argo was now supplementing its list of educational
spoken-word recordings with titles for the expanding folk market.[160]
With Decca's cash behind the venture, Argo could even pay advances
on recordings, something rare among the specialist folk labels.[161]
Argo record producer Harley Usill admired the work of MacColl
and Seeger. He recognised that the label's educational remit suited
serious artists who were always keen to fill their record sleeves with
scholarly essays, song notes, even bibliographies. With Usill's backing, it
became possible for Seeger and MacColl to embark on some ambitious
recording projects.

The best six *Radio Ballads* were finally issued on vinyl, and between
1966 and 1968 MacColl and Seeger recorded *The Amorous Muse*,
*The Wanton Muse* and *The Angry Muse*, a trilogy of LPs that grouped
British and American folksong thematically.[162] The latter presented an
historical survey of protest song from 1689 to the present; hitting just
the right balance between radical cultural archaeology and abrasive
contemporary work, it proved one of their best records of the 1960s.
They were also able to record *The Paper Stage*, a two-album set
exploring connections between early broadside-ballads and famous
Elizabethan plays: it was a scholarly project in which MacColl's parallel
passions for theatre and vernacular culture converged.[163] And they
undertook their most ambitious recording venture to date. An epic ten-
LP ballad survey, *The Long Harvest*, wasn't for the folk dilettante.[164]
Released in late 1967 and 1968, it ran to over seven hours of music,
with each disc presenting back-to-back British and American variants
of four or five prominent ballads.[165] Exhaustive in scope and serious
in purpose, the project was aimed at the school, college and university

library market. The critical consensus was that the quality of the singing and musicianship found MacColl and Seeger at their 'monumental best' and lifted the series from its narrowly educational niche.[166] Owning the entire set became a badge of commitment among the revival's traditionalists.

CB80

Authoritarian, self-aggrandising, irascible: the Critics Group encountered all these facets of MacColl's persona in their weekly meetings, but there was no doubting the depth of his commitment to them. 'There was so much talent,' he'd say in later years. 'The future looked very, very rosy indeed.'[167] He pushed work their way and initiated projects likely to sharpen learning curves. In 1966 he instigated a Critics Group radio play, *Romeo and Juliet*. Broadcast on BBC Home Service for Schools on 18 and 25 May 1966, the production relocated Shakespeare's play to the modern East End and grew out of improvisation sessions held during Critics Group meetings. Charles Parker produced; Seeger directed the music; MacColl structured the improvisations, shaped the script, directed the cast, and wrote five new songs including Romeo's ravishing outpouring, 'Sweet Thames Flow Softly'.[168] Wherever possible the Critics were drawn into MacColl and Seeger's own recording projects: Denis Turner supplied the artwork for *The Long Harvest* records; various Critics were involved in two series of Argo's records for schools, *Poetry and Song* and *Voices*;[169] Turner, John Faulkner, Terry Yarnell, Sandra Kerr and Jack Warshaw provided chorus and instrumental backing on some of MacColl and Seeger's late 1960s Argo recordings.

And through the revitalised Argo records, the Critics Group cut six records of their own between 1966 and 1971, with MacColl working as overall director and Seeger as musical director.[170] The first two LPs, *Sweet Thames Flow Softly* (1966) and *A Merry Progress to London* (1967) recovered the broadside traditions of London; the last two, *As We Were A' Sailing* (1970) and *Ye Mariners All* (1971), dealt with sea songs; *Waterloo: Peterloo* (1968) presented political songs from the period 1780–1830; *The Female Frolic* (1968) was a collaboration between Peggy Seeger, Sandra Kerr and Frankie Armstrong that contested the often chauvinistic repertoire of the folk revival by presenting songs chronicling women's lives and experiences.[171]

The records brought into focus the basic contradiction in which the Critics Group project was always caught. MacColl and Seeger were working to develop the individual talents of a gifted group of young singers and instrumentalists; the Critics Group's ample abilities were abundantly reflected on all their recordings. At the same time, MacColl and Seeger possessed forceful, charismatic personalities, a low opinion of most other folk revival artists, and rigid ideas about what was worth singing and how to sing it. They had developed a particular way of researching material, accompanying songs, sequencing tracks and writing sleeve-notes. Codifying and transmitting their version of folk authenticity was the Group's *raison d'être* and it was inevitable that in appearance, content and style the Critics Group records would resemble their own. Unsympathetic reviewers had a field day.[172] An unsigned article in Karl Dallas's magazine (now rebranded as *Folk Music Ballads and Songs*), observed of the first two Critics Group records:

> What is distressing is to find so many of MacColl's mannerisms, as opposed to his technique, cropping up in all but one of the main singers on the record ... John Faulkner and Sandra Kerr are the real disappointments ... If MacColl's techniques can turn two of the brightest young singers in the revival into the dull, spiritless voices we are offered here, it is an indictment of those techniques indeed![173]

Jokes circulated that the Critics Group was an elaborate wheeze in which MacColl had jealously taken the best singers on the scene and ruined them.[174] 'Listening to these albums,' wrote Ian Campbell in *Sing* magazine, 'I experienced that disconcerting feeling one gets when watching a television puppet show ... Four young men sing on these records, but the accent is so similar as to become quite indistinguishable.'[175] It was a dispiriting business in which the Critics absorbed blows really intended for MacColl. He imputed the 'purposeful misrepresentation' to ignorance, malice or hidden political motivations, but the fervour with which the cloning charges were discussed by the Critics Group indicated just how seriously they were taken.[176] It was a reminder, if anybody needed reminding, that to work with MacColl was always to be drawn into a vortex of controversy.

◦◦◦

While the loyalists were being bludgeoned by the critics, one lapsed member was riding high in the pop charts. Luke Kelly was too recalcitrant a personality to endure MacColl's tutelage for long – after a few months of Beckenham meetings he retreated to Ireland and resumed relations with the hedonistic and hirsute kindred spirits who became famous as The Dubliners. In 1967 the band recorded *A Drop of The Hard Stuff*, their debut album, which included 'Seven Drunken Nights', a song originally from the repertoire of Joe Heaney. This tale of drunken confusion and cuckoldry became an overnight cult classic on the pirate station Radio Caroline; The Dubliners' record company promptly issued the track as a single. Instantly banned in Ireland, 'Seven Drunken Nights' reached the top ten of the British Hit Parade in May 1967. ('Silence is Golden' by The Tremeloes was number one.)

Neither The Tremeloes nor The Dubliners were music to MacColl's ears, and if Kelly's sell-out wasn't bad enough, The Dubliners also breached folk scene protocol and copyrighted all of the traditional songs on their album, some of which they'd learned from earlier MacColl and Seeger song anthologies. Future artists recording the songs would now pay royalties to The Dubliners, rather than to folk sources such as Joe Heaney, or Harry Cox, the origin of the song 'Black Velvet Band'. Karl Dallas spoke out in the *Morning Star*;[177] MacColl and Seeger alerted their publishers to the situation, and the Workers' Music Association eventually overruled the copyrighting of one song collected by MacColl.[178] Nothing more came of the matter, which Peggy Seeger remembers being slowly 'drowned in lawyers' and the murky waters of copyright legislation.[179] But for MacColl it was another example of the talented being seduced and the virulent culture industry devouring the organic culture of the people.

෬৪৩

A series of purposefully provocative articles written by Karl Dallas in late 1967 and 1968 further rattled MacColl.[180] Like MacColl, Dallas was a man of the left, a Singers' Club regular and political folk activist. Unlike MacColl, who for most of the 1960s had never heard of iconic footballer George Best, Dallas kept abreast of shifts in popular culture. Still writing for the *Melody Maker*, Dallas had revised his earlier thinking and now argued that popular music had come a long way since the saccharine 1950s schmaltz against which the revival had originally defined itself. 'The pop of today', he wrote in September 1967, singling out The Beatles for particular praise, 'is increasingly vital, creative and really popular, for the first time since mass-produced entertainment killed off the music halls.'[181] By contrast, he detected a new hesitancy among the folk scene: 'Is the revival to remain just a minority movement,' he asked; 'is its glance always to be cast backwards, or is there a way of developing it without destroying its very essence?' Folk and pop people were, he claimed, 'in the same business, revitalising popular music': while folk prided itself on grassroots independence from the cultural mainstream, 'the new pop people' now virtually controlled the mass media. Folk should, Dallas argued, be engaged in a creative dialogue with pop music that would enrich both. He singled out MacColl, advising that familiarity with Frank Zappa's work might sharpen MacColl's satirical writing. 'It's nice and safe up there in your room over the pub,' he concluded. 'The pressures are less and so are the temptations. But it's time we came back down into the market-place.'

MacColl's satirical pub-room *Festival of Fools* responded to Dallas's critique. The 1967–8 show ridiculed the summer of love and its hippy soundtrack as a festival of drug-induced civil obedience ('It's what you feel not what you do, quiescence is the creed' ran his song 'The Flower People'); the 1968–9 festival parodied The Beatles' 'Eleanor Rigby' and made sport of Dallas's claim that pop musicians were now running the culture industry. MacColl wouldn't entertain the idea that progressive, nuanced popular culture might be produced from those with major recording contracts (how this squared with his own major label arrangements wasn't clear). He saw big business as a ruthless censorship machine that conspired to debase public taste and disseminate bourgeois ideology. Wherever music was concerned, MacColl's thinking was locked into an intractable opposition: on one side he saw folk music – an uncontaminated cultural tradition that encoded working-class consciousness and needed safeguarding in the folk scene's non-commercial enclave; on the other hand there was pop, the brain-softening pulp canned by the culture industry. 'He didn't know enough about it,' Peggy Seeger told me. 'I think it was his Achilles heel ... he condemned it without thinking. It's a shame his mind was closed.'[182] By now the fifty-year-old MacColl had too much invested in folk music's radical authenticity to revise his opinions. Dallas got the better of the argument: his central point was that if a figure with MacColl's manifold abilities broke out from internal cultural exile within the folk scene, he might hugely enrich Britain's progressive popular music. The appeal fell on deaf ears.[183]

ⱽⱽ

During the second half of the 1960s MacColl came to support what he knew of Chairman Mao's Great Proletarian Cultural Revolution. Always trusting where self-proclaimed socialist states were concerned, MacColl disregarded Western media reports of Chinese economic instability, political chaos and bloodshed as bourgeois propaganda, and preferred to take the Chairman's proclamations at face value.[184] For MacColl and his fellow British Maoists, the Cultural Revolution was not a ruthlessly executed power struggle to shore up Mao's disastrous leadership, but exactly what the Chairman claimed – an ongoing revolution with cultural questions at its heart.

Maoism was never compulsory for Critics Group members, although neither was it hidden. There was the political reading group; Maoist publications were sold at meetings; *Festival of Fools* sketches spelt out MacColl's position on global communism and the Sino-Soviet split; prominent members visited the Maoist Albania in 1966.[185] On occasions Maoist sectarian righteousness fused with MacColl's cultural purism and coloured the atmosphere of meetings. One visitor to a Critics Group session couldn't help but observe the unnerving number of Chairman Mao style chin-strap beards.[186] The notion of constructive criticism had always been central to the Critics Group. Mao's cult of criticism and self-criticism – regarded by the Chairman as a dis-tinguishing hallmark of the Chinese Revolution – was increasingly used to provide ideological justification for MacColl's authoritarian tendencies.[187] The irony was that MacColl had never been good at taking criticism himself. He seldom listened to feedback about the *Festival of Fools* script (on one occasion he magnanimously invited criticism, then responded furiously when it was offered).[188] 'Those members who would voice criticisms on behalf of the group,' remembers Frankie Armstrong, 'would often be verbally annihilated by his articulate, mind-blitzing self-defence.'[189]

Gifted members such as Denis Turner and Phil Colclough now left amid acrimonious bust-ups. Gordon McCulloch, who had become disillusioned with MacColl, had also withdrawn: 'When he got to the end of what he knew about something', McCulloch told me, 'he made it up.'[190] Poet and broadcaster Mike Rosen, who joined the group in 1970, recalled:

> People stepping out of line or deemed to be soft, middle class or in some way objectionable were on several memorable occasions publicly humiliated and told that eating shit was good for them. Any suggestion that personal politics needed to be looked at was derided as a luxury because the show had to be got on the road.[191]

MacColl's impatience with group grievances was heightened by his own exhausting work-rate, which was as prodigious as ever. In 1970, for example, he and Seeger drove over 2,500 miles per month to play sixty-three concerts up and down Britain.[192] That year his longstanding US visa problems finally came to an end. The American Embassy granted him a 'waiver of ineligibility' on the condition that he didn't deviate from a rubberstamped itinerary.[193] He and Seeger toured the east coast and Canada in May before returning to play the west coast in October. Over the summer they appeared at a festival in Lugano, Italy with four members of the Critics Group. There were also recording commitments: MacColl and Seeger hired radio ballad veterans Brian Daly and Bruce Turner to add instrumental colour to *The World of Ewan MacColl and Peggy Seeger*, a commercially oriented 'best of' collection that became their best-selling record of the 1970s.[194] The year's work culminated in the usual punishing routine of writing, rehearsing and directing the *Festival of Fools*.

The show hit its peak that year. Now in its fourth year, the logistics of organising the show and co-ordinating parallel rehearsal sessions for a cast of twenty-five actors and as many scenes had been refined by Peggy into almost military efficiency. MacColl's twenty-year-old son Hamish was currently following Jean Newlove's footsteps into the world of contemporary dance: MacColl recruited him to choreograph scenes and sharpen the group's movement. The folksiness of the early shows had receded – the election of a Lord of Misrule was now an occasion for satire rather than integral to the show; there were no longer in-jokes about MacColl's folk scene adversaries. The show's politics had broadened while the writing had become more concise. MacColl retained the agitprop conclusion, now paying homage to the Black Panthers and guerrillas in South Africa, Mozambique, Angola and the Middle East. Under pressure from the women in the group, he wrote scenes that explored connections between patriarchy and capitalism.[195] He wrote new songs about Enoch Powell, Vietnam, Ted Heath's cabinet.[196] He wrote surreal, satirical monologues that exposed the brutal histories of colonialism. He was now fully exploiting the theatrical possibilities created by the three-staged performance area. The 1967 seizure of Greece by US-backed ultra right-wing colonels became a key radical cause in the late 1960s. The show's best scene was an elaborate triptych that gave theatrical form to the rhythms of contemporary history: one stage was used to narrate the testimonies of a Greek political activist tortured by the colonels' henchman; a second dramatised the court cases of radicalised Cambridge University students who had participated in a violent demonstration against the junta; a third showed the political complicity of English holidaymakers who sunned themselves on Greek beaches.[197] The combination of lighting, songs and greatly improved acting combined to produce a powerful theatrical effect.[198] The show ran four nights a week between 2 January and 7 February 1971. The 1967–8 show had been savaged by the *Guardian* as 'a verbose, unfunny mixture of would-be satire, pompous moralising and revue sketches'.[199] By 1970 the *Festival of Fools* was becoming a significant fixture in London's radical calendar. Clive Barker, who went on to become a Professor of Theatre Studies, remembers them as 'knock-out'.[200] Billie Whitelaw was a *Festival of Fools* regular. Joan Littlewood turned out for the 1970/1 show and was impressed by what she saw.

CB&infin;CO

MacColl was seldom in good health – he'd been a sickly child and illness had dogged him ever since. 'He was a smoker and he loved good wines, fatty meats and cream on his desserts,' says Peggy; 'he was a type-A compulsive worker and didn't do enough exercise.'[201] He could barely swim and wasn't interested in walking unless mountains were involved. He suffered from longstanding bronchial complaints, insomnia and a recurring slipped disc. 'Every year he would come down with some dire ailment that would confine him to bed,' says Peggy.[202] His son Hamish remembers bouts of depression.[203] 'He would exhaust himself, physically and mentally,' Sandra Kerr remembers, 'and he would just go right down and have to go to bed.'[204]

The 1970/1 *Festival of Fools* took more than the usual toll. Three weeks into the run MacColl turned fifty-six. On 25 January, the night of his birthday, he lost feeling in his limbs and suffered a heavy nosebleed – the haemorrhage was the first manifestation of the arteriosclerosis that would wreak havoc in the final decade of his life. 'I was afraid to go to sleep that night,' he remembered. 'I thought, if I go to sleep, I've had it. My heart will just stop beating.'[205] Though he recovered physically, he remained deeply shaken by this premature glimpse of his own mortality. Already on the edge of emotional and nervous exhaustion, he yielded to gloomy broodings on his status, achievements and relationship with the Critics Group. John Faulkner and Charles Parker called round to Stanley Avenue on 10 February 1971 and spent the evening with MacColl. Forever alert to the importance of MacColl's words, Parker recorded the conversation.[206]

That night he talked fast, openly and intensely about his recent thoughts and feelings; the tape makes uncomfortable listening. His mood swings from self-loathing to euphoria. He talks about how much he'd learned from his work with the Critics Group, and how much talent they possess. He repeatedly berates himself for his self-isolating and dictatorial manner. 'To know people for all those years, to be in their company, to work with them, and not know them,' he says; 'I curled up when I first began to think that. I lay in bed, blushing from the toes to the roots of my hair at being so obtuse. And being such a cunt.' He says he'd only made real human contact with three members of the group: Brian Pearson, John Faulkner and Brian Byrne, a young socialist Irishman who'd died in 1967 of a rare bone disease. 'All I've done is just sit there and pontificated like God,' he says, sounding increasingly agitated:

> I've never got through to them. I've just built a big bloody hard shell around myself. A big, dirty, fucking callus. I've never really done what I should have done ... It's the old business of being able to communicate with a lot of people, but not being able to communicate with many individual people. It's a terrible thing ... I suddenly found myself wanting to expiate in some way. To make up for being callous, for being so unobservant. For not taking the trouble to find out about people ... I've come to the conclusion that a lot of the weaknesses, or the comparative lack of development through the group is me ... everybody needs to be understood, loved, admired. I've even gone out of my way to contradict this basic truth at classes, saying

'I don't give a fuck what these people think about me.' Of course I give a
fuck what they think about me.

This insight, he says, represents a 'revolutionary jump ... in these
last two or three days I've experienced what it will be like to be alive
under Communism. A kind of sense of the possibilities of human
communication.' 'I'm going to work,' he concludes as the tape runs
out, 'in a completely different way.'[207]

∞

He called the group together at Beckenham at the end of the following
week and spelt out his vision for the future. They were, he announced,
to spend the next eighteen months transforming themselves into what
he called 'a permanent, professional revolutionary theatre group'.[208]
They were to ditch the name Critics Group – always an albatross
around their necks – and start afresh. He envisaged a team of eight
to ten with a good truck and lightweight aluminium equipment. All
should be able to act, move, sing and play instruments. They would
give political shows in working-class communities and supplement their
income with folk club appearances. He hadn't felt so enthusiastic about
a new project, he told them, since the launch of Theatre Workshop
in 1945. He was going to delegate responsibility by appointing three
directors (he suggested Sandra Kerr, Jim O'Connor and Brian Pearson).
'I've been in a rut,' he told them. 'I've been living on past skills, past
glories, all the rest of that fucking nonsense. I don't want to do it any
longer. I want the fun ... I want the fun of doing new things.'[209] He
hoped that as many as possible would embrace the new venture.

It was an annunciation of a new start, but cast in an old, familiar
manner – there'd been little consultation and the style was still top-down
with MacColl doing the talking. Many Critics had already fallen by
the wayside; many were still licking wounds inflicted during MacColl's
rages. Sensing trouble brewing, Frankie Armstrong and Brian Pearson
now also withdrew.[210] Others were disappointed that singing had been
sidelined: parallel Singers' Workshops were maintained, but it was
all too obvious that MacColl's enthusiasm was now with the theatre
project. Bob Blair, one of the most skilful singers to pass through
the group, also left. 'I came to the conclusion that I would be much
better involved as a trade union activist to further the revolution,' he
remembers. 'Ewan and I had a serious falling out about it ... He said

"we've got plenty of trade union organisers, but we haven't got any fucking singers".[211]

cs℘

MacColl was instructed to rest up through 1971, but relaxation never came easy. He and Peggy appeared seventeen times at the Singers' Club, and took sixty bookings in other clubs. He cut a new record, issued the following year as *Solo Flight*; with members of the Critics Group he recorded a collection of songs from the radio ballads and worked on the music for a BBC film.[212] There was an ongoing censorship wrangle to occupy his mind: Argo had recorded *The Festival of Fools* for commercial release but now insisted that a sketch critiquing apartheid should be cut – the Critics wouldn't agree, and the record was pulled.

In the late spring of 1971 a television crew visited Beckenham to shoot *A Kind of Exile*, an ATV documentary about thirty-six-year-old Peggy.[213] The film catches dinner table conversations about the leadership of the Black Panthers. We see Calum and Neill playing football on the suburban gravel drive while a spectral Betsy hovers in the background. MacColl displays a paternal pride in Peggy's creative progress: 'It was absolutely vital to her, to me', he says, 'that she continued to develop as an artist.' From the book-lined workroom Peggy explains that MacColl has enabled her to recognise that folksong is the 'direct expression of social antagonism' and 'the only form of cultural expression that the working class have'. She berates the 'cultural prostitutes in the folk music world' (Judy Collins and Joan Baez are mentioned shortly afterwards). 'The only way to take over is to come up from the bottom,' she says, when describing the grassroots folk scene where they play most of their concerts. Establishing a travelling theatre company is their 'next job'; 'there's going to be a big blow-up soon in the Western world', she says. 'I stand on the side of Mao Tse Tung who says it's going to be a basic, elemental jungle struggle for a while.' A number of TV reviewers poked fun at these indomitable suburban revolutionaries. 'She is a very formidable lady,' observed the *Guardian* TV writer Nancy Banks-Smith. 'A musician through and through and madder than a wet hen.'[214]

cs℘

MacColl liked the idea of devolved power, but it had never been his style. He issued a comprehensive reading list for the new theatre group, and took the odd meeting.[215] ('It would be false modesty to pretend I couldn't help', he'd told them.)[216] It wasn't always easy to spot the difference between the old format and the new. Mike Rosen remembers those meetings:

> He would sit in the dentist's chair. The anglepoise would be on him. We'd all be in the dark and MacColl would give us a one-hour lecture on the history of left wing theatre, a one-hour lecture on the relationship between folk music and the proletariat. They were fascinating lectures. But they were lectures. They weren't discussions ... He was very keen that we should write songs or sketches. To be fair to him, I don't think he knew exactly how to do it, how to create an environment in which that was easy to do.[217]

The group was now encouraged to meet up independently, and they enjoyed the contrast in atmosphere. 'We had a wonderful time,' remembers Sandra Kerr. 'It was so exciting, it was us doing it all by ourselves, we were all now pushing thirty, thirty one ... grown up as singers and actors ... It was like kids playing when Mum and Dad were away.' They were expected to report back to MacColl, who seldom liked what they'd done. On one occasion, she remembers, 'he immediately got into one of his black strop moods ... he didn't like not having control ... And I think he found that very hard indeed.'[218]

To relieve the still fragile MacColl from the pressure of writing a new *Festival of Fools* for 1971/2, it was agreed that the next show should be mainly a revue of previous shows. MacColl and Seeger had high hopes for 1972 and the future. Peggy was busy organising a support party to generate funds for the new touring theatre company – celebrities including Spike Milligan, Kenneth Tynan, Ken Loach and Michael Redgrave were to be invited.[219] An independent film company was coming to record the show.[220] As usual, the ever hospitable Ewan and Peggy hosted a New Year's Eve drinks party at Beckenham for all those involved in *Festival*.

All seemed well on the surface, but tensions within the group were now reaching breaking point. 'Groups that are together too long get incestuous,' says Peggy (she wasn't being merely metaphorical: sexual liaisons within the group weren't unheard of). 'It was a very patriarchal group. I don't think there was enough praise for the things people did well.'[221] MacColl's leadership-style had created a dynamic that couldn't be easily converted into something more co-operative; though he understood that the group needed more space for creativity, he couldn't let go. It was like a Freudian psychodrama in which the survival of the children required that the father had to be slain. 'If he had learned to be challenged, it would have been brilliant,' Peggy told me.[222] 'We hadn't been treated the way grown-ups should be treated,' says Sandra Kerr. 'And I think you can take that when you're not grown up, and so in awe of someone. But we weren't so in awe anymore.'[223] 'I was trying to find, along with others, a kind of popular left-wing form of entertainment that was also a pleasure to work with,' says Mike Rosen. 'We'd come to a point where it wasn't pleasurable anymore.'[224] MacColl wanted to relive his theatre career vicariously; he needed the group to overcome all the obstacles upon which Theatre Workshop had foundered. 'They're going to go a long way past where I've gone, if I've got anything to do with it,' he'd proudly told Charles Parker. 'Then I'll feel I've achieved something.'[225] 'He wanted them to take theatre out on the road,' says Peggy, 'to the places he figured it was really valuable, as Theatre Workshop had done … into mining communities, textile communities, carrying forth Ewan MacColl's dream. But the dream of the Critics Group was not Ewan MacColl's dream.'[226]

Weariness and anger prevailed among the 'new young singers' who felt neither new nor young. There was little enthusiasm for doing a retrospective *Festival of Fools*: the whole point of the show that it was supposed to be cutting-edge. Nor was there enthusiasm for the few additional scenes and songs that the exhausted MacColl had managed to write. Apart from 'I'm Gonna Be an Engineer', a new song added by Peggy that was later taken up by the women's movement, the *Festival* that year was professional but flat.[227] 'The atmosphere got worse and worse,' Sandra Kerr remembers. 'There were lots of midnight calls between us saying we can't go on like this.'[228]

Behind MacColl and Seeger's back, the key members of the remaining Critics held a meeting on New Year's Day 1972. They decided to see out the run, dissolve the group, and set up a new outfit without MacColl.[229] While MacColl and Seeger were talking to the press after the last show of the 1971/2 *Festival of Fools*, the group stripped the room of all the equipment they'd accumulated over the years. Sandra Kerr:

We took this bizarre decision that on the last night of the show we were going to dismantle everything and take it ... I don't know what we were thinking of. It was as though the equipment equated with power ... We did feel that we'd bought all that stuff ... We were going to take it away somewhere else.[230]

'They all stood there in a bunch,' remembers Peggy. 'We said "Where is everything gone?" They said, "It's in the truck and you'll never find it."'[231] 'It all ended horribly,' says Sandra Kerr, 'literally shaking fists at the stage door.'[232] Mike Rosen: 'Ewan said something to the effect of "Fuck the lot of you. I shall carry on on my own. I'll start again. I don't get knocked down." And he walked out.'[233]

# 10
# *Sanctuary*

His parting shot to the Critics Group was a bravura performance of
defiance and tireless commitment, but nothing could have been further
from the way MacColl felt. He retreated to Beckenham. 'Ewan's doing
a fantastic amount of gardening,' Peggy wrote in a letter to Charles
Parker three months later. 'He just doesn't want to embark on anything
right now ... he shows a definite disinclination to begin again.'[1] Over
the next four years he made just one record and wrote three songs.
In terms of creativity, the early to mid 1970s was the quietest period
in his life.

ଔୠ

The former Critics rebranded themselves as Combine, started a new
folk club at the Knave of Clubs pub in the East End, and continued
their experiments with folksong, agitprop and documentary theatre.
They wrote political songs, issued songbooks and gave performances to
striking workers.[2] Doing without 'a permanent director or leader of any
kind' was emphasised, and Combine became part of a broader scene
of like-minded early 1970s radical theatre groups that included John
McGrath's 7:84 and the Banner Theatre of Actuality in Birmingham,
in which Charles Parker was a significant figure.[3] Combine would
last for three years. A couple of members continued to appear at the
Singers' Club, but never when MacColl was around. As far as he was
concerned they were now *personae non gratae*.

On occasions he'd attribute the Critics Group's demise to the conspiratorial machinations of agents provocateurs and middle-class
intellectuals.[4] 'It's so much easier to deal with if its someone else's fault,'
Sandra Kerr told me. 'It meant he didn't actually have to look at how

it had developed and realise that he could have gone another way.'[5]
On other occasions he took some responsibility for the Critic Group
ructions. 'It went on so long and it tended to become incestuous,' he
said in one interview. 'We tended to feed off each other. This was a
mistake, but it was my mistake, not theirs.'[6] Elsewhere he'd brush off
the whole business as a long-forgotten trifle. It was ten years after the
split before Mike Rosen saw MacColl again. 'I wanted to apologise
because although we'd had disagreements,' Rosen remembered, 'we'd
probably gone about it in the wrong way.' MacColl was the embodiment
of charm. 'It's all forgotten,' he said. 'I never gave it a second thought.'[7]
But behind the closed doors of Stanley Avenue, it was obvious that the
group's mutiny had shaken him profoundly. '[T]he actions of the Critics
Group hurt Ewan more than anyone will ever know,' wrote Peggy at
the time.[8] 'I think that was a big turning point in his life,' says his son
Calum. 'He became very disillusioned, very angry, very bitter.'[9] 'It was
almost like having someone die in the family,' remembers Calum's older
brother Neill. 'For the first time ever, he seemed emotionally needy ...
It was very definitely at that point that his health started to go ... I
don't think he ever recovered from that.'[10]

CS80

MacColl's problems grew worse later that year. In 1970 the BBC had
restructured radio programming – dumbing down, many called it –
and Charles Parker was rendered effectively redundant.[11] His formal
lay-off was confirmed in 1972, and a campaign formed to oppose a
redundancy widely regarded as politically motivated. While Parker's
achievements were by no means confined to the radio ballads, it was
inevitable that these award-winning programmes – currently enjoying
a return to the airwaves in the form of specially adapted television
documentaries – should be singled out as outstanding examples of
Parker's contribution to innovative broadcasting.[12] The ambiguity that
had always surrounded the authorship of the radio ballads resurfaced.
Sympathetic journalists emphasised Parker's role, sometimes at the
expense of MacColl, while Seeger's contribution was frequently
overlooked.[13] Still reeling from the break-up of the Critics Group,
MacColl felt aggrieved that the radio ballads were now becoming
widely known as 'Charles Parker's Radio Ballads'. While Peggy Seeger
did nothing to claim her own share of the credit – and she, above all,

had a grievance – she was fiercely protective of the fragile MacColl, and insisted that Parker should do more to set the record straight. 'These kinds of "slips" would be impossible if proper credit had been given in the first place,' she wrote in one letter.[14] 'To me they are Ewan's radio ballads and they are so often reported as Charles Parker's radio ballads that I must object, and intend to make Ewan accept what is his as credit.'[15] 'I think a public rebuttal of the solo authorship is due,' she told Parker. 'It is your duty not as a friend but as a Maoist, and in the interest of intellectual honesty.'[16]

Parker pointed out that he was unwell and fighting to save his BBC career, but proved otherwise contrite. 'I have my share of bourgeois possessiveness and capacity to appropriate,' he confessed, before rebuking himself for 'uncritical worship' of MacColl.[17] He dutifully wrote letters to newspapers stating that the radio ballads' 'origination and overall conception remains with Ewan MacColl'.[18] The issue would smoulder for years, sporadically flaring up whenever the radio ballads were newsworthy: the following year Parker was interviewed by *Guardian* journalist Carol Dix, and the ensuing article referred to 'his ballads' and implied that he'd been the creative force behind *The Ballad of John Axon*.[19] Bracing himself for the inevitable backlash from Seeger and MacColl, Parker scribbled them a note regretting his 'incorrigibly garrulous tongue' and for being 'disarmed by a pretty face'.[20] Seven years later, on 10 December 1980, the sixty-one-year-old Parker died prematurely of a stroke. In MacColl's view the obituaries of his old comrade further ingrained the perception that Parker had created the radio ballads. 'Charles Parker was a painstaking producer, a tape-editor of enormous skill and a radio man to his fingertips,' wrote MacColl in grouchy response to one obituary that had described Parker as 'the producer and co-author of the radio ballads'. 'He was also a dear friend and I think he would choose to be remembered for the virtues he possessed rather than those friends would thrust upon him.'[21]

കജ

The ugly exchanges ultimately revealed more about MacColl's embattled state of mind than about the radio ballads. He felt that the Critics Group, like Theatre Workshop, had benefited from his vision and then turned their backs on him; without his revolutionary theatre ensemble, the radio ballads were now his most concrete achievement. At a low ebb, emotionally, physically, psychologically and creatively, MacColl couldn't bear to be publicly demoted to Charles Parker's sidekick or collaborator. He knew he was the primary creative force behind the radio ballads, and needed to be recognised as such.

Solace came, however, from the most unlikely source. While the nebulous collectivism of the radio ballads had resulted in some uncomradely displays, the cut-throat efficiency of the culture industry did, at least, keep the records straight. For the last ten years, 'The First Time Ever I Saw Your Face', which MacColl had dashed off in a warm glow of lovesickness and whisky back in 1957, had taken on a life of its own.[22] Covered by The Kingston Trio in 1962, 'The First Time Ever' was subsequently picked up by a string of lesser-known artists including African-American soul singer Roberta Flack, who included the song on her 1969 debut album. MacColl and Seeger paid little attention – they consigned most pop cover versions of their music to what they called their 'Chamber of Horrors file'.[23] The song remained a relatively obscure album track until featured in *Play Misty For Me* (1971), a Hollywood thriller directed by the young Clint Eastwood. Flack's label then released the track as Atlantic K 10161, and the single reached the top of the American billboard chart on 15 April 1972, where it spent the next six weeks (in Britain it reached number fourteen a month later). Within a year it had sold a million copies. In 1973 it won two Grammies, including song of the year.[24] The song was later sold for use in a face cream commercial, and covered by the likes of Elvis Presley and Johnny Cash. By 1985 it had been broadcast two million times; by 1995, three million, ranking it along airtime standards including Van Morrison's 'Brown Eyed Girl' and the Rolling Stones' 'Satisfaction'.[25]

Royalties had previously trickled into Beckenham, notably when Rod Stewart recorded 'Dirty Old Town' in 1969, but a number one single was another story. 'We couldn't believe it,' Peggy remembers.[26] Even MacColl, who was virtually oblivious to pop culture, was soon aware of the hit on his hands. The money poured in. MacColl suffered spasms of guilt that something he'd created so effortlessly had now bloomed into a golden goose, but he then began to enjoy the alleviation of financial pressure. 'There was a huge change,' recalled Neill MacColl, who was fourteen at the time. 'We became slightly nouveau riche.'[27]

They took a holiday, bought a new car and a cottage near Lockerbie in Dumfries and Galloway. MacColl supplemented his collection of books and broadsheet ballads with new items. He could suddenly afford to indulge his passion for good meat and cheese. He joined a wine club. Indian food was a longstanding favourite with MacColl, who now took up occasional cooking. Preparing everyday fare didn't interest him, but in flurries of culinary creativity he mounted ambitious productions of colour and spice, liberally spattering the small Beckenham kitchen with ingredients. 'It was like Napoleon had hit,' says Peggy.[28]

Calum was sent to join Neill at Alleyn's in Dulwich, an independent day school whose old boys included C. S. Forester and V. S. Pritchett. The MacColl brothers were often ribbed for being the privately educated children of Beckenham's most notorious Maoists. Seldom daunted by MacColl's authoritarian style, Calum challenged his father about the contradiction. MacColl reassured him that what appeared a compromise was actually a long-term anti-bourgeois strategy. 'If I send you here,' Calum remembers being told, 'you can have the education I didn't have. You'll also get into university and then you'll be an officer in the People's Army. You'll be a leader.' 'It was always', Calum told me, 'a very leaky argument. Let's face it.'[29]

CB80

There was a welcome new addition to the family on 2 December 1972 when Peggy gave birth to Kitty, the fifty-seven-year-old MacColl's fifth child and second daughter. 'The smell of ironing, cooking, milk-fed baby, and baby clothes warming on the radiators were the smell of the home,' Peggy remembered.[30] Ten-year-old Calum helped out with baby-care, and they hired Alice Dawson, a live-in au pair who would become a second mother to Kitty up until her early teens. The house was so crowded that Kitty slept in the dining room. A couple of years later eighty-nine-year-old Betsy voluntarily moved out into a nearby nursing home, where she lived out the rest of her ninety-six years.

Without radio ballads, Critics Group meetings or the *Festival of Fools* there was suddenly more time for the family, and the influx of royalties relieved the pressure to accept endless club tours. 'I was at home more by the time Kitty was born and spent more time with her,' Peggy remembered. 'She was my little companion right into her early teens.'[31] MacColl also doted on his new daughter and soon warmed to the quieter, home-based set-up. Never one to change nappies, he was nonetheless a loving, affectionate father, particularly when the children were young, and he thoroughly enjoyed inventing bedtime stories featuring characters such as Polly the Androgynous Polyp.[32] 'Our new way of life is as novel and exciting as the old one,' Peggy wrote to their old friend Alan Lomax in 1976.[33] On MacColl's sixty-second birthday, 25 January 1977, Ewan MacColl and Peggy Seeger got married at Bromley Civil Registry. Neither subscribed to the matrimonial institution, but with money now in the bank, marriage had become advisable. MacColl played the part. 'He was never much of a one for ritual,' Peggy remembers, 'but he got me some flowers and a bottle of champagne.'[34]

CB80

MacColl pottered with the projects that most appealed. He and Peggy wrote and recorded passages of new music for the three BBC television radio ballads produced by Philip Donnellan, a like-minded cultural activist who shared their commitment to radical causes, innovative documentary and the people's music.[35] MacColl and Seeger also researched and performed music for *The Ideas of Karl Marx*, an audio-visual classroom aid designed to introduce schoolchildren to nineteenth-century cultural history and dialectical materialism.[36] And in collaboration with academics from the University of Dundee, MacColl embarked on a screenplay about the life and work of his old hero, Robert Burns. Though the film was to be partly sponsored by a prominent whisky manufacturer, MacColl began enthusiastically.[37] He jettisoned the project as soon as script revisions were suggested. Working with commercial sponsors, he reasoned, tended to result in work of 'stupefying blandness'.[38] 'I have reached the age', he wrote in a weary letter of resignation, 'when the prospect of having to edge crabwise in the hope of sounding out the weak points of a sponsor's defences is no longer a challenge.'[39] Back in 1969 he and Peggy had accepted a tedious but lucrative job writing and performing music for a television documentary about celebrity racing driver Jackie Stewart; the following year he'd accepted a one-off television acting job.[40] Now there was no need to take on projects that didn't interest them.

CB80

He'd always had a vexed relationship with institutions of education. In 1969 he and Seeger had been approached by the new University of Sussex to run folk music courses. MacColl was flattered, expressed interest and promptly allowed the matter to drop.[41] Between 1974 and 1976 at least three American universities wanted to hire him for short-term guest professorships – none came to anything.[42] The official explanation was that he was tired of teaching, but the feelings of inadequacy deeply embedded during his days in the Grecian Street schoolroom were stirred up anew whenever formal education was mentioned. It meant a great deal to him that professors such as Boris Ford of Sussex University and George Thomson at Birmingham valued his work; he enjoyed preparing material for the new Open University or teaching one-off short courses. But contractual responsibilities were another matter.[43] 'Ewan was intellectual in all sorts of ways, but he was very suspicious of university education,' remembers musician and academic Vic Gammon. 'There was, for all his outward show – a moderately aggressive sort of stance – a tremendous insecurity about him.'[44]

Three years before his death it seemed that the ghosts of Grecian Street had finally been put to rest when he accepted an honorary D.Litt. from the University of Exeter – the formal recognition delighted him. 'He was the proudest man on earth,' remembers his son Calum.[45] He was then offered an honorary MA at the University of Salford, two hundred yards from the now bulldozed Coburg Street. It was too close to the world of childhood humiliation and shame. On the day of the degree ceremony MacColl, who'd barely experienced a moment's stage fright in his entire professional life, was overwhelmed by feelings of apprehension and nausea. He panicked, couldn't go through with it, and wanted to turn down the honorary degree altogether. Peggy sent apologies: 'He feels the whole occasion is beyond him,' she wrote.[46] The degree was eventually awarded posthumously.

CＺℵℶ

Scholarly pursuits at home in Beckenham were another matter. Every morning he'd be at his desk by seven, where he'd stay until lunchtime. He worked on the story of Ben Bright, a septuagenarian Welshman whose life combined restless seafaring and radical political commitments across Britain, America and Australia. Bright, who came to MacColl's attention through Charles Parker, was like Sam Larner with Marxist politics to boot. MacColl and Seeger first visited Bright's gloomy North London flat in October 1972 and were regaled with political songs, sea-songs, and colourful stories of the Wobblies, the Ku Klux Klan and rides on freight trains from New Orleans to California. They eagerly returned for two more interviews. The militant mariner's testimony spoke to MacColl's abiding obsessions – class-consciousness and political radicalism expressed through and reinforced by the music of the people. It moved MacColl to creativity. 'Shellback', recorded in 1973, was the first song he'd written since the Critics Group split.[47] A decade later he would draw on Bright's life again for his theatrical comeback, *Shore Saints and Sea Devils* (1983). In his mind's eye he also saw a new television radio ballad with Bright in the lead role.[48] True to form, the itchy-footed seaman took a boat to Australia before he'd told MacColl and Seeger the whole story.[49] They transcribed the tapes they'd already made, researched the origins of Bright's songs, and glossed the political and historical references. The resulting pamphlet, *Shellback: Reminiscences of Ben Bright, Mariner* (1978), was issued by the new 'history from below' publication, *History Workshop Journal* where MacColl struck up a rapport with Raphael Samuel, a Ruskin College-based Marxist historian with whom he'd collaborate again in the future.[50]

CȜƎO

MacColl was also busy with a new book, provisionally entitled *Scots and English Folksongs*. Back in 1967 Bert Lloyd had published his magnum opus, *Folk Song in England*, a historical survey of the nation's traditional song that remains the standard work forty years later.[51] MacColl and Seeger envisaged a parallel, scholarly compendium of 240 folksongs based on the racks of field recordings in Stanley Avenue. 'There's a lot of disagreement about what folk music is,' MacColl explained, 'and this to some extent is based on not knowing what current repertoire is. There's a lot of misunderstandings about how much still survives and where it survives ... a book might clarify a lot of points on this particular issue.'[52]

Their book was to cover all points between Banffshire and Dorset; bolstered by scholarly notes detailing the provenance and history of each song, it would run to over 600 pages. The repertoires of Sam Larner, the Elliotts of Birtley, the Stewarts of Blairgowrie, Ben Bright and the Black Country chain-maker George Dunn would be integral to the project.[53] It was a characteristically ambitious venture, but they were one step behind rival folklorist Peter Kennedy, who published his *Folksongs of Britain and Ireland* in 1975.[54] The shrinking market for folksong anthologies couldn't absorb a competing title, and MacColl and Seeger had to rethink their plans.

Song collecting over the past fifteen years had only confirmed their long-held belief that 'the travelling people have become the real custodians of English and Scots traditional song'.[55] Noting that no song collection dealing with the repertoire of Britain's travelling people had been published in fifty years, they now transcribed recordings of 131 songs collected from eighteen travellers between 1962 and 1975.[56] The material ranged from ancient ballads, songs of labour and erotic pieces to fragments that had passed through music-hall. The songs were typed up exactly as they had been sung – the point was to produce a record of folksong's current status within travelling communities. Preparing the book was a family effort. Hamish MacColl, now twenty-six and training in Chinese Medicine, was dispatched to the British Museum to research the songs' former incarnations in printed broadsides; his sixteen-year-old sister Kirsty, who'd just enrolled at Croydon Art School, helped with statistical analysis; Calum (13) and Neill (17) were recruited for proofreading. *Travellers' Songs from England and Scotland* was published in 1977. Previous MacColl/Seeger songbooks had been revival manuals and manifestoes; this was a sober piece of recovery scholarship, which sifted through collective traveller memory and explored the residual song culture of some of post-war Britain's most marginalised communities. 'A well-researched, scrupulously edited and beautifully produced book,' wrote Hamish Henderson in his review; poet Douglas Dunn wasn't alone in applauding a project that brought to light the cultural riches of a much-maligned submerged population.[57]

CI380

The Stewart family of Blairgowrie, Perthshire, had enabled MacColl and Seeger to get a foot in the door of the wary communities of Scottish travellers. Made up of matriarch Belle Stewart, her piper husband Alec, and singing daughters Cathie and Sheila, the Stewarts themselves possessed a living oral culture and had become 'traditional' stalwarts of the folk revival.[58] MacColl and Seeger had first recorded them back in 1961 and sporadically since; the Stewarts were now recording artists and regular guests at the Singers' Club and Stanley Avenue.[59] Always central to MacColl and Seeger's ideas about the ways in which folk music could reinforce cultural identity, the Stewarts' family folklore was considered too rich and various to be amply accommodated in *Travellers' Songs from Scotland and England*. MacColl and Seeger planned a separate, parallel volume.

They wanted to create 'an accurate picture of a traditional culture operating within the somewhat confined space of a family circle', which would sample the broader oral culture – cant, folktales, riddles, children's rhymes – of which the Stewarts' music was a part.[60] A genre-defying blend of biography, cultural anthropology, folklore, ethnomusicology and social history, the book presented obvious marketing problems and would be rejected by several publishers.[61] When finally issued in 1986 by Manchester University Press, *Till Doomsday in the Afternoon: The Folklore of a Family of Scots Travellers, The Stewarts of Blairgowrie*, was admired by the Stewarts and critically well-reviewed, although one traveller pressure-group took issue with MacColl and Seeger's elegiac obituary for a passing oral culture. MacColl and Seeger claimed that the Stewarts' family repertoire had 'crystallised at some point before 1960'; the reviewer pointed out that travelling folk had always been eclectic in their assimilations and adept in negotiating the commercial world.[62]

The book illustrated a number of contradictions in which MacColl's visions for folk culture in contemporary society were always caught. From the early 1960s the plan had been to work through politically oriented folk institutions in order to reintroduce folk culture's forgotten riches to a modern population; MacColl and Seeger now noted that those very institutions had actually made the folk into minor celebrities whose songs and stories were 'now being used, almost exclusively, to entertain the visiting folklorist, journalist and television crew'.[63] 'Twenty years ago', he and Seeger wrote in the introduction, 'the Stewarts saw themselves as Travellers', now they were 'observers – sympathetic, but detached observers'.[64] Singing for the folk scene had, they noted, not only eroded the Stewarts' identity but also their authenticity, introducing self-consciousness into performance

– 'stereotyped formats of presentation, borrowed from the music hall, the cinema and television'.[65]

MacColl and Seeger wanted the folk to be unselfconsciously authentic (their songs and stories should be what Seeger called 'a natural function of their everyday life') *and* knowingly to embody and preserve the pure artistic practices MacColl and Seeger associated with the tradition (to sing like Joe Heaney, not like the voices heard on the radio).[66] They wanted the folk to function as models for those swimming against the tide of the cultural mainstream, but they didn't want the folk to get their feet wet. 'It's unfortunately true that people like us are – to some extent at any rate – responsible for the alienation of travellers from their communities,' MacColl admitted in a 1980 television documentary. 'Our intentions were good – *are* good. We have tried to liberate whole areas of a submerged but living culture – the survival of which is, we think, vital to social and political progress.'[67] Whereas in the past MacColl had been fluent with the answers – start folk clubs, set up study groups, analyse the folk, engage in self-criticism – now in his early sixties, he began to wonder whether it was really possible to expect the fragile resources of 'a submerged but living culture' to withstand the structural force of a rapacious culture industry forever 'encouraging us to live out our lives in the flickering half-light of someone else's dreams'.[68]

⊂୫୬⊃

The folk weren't what they used to be, and neither was the folk scene. Writing in the *New City Songster*, Peggy Seeger described 'young people' as 'the most creative and receptive elements' of contemporary life 'whose presence at the beginning of the revival gave its energy, its forward looking optimism'.[69] By the mid-1970s, contributions to the *New City Songster* were drying up, and youth in folk clubs was thin on the ground.[70] There was consensus that while the political revival had begun as a vibrant subculture that strove to transform cultural reality, twenty years later folk clubs seemed less a vanguard for democratising contemporary culture than a strategy for coping with it.[71] 'The social/ political involvement and sense of urgency that was central to the early folk song revival', wrote Combine cultural activist Doc Rowe, 'has largely slid into either irrelevant elitism or antiquarianism or "third rate cabaret".'[72] 'Folk clubs should be hives of subversion,' argued political songwriter Leon Rosselson, 'not nests of nostalgia.'[73]

Aspects of the folk revival made MacColl feel 'dismal'; if the folk scene was all it should be, he said, 'I wouldn't be involved with it anymore. I'd have moved on to something else.'[74] He had no time for the many folk traditionalists who were 'antiquarian or twee or just plain bloody reactionary' and was depressed by the poor quality of performance – in one interview he explained to a flabbergasted Charles Parker that in terms of technique and vocal control, most folk artists could learn plenty from pop-singer Lulu.[75] MacColl was naturally sympathetic to the analysis and initiatives of activists such as Trevor Fisher, Doc Rowe and Charles Parker who sought to repoliticise the revival and return a more 'authentic popular culture' to the working class.[76] But still recovering from the Critics Group, he was reluctant to become directly involved.

In part, however, he was insulated from the broader revival's decline. He and Seeger gave an average of around forty folk club shows per year in the mid-1970s, and frequently played to full houses that bucked the general trend of dwindling attendances.[77] In October 1976 they embarked on a critically acclaimed three-week tour of Australia hosted by the country's biggest trade union, the Amalgamated Metal Workers' Union.[78] Back home, their own Singers' Club was by no means representative of the national scene. It had begun life as the medium of tradition, and had survived long enough to become a tradition in itself – for ten unbroken years the club had been hosted at the Union Tavern, before looping full circle back to the Princess Louise in the autumn of 1976, and then on to the Bull and Mouth on Bloomsbury Way in January 1977. Though questionably branded as 'the oldest folk club in Britain', it was not a nest of nostalgia. 'The accusation that we are politically biased is one that most of us involved in the club would happily plead guilty to,' club resident Jim Carroll would write in January 1980.[79] Visits from Ravi Shankar were a thing of the past, but audiences could regularly hear A. L. Lloyd, former Critics (though not when MacColl or Seeger were in attendance), and MacColl and Seeger themselves, who appeared for a discounted fee of £14 (around £80 today) some twenty times per year in the mid-1970s.[80] The club also ran benefit nights for organisations such as the National Council for Civil Liberties (14 September 1974) and booked newer artists such

as Dick Gaughan (8 June 1976), June Tabor (25 January 1975) and
Fiddler's Dram, with whom MacColl shared a stage on 10 January
1976, and who would have a top-five hit with their novelty record
'Day Trip to Bangor' four years later.[81]

છ૪ૐ

In the late 1960s and early 1970s Argo Records were receptive to most
proposals drawn up by MacColl and Seeger; the decline of the revival
inevitably had an impact on the sales of serious folk records, and when
Harvey Usill retired from the company's frontline, MacColl and Seeger
were dropped by the label – 1,000 unsold copies of The Long Harvest
were destroyed as a result.[82] Argo's volte-face only confirmed MacColl's
theories about the fickle culture industry, and he now proposed they
cut their losses, use proceeds from 'First Time Ever' to build a small
studio at Stanley Avenue, and establish their own independent label.
It would, he argued, represent freedom from political interference (he
hadn't forgotten the row with Argo over Anti-Apartheid material).
They would be liberated from record company profit margins and
schedules, would be free to issue topical songs as seven-inch singles,
and able to sell the records more cheaply.[83] 'Once again it was a good
idea and I did the work,' remembers Peggy.[84] Their label, Blackthorne
Records, was formally founded on 30 July 1976 and incorporated
three weeks later.[85]

'We didn't do our homework,' Peggy told me; 'I was not a business
person.'[86] British distribution would prove difficult – large retailers were
reluctant to deal with such a small company, and most Blackthorne
products would have to be sold mail order and at concerts.[87] The
bulging eaves of Stanley Avenue became the Blackthorne warehouse,
and in 1979 valuable stock was lost in a house fire. Sound quality on
early productions was tinny – neither MacColl nor Seeger knew much
about sound technology and Calum, Neill and volunteer engineer Steve
Hardy had first to build Blackthorne's studio, and then learn how to use
it. The company was never financially viable, and repeated injections
of 'First Time Ever' cash were required to balance Blackthorne's books,
but the label at least enabled them to make a spate of new recordings.[88]
MacColl and Seeger had recorded just one album since the end of the
Critics Group (further recordings lay unreleased in the Decca vaults);
between 1976 and the turn of the decade Blackthorne would issue

two political singles, two Peggy Seeger albums of songs by and about women, a live album from the Singers' Club, and two new Seeger/ MacColl studio records, *Cold Snap* and *Hot Blast*.[89]

The recording possibilities stirred MacColl's dormant muse, and he found his best songwriting form since the radio ballads. He wrote 'The Tenant Farmer', a song in a folksong style recounting the hardships faced by a Lockerbie neighbour and recorded on *Hot Blast*.[90] Written in 1975 and released as a Blackthorne single two years later, 'Parliamentary Polka' blended the rhythms of Irish dance music with theatrical gusto to lambast the desperate economic policies of Harold Wilson's moribund Labour government.[91] 'Father's Song' was a *Hot Blast* album track that recast the lullaby genre – the hushed tones masked a political message more likely to induce nightmares than sweet sleep in a slumbering child: 'There's no ogres, wicked witches,' he sang gently; 'Only greedy sons of bitches / Who are waiting to exploit your life away.'[92] Two MacColl compositions found a new, more lyrical language to explore the depression-era that had shaped his political consciousness. Recorded for *Kilroy was Here* (1980), the stark 'Nobody Knew She Was There' tracked Betsy's dawn-time cleaning work across the monochrome landscape of 1930s Manchester; through its fusion of melody and poetry, the song retrospectively illuminated a figure who'd been invisible to her employers and sometimes taken for granted by her son and husband.[93] Written as MacColl passed the age at which his father had died, 'My Old Man' paid tender homage to Will Miller's militancy and became a regular fixture on concert set-lists.[94]

છ૪૦

'Purism was a big, big thing in our lives when we were growing up,' Calum MacColl told me, 'musically and politically.'[95] Peggy took a hard-line on folk music as 'a finished art form ... controlled, deliberate' with its 'own disciplines and limitations'.[96] And both Calum and Neill came up against their father's doctrinaire tendencies during his volatile moods of the 1970s. Thirteen-year-old Neill once covered his bedroom walls with posters of footballers and pop stars; he returned from school to find his collage torn down by an enraged MacColl. 'We never talked about it at all,' Neill remembers; 'I wasn't going to show him any annoyance, even though I was absolutely gutted.'[97] Calum remembers the day he bought his first electric guitar. 'He didn't really speak to me for three weeks. It was a real Judas moment.'[98]

Both Neill and Calum would follow their parents into the music business and enjoy successful careers as recording artists, session musicians, producers and sound track composers. Still in their teens during the early days of Blackthorne, they began to work with their parents in the studio and on-stage. They were quickly struck by the discrepancy between the rigid, official edicts and the flexibility of MacColl's writing and working practices. 'Although he wanted, nominally, a workers' music,' says Neill:

> what he actually wanted was his music which, a lot of the time, had nothing to do with tradition. He made it up as he went along. In the same way that The Beatles songs drew on lots of different styles, so did he. He drew on music-hall, on 1940s show tunes, as well as on hardcore traditional music.[99]

Touring with MacColl was also an eye-opener. He was relaxed, professional, encouraging and brimming with pride to be working with his sons; 'there was an absolute lack of purism about him when it came to doing their stuff', says Neill. 'We can be jazzy where we wanted to, do what we liked really ... I never even questioned it, never thought, "hang on, this isn't what you say to everyone else!"'[100] Calum also enjoyed the shows, even if the sober atmosphere of MacColl/Seeger concerts sometimes fell short of his youthful rock and roll expectations: 'Very polite,' he remembers. 'A lot of vegan nut loaves. And people knitting their own instruments.'[101]

ᎄᏸ

MacColl and Seeger returned to Australia early in the new year of 1979, and played ten dates punctuated by the odd day of sightseeing. February they spent in Beckenham preparing for a spring British tour, which began in Hemel Hempstead on 1 March. A week later they were up in Glasgow for an anti-Nazi benefit concert, where their performance drew the fire of former Critics Group member Gordon McCulloch; his review took issue with Seeger's 'excruciating priggishness' on-stage and 'the self-righteous hectoring quality' of MacColl's songs, 'magnified', McCulloch wrote, 'by the attitude of magisterial condescension which he unwittingly brings to his stage presence'.[102] Similar reviews in the 1970s weren't uncommon – MacColl and Seeger now divided opinion between those who found their work reassuringly oblivious to 'musical fashions', and those who considered it politically hectoring or stuck in the late 1950s.[103]

The tail end of the tour was played against the backdrop of the general election campaign fought out between Jim Callaghan and Margaret Thatcher. In late April MacColl and Seeger drove back up to Scotland to their Lockerbie cottage for a break; in May they were due to play concert dates in the US.[104] The cottage, situated in Eskdalemuir pine forest in Scotland's southern uplands, provided a welcome retreat and MacColl enjoyed the back-to-basic lifestyle in a country he'd always considered his homeland. He was chopping wood in the barn when he suffered the shooting pains and racing rhythm of his first major angina attack. He staggered back into the kitchen gasping for breath and Peggy bundled him into the car. They made the half-hour journey to Moffat Cottage hospital in less than twenty minutes. 'That was a nightmare ride,' she remembers. 'He took it very well. He didn't panic.'[105] Once in hospital the sixty-four-year-old MacColl made good progress and pledged to stop smoking. He was discharged and returned to Beckenham shortly afterwards. By the time he was up and about, Margaret Thatcher was making herself at home in Downing Street. She'd still be there when he died a decade later.

# 11
# Endgame

MacColl was eligible to draw his old age pension from January 1980, and the years began to weigh heavily on him. He could now add a heart attack to a growing list of medical complaints that included angina, arteriosclerosis, gouty arthritis, hiatus hernia, hypertension and intestinal disorders. Heroes, comrades and friends were dying. Mao Tse Tung lasted until 1976; the pro-market reforms of Mao's wily successor Deng Xiaoping did nothing to tranquillise MacColl's erratic blood pressure. In September 1978 MacColl's old mentor Hugh MacDiarmid died, followed by Peggy's father, Charles Seeger, in February 1979 – though MacColl would sometimes impersonate Seeger's purposeful stride and patrician mannerisms, he always felt profound admiration for the radical musicologist. Charles Parker died in December 1980, then Bert Lloyd in September 1982. The vexed question of the radio ballads' authorship had put a strain on relations with Parker; Lloyd had grown distant during the high Maoism of the 1960s (Lloyd remained solidly CP to the end), but these men had been key comrades in culture wars since the 1950s. Failing health, funerals to attend, the folk revival in decline, the left in disarray, a monetarist in Downing Street: it was difficult not to succumb to feeling that the stories in which he'd been a protagonist were losing momentum.

ↂ

MacColl's eldest son Hamish was now qualified to practise Chinese Medicine and treated his ailing father on a weekly basis.[1] MacColl proved responsive to acupuncture and also began yoga – each morning he'd prepare for the day with relaxation exercises performed to the music of Bach.

Work had always been a compulsion, and he didn't ease up now. 'Ewan definitely had a heroic aspect,' Peggy Seeger told me. 'He had that apocalyptic vision of how everyone's voyage is huge ... just the fact that we keep going despite this huge gorgon waiting at the end of our lives to swallow us up. That is why he was such a good ballad singer.'[2] The looming form of his own gorgon put him in the frame of mind to sing the big songs he regarded as akin to 'the great classic roles of Hamlet, Lady Macbeth, Clytemnestra and King Lear'.[3] Two ballad albums from *The Long Harvest* series had been recorded and never released.[4] Blackthorne now enabled the work to continue, and MacColl and Seeger planned to issue one album of lesser-known Scottish and North American ballads per year. *Blood and Roses* was to be the series title, an allusion to the ballads' combinations of violence and love neatly illustrated in 'Sheath and Knife', a tale of incest, murder and self-castration that frequently cropped up in MacColl concerts.[5] The first volume appeared to critical acclaim in 1979 and found the now non-smoking MacColl in excellent voice.[6]

Critics responded with equal enthusiasm to an album of mostly new material, *Kilroy Was Here* (1980).[7] The record reflected a songwriting pattern that would continue for the rest of his life. He was still producing pieces in the worker-as-hero mode of the radio ballads: 'Seven Days of the Week' and 'Kilroy Was Here' were heartfelt hymns of praise to industrial labour that acquired elegiac overtones in an era of deindustrialisation.[8] Songs in the vein of 'Nobody Knew She Was There' and 'My Old Man' found a more personal and persuasive take on the same subject matter.[9] The majority of the remaining songs were direct lampoons of the Thatcher administration, a subject that would draw more heat than light from MacColl throughout the decade. Confronted with an administration intent on tearing up the post-war consensus, privatising public assets and dismantling the welfare state, MacColl was stunned into name-calling that gained little purchase on the profound political shifts taking place. Splenetic anti-Thatcher diatribes with titles like 'The Androids', 'Dracumag', 'Rogues' Gallery' and 'Collection of Second-Rate Chancers' came thick and fast as the Iron Lady tightened her grip on political power.[10]

ೞ

Another MacColl entered the public stage in the summer of 1981 when twenty-one-year-old Kirsty had a top-twenty hit single with 'There's A

Guy Works Down the Chip Shop Swears He's Elvis'. Co-written with Phil Rambow, the song's quirky, tabloid-style narrative made good copy for journalists, as did the notorious anti-pop views of Kirsty's famous father. 'It's a very good, very witty song,' Ewan told one reporter who phoned Stanley Avenue. 'If she wants to work in pop music, I want her to be as successful as she can be doing it,' he said before adding, 'I'd feel the same if she wanted to be a bricklayer. I'd want her to be a good bricklayer.'[11]

Kirsty's interviews reciprocated the appreciation – 'I'd like to think I could become as good a writer as he is,' she told another reporter – but also measured her distance from MacColl.[12] She'd never lived with her father, and hadn't set foot in Stanley Avenue until the late 1960s. 'I wasn't a great part of my father's life,' she'd say in another interview, 'and I felt very detached from him'.[13] Her future husband, record producer Steve Lillywhite, partly attributed Kirsty's creativity to the fact that she hadn't been brought up under her father's 'overpowering influence'. Her talent, he reflected, 'was allowed to develop more because she wasn't part of that'.[14]

'I wanted to be *that man on the stage*,' she later explained; 'I never thought of myself as a girl.'[15] After leaving the local comprehensive she'd drifted through Croydon Art School, finding herself within the orbit of Stiff Records, whose roster numbered Ian Dury, The Damned and Elvis Costello. Possessing an unerring melodic sense, and all of her father's vocal and literary skills without his purism or political super ego, Kirsty cut her first single, the self-penned Motown-influenced 'They Don't Know', in June 1979.[16] The success of 'There's a Guy Works Down the Chip Shop' two years later set her career firmly on track. She would go on to record with artists including Van Morrison, Talking Heads, Robert Plant, The Rolling Stones and The Smiths. She'd keep company with the aristocracy of 1980s pop music. On 18 August 1984 she married Steve Lillywhite; their glamorous rock 'n' roll lifestyle was a long way from the Singers' Club. MacColl was concerned that he couldn't afford to foot the bill for a London celebrity wedding whose guests included U2's Bono and the lead singer of Frankie Goes to Hollywood.[17] He wasn't asked to pay, but proudly put on a top hat and tails and led Kirsty down the aisle.

಄

MacColl was unstintingly open-handed when it came to sharing his memories, opinions and writings with those interested in exploring and developing traditions of radical working-class culture.[18] He made his old plays available to companies interested in performing them, and would waive royalties for smaller groups.[19] He made himself available to researchers of radical drama, whether callow undergraduates or distinguished professors. He collaborated with left-wing academics Raphael Samuel and Stuart Cosgrove on *Theatres of the Left 1880–1935: Workers' Theatre Movements in Britain and America* (1985), a sourcebook that anthologised scripts, documents and interviews with surviving figures from an earlier period of political drama.[20] He encouraged his old friend Howard Goorney to write the inside story of Theatre Workshop, formally disbanded in 1978.[21] Goorney was largely sympathetic to MacColl's view that the political commitments integral to Theatre Workshop's early years had been underplayed during the London heyday; by emphasising those formative years, the book sought to set the record straight.[22] Goorney and MacColl continued the work by co-editing *Agit-Prop to Theatre Workshop: Political Playscripts 1930–1950* (1986), a collection of early Theatre of Action, Theatre Union and Theatre Workshop scripts prefaced by a long MacColl essay, which again attempted to bring the company's political pre-history back into view.[23]

CBED

MacColl found a new kindred spirit in Marxist intellectual, writer and director John McGrath, whom he'd first come across during the Centre 42 initiative of the early 1960s when McGrath was writing the groundbreaking BBC television police drama *Z Cars*. In 1971 the thirty-one-year-old McGrath had founded 7:84, a theatre company whose name derived from a 1966 statistic revealing that 84 per cent of Britain's wealth was owned by 7 per cent of the population. Like their politics, 7:84's collective ethos, non-naturalistic aesthetic and commitment to performing in theatrically deprived working-class communities were solidly in the tradition of Theatre Workshop's early days.[24] When the company formed a Scottish wing in 1973, McGrath's roving Marxist ensemble soon found itself reminding older audience members of shows by Theatre Workshop and their 1940s and 1950s contemporaries.[25] Keen to position their repertoire in a continuing tradition of Scottish working-class culture, 7:84 proposed a season reviving those earlier plays, and began to search for suitable texts and the actors, directors, designers and technicians who'd first staged them. Honorary Scot MacColl was high up McGrath's list. The Glasgow 'Clydebuilt' season ran from February to May 1982 and consisted of four plays, including *Johnny Noble* (1945).[26]

Theatre Workshop founder member David Scase, who'd played the lead in the original production and now worked as Artistic Director at the Manchester Library Theatre, was hired by 7:84 as guest director. The action was relocated from Humberside to north-east Scotland, and the MacCollesque Communist Scottish folksinger Dick Gaughan took MacColl's old part of singing narrator.[27] Gaughan vividly remembers making his acting debut at Glasgow's Mitchell Theatre on 6 April 1982: 'I walked on, very nervous, started singing the opening lines of the play and made the mistake of looking down at the front row – straight at Ewan.'[28] Gaughan gave a strong performance in a production true to the spirit of the original version, and MacColl enjoyed the show. Reviewers were quick to point out that the play's themes of industrial crisis, unemployment, housing shortages and working-class wartime sacrifice seemed all too topical in the fourth year of Thatcherism and as the British naval fleet massed in Portsmouth Harbour preparing to reconquer the Malvinas/Falkland Islands.[29]

It was a moving occasion. MacColl had always imagined Theatre Workshop settled in Glasgow, and he now encountered in McGrath's troupe the type of skilful and politically uncompromising outfit that he felt the Critics Group might have become. Regret was tempered by a pride that his earlier work was now a precedent for a new generation of cultural activists; the link was consolidated when MacColl was invited to join the 7:84 board as a director.[30] True to the Theatre Workshop tradition, 7:84 would have running battles with the Arts Council, and MacColl helped out when he could. When he later heard that 7:84's Scottish Art's Council grant had been cut, he fired off a furious letter of protest. 'What possible excuse can there be for such a move?' he asked. 'Who else has striven so consistently and so well to create a truly popular theatrical style?'[31]

CЗ୫Ͻ

On 2 May 1982 MacColl was back at the 'Clydebuilt' season in Glasgow for an afternoon seminar about his plays; that evening he shared the stage with Peggy and Dick Gaughan in a concert devoted entirely to his songs. Seeger and MacColl gave concerts in Lancaster and Blackpool on the way back down to London, and appeared at a CND benefit in Deal, Kent, before flying out to Italy for two shows.[32] It was here that MacColl suffered his second major heart attack, and spent three days on an intensive care ward in Venice. 'Time was I could look at the Grand Canal and see it overlaid with the vision of Canaletto and Guardi,' he'd write a few years later. 'Now I see, hovering in the background, Goya's *Satan Devouring One of His Sons*.'[33] He made just one concert appearance over the next four months. 'He is beginning to feel that his time is limited,' Peggy wrote in a letter that September, 'and his desperation at not getting to the work he really wants to do is beginning to take a toll on his health.'[34]

CঙৎৎO

'Clydebuilt' compounded MacColl's feeling that he had plays left to write – the recursive return to theatre was one of the basic rhythms of his career. He touched up *Operation Olive Branch* and gave *Uranium 235* a new anti-nuclear ending. He sent the scripts to McGrath hoping for further 7:84 revivals: 'Both plays', MacColl wrote, 'are made daily more relevant by the worsening international situation.'[35] Neither was taken up.

A new full-length play had been on his desk since at least 1981. 'Clydebuilt' seemed to galvanise his efforts, and he completed *Shore Saints and Sea Devils* shortly afterwards. The script was rejected by 7:84, the Royal Court and Theatre Workshop's former home at Stratford East – all cited the cost implications of the large cast.[36] He had more luck at Manchester's Library Theatre. David Scase always had a high regard for MacColl's work, and proposed that the Library Company produce MacColl's theatrical comeback; Scase also offered to return from retirement and play the lead. Directed by Howard Lloyd-Lewis, *Shore Saints and Sea Devils* opened on 9 November 1983 in the Library Theatre, where *The Other Animals* and *Rogues' Gallery* had been premiered thirty-five years before.

Appropriately, the play's subject was the passage of time. Set in a London dockside boarding house in 1905, *Shore Saints* drew for local

colour on the testimony of Ben Bright. MacColl's protagonist was
Robert Guthrie, a demagogic and distinguished Presbyterian Scottish
sail-ship captain now rendered redundant by the shipping industry's
transition to steam vessels.[37] MacColl described his new play as 'an
almost perfect metaphor for the final period of laissez-faire capitalism
and the beginnings of monopoly capitalism', but that was the least
interesting thing about *Shore Saints*.[38] MacColl was using the past
to unsettle the present, something his new songs couldn't always
manage. He'd been recently captivated by *Boys From the Blackstuff*,
Alan Bleasdale's BBC TV drama about a group of laid-off Liverpudlian
tarmac workers struggling to cope with the social and political realities of
Thatcher's Britain.[39] *Shore Saints* was his own version of the same story
– MacColl too was writing about economic forces shattering established
communities and plunging conventional models of masculinity into
crisis. Though he was surprised at the suggestion, he was also writing
about himself.[40] The overreaching Scot Guthrie was MacColl's age,
magnetic, articulate. 'Ay Blaw! Blow! Blow your guts oot … ye've fairly
marked me for destruction!' Guthrie yawped like Lear on the heath. 'My
trade, my ship, my livelihood a' gane … My reputation, a mockery! D'ye
ken what I am noo?'[41] Through Guthrie MacColl vented his feelings of
being out-of-time, and the core human drama was tragically compelling:
the Ahab-like Guthrie was MacColl's greatest fictional creation. But the
surrounding play was a ragged mix of spiritual autobiography, searing
poetry and plodding documentation. The critics were bewildered. It
was simultaneously 'one of the most powerful plays I've seen for years',
wrote the *Guardian* reviewer, and 'becalmed in the doldrums of its
own verbosity'.[42] 'It has a tang that is overwhelmed by the smell of
the musty volumes that the author has poured [sic] over in his effort
to give the tale authenticity,' wrote the *Manchester Evening News*.[43]
MacColl needed an editor, and no one at the Library Theatre took on
the job. Joan Littlewood, who had been leading an itinerant lifestyle
since Gerry Raffles' untimely death eight years before, dropped in to
have a look at the show. She scribbled a cruelly accurate diagnosis to
Stanley Avenue on a homemade postcard:

> thought it had great potential – but only understood about 10%, not the
> actors [sic] fault – production puerile and you to blame, indulging in brilliant
> linguistic exercises at the expense of contact and conflict … I didn't know
> where I was, I don't buy programs … To tell the truth – the real killer was

your construction. It is arsy varsy – the straight-forward simple movement of the last 'act' – should come first ... I could put it right in a week but hesitated to say so for fear of opening old wounds. My best to Peggy and family, J.[44]

 C3ᘓ)

Halfway through *Shore Saints*' fortnight run, Peggy Seeger was one of 297 women arrested outside Parliament during a daytime protest against the installation of American Cruise Missiles at Berkshire's Greenham Common Airfield.[45] She was shunted from overcrowded police cells to wagons, and finally charged at Holborn station at midnight. Summoned to appear in Highbury Magistrates' Court the following February, she greeted the bench with a protest song specially written for the occasion. The magistrate stopped her after the first line, threatening her with contempt of court.[46] She was found guilty of obstruction and attending an illegal demonstration, fined and bound over to keep the peace for a year.

'It's as if all of a sudden the country is coming alive again,' she wrote in a letter the following month, though her own political energy had never ebbed.[47] She was currently involved in feminist politics, anti-nuclear work and was a regular visitor to the Women's Peace Camp at Greenham. With and without MacColl, she was playing so many political fundraisers that she'd written a song for singing as the collection-bucket went round.[48] Whereas events of the 1970s had drawn few songs from MacColl, she'd been more prolific than ever. 'I'm Gonna Be an Engineer' (1971) had become popular within the burgeoning women's movement;[49] her songs were featured in the pages of new radical feminist magazines such as *Spare Rib* (July 1976);[50] compositions including 'Housewife's Alphabet' (1976) and 'Nine Month Blues' (1976) provided material for her critically acclaimed Blackthorne albums of women's songs.[51] 'When a future social historian seeks to document the changes in women's consciousness that have been, perhaps, the most significant and lasting aspect of the sixties and seventies', ran one review, 'if he/she fails to include the lyrics of Ms Seeger alongside the work of Ms Millett and Greer, he/she will be missing an important part of the picture'.[52]

Seeger was now using the interviewing and songwriting techniques honed during the radio ballads to articulate a feminist politics sensitive to issues of class. In the summer of 1977, 160 mostly Asian women workers struck at the Grunwick mail-order photographic laboratory in north London. The service sector dispute didn't conform to MacColl's model of male-dominated working-class struggle in traditional industries, and didn't move him to song. Seeger wrote 'Union Woman II', based on interviews with newly radicalised strike leader, Jayaben Desai.[53] Through 1977 Seeger visited a refuge for victims of domestic violence, wrote songs based on the testimony, and proposed to MacColl that these and other women's stories might form the basis of a new radio ballad.[54] He was shocked by the brutality of the experiences and uneasy with the women's attitude to men; the project was dropped. 'He felt very threatened by feminism,' Peggy remembers.[55] He was simultaneously proud of her mounting militancy and removed from it. On 9 January 1984 he accompanied Peggy to Greenham and wrote the poem 'Greenham Woman' about the experience. Seeger is the dynamic figure in the piece, confidently confronting the military personnel massed behind the perimeter fence. MacColl stands aside, an onlooker without a role, trying to find a connection.[56]

○ਤੈੴ

The 1984–5 miners' strike was another story. He'd first met the teenage Young Communist Leaguer Arthur Scargill during the Ballads and Blues days of the mid-1950s, and had been pleased to observe the charismatic firebrand's rapid climb through the hierarchy of the National Union of Mineworkers. 'I've always liked miners,' he said in a 1985 television interview, colourfully adding, 'I number among my personal friends I would guess fifty or sixty coal miners and their families. So when the strike came, I naturally threw in any talents I possess – I put them at the disposal of the miners.'[57]

If the demographic and sociological subtleties of the Grunwick dispute eluded the conventional workerist instincts of his muse, MacColl was thoroughly exercised by this epic upsurge of militancy in which 150,000 big hewers downed tools, not for money, but to safeguard the future of industrial communities. In March 1984 he hadn't written a song for two years; in the first four months of the strike he wrote half a dozen. He wrote about the police – 'Remember the chap in the comical hat is one of humanity's crosses', he sang. 'Whenever there's trouble, whenever there's struggle, he'll be on the side of the bosses.'[58]

He vilified blacklegs who'd been bought off by consumer goods and had 'forgotten the old-timers who made the union strong'.[59] He took a line against the 'talking machine' that 'works overtime to prove that black is white'.[60] 'Daddy, What Did You Do in the Strike?' provided an alternative account of events, and presented the strike as modern class-war in which miners had to stand and be counted (it was left to Peggy to write a song about the Women Against Pit Closure groups who worked alongside the NUM to keep the strike going).[61]

The best of the new songs were quickly recorded, interspersed with testimony gathered from mining communities, and issued as a Blackthorne six-track cassette.[62] All profits went to the NUM and the cassette was sold during the extensive fundraising and coalfield touring undertaken by MacColl, Seeger, Calum and Neill in the course of the year-long dispute.[63] The first six months of the strike both revived and overtaxed the sixty-nine-year-old MacColl. In September he was too ill to play dates in West Germany; that November he suffered his third heart attack on tour in America and was admitted to an emergency ward in New England Medical Center. Two days later he was back on-stage at a NUM benefit concert in New York.

C3&0

MacColl envisaged the strike as the beginning of a new fight-back against Thatcherism, but on 21 January 1985 593 miners returned to work in Scargill's Yorkshire stronghold. When the history of the strike came to be written, that day would be known as 'black Monday'.[64] It was a cruel blow that this pivotal moment in post-war industrial and political relations coincided with the edifying fanfare of MacColl's seventieth birthday Royal Festival Hall tribute concert. Neill MacColl recalls the boost his father had received from the strike:

> He went on about the working classes but had no contact with them, he didn't know who they were any more. But I think the strike brought out the last lot of really good writing ... he wrote a lot of songs which were a banner for the striking miners to stand under ... I was getting sceptical by this point, that actually it didn't do any good at all, but when he got up on that stage and started 'Daddy, What Did You Do in the Strike?' ... [the] miners knew it. The songs obviously spoke to them. He'd still retained that skill, over twenty years or so in a bubble in Beckenham.[65]

C8&O

A film crew visited Stanley Avenue in July to shoot an interview with MacColl for a Granada biographical television documentary, also called *Daddy, What Did You Do in the Strike?*, eventually broadcast on 15 December 1985. 'Peggy Seeger kept interrupting our recording session with trays of coffee for the crew,' recalled the programme's producer, David Boulton, 'which seemed to demonstrate an unexpected tenderness for capitalist media hacks until it dawned on me that it was her way of giving "the old man" regular breaks from the long interrogation under hot lights.'[66]

Despite frail health, the now white-haired MacColl was in feisty form. Wearing a checked shirt and seated in his favourite leather armchair, he was asked about his 1953 panegyric to Stalin. He was unrepentant. 'It was an *excellent* song,' he grinned, 'and the things it said were good things. It dealt with the positive things that Stalin did. Stalin did a lot of positive things.' Boulton then asked MacColl how he squared his political beliefs with selling his most famous love song for use in a face cream commercial. 'That has allowed me to do all kinds of work that I couldn't have done otherwise,' MacColl said. 'It's sustained us for twenty years.' 'This is your seventieth birthday year,' Boulton summed up:

> Looking back on a long life of intense political cultural activity, you can look back on a revolutionary theatre which is now, to most people, simply a historical curiosity. You can look back on a folk revival which came and has since receded. You look back at a political party which is now divided and whose leadership, I suspect, you would dismiss as revisionist and right wing. And you look back on a working class which has consistently failed to grasp the message that you've been putting across over that period. Is it a happy seventieth birthday?

'Yes it is,' replied MacColl puckishly:

> It's not true that the working class has failed to grasp the message. A lot of the working class, or some of the working class, have grasped it. It's better now than it was. And the struggle itself has been good. The struggle has been marvellous![67]

'What was disturbing was the extent of MacColl's political commitment,' complained the *Sunday Times* reviewer.[68] The *Daily Telegraph* critic had to pinch himself not to be mesmerised by a 'remarkably handsome old man' whose 'voice still has the timbre of a baritonal Paul Robeson'.[69]

CﬡBO
•

Long-term MacColl advocates Karl Dallas and Bruce Dunnet had always envisaged the seventieth birthday concert as the first in a series of rolling events honouring MacColl's career. A three-day event, *The Artist: Maker or Tool?: A Symposium on Cultural Politics Organised in Celebration of Ewan MacColl's 70 Years of Creative Struggle* was held at the GLC's County Hall over the first weekend of March 1986. (The GLC would defiantly mark its own dissolution with a £250,000 one-day free-festival four weeks later.)[70]

Alan Lomax was flown over for the MacColl symposium.[71] Hamish Henderson and MacColl were reunited after a long separation; Sandra Kerr came into awkward contact with MacColl and Seeger for the first time since 1972. There were tribute concerts featuring 1960s revival artists such as Ian Campbell and Ray Fisher, while the Stewarts of Blairgowrie represented MacColl's links with the travelling people.[72] Playwrights and actors including John McGrath and Howard Goorney discussed contemporary political drama and the Theatre Workshop's legacy. Films were shown including Philip Donnellan's *The Other Music* (1981), a BBC documentary charting the revival's decline from cultural vanguard to Fiddler's Dram.[73] Historians and cultural theorists debated the politics of folksong – one session featured a presentation from Dave Harker, the first intellectual from the left to apply sustained critical pressure to the workerist romanticism and shaky scholarship sometimes underpinning the political revival's construction of an authentic, working-class music.[74] Though MacColl missed the session, and dismissed as laughable Harker's theories of a homogeneous revival obediently moulded around the cultural policy of the Communist Party, he was rattled by Harker's writings and the challenges to the revival's intellectual foundations they represented.[75]

CﬡBO

On the Sunday evening MacColl and Seeger slipped away from the political revival's post-mortem to appear across town at a sell-out Royal Albert Hall concert marking the anniversary of the miners' defeat. The line-up included two of MacColl's political heroes, Tony Benn and Dennis Skinner, and musicians Paul Weller, Tom Robinson, Lindisfarne and the political a cappella group the Flying Pickets (some of whom were former members of John McGrath's 7:84).[76] 'The place was absolutely filled with miners,' remembers Neill MacColl, who joined his parents on-stage. 'It was incredibly moving.'[77] The following night, 4 March 1986, MacColl and Seeger had been invited to share a stage with Billy Bragg and pro-Labour pop coalition Red Wedge at an East End benefit for striking print-workers, but had a prior booking and regretfully declined.[78]

The revival might be in trouble, but MacColl and Seeger had always been part of this other, overlapping story – professional musicians lending their talents to radical causes. Bragg's punk-influenced electrified protest seemed a long way from the Singers' Club, but he saw himself as belonging to a formation of radical British music that included MacColl and Seeger. He'd later recall the impression that Peggy's solo performance of 'Four Minute Warning' had made at an early 1980s CND rally:

> I was really, really impressed by that. This woman getting up there on her own and singing. And I think seeing Peggy sing like that gave me encouragement that I could do it on my own, that I didn't need a band … Seeing Peggy, the power of a solo political performer, I suppose the integrity of what she'd done, keeping that alive until it was time for people like me to pick up on it, was quite important. I was of the opinion that folk music was all about The Wurzels. I didn't really think of it as being political. Peggy's role is the link, not with just tradition, but with the revival, which is really important.[79]

MacColl didn't always enjoy the music made by Kirsty's friends such as Bragg and The Pogues (they'd covered 'Dirty Old Town' in 1985).[80] 'It's too raw for me, too hectoring,' he said in one interview, before enthusiastically adding, 'It's a long time since people have been subjected to this kind of harassment!'[81] But the idea that all pop was intrinsically bourgeois made no sense in such company, and Billy Bragg was later invited to dine at Stanley Avenue – MacColl even responded warmly to Bragg's idea of updating the lyrics to 'The Internationale'.[82] From now on, in public at least, MacColl would couch his disapproval of pop music in terms of personal preference rather than political rectitude. Seeger went further, insisting that there were lessons to be learned from the flourishing new scene. 'Billy was getting political audiences the like of which Ewan and I would never get,' she told me. 'He knew how to reach to a mass of people. We didn't know how to do that. And we pretended that we did.'[83]

cs℘ꝏ

The new generation rejected the regimented earnestness of the folk scene, but brought cultural energy to some of the political campaigns with which the revival was long associated, notably CND (famously twinned with the Glastonbury festival in the early 1980s) and the movement against Apartheid. In December 1980 the United Nations had passed Resolution 35/206 calling for a cultural boycott of South Africa.[84] Frustrated by the resolution's frequent evasion, Jerry Dammers, formerly of ska band The Specials, formed the Artists Against Apartheid pressure group in April 1986.[85] In the summer of 1986 MacColl and Seeger set about producing a fundraising Blackthorne cassette of eleven anti-apartheid songs to support the campaign.

The material reflected the length of their commitment to the cause. MacColl's first anti-apartheid song was provoked by the 1960 Sharpeville massacre; three years later Peggy Seeger had written 'I Support the Boycott' (1963) in support of consumer sanctions, while MacColl's starkly poetic 'Black and White' (1963) was one of his most potent political songs of the 1960s.[86] The new cassette also included 'White Wind, Black Tide', a post-Soweto eighteen-minute song cycle first recorded on *Hot Blast* (1978), written in a period when MacColl and Seeger's political and cultural activities against apartheid had been redoubled by contact with Ahmed Timol, a South African political exile and Singers' Club regular.[87] Timol had been tortured and killed after returning to Johannesburg in 1970;[88] MacColl wrote for the cassette a new song pointing the finger at Western corporations who propped up apartheid.[89] Another new composition celebrated shop-workers in Dunnes' store, Dublin, who'd recently gone on strike rather than handle South African goods.[90] They also included a version of Hamish Henderson's tribute to Nelson Mandela, 'Men of Rivonia', and Peggy Seeger's 'No More', which drew upon the melodic patterns of South African choral singing to stirring effect.[91] Released in November 1986 and distributed through the Anti-Apartheid Movement, the cassette took their music beyond the shrinking confines of the folk revival and raised in the region of £8,000; on 23 January 1987 they appeared alongside fellow Artists Against Apartheid Jerry Dammers, Peter Gabriel and Aswad on the BBC 2 television show *Ebony*.[92]

cs℘ꝏ

In the summer of 1986, MacColl, Peggy and thirteen-year-old Kitty took a holiday in Scotland – the Lockerbie cottage had been sold a few years before, but they were still frequent visitors north of the border, especially to the Western Highlands. The three of them set out for a day's hill walking near Inverpolly. 'They streaked ahead of me and I saw them getting smaller and smaller,' MacColl would explain during a concert performance the following year:

> and I felt smaller and smaller. And about halfway up I just gave up. I sat down in that great tumbled mass of rock, in that great beautiful desolation. I thought, well this is the end. I've reached the end of the road. I really felt very sorry for myself. And I brooded about it for the next three or four days and wrote a song. The song is called 'The Joy of Living'.[93]

The stately, hymn-like tune was borrowed from a tape of Sicilian folk music – this was MacColl's characteristically restrained version of what later became known as fusion. The lyric longed for an irrecoverable past, and gave full rein to his flair for self-dramatisation. He grandly bade farewell to the places and people he loved best – Peggy who'd 'held the night at bay', his five children 'Flesh of my flesh, my future life, bone of my bone.' Fifty-four years earlier his first enduring song, 'The Manchester Rambler', had been written in response to the natural world; it was fitting that his last big song brought the story full circle. The final verse caught a glimpse of the world beyond his death and spelt out instructions for the disposal of his ashes. 'Take me to some high place of heather, rock and ling,' he sang. 'Scatter my dust and ashes, feed me to the wind.' He rounded off with a pantheistic vision of his individual spirit suffused through the four corners of nature's domain: 'I'll be riding the gentle wind that blows through your hair. / Reminding you how we shared in the joy of living.'[94] The song was premiered in September 1986 and instantly became a concert standard.[95]

Cঔৎঔ

Between 1986 and 1988 Seeger and MacColl gave an average of thirty-five concerts per year, divided between lucrative arts centre bookings, benefit concerts, which they played for nothing, and the Singers' Club, which had been forced to close for a year in 1982, but now limped forward on a fortnightly basis.[96] The club had reopened in the old Union Tavern room, but soon resumed the meandering pattern of previous years, with brief spells back at the Cora Hotel, over at the

Marquis of Cornwallis off Russell Square, up in a gloomy room at the Belvedere Hotel near Holloway Prison, and eventually down in the basement of Finsbury Library. Audiences averaged around sixty people;[97] MacColl and Seeger were now the club's only prominent names and became closely involved in everyday committee affairs – MacColl enjoyed the contact and was a cheerful presence at meetings, full of good ideas about everything from benefit concerts to reupholstering clubroom chairs.[98]

Touring was now difficult. MacColl could no longer drive, struggled to climb stairs, felt sluggish in the mornings and needed to rest after lunch.[99] Few of Britain's surviving folk clubs could afford their fees, or the decent hotel accommodation that MacColl required. Angina attacks frequently disrupted schedules – shows were either cancelled or performed solo by Peggy.[100] Foreign touring was increasingly risky, even though the big stages never lost their allure for MacColl. Calum joined his parents for their American tour in the spring of 1986, and remembers the strain:

> It became partly looking after dad and making sure he didn't have a heart attack on stage. Which he sometimes did – I saw him turn blue [one night], while he was in the middle of a song. Mum would be trying to get him off. It was madness. He shouldn't have been there. Yet he was driven.[101]

The following year they followed up an irresistible invitation from the Alaskan Wobblies for a shorter tour.[102] In February 1988, the seventy-three-year-old MacColl gave his final overseas performance at the East Berlin Festival of Political Song. The Berlin Wall would outlive him by three weeks.

❧

Encouraged by his old friend Alan Lomax, MacColl began to write his autobiography in 1986.[103] He had mixed feelings from the outset, which Peggy attributed to the fact that his 'life was a tangle of security on one level, insecurity on another'.[104] He was suspicious of the confessional mode that the genre seemed to require; he wondered who'd be interested in his story; though he'd written over 300 songs and a dozen full-length plays, he hadn't written a book since his unpublished 1930s novel, and always preferred performance to print. He described writing his autobiography as 'the most unrewarding thing I've ever done, a very lonely occupation'.[105] *Journeyman: An Autobiography* would eventually be published nine months after his death.

Perched up in the top room of Stanley Avenue, the seventy-one-year-old MacColl immersed himself in memories of his parents and childhood. He was reconnecting with material that he'd often mined for vivid anecdotes, but had rarely discussed or written about – 'My Old Man' and 'Nobody Knew She Was There' were exceptions. It was painful to revisit the shame and humiliation of childhood poverty and the endurance of Betsy and Will. 'He'd sometimes come downstairs from writing his book,' says Peggy, 'and it was obvious he'd been crying.'[106] Spun from his innermost feelings, MacColl's account of those years is a moving, poetic and densely textured memoir of a slum childhood. It was a resolutely unsentimental affair that managed to chronicle extreme deprivation while retaining the wonderment experienced by his opening consciousness.

In places he indulged in colourful dramatisation. Plausible exaggeration is the essence of strong storytelling: deeply aware of the discrepancy between his middle-class lifestyle and preferred working-class identity, he made much of his short career as a car mechanic.[107] And as if to compensate for a loss of potency – 'the spirit is still willing', he confessed later in the book, 'but the flesh, at times, finds it difficult to rise to the occasion' – he vividly revisited his adolescence, cheerfully alluding to the size of his penis ('"Not bad," she said, "not bad at all" and fell to caressing it') in graphic passages detailing early sexual exploits.[108]

The manuscript was ghostwritten by feelings of loss and failure; retreat from what he regarded as cultural and political defeats structured his text. The distant past in Lower Broughton was as exotic as another country: eleven long chapters covered his first fifteen years; another six slowly recreated his young manhood. But Theatre Workshop was a familiar story with an unhappy ending. He wasn't interested in writing it up, so treated it summarily, then dismissed the whole enterprise through a jaundiced squint: 'Theatre Workshop', he wrote, 'did not ... make any lasting impression on the English theatre as a whole. For a short time I believed that we had, but twenty years of theatregoing has since disabused me of any such notion.'[109] He was most famous for his work in the folk revival, whose dwindling ranks were likely to be the book's primary target audience (the literary agent who later handled the book hoped it would become a dependable 'reference work' on the subject').[110] There were enough songbooks, magazines, letters, records and tapes in MacColl's study alone to write an authoritative inside history, but he didn't cross the room to consult any of them. He dealt with the revival in three cursory chapters, and spliced in a lightly revised version of a twenty-year-old article about the radio ballads in which he wearily rehearsed his grievances about accreditation.[111] As with Theatre Workshop, he was too dispirited by the outcome to enjoy writing about the origins. 'It was with a real sense of shock', he admitted, 'that we – those of us who had been present at its concept and birth – saw the revival slipping away.'[112]

The book's most illuminating moments are its silences. MacColl didn't always find it easy to straddle the generation gap and communicate with his children: communicating about them was no more straightforward, so he largely left them out. The narrative jumps from 1939 to 1945 without comment. There was no war, no arrest, no imprisonment, no Stalin, no Mao. Those he'd felt hurt by were consigned to anonymity. Frankie Armstrong, Bob Blair, John Faulkner, Sandra Kerr, Gordon McCulloch, Jim O'Connor, Brian Pearson, Denis Turner, Jack Warshaw – these and others were close allies of the 1960s, but none made it into MacColl's book. The manuscript had burst into life, dipped into diminuendo, and faded out around the time of the Critics Group split (now attributed to 'internal dissension').[113] He pasted into the text a couple of his favourite long ballads and described the complexities of singing them.[114] At the beginning of 1988 he declared he was finished. He hadn't so much finished telling his life-story as abandoned it. '[H]e seemed almost to forget about it,' Peggy remembers. 'It sat in his office for nearly a year.'[115]

CፄᎦᎧ

'The whole last three years of his life he was confused,' says his son Calum; 'he felt redundant, he felt it was a world he didn't understand anymore.'[116] There were moments of respite: the English Folk Dance and Song Society decorated him and Peggy with a Gold Badge for services to folk music;[117] they were made honorary lifelong members of the NUM for their commitment during the strike.[118] 'By and large he ended up quite lonely,' adds Neill. 'He'd alienated so many friends, and lots of his family as well, and didn't really understand why. And nobody had a language to explain it to him because that had never been there between us.'[119] Apart from Peggy, he had no confidants; he had few friends outside his professional life; he'd previously enjoyed post-production parties, but his receding health took with it much of his remaining social life. He suffered bouts of depression. Dull and morose, he'd watch endless hours of television. 'Looking for a Job', a late MacColl composition ostensibly written in response to the return of 1930s levels of mass unemployment, includes the lines 'Another twelve months gone /...Frittered away on the box, / The box is eating my life.'[120] 'If you listen to the way he sings it,' says Calum 'that's him. That's him in the eighties. I can't listen to it. I just get an image of him sitting in that red leather chair, watching telly.'[121]

For almost thirty years he and Peggy had seldom been apart. Their meeting, Peggy later wrote, 'completed him as it completed me ... We worked together so well that we developed an ESP both off and on stage ... We were an almost perfect working team.'[122] Now for the first time their political and creative energies weren't in synch. MacColl stayed at home; Peggy was busy with Beckenham Anti-Nuclear Group, women's politics, environmental campaigning. She was working with Jade, a new four-piece women's vocal outfit, and also singing with Irene Scott, who sometimes went with Peggy to MacColl/Seeger bookings when MacColl was too unwell to perform. (Irene, a member of Jade, had been a friend and political ally since the 1960s and would later become Peggy's partner in life.)[123] MacColl needed Peggy and needed her to need him. 'He coped very badly with her doing anything without him,' says Neill. 'They'd always been together. He felt quite alone and frail without her.'[124] 'It's hard being around someone who is depressed the whole time,' says Calum; 'she perceived another life for herself, while he was acting like life was finished.'[125] 'Each passing year a new malady appeared to drain his body and besiege his mind,' Peggy Seeger later wrote. 'At first these afflictions drew us together but gradually, as the song says, we drifted ... The prospect of losing him haunted me for at least five years before his death.'[126]

CB℘

She persuaded him to have another look at the autobiography. 'I suggested that he write about NOW,' she remembered, 'a time in which he was reverting to being at the mercy of his own body, ageing and ill as it was becoming.'[127] The result was two fresh chapters and an epilogue yielding an unprecedented glimpse of his inner life. He described the limbo state induced by serious illness. 'I find myself these days hesitating before buying a new pair of shoes or a shirt,' he confessed. 'Will I be around long enough to make them worth the price?'[128] He paid tribute to the qualities of Jean Newlove and Joan Littlewood, and described his love for his children and Peggy.[129] He added a new chapter about the process of writing the songs that would become his most enduring legacy.[130] And he returned to the question that documentary filmmaker Dave Boulton had asked about the Communist Party, which was now irreconcilably polarised between advocates of traditional class politics and a modernising wing. MacColl had his differences with the old-guard class warriors now digging in around the *Morning Star* newspaper – they'd never grasped the significance of Mao, cultural activity in general or the people's music in particular – but his contempt was entirely reserved for the modernisers currently talking of new times in their highly successful journal, *Marxism Today*.[131] For MacColl, these people were designer socialists, 'upwardly mobile cacodemics' who seemed more interested in scrutinising counter-hegemonic cultural formations than in fighting the class struggle.[132] His final warning to the party he called 'my university' was against further revisionism.[133] 'So the party I had served was moribund,' he wrote, 'but the ideas and concepts which gave rise to it are still as alive as ever they were. Has there ever been such a desperate need for a revolutionary party as there is today?'[134]

⋇

'The working class should not forget its heroes,' MacColl said in a late interview, with perhaps a twinge of anxiety about his own posterity:

> we have our own heroes and too many of them are forgotten. When we can find those who are still on record and make use of them, it's our job to keep them alive. Revolutions don't start now and then finish. It's a constant process. There should be a sense of continuity in the way we look at life, the way we look at struggle.[135]

To protest against Margaret Thatcher's poll tax, he and Peggy wrote 'Bring the Summer Home', a folk cantata commemorating the Peasants' Revolt provoked by the poll tax of 1381. The songs needed a range of male voices. MacColl did some recruiting at the Singers' Club, but his volunteers weren't experienced singers. 'They couldn't get the oomph into it, the passion,' Peggy remembers.[136] MacColl resorted to his old Stanislavski methods, and told them to imagine they were sailors who hadn't seen a woman for three months singing about returning to port. Two of his choir replied they were gay. MacColl was dumbfounded to hear such a thing from men whose company he enjoyed and whose politics he shared. 'He was seventy four and still learning,' says Peggy. 'I don't recall hearing any homophobic jokes from him from that time.'[137] 'Bring the Summer Home' was premiered at a benefit for Amnesty International at Hammersmith Town Hall on 9 June 1989. It was his final public performance outside the Singers' Club, where he appeared for the last time on 8 October.

ᗧᗤ

He wrote four new songs and went into the studio to record his last record, but 1989 was largely a miserable year for MacColl.[138] He was besieged by angina and heart attacks, and managed just a handful of public performances. His doctor recommended an angioplasty operation to widen his coronary arteries and increase the blood-flow to his heart. MacColl was admitted to Royal Brompton Hospital, Chelsea on 21 October 1989. He was warned that the operation might have no effect, but MacColl was emphatic that he wanted to take the risk, and that he'd rather die than revert to a housebound life.[139] He went into hospital in good spirits. The BBC were making a new documentary about his life to coincide with his seventy-fifth birthday the following January; the poll tax was galvanising opposition to Margaret Thatcher; the four men wrongfully imprisoned for the 1974 Guildford bombings had just been cleared in the light of new evidence about police brutality and corruption – MacColl had long supported their cause. On the hospital ward he made light of the situation, joking about the 'lang syringes' piercing him.[140] He was anaesthetised and wheeled off; as he later recovered consciousness, he became aware that the operation hadn't worked. A couple of hours later, he began to glide in and out of consciousness.

Peggy and all of his children gathered round the bed in the late afternoon and sang his favourite songs, including the Jacobite 'A Parcel of Rogues is a Nation'. 'My shoulders are sore,' murmured MacColl, and Neill went round the bed to rub them. MacColl then repeated the phrase. 'My shoulders are sore, my shoulders are sore,' then became 'my soldiers ashore', then 'soldiers ashore'. His final words were 'the soldiers have come to the shore of my body'.[141] The death certificate gave heart attack and myocardial infarction – destruction of heart muscle resulting from the blockage of a coronary artery – as the cause of death.

৻৵৪৹

News of MacColl's death was widely reported on British news the following day. BBC 2's arts programme *The Late Show* ran a tribute to the man described as 'Britain's Woody Guthrie'.[142] 35 Stanley Avenue was inundated by hundreds of cards and letters of condolence. The broadsheets ran full-page obituaries of 'the people's singer'.[143] 'He had a significance in my life exceeded only by my parents,' said Dick Gaughan in one tribute. 'If it were not for the work of Ewan MacColl I would probably still be working as a plumber on Edinburgh building sites.'[144] 'His influence on the culture we live through now', wrote Fintan O'Toole in the *Irish Times*, 'is so pervasive as to be almost invisible, so much taken for granted that we hardly bother to see it.'[145]

৻৵৪৹

MacColl was cremated in a secular ceremony in Beckenham the following week, and the family set about planning to scatter his ashes along the lines laid down in 'The Joy of Living'. Scotland was naturally the first choice, especially Suilven or Stac Pollaidh in the Highlands, and the appropriate authorities were contacted about the possibility of a small commemorative plaque. The privately owned Suilven was a non-starter, and the Nature Conservancy Council, which looked after Stac Pollaidh, was concerned about thronging pilgrims.[146] For the last time, MacColl's pitch for Scottishness was gently rebuffed. In May 1990 Peggy Seeger and the immediate family climbed Bleaklow Hill and fed his ashes to the winds billowing over the Peak District landscape of his youth.

# Notes

## Prologue, 'Minstrel of Labour'

1. Unsigned article, 'Thatcher Sees Pit Victory Within Grasp', *Guardian*, 22 January 1985.
2. *Guardian*, 21 January 1985; *The Times*, 21 January 1985.
3. A videotape of the concert, produced and directed by David E. Naughton, is held in the Ewan MacColl/Peggy Seeger Archive, Ruskin College, Oxford.
4. Programme for Ewan MacColl's 70th Birthday Folk Concert, MacColl/Seeger Archive.
5. Karl Dallas, interview by author, 22 October 2003, Bradford.
6. Dave Brock, 'Protesting Folk', *City Life* (Manchester), 15–29 March 1985.
7. Videotape of concert; Arthur Scargill to Ben Harker, 4 April 2003.
8. Peggy Seeger, interview by author, 16 November 2003, York.
9. *Class Against Class: The General Election Programme of the Communist Party of Great Britain, 1929* (London, 1929), p. 5.
10. Notably André Gorz, *Farewell to the Working Class: An Essay on Lost Industrial Socialism* (London: Pluto, 1982).

## Chapter 1, 'Lower Broughton'

1. Friedrich Engels, *The Condition of the Working Class in England* (1845; Oxford: Oxford University Press, 1993), p. 74.
2. Ewan MacColl, interview in Dave Boulton's film, *Daddy, What Did You Do in the Strike?*, Granada Television, broadcast 15 December 1985.
3. Engels, *Condition of the Working Class in England*; Salford was dubbed 'The Classic Slum' in Robert Roberts' famous sociological memoir *The Classic Slum: Salford Life in the First Quarter of the Century* (1971; Harmondsworth: Pelican, 1973).
4. Betsy Miller, interview by Charles Parker, 6 February 1962. Recording held in the Charles Parker Archive, Birmingham Central Library. CPA MS 4000/5/1/3/3.
5. Ewan MacColl, *Journeyman: An Autobiography* (London: Sidgwick & Jackson, 1990), p. 15.
6. Betsy Miller, interview by Charles Parker, 29 January 1969. CPA MS 4000/5/1/3/5D.
7. Betsy Miller, interview by Charles Parker, 6 February 1962. CPA MS 4000/5/1/3/3.

8. Betsy Miller, interview by Charles Parker, 6 February 1962. CPA MS 4000/5/1/3/3.

9. MacColl, *Journeyman*, pp. 13, 1, 27.

10. Betsy Miller, interview by Charles Parker, 29 January 1969. CPA MS 4000/5/1/3/5D.

11. Betsy Miller, interview by Charles Parker, 29 January 1969. CPA MS 4000/5/1/3/5D; Betsy Miller, interview by Charles Parker, 6 February 1962. CPA MS 4000/5/1/3/3; MacColl, *Journeyman*, p. 21.

12. MacColl, *Journeyman*, p. 53.

13. MacColl, *Journeyman*, p. 29.

14. MacColl, *Journeyman*, p. 21.

15. MacColl, *Journeyman*, p. 13.

16. MacColl, *Journeyman*, p. 21.

17. Betsy Miller, interview by Charles Parker, 6 February 1962. CPA MS 4000/5/1/3/3.

18. Betsy Miller, interview by Charles Parker, 29 January 1969. CPA MS 4000/5/1/3/5D.

19. *Ordnance Survey Map, Manchester (NW) and Central Salford 1915* (Consett: Godfrey, 2001).

20. MacColl, *Journeyman*, p. 10.

21. MacColl, *Journeyman*, p. 181.

22. MacColl, *Journeyman*, p. 182.

23. MacColl, *Journeyman*, p. 20; Harry McShane and Joan Smith, *Harry McShane: No Mean Fighter* (London: Pluto, 1978).

24. MacColl in Raphael Samuel, Ewan MacColl and Stuart Cosgrove, eds, *Theatres of the Left 1880–1935* (London: Routledge, 1985), pp. 205, 209; Dave Sherry, *John Maclean* (London: Socialist Workers Party, 1998).

25. MacColl in *Theatres of the Left*, p. 209.

26. MacColl, *Journeyman*, p. 26.

27. Betsy Miller, interview by Charles Parker, 6 February 1962. CPA MS 4000/5/1/3/3.

28. Betsy Miller, interview by Charles Parker, 29 January 1969. CPA MS 4000/5/1/3/5D; MacColl, *Journeyman*, p. 34.

29. Betsy Miller, interview by Charles Parker, 6 February 1962. CPA MS 4000/5/1/3/3.

30. MacColl in *Theatres of the Left*, p. 207.

31. MacColl, *Journeyman*, p. 36.

32. MacColl, *Journeyman*, pp. 59, 65.

33. MacColl, *Journeyman*, p. 60.

34. MacColl, *Journeyman*, p. 65.

35. MacColl in *Theatres of the Left*, p. 213; MacColl, *Journeyman*, p. 55.

36. MacColl, *Journeyman*, p. 47.

37. MacColl, *Journeyman*, p. 50.

38. MacColl, *Journeyman*, p. 53.

39. MacColl, *Journeyman*, p. 71.

40. MacColl, *Journeyman*, p. 69.

41. MacColl, *Journeyman*, p. 107.

42. MacColl in *Theatres of the Left*, p. 209.

43. *North Grecian Street Primary School Inspection Report, Dates of Inspection 21–24 May 2001*; Alan Kidd, *Manchester* (1993; Edinburgh University Press: Edinburgh, 2002), p. 122.
44. MacColl, *Journeyman*, p. 111; MacColl in *Theatres of the Left*, p. 207.
45. MacColl, *Journeyman*, p. 40.
46. MacColl, *Journeyman*, pp. 43–4.
47. MacColl, *Journeyman*, p. 125.
48. MacColl, *Journeyman*, p. 125.
49. MacColl, *Journeyman*, pp. 124, 131.
50. MacColl, *Journeyman*, p. 130.
51. MacColl in *Theatres of the Left*, p. 209; MacColl, *Journeyman*, p. 105.
52. MacColl, *Journeyman*, p. 106.
53. Betsy Miller, interview by Charles Parker, 29 January 1969. CPA MS 4000/5/1/3/5C.
54. Neill MacColl, interview by author, 27 February 2006, London.
55. MacColl, *Journeyman*, p. 110.
56. MacColl, *Journeyman*, p. 74.
57. MacColl, *Journeyman*, p. 129.

## Chapter 2, 'Red Haze'

1. Ewan MacColl, 'Theatre of Action, Manchester', in *Theatres of the Left 1880–1930*, ed. Raphael Samuel, Ewan MacColl and Stuart Cosgrove (London: Routledge, 1985), p. 226.
2. Matthew Worley, *Class Against Class: The Communist Party in Britain Between the Wars* (London and New York: I. B. Tauris, 2002), p. 173; Edmund and Ruth Frow, *The Battle of Bexley Square: Salford Unemployed Workers' Demonstration – 1st October, 1931* (Salford, 1994), pp. 4–6.
3. MacColl in *Theatres of the Left*, p. 214.
4. Ewan MacColl, *Journeyman: An Autobiography* (London: Sidgwick & Jackson, 1990), pp. 149, 143; MacColl in *Theatres of the Left*, p. 214.
5. MacColl in *Theatres of the Left*, p. 215.
6. MacColl in *Theatres of the Left*, p. 214; MacColl, *Journeyman*, p. 175.
7. MacColl, *Journeyman*, p. 155.
8. MacColl, *Journeyman*, pp. 135, 155.
9. Ewan MacColl, 'The Evolution of a Revolutionary Theatre Style', in *Agit-prop to Theatre Workshop*, ed. Howard Goorney and Ewan MacColl (Manchester and New York: Manchester University Press, 1986), p. xvii. MacColl, *Journeyman*, pp. 155, 201.
10. MacColl in *Theatres of the Left*, p. 210.
11. MacColl, interview by Dave Boulton, in Boulton's documentary film about MacColl, *Daddy, What Did You Do in the Strike*, Granada Television (1985).
12. *Manchester and Salford Workers' Film Society Report, Season 1930–1*. Original in Working Class Movement Library, Salford.
13. Manchester and Salford Workers' Film Society pamphlet, *The cinema and its application to social questions*. Original in National Labour History Archive and Study Centre, Manchester (hereafter NLHASC), NMLH/MSFS/2.

14. MacColl in *Agit-prop*, p. xvi.
15. Manchester and Salford Workers' Film Society, 'Prospectus for Second Season, 1931–2'; handbill for performance given on Saturday 18 April 1931. Originals in Working Class Movement Library, Salford.
16. MacColl in *Agit-prop*, p. xvi.
17. Betsy Miller, interview by Charles Parker, 29 January 1969. Charles Parker Archive, Birmingham Central Library. CPA MS 4000/5/1/3/5D.
18. MacColl, interview by Boulton, *Daddy* (1985).
19. MacColl in *Agit-prop*, p. viv.
20. MacColl in *Agit-prop*, pp. xiv–xv.
21. MacColl recalled Harrison in a number of interviews and written pieces over the years, but he frequently confused Harrison's first name: sometimes it was given as Stanley, at others as Charlie. See MacColl in *Agit-prop*, p. xvii; MacColl in *Theatres of the Left*, p. 233; MacColl, *Journeyman*, pp. 143, 155.
22. MacColl, *Journeyman*, p. 143.
23. MacColl in *Agit-prop*, p. xviii; MacColl in *Theatres of the Left*, p. 223.
24. MacColl in *Theatres of the Left*, p. 224.
25. MacColl in *Agit-prop*, p. xix.
26. Francis Beckett, *Enemy Within: The Rise and Fall of the British Communist Party* (1995; London: Merlin, 1998), pp. 9–16. Also Willie Thompson, *The Good Old Cause: British Communism 1920–1991* (London: Pluto, 1992).
27. Kevin Morgan, *Harry Pollitt* (Manchester and New York: Manchester University Press, 1993), p. 62.
28. Morgan, *Pollitt*, p. 63.
29. John Stevenson and Chris Cook, *The Slump: Society and Politics During the Depression* (London: Quartet, 1979), p. 128; MacColl quotation from Robin Denselow, *When the Music's Over: The Story of Political Pop* (London: Faber & Faber, 1989), p. 19.
30. Andrew Thorpe, *The British Communist Party and Moscow, 1920–1943* (Manchester and New York: Manchester University Press, 2000), p. 284.
31. Worley, *Class Against Class*, p. 259.
32. MacColl, *Journeyman*, p. 155.
33. MacColl in *Theatres of the Left*, pp. 205, 216.
34. MacColl in *Theatres of the Left*, p. 206, 217; Betsy Miller, interview by Charles Parker, 29 January 1969. CPA MS 4000/5/1/3/5D.
35. MacColl, *Journeyman*, p. 155.
36. MacColl, *Journeyman*, p. 156.
37. MacColl in *Theatres of the Left*, p. 222.
38. Ewan MacColl, interview in *Parsley, Sage and Politics* (1985), a nine-part radio documentary produced by Michael O'Rourke and Mary Orr and subsequently issued on audiocassette and CD.
39. MacColl, *Journeyman*, p. 182.
40. *Daily Worker*, 1 January 1930.
41. MacColl in *Theatres of the Left*, p. 222.
42. MacColl in *Theatres of the Left*, pp. 219–21; MacColl, *Journeyman*, p. 357; Ruth Frow, interview by author, 29 September 2003, Salford.

43. *Ward and Goldstone Spark*, 24 July 1930. Original in Working Class Movement Library, Salford.
44. MacColl in *Theatres of the Left*, p. 220.
45. Ruth Frow, interview by author, 29 September 2003, Salford; MacColl in *Theatres of the Left*, pp. 219, 221.
46. MacColl, *Journeyman*, p. 183.
47. MacColl, *Journeyman*, p. 183.
48. MacColl in *Theatres of the Left*, pp. 221–2.
49. MacColl in *Theatres of the Left*, p. 224.
50. MacColl in *Theatres of the Left*, p. 224.
51. MacColl in *Agit-prop*, p. xx.
52. Tom Thomas, 'A Propertyless Theatre for the Propertyless Class' in *Theatres of the Left*, p. 83; MacColl in *Agit-Prop*, p. xix; Thomas had earlier scripted the stage adaptation of *The Ragged Trousered Philanthopists* in which Miller had been involved.
53. Thomas in *Theatres of the Left*, p. 87.
54. *Daily Worker*, 10 May 1930, cited in Worley, *Class Against Class*, p. 206.
55. In his later life MacColl often dated the formation of the Manchester and Salford WTM as 1930, and the dating has been reproduced in various books and articles. But the first edition of the WTM journal, *Red Stage,* appeared in November 1931 and the Manchester and Salford branch is reported as being a recent organisation. Mid-1931 seems more likely.
56. MacColl, *Journeyman*, pp. 160, 165.
57. MacColl in *Theatres of the Left*, pp. 216, 225.
58. Edmund and Ruth Frow, 'The Workers' Theatre Movement in Manchester and Salford, 1931–1940', *North West Labour History Journal*, 17 (1992–3), pp. 66–75, at p. 67.
59. MacColl in *Theatres of the Left*, p. 225.
60. Edmund and Ruth Frow, 'Workers' Theatre Movement', p. 67; MacColl, *Journeyman*, pp. 187–8.
61. MacColl, *Journeyman*, p. 207.
62. *Red Stage: Organ of the Workers' Theatre Movement*, No. 1 (November 1931). Originals in Working Class Movement Library, Salford.
63. *Red Stage*, No. 2 (January 1932); Richard Stourac and Kathleen McCreery, *Theatre as a Weapon: Workers' Theatre in the Soviet Union, Germany and Britain, 1917–1934* (London and New York: Routledge & Kegan Paul, 1986), p. 305.
64. *Red Stage*, No. 2 (January 1932).
65. Stourac and McCreery, *Theatre as a Weapon*, p. 206.
66. Stourac and McCreery, *Theatre as a Weapon*, p. 108.
67. Notably the International Workers' Dramatic Union (IWD). Stourac and McCreery, *Theatre as a Weapon*, p. 208.
68. André van Gyseghem, 'British Theatre in the Thirties: An Autobiographical Record', in Jon Clark, Margot Heinemann, David Margolies and Carole Snee, eds, *Culture and Crisis in the Thirties* (London: Lawrence & Wishart, 1979), pp. 209–19, at p. 212.
69. See *Daily Worker*, 11 June 1930, 3 January 1931, 12 January 1931.

70.  MacColl in *Theatres of the Left*, p. 229; MacColl *Journeyman*, p. 159.

71.  MacColl in *Theatres of the Left*, p. 229.

72.  The new name coincided with the acquisition of 'a new uniform, which is meeting with the workers' approval'. *Workers' Theatre Movement Monthly Bulletin*, No. 3 (February 1933).

73.  MacColl in *Agit-prop*, p. xxi.

74.  *The Meerut Trial, Facts of the Case* (pamphlet issued by the National Meerut Prisoners' Defence Committee, August 1929), NLHASC, CP/ORG/MISC/10/04. See also Worley, *Class Against Class*, p. 227.

75.  The text was updated by the WTM to reflect the changing situation; the 1933 version is reprinted in *Theatres of the Left*, pp. 114–17, as are Charlie Mann's guideline for performers, 'How to produce *Meerut*', pp. 106–8.

76.  MacColl in *Agit-prop*, p. xxiii; MacColl in *Theatres of the Left*, p. 231.

77.  *Red Stage*, No. 2 (January 1932).

78.  Promotional handbills and a copy of the programme in Working Class Movement Library, Salford. For the group's own write-up see *Red Stage*, No. 4 (March 1932).

79.  *Red Stage*, No. 4 (March 1932).

80.  Andrew Davies, *Leisure, Gender and Poverty: Working-Class Culture in Salford and Manchester, 1900–1939* (Buckingham and Philadelphia: Open University Press, 1992), pp. 123–39.

81.  MacColl in *Agit-prop*, p. xxiii; for Trafford Road docks, see Davies, *Leisure*, p. 37.

82.  MacColl in *Agit-prop*, p. xxiii.

83.  Wal Hannington, *A Short History of the Unemployed* (London: Victor Gollancz, 1938), p. 57.

84.  By December 1930 the £56 million debt was increasing by £7 million a week. Hannington, *Unemployed*, p. 57.

85.  Richard Croucher, *We Refuse to Starve in Silence: A History of the National Unemployed Workers' Movement 1920–1946* (London: Lawrence & Wishart, 1987), p. 117.

86.  MacColl, *Journeyman*, p. 195; Croucher, *We Refuse to Starve*, p. 120; Hannington, *Unemployed*, pp. 61–3.

87.  Croucher, *We Refuse to Starve*, pp. 39–57; Worley, *Class Against Class*, p. 7.

88.  Worley, *Class Against Class*, p. 176.

89.  Worley, *Class Against Class*, p. 281.

90.  Edmund and Ruth Frow, *The Battle of Bexley Square: Salford Unemployed Workers' Demonstration – 1ˢᵗ October 1931* (Salford, 1994), p. 7.

91.  MacColl, *Journeyman*, p. 201.

92.  Edmund and Ruth Frow, *Bexley Square*, p. 7.

93.  Edmund and Ruth Frow, *Bexley Square*, p. 11; MacColl, *Journeyman*, pp. 195–6.

94.  *Red Stage*, No. 1 (November 1931).

95.  MacColl, *Journeyman*, p. 200; for Margaret Bondfield, see Stevenson and Cook, *The Slump*, pp. 148, 252.

96.  The WTM published this version of 'Billy Boy' in *Red Stage*, No. 4 (March 1932) where it's credited to the journal's editor, Charlie Mann. MacColl

remembered singing the song on the day, but he usually referred to it as something he'd written himself. It may be that he did write a version; it's also possible that he had access to the WTM version prior to its official publication but later forgot the song's origin and assumed he'd written it. For MacColl's memories of performing at the Bexley Square demonstration, see MacColl, *Journeyman*, pp. 199–200; MacColl in *Agit-prop*, p. xxi.

97. The Manchester WTM considered the demonstration as 'our first real experience of open-air work' and were confident that 'there is ample scope to reach large masses of workers in this way'. *Red Stage*, No. 1 (November 1931).

98. The charter demanded fair wages, fair levels of relief, free coal during the coming winter and free milk for children under five. *Salford City Reporter*, 9 October 1931, cited in Edmund and Ruth Frow, *Bexley Square*, p. 24.

99. Walter Greenwood, *Love on the Dole* (1933; Harmondsworth: Penguin, 1969), pp. 194–209.

100. Greenwood, *Love on the Dole*, p. 199.

101. Edmund and Ruth Frow, *Bexley Square*, pp. 18–23.

102. Ruth Frow, interview by author, Salford, 26 September 2003.

103. Nellie Wallace, interview by Michael O'Rourke and Mary Orr, in *Parsley, Sage and Politics* (1985), a nine-part radio documentary about Ewan MacColl and Peggy Seeger subsequently issued as audiocassette and CD.

104. MacColl, *Journeyman*, pp. 195–200.

105. MacColl, *Journeyman*, p. 195.

106. MacColl, *Journeyman*, p. 200.

107. This grievance is voiced by the Manchester and Salford WTM branch in *Red Stage*, No. 3 (February 1932).

108. Croucher, *We Refuse to Starve*, p. 134.

109. The text is reprinted in *Theatres of the Left*, p. 239. MacColl reminisces about political songs from the period in CPA MS/4000/5/1/12/4.

110. Maurice Levine, letter to the *Guardian*, 31 October 1989.

111. Worley, *Class Against Class*, p. 169.

112. Stevenson and Cook, *The Slump*, p. 13, table A10.

113. Worley, *Class Against Class*, p. 296.

114. MacColl in *Theatres of the Left*, p. 235.

115. MacColl in *Theatres of the Left*, p. 235; MacColl in *Agit-prop*, p. xxv.

116. MacColl in *Theatres*, pp. 236–69; MacColl in *Agit-prop*, p. xxv.

117. MacColl in *Agit-prop*, p. xxv.

118. Ewan MacColl, 'Grass Roots of Theatre Workshop', *Theatre Quarterly*, III, 9 (January–March 1973), pp. 58–69, p. 60; MacColl in *Theatres of the Left*, p. 238.

119. *Red Stage*, No. 6 (June–July 1932).

120. Tom Thomas, 'The Workers' Theatre in Britain', *International Theatre*, No. 1 (1934), pp. 22–4.

121. Sheffield unemployment figure from Dave Cook, 'The Battle for Kinder Scout', *Marxism Today* (August 1977), pp. 241–3, at p. 241; MacColl in *Theatres of the Left*, p. 227.

122. MacColl, *Journeyman*, p. 184.

123. MacColl in *Theatres of the Left*, p. 232; MacColl, *Journeyman*, p. 167.

124. MacColl, *Journeyman*, p. 178.

125. MacColl in *Theatres of the Left*, p. 227.

126. MacColl, *Journeyman*, p. 185.

127. Frow, interviewed by O'Rourke and Orr, *Parsley, Sage and Politics*.

128. Phil Barnes, *Trespassers Will Be Prosecuted: Views of the Forbidden Moorland* (Sheffield, 1934), cited in John Lowerson, 'The Battle for the Countryside' in Frank Gloversmith, ed., *Class, Culture and Social Change: A New View of the 1930s* (Brighton: Harvester, 1980), pp. 258–80, at p. 277 and Cook, 'Kinder Scout', p. 241.

129. Cook, 'Kinder Scout', p. 241; Lowerson, 'Battle', p. 277.

130. Lowerson, 'Battle', p. 273.

131. *Communist Review* (February 1930), cited in Worley, *Class Against Class*, p. 223.

132. Worley, *Class Against Class*, p. 211.

133. Bernard Barry, 'Not Just a Rambler', *Working Class Movement Library Bulletin* (1998).

134. *BWSF Camp Souvenir*, undated, cited in Worley, *Class Against Class*, p. 212. The Working Class Movement Library, Salford, has a photograph of Frow on the camp.

135. Cook, 'Kinder Scout', p. 242.

136. 'Extract from CC Salford report re the British Workers Sports Federation', 29 April 1932. National Archives. KV2/2175/48.

137. MacColl, interview by Dave Boulton, *Daddy* (1985).

138. Cook, 'Kinder Scout', p. 242.

139. On Monday 25 April both the *Daily Dispatch* and the *Daily Telegraph* estimated four hundred; the *Manchester Guardian* claimed 'four or five hundred'.

140. MacColl estimated 3,000 in the television interview with Dave Boulton; for the higher figure, see Denselow, *When The Music's Over*, p. 20.

141. Lowerson puts the figure at 8. 'Battle', p. 276.

142. *Manchester Guardian*, 25 April 1932.

143. Cook, 'Kinder Scout', p. 243.

144. *Daily Worker*, 22 July 1932.

145. Cook, 'Kinder Scout', p. 243.

146. *Daily Worker*, 22 July 1932.

147. Benny Rothman's untitled and undated account of events is held in the Benny Rothman Papers at the Working Class Movement Library, Salford.

148. *Worker Sportsman* (August 1932), p. 9.

149. Lowerson, 'Battle', p. 286.

150. *The Times,* 7 March 1939, cited in Lowerson, 'Battle', p. 274.

151. Rothman's undated and untitled account of Mass Trespass, Working Class Movement Library, Salford.

152. MacColl, interview by Howard Goorney (unpublished), late 1970s.

153. MacColl in *Theatres of the Left*, p. 232; MacColl, *Journeyman*, p. 167.

154. 'Mass Trespass 1932', reprinted in Peggy Seeger, ed., *The Essential Ewan MacColl Songbook: Sixty Years of Songmaking* (New York: Oak Publications, 2001), p. 279.

155. Natt Frayman, interview by O'Rourke and Orr, *Parsley, Sage and Politics*.
156. Natt Frayman, interview by O'Rourke and Orr, *Parsley, Sage and Politics*.
157. Ewan MacColl, *Journeyman*, p. 358. The song is reprinted in Seeger, ed., *Ewan MacColl Songbook*, p. 370.
158. MacColl, quoted in Peggy Seeger, introduction to MacColl, *Journeyman*, p. 1.

## Chapter 3, 'Welcome Comrade'

1. Ewan MacColl, *Journeyman: An Autobiography* (London: Sidgwick & Jackson, 1990), pp. 205–6.
2. MacColl, *Journeyman*, p. 201.
3. MacColl, *Journeyman*, p. 202.
4. MacColl, *Journeyman*, p. 203.
5. MacColl, *Journeyman*, pp. 201–3.
6. MacColl, *Journeyman*, p. 161.
7. D. G. Bridson, *Prospero and Ariel: The Rise and Fall of Radio* (London: Victor Gollancz, 1971), pp. 36, 32; Olive Shapley with Christina Hart, *Broadcasting a Life* (London: Scarlet, 1996), p. 54.
8. Asa Briggs, *The Age of the Wireless* (London: Oxford University Press, 1965), p. 329. The North Region could count two million licence holders between the Scottish borders, the Potteries, Lincolnshire and Lancashire, double the number for the Midlands and four times that for Scotland. Paddy Scannell and David Cardiff, *A Social History of British Broadcasting: Volume One 1922–1939* (Oxford: Blackwell, 1991), p. 334.
9. *Crisis in Spain* (1931) was a reportage programme about the fall of the Spanish monarchy. The original recording was wiped, but the programme was remade for training purposes in the late 1930s. BBC SAL T28022; National Sound Archive CPRD 28022, sequence T. Script in BBC WAC, Scripts. The second programme was *New Year Over Europe*, broadcast on 31 December 1932. Script in BBC WAC, R19/825/1.
10. Olive Shapley interviewed on *Vox Pop: The Story of the First Feature Programme*, BBC Radio 4, 23 December 1985. National Sound Archive B514, disk 1.
11. Bridson, *Prospero*, p. 35.
12. Bridson, *Prospero*, p. 33; MacColl, *Journeyman*, p. 233; *The Times*, 18 and 19 July 1934.
13. Ewan MacColl, interview by Fred Woods, *Folk Review*, 2.7 (May 1973), p. 4. No BBC contracts have survived for Miller's earliest appearances, but in May 1936 he was paid 5 guineas for his work on a second version of *May Day*. The fee covered 14 hours of rehearsals plus the recording. Details from BBC WAC/R Cont 1/Miller, James/Artist File, 1935–62. For average weekly earnings in the mid-1930s, see Philippa Polson, 'Feminists and the Woman Question', *Left Review* (September 1935), pp. 500–2. The average weekly wage for a coal miner in 1934 was £2 15s per week. George Orwell, *The Road to Wigan Pier* (1937; London: Penguin, 1962), p. 36.

14. MacColl, *Journeyman*, p. 233.
15. MacColl, *Journeyman*, p. 229.
16. Bridson, *Prospero*, p. 30.
17. In Manchester's Free Trade Hall in March, then again at a rally at the city's Belle Vue in October. John Stevenson and Chris Cook, *The Slump: Society and Politics During the Depression* (London: Quartet, 1977), p. 202.
18. Membership took an upward turn, more than doubling from 5,000 to 11,000 between February 1934 and October 1936. For membership figures, see Andrew Thorpe, *The British Communist Party and Moscow, 1920–43* (Manchester: Manchester University Press, 2000), p. 284.
19. The tension was present as early as the first WTM National Conference in June 1932 when the aptly named Rebel Players had outraged the agitprop majority by presenting a naturalistic play set in a Russian peasant home. The rift became more pronounced in the May of 1933 when the cream of British groups made their way to the Moscow Olympiad, only to discover that the Mecca of the agitprop form was itself turning to longer, more naturalistic plays. The Rebels felt vindicated, the champions of agitprop confused. Richard Stourac and Kathleen McCreery, *Theatre as a Weapon: Workers' Theatre in the Soviet Union, Germany and Britain, 1917–1934* (London and New York: Routledge & Kegan Paul), pp. 230–3, 241–2.
20. Adolphe Appia, 'Actor, Space, Light, Painting' (1919) and extracts from *Music and the Art of Theatre* in Richard C. Beacham, ed., *Adolphe Appia: Texts on Theatre* (London and New York: Routledge, 1993), pp. 114–16, 29–59.
21. Léon Moussinac, *The New Movement in Theatre: A Survey of Recent Developments in Europe and America* (London: B. T. Batsford, 1931).
22. Stuart Cosgrove, 'From Shock Troupe to Group Theatre' in Raphael Samuel, Ewan MacColl and Stuart Cosgrove, eds, *Theatres of the Left, 1880–1935* (London: Routledge & Kegan Paul, 1985), pp. 267–8.
23. Cosgrove, *Theatres of the Left*, p. 270.
24. Cosgrove, *Theatres of the Left*, p. 271.
25. Cosgrove, *Theatres of the Left*, p. 279.
26. Ewan MacColl in *Theatres of the Left*, p. 245. The contact was Benny Segal, a waterproof garment worker who lived in Lower Broughton. For Segal, see also Ewan MacColl to Denis Mitchell, 10 October 1973, General Correspondence file, Ewan MacColl and Peggy Seeger Archive, Ruskin College, Oxford.
27. MacColl, *Theatres of the Left*, p. 247.
28. *Manchester Guardian*, 18 May 1935.
29. Joan Littlewood, *Joan's Book: The Autobiography of Joan Littlewood* (London: Methuen, 1994), p. 70. On 1 and 2 September 1933 she played Cleopatra in 'Scenes from Shakespeare' broadcast on the Empire Service. BBC WAC/Joan Littlewood/Artist file/1933–62.
30. Littlewood interviewed on *Vox Pop: The Story of the First Feature Programme*.
31. Littlewood, *Joan's Book*, pp. 7, 79, 81.
32. Littlewood, *Joan's Book*, p. 85.

33. Ronald Mackenzie's *The Maitlands*. *Daily Dispatch*, 21 September 1934. Programme in Manchester Central Library Theatre Collection.
34. *Manchester Guardian*, 18 December 1934. Programme in Manchester Central Library Theatre Collection.
35. Programmes in Manchester Central Library Theatre Collection.
36. MacColl, *Journeyman*, p. 211.
37. Littlewood, *Joan's Book*, p. 88.
38. Littlewood, *Joan's Book*, p. 89.
39. Littlewood, *Joan's Book*, p. 89.
40. Littlewood, *Joan's Book*, p. 89.
41. Littlewood, *Joan's Book*, p. 91. Rosalie Williams also recalls Miller using the phrase at this time. Rosalie Williams, interview by author, 1 October 2003, Manchester.
42. Littlewood, *Joan's Book*, p. 93.
43. MacColl, *Journeyman*, p. 211.
44. MacColl, *Journeyman*, p. 211.
45. Cosgrove, *Theatres of the Left*, p. 269. Ewan MacColl, 'The Evolution of a Revolutionary Theatre Style' in Howard Goorney and Ewan MacColl, eds, *Agit-prop to Theatre Workshop: Political Playscripts 1930–1950* (Manchester: Manchester University Press, 1986), p. xxxi. MacColl was a keen reader of the American *New Theatre* magazine and kept abreast of developments in the US. See p. xxxiv.
46. For the smaller venues, see MacColl, *Agit-prop*, p. xxi and Littlewood, *Joan's Book*, p. 93. The precise dating of the Ancoats show presents some difficulty. In *Agit-prop* (p. xxi), MacColl gives the date as 'February or March 1934'. This is impossible: Littlewood was definitely involved in the show, and didn't arrive in Manchester until the summer; the undated production handbill reveals that the group were already calling themselves 'Theatre of Action'. Given that the Americans didn't come up with the name until 1935, and that Miller's group can't have begun using it until at least then, spring 1935 seems the most likely date. The production doesn't seem to have been reviewed in the local press.
47. The handbill is reprinted in Ewan MacColl, 'Grass Roots of Theatre Workshop', *Theatre Quarterly*, III, 9 (January–March 1973), p. 61 and in Howard Goorney, *The Theatre Workshop Story* (London: Methuen, 1981), pp. 11–12.
48. The handbill recycles Alfred Saxe's article, '"Newsboy": from Script to Performance' published in *New Theatre* (July–August 1934) and reprinted in *Theatres of the Left*, pp. 289–96.
49. MacColl, *Agit-prop*, p. xxxi.
50. Cosgrove, *Theatres of the Left*, pp. 273–5. The American adaptation is reprinted in *Theatres of the Left*, pp. 316–22.
51. The British adaptation is reprinted in *Agit-prop*, pp. 13–21.
52. *Agit-prop*, p. 14.
53. MacColl, *Journeyman*, p. 212.
54. The script is held in the Merseyside Left/Unity Theatre Archive, Box 12, file 1. MacColl's memory was often hazy about this. He always referred to

the play as 'Hammer', confusing the author's surname with the play's title. MacColl, *Agit-prop*, pp. xxiii–iv.

55. *John Bullion: A Ballet with Words* is reprinted in *Agit-prop*, pp. 2–11.

56. Littlewood, *Joan's Book*, p. 101.

57. The season included adaptations of two Brontë novels and a version of Thomas Hardy's *Tess of the D'Urbervilles*. Season programme in Manchester Central Library Theatre Collection.

58. Littlewood, *Joan's Book*, pp. 95–7 and MacColl, *Theatres of the Left*, pp. 249–50; *Agit-prop*, pp. xxxii–iv.

59. Written up in the *Daily Worker*, 19 February 1935.

60. Littlewood, *Joan's Book*, p. 101.

61. Littlewood, *Joan's Book*, p. 96.

62. *Daily Dispatch*, 15 February 1935; *Manchester Evening News*, 12 February 1935; *Manchester Guardian*, 12 February 1935.

63. Littlewood, *Joan's Book*, p. 96. Littlewood inaccurately claims that Theatre of Action quarrelled with director Dominic Roche and didn't make the trip to London. MacColl remembered the performance and mentioned it on a number of occasions; Theatre of Action's input is also discussed in the *Daily Mail* review of the London show, 13 May 1935.

64. The *Daily Mail* critic dismissed the performance as an 'extraordinary hotchpotch'. One unsourced review held in the Theatre Museum, Covent Garden describes the performance as making 'a braver show as propaganda than as a work of art'.

65. MacColl, *Agit-prop*, p. xxxii.

66. Littlewood's autobiography suggests that she parted company with the Manchester Rep immediately after the London show (p. 97). According to newspaper reports, however, she worked on for another month. Her last appearance seems to have been in *The Blind Goddess*, a second Toller play in which her performance was singled out for praise in the *Manchester Guardian* on 4 June 1935.

67. MacColl, *Journeyman*, p. 35; Littlewood, *Joan's Book*, p. 99.

68. Littlewood, *Joan's Book*, p. 98.

69. Littlewood, *Joan's Book*, p. 102.

70. Littlewood, *Joan's Book*, p. 104

71. Littlewood, *Joan's Book*, p. 99.

72. R. J. Finnemore, 'Is There A Crisis in Theatre?', *Daily Dispatch*, 17 May 1935, p. 4. Also *Daily Worker*, 14 April and 30 April 1935.

73. For André van Gyseghem, see van Gyseghem, 'British Theatre in the Thirties: An Autobiographical Record' in Jon Clark, Margot Heinemann, David Margolies and Carol Snee, eds, *Culture and Crisis in Britain in the Thirties* (London: Lawrence & Wishart, 1979), pp. 209–18.

74. Michael Denning, *The Cultural Front: The Labouring of American Culture in the Twentieth Century* (London and New York: Verso, 1997), pp. xiv–xv and Harold Clurman, *The Fervent Years: The Group Theatre and the 30s* (1957; New York: Da Capo Press, 1983), pp. 141, 145–9. The text is reprinted in *Theatres of the Left*, pp. 326–52.

75. For the controversy, see Colin Chambers, *The Story of Unity Theatre* (London: Lawrence & Wishart, 1989), pp. 41–2 and Stourac and McCreery, *Theatre as a Weapon*, p. 248.

76. As with all of the early Theatre of Action productions, the precise dating of *Waiting for Lefty* is difficult. Performances were for members only, runs were very short, handbills were often undated and the productions were seldom reviewed. According to the local press, Theatre of Action had staged the play by August. *Daily Dispatch*, 16 August 1935.

77. Exactly what happened next is contested – MacColl would tell the story of the group's sudden implosion on a number of occasions, and there are discrepancies between each. According to one version, the Communist Party were reluctant arbiters in an internal dispute (MacColl, *Journeyman*, pp. 214–17); in another they weren't involved at all (MacColl, *Agit-prop*, pp. xxv-xxxvii); in a third it was the party that initiated proceedings – the apparatchiks were apparently eager to mobilise this now prominent group for fundraising and recruitment work and to wrest control from a pair of prima donnas trying to 'dance their way through the revolution' (MacColl, *Theatres of the Left*, pp. 250–2).

78. The new Theatre of Action would emphasise 'social protest' and perform a less experimental repertoire including Odets' new play *Till the Day I Die* and, pointedly, the original version of John Hammer's *Slickers Ltd.* They performed this double-bill at the Stockport Garrick Theatre for the Stockport District Anti-War Council on 31 October 1935. See *Manchester Guardian*, 19 October 1935. They also presented *Till the Day I Die* at the Hyde Socialist Church on 3 November. The Working Class Movement Library, Salford, holds correspondence relating to these productions. The inaugural meeting of the New Theatre League was held in London on 1 and 2 February 1936.

79. MacColl, *Journeyman*, p. 216.

80. For the Academy, see Herbert Marshall's three autobiographical essays in *The Listener*, 22 March, 29 March and 5 April 1973. See also Cosgrove, *Theatres of the Left*, p. 271. A year previously Miller's WTM acquaintance André van Gyseghem had recognised Jimmie's talents and encouraged him to apply. When Littlewood arrived on the scene they'd hastily applied for her too.

81. Jimmie's passport application was later passed on to MI5. National Archives, KV/2/2175/32.

82. MacColl, *Journeyman*, p. 217 and *Theatres of the Left*, p. 251; Littlewood, *Joan's Book*, pp. 101, 104. Littlewood's memory of the dates is hazy here.

83. MacColl, interview by Howard Goorney (unpublished), late 1970s.

84. Littlewood to Robin Whitworth, 8 November 1935. BBC WAC/Joan Littlewood/Artist file/1933–62.

85. Miller to Robin Whitworth [nd]. BBC WAC/Miller, James/Artist file/1935–62.

86. BBC Memo, 15 November 1935. BBC WAC/Joan Littlewood, Artist file/1933–62; BBC Memo, 17 December 1935. BBC WAC/James Miller, Artist file/1935–62.

87. MacColl, interview by Howard Goorney (unpublished), late 1970s.
88. Miller to Robin Whitworth, 24 January 1936. BBC WAC/James Miller/Artist file/1935–62.
89. Miller to Whitworth, 8 March 1936. BBC WAC/James Miller/Artist file/1935–62.
90. MacColl, interview by Howard Goorney (unpublished), late 1970s.
91. Richard Taylor, introduction to *The Eisenstein Reader* (London: BFI, 1998), p. 21.
92. BBC WAC/James Miller/Artist file 1935–62.
93. Rosalie Williams, interview by author, 1 October 2003, Manchester.
94. Littlewood, *Joan's Book*, p. 117.
95. The initiative was typical of Popular Front anti-fascist cultural and political allegiances. The *Daily Worker* now vowed to transform itself from 'a narrow party organ into a fighting daily newspaper of the United Front, a mouthpiece for unity' (*Daily Worker*, 7 January 1936); by 1936 Manchester's Left Book Club numbered over 1,000 members and its claim to be 'a most efficient revitalising factor in the political life of the city' contained some truth. See Jon Heddon, 'The Left Book Club in Manchester and Salford', *North West Labour History*, 21 (1996–7), pp. 58–67, at p. 61.
96. MacColl, 'Theatre of Action, Manchester', p. 59; 'Grass Roots', p. 64; 'Evolution', pp. xxxviii–ix.
97. *Daily Dispatch*, 2 July 1937; *Manchester Evening News*, 10 July 1937.
98. MacColl, *Journeyman*, p. 234.
99. Littlewood to Leslie Stokes, nd [February 1938]. BBC WAC/Joan Littlewood/ Scriptwriter File/1934–62.
100. Scannell and Cardiff, *A Social History*, pp. 350, 341; Bridson, *Prospero*, p. 47
101. Bridson, *Prospero*, p. 64.
102. Briggs, *Wireless*, p. 329.
103. Broadcast on BBC North Region Home Service, 6 September 1938. Scannell and Cardiff, *A Social History*, pp. 346–7.
104. Script in BBC WAC/North Region scripts. Jimmie also wrote two of the scripts for *Northern Nationalities*, a series about the cultures of the North's ethnic communities, broadcast in late August and September 1937. BBC to James Miller, 19 March 1937; BBC to James Miller, 7 October 1937. BBC WAC/James Miller/Copyright file 1/1937–62.
105. There's a copy of the script in the Ewan MacColl/Peggy Seeger Archive, Ruskin College, Oxford. Pre-production correspondence is kept in BBC WAC R 47/981/1.
106. *Manchester Evening News*, 19 November 1937.
107. Valentine Cunningham, *British Writers of the Thirties* (Oxford: Clarendon Press, 1989), pp. 135, 149. John Pudney, 'Generals', *Left Review* (May 1937), p. 37.
108. BBC Internal Memo, 28 October 1937. BBC WAC/Joan Littlewood/ Scriptwriter File 1/1934–62. *Lines on the Map* was a series on the BBC Empire Service exploring communications. Pudney hired Miller to write the second in the series, a programme entitled *The Seafarers*, broadcast on 25

February 1938. BBC Internal Memo, 29 December 1937. BBC WAC/James Miller/Copyright File 1/937–62.

109. Broadcast on BBC North Region Home Service, 21 December 1937. Script MacColl/Seeger Archive.

110. John Pudney to Felix Felton, 19 November 1937. BBC WAC R19/157/The Chartists' March 1937–8.

111. John Pudney to Felix Felton, 19 November 1937. BBC WAC R19/157/The Chartists' March 1937–8.

112. Rowland Hughes to John Pudney. BBC Internal Memo, 12 March 1938. BBC WAC R19/157/The Chartists' March, 1937–8.

113. Pudney to Miller, 6 April 1938. BBC WAC/R19/157.

114. The undated manuscript is in the MacColl/Seeger Archive. Littlewood remembers Jimmie working at the novel during this period. Littlewood, *Joan's Book*, p. 106.

115. 'Damnable Town', unpublished manuscript, p. 186.

116. 'Damnable Town', p. 187.

117. LB [?] to Joan Littlewood, 10 February 1944. This is the only evidence of the novel being sent to publishers. Littlewood later passed the rejection letter to MacColl. Joan Littlewood to Ewan MacColl, 29 December 1985. General Correspondence File, MacColl/Seeger Archive.

118. Figures from Francis Beckett, *Enemy Within: The Rise and Fall of the British Communist Party* (London: Merlin, 1995), pp. 49–50.

119. *Greater Manchester Men Who Fought in Spain* (Manchester: Greater Manchester International Brigade Memorial Committee, nd), pp. 9, 10.

120. *Greater Manchester Men Who Fought in Spain*, pp. 10, 49, 62.

121. Ewan MacColl, ed., *Personal Choice of Scottish Folksongs and Ballads* (New York: Hargail, nd), pp. 38–9. The final verse was dropped from MacColl when he performed the song during the folk revival, and was cut from subsequent reprintings in *Ewan MacColl Peggy Seeger Songbook* (1963; New York: Oak, 1963), p. 19 and Peggy Seeger, ed., *The Essential Ewan MacColl Songbook: Sixty Years of Songmaking* (New York: Oak, 2001), p. 76.

122. Jimmie Miller, 'The Damnable Town', unpublished manuscript, p. 169.

123. National Archives, KV/2/2175/48 reports on a lecture given by Jimmie on 'The Chartists' Revolt' in June 1938.

124. Wat Tyler, Oliver Cromwell, Feargus O'Connor and William Cobbett loomed large on banners in these public attempts to dispel the perception that communism was alien to Britain's radical traditions. As one headline in the *Daily Worker* put it, 'Communism Grows from English Soil', *Daily Worker*, 14 September 1936; also *Daily Worker*, 12 July 1937; *Manchester Guardian*, 12 July 1937. Osmond Robb, 'Players to the People', *Daily Worker*, 1 September 1952 gives a retrospective account of Jimmie and Joan's involvement in these pageants. Also Paul Hogarth, *Drawing on Life: The Autobiography of Paul Hogarth* (London: David & Charles, 1997), p. 15.

125. On Tuesday 17 January 1937 a rally was held at the Free Trade Hall to raise funds for the Manchester Foodship for Spain, the first of a rolling series of rallies in the city centre. Handbill reprinted in *Greater Manchester Men Who*

*Fought in Spain*, p. 31. Jimmie's MI5 file, National Archives, KV2/2175/47, includes details about a pro-Soviet celebration held in December 1938. Pinpointing the precise meetings at which Miller performed is difficult – handbills and write-ups usually list only the speakers; meetings often blur together in the memories of those involved. Howard Goorney remembers sharing a stage with Harry Pollitt during the late 1930s (interview by author, 9 April 2003, Bath). It seems likely that Miller performed at the Free Trade Hall Concert to welcome home local International Brigaders, as discussed in Fyrth, *Signal*, p. 200. For MacColl's own memories, see *Agit-prop*, p. xli. MacColl often recalled sharing stages at these events with Paul Robeson, who indeed made extensive appearance in Britain at public meetings supporting the Republican cause. See Martin Duberman, *Paul Robeson* (London and New York: New Press, 1989), pp. 210–32.

126. National Archives, KV2/2175/47.

127. National Archives, KV2/2175/48.

128. Jimmie Miller to Mick Jenkins [labelled September 1938], KV2/2175/47.

129. Inspector J. M. Robinson to Chief Constable, 28 April 1939. National Archives, KV/2/2175/28.

130. National Archives, KV2/2175/28; report by Sergeant S. Watkins, 11 October 1939, National Archives, KV/2/2175/46.

131. National Archives, KV2/2175/28, KV2/2175/46.

132. Once again, the choice of name signalled a connection to an international scene: the American Theater Union had been formed in 1933. Cosgrove, *Theatres of the Left*, p. 268.

133. Programme for Theatre Union's *The Good Soldier Schweik* [1939], People's History Museum, Manchester.

134. 'Who Are These People' [list of Theatre Union personnel]. I'm very grateful to Nadine Holdsworth for sharing this material with me.

135. Goorney, *Theatre Workshop Story*, pp. 17–18.

136. *Hugh MacDiarmid: New Selected Letters*, ed. Dorian Grieve, Owen Dudley Edwards and Alan Riach (Manchester: Carcanet, 2001), p. 554.

137. Theatre Union Manifesto, programme for *Fuente Ovejuna* [1939], p. 3. Theatre Royal Archive, Stratford, London.

138. Theatre Union Manifesto, programme for *Fuente Ovejuna* [1939], p. 3. Theatre Royal Archive, Stratford, London.

139. *Four Plays by Lope de Vega*, translated by John Garrett Underhill (New York: Scribner's Sons, 1936). Miller owned a copy of this edition.

140. The *Manchester Guardian* reviewer reassured the hesitant that, despite Theatre Union's politics, the play's 'aesthetic qualities will be a delight to all'. *Manchester Guardian*, 22 February 1939.

141. La Barraca, Lorca's travelling left-wing theatre group, had performed it in the spring of 1931. The link between the Granada poet and *Fuente Ovejuna* was not lost on the *Manchester Guardian*. *Manchester Guardian*, 9 February 1939.

142. Merseyside Left/Unity Theatre Archive, Liverpool has a copy of the script, Box 14, file 6.

143. *Manchester Guardian*, 9 February 1939; *Daily Dispatch*, 17 February 1939.

144. D.S., 'Theatre Union: A New Movement in Manchester', *Manchester Guardian*, 22 February 1939, p. 13.
145. Script in Merseyside Left/Unity Theatre Archive, Liverpool.
146. Handbill, People's History Museum, Manchester; *Manchester Evening News*, 15 May 1939.
147. Rosalie Williams, interview by author, 1 October 2003, Manchester.
148. Rosalie Williams, interview 1 October 2003.
149. Anthony Burgess, *Little Wilson and Big God* (London: Heinemann, 1987), pp. 182–3.
150. Littlewood, *Joan's Book*, p. 122.
151. Harry Pollitt, 'A working-class peace policy', *Labour Monthly* (May 1936) and 'The Seventh Congress of the Communist International', *Labour Monthly* (October 1935). Sourced from Kevin Morgan, *Harry Pollitt* (Manchester and New York: Manchester University Press, 1993), p. 107.
152. One chronicled the hardship faced by fairground workers unable to earn their living owing to petrol rations and the blackout; a second showed the problems created for Manchester workers by restrictions on public transport; a third, which was made and broadcast, sampled the public's views on the rationing system. Proposals for the first two were sent to Bridson; he forwarded them to Laurence Gilliam on 30 November 1939. BBC WAC/Joan Littlewood/Scriptwriter/1934–62. 'Four Ounces a Head', the feature on rationing researched and presented by Miller and Littlewood, was broadcast on BBC Home Service, 18 January 1940.
153. 12 October 1939. 'I do not understand why the BBC continues to use them,' wrote one MI5 officer in Jimmie's file. 'Could they be warned to drop them if other people are available?' National Archives, KV/2/2175/29. Also Littlewood, *Joan's Book*, pp. 115–16. Miller's last appearance was for Children's Hour, 14 March 1940 (BBC /WAC N18/3,389/1/Jimmy Miller/ Personal File), Littlewood's on 18 April. She resumed BBC work in 1941 (BBC WAC/Joan Littlewood/Artist File/1933–62).
154. Minutes for Theatre Union meeting, 6 November 1939. Pre-1953 file, Theatre Royal Archive, Stratford, London.
155. 'Report on Living Newspaper, 6 November 1939' and 'Memorandum on Living Newspaper on the war' [nd], Theatre Royal Archive, Stratford, London.
156. Burgess, *Little Wilson*, pp. 180–1.
157. Sections of the script are reprinted in *Agit-prop*, pp. 21–35. The whole text is held in the MacColl/Seeger Archive.
158. Reprinted in *Agit-prop*, p. ix.
159. Written shortly after the end of the Spanish Civil War, MacDiarmid's poem was eventually published as *The Battle Continues* (Edinburgh: Castle Wynd, 1957).
160. Reprinted in Peggy Seeger, ed., *The Essential Ewan MacColl Songbook: Sixty Years of Songmaking* (New York: Oak, 2001), p. 300.
161. *Last Edition* handbill, People's History Museum, Manchester. Upbeat reviews from the *Daily Dispatch* and *News Chronicle* were sampled in the *Manchester Evening News*, 9 May 1940.

162. Script in Theatre Royal Archive, Stratford, London; Miller to D. Samuels, 22 April 1940. Miller was eager to also present the show as a *Daily Worker* fundraiser at the Picton Hall, Liverpool and dealt directly with the *Daily Worker* League. Some confusion arose, but eventually the Merseyside Left Theatre Club booked the production for Saturday 8 June at the David Lewis Theatre. *Merseyside Left Theatre Club Bulletin* (29 May 1940). The handbill is reprinted in Jerry Dawson, ed., *Left Theatre: Merseyside Unity Theatre* (Liverpool: Merseyside Writers, 1985), p. 86.

163. Hogarth, *Drawing on Life*, p. 15; MacColl, 'Grass Roots', pp. 65–7. Once again, pinpointing the precise dates of these performances is difficult – no handbills have turned up so far, and unlicensed shows attracted little press coverage, especially during the war. Jim Barnes of Blackburn recalls seeing Theatre Union at the Co-op Hall in Bacup: 'apart from teaching us the history of our class,' he wrote, 'Theatre Union gave us a hearty culture.' Undated letter, Theatre Royal Archive, Stratford, London. In an unsigned letter of 10 September 1940, the acting Theatre Union secretary refers to 'our Bacup friends' attending a training class. Merseyside Left/Unity Theatre Archive, Box 8, file 1, Liverpool. Littlewood probably exaggerated when she writes 'Theatre Union clubs sprang up all over Lancashire after *Last Edition*'; she recalls working on a spin-off living newspaper called *Cotton*, possibly based on her radio feature of the same name. Littlewood, *Joan's Book*, p. 117.

164. Letter from Hyde Chief Constable, 26 April 1940. National Archives, KV/2/2175/45.

165. Angus Calder, *The People's War: Britain 1939–1945* (1969; London: Pimlico, 2000), p. 81.

166. Rosalie Williams, interview by author, 1 October 2003, Manchester. Littlewood, *Joan's Book*, pp. 110–11.

167. National Archives, KV/2/2175/43.

168. Littlewood, *Joan's Book*, p. 113.

169. *Daily Worker*, 3 June 1940. Cutting in National Archives, KV/2/2175/44. Unsigned Theatre Union Secretary to Jerry Dawson, 10 August 1940. Liverpool Left/Unity Theatre Archive, Liverpool, Box 8, file 1.

## Chapter 4, 'Browned Off'

1. Angus Calder, *The People's War: Britain 1939–1945* (1969; London: Pimlico, 2000), pp. 51, 119; James Henry Miller, Military Records, Army Personnel Centre.

2. MacColl describes some of these experiences during a Critics Group meeting held on 31 January 1968. Charles Parker Archive, Birmingham Central Library. MS 4000/5/4/2/171C and 172C.

3. Joan Littlewood, *Joan's Book: The Autobiography of Joan Littlewood* (London: Methuen, 1994), p. 130.

4. W. A. Alexander to Colonel Tomes, 11 December 1940. National Archives, KV/2/2175/40.

5. Internal Security of HM Forces Report, 16 December 1940. National Archives KV/2/2175/40.

6. Reprinted in Peggy Seeger, ed., *Essential Ewan MacColl Songbook* (New York and London: Oak, 2001), p. 298. MacColl later recorded the song on Ewan MacColl, *Barrack Room Ballads*, 10 inch disc, 10 T25, Topic, 1958.

7. Major W. A. Alexander to Captain Rutherford, 4 January 1941. National Archives, KV/2/2175/40.

8. Alexander to Rutherford, 4 January 1941.

9. Manchester City Police Force: Detective Officer's Report of Result of Enquiries, 11 November 1940. National Archives, KV2/2175/41.

10. A version of the play was presented at the Left Book Club Summer School at Wennington Hall in August 1940; the main premiere took place at the Milton Hall, Deansgate on 18 January 1941.

11. National Archives, KV2/2175/40 and 41.

12. Manchester City Police Force: Detective Officer's Report of Result of Enquiries, 11 November 1940. National Archives, KV2/2175/41.

13. James Henry Miller, Military Records, Army Personnel Centre.

14. Secret and Personal Report, 16 December 1940. National Archives, KV/2/2175/40.

15. James Henry Miller, Military Records, Army Personnel Centre.

16. James Henry Miller, Military Records, Army Personnel Centre.

17. Betsy Miller, interview by Charles Parker, 29 January 1969. CPA MS /4000/5/1/3/6D.

18. Hyde Borough Police Report, 2 September 1943. National Archives, KV/2/2175/37.

19. Alan Kidd, *Manchester*, 3rd edn (Edinburgh: Edinburgh University Press, 2002), p. 197. *Our Blitz: Red Skies Over Manchester* (1945; Manchester: Manchester Evening News, 1999), p. 16.

20. Rosalie Williams, interview by author, 1 October 2003, Manchester.

21. Littlewood's attempts to secure a permanent contract were rebuffed on political grounds: her protestations to have severed ties with the Communist Party were regarded with due suspicion, and it was widely viewed that Jimmie had deserted 'with the connivance of the rest of the family'. National Archives, KV/2/2175/37.

22. *Bulletin: Monthly Organ of Theatre Union*, nd [1940]. People's History Museum, Manchester.

23. *Hell is What You Make It*, cue 1209. Script in Ewan MacColl and Peggy Seeger Archive, Ruskin College, Oxford. MacColl would later claim to have written the play in 1939, but 1941 seems more likely.

24. The original version was handwritten in an exercise book from Urmston Grammar School, where Rosalie Williams' father worked. Script in MacColl/ Seeger Archive.

25. Ewan MacColl, *Journeyman* (London: Sigwick & Jackson, 1990), p. 268.

26. Littlewood, *Joan's Book*, pp. 277, 248; MacColl, *Journeyman*, p. 268.

27. Jimmie to Betsy Miller, nd. MacColl/Seeger Archive.

28. D. G. Bridson, *Prospero and Ariel: The Rise and Fall of Radio* (London: Victor Gollancz, 1971), p. 86. In this period Littlewood was commissioned to work on 'Salute to Joseph Stalin' for the Home Service. Undated memo,

BBC WAC/Joan Littlewood/Artist File/1933–62. She was also in the cast of *The Red Army*, broadcast on 23 February 1945. National Archives, KV/2/2175/35.

29. For discrimination against communists in the armed forces, see Noreen Branson, *History of the Communist Party of Great Britain 1941–1951* (London: Lawrence & Wishart, 1997), pp. 53–7.

30. Ewan MacColl, *Landscape with Chimneys*, cue 653. Script in MacColl/Seeger Archive.

31. MacColl later told historian Raphael Samuel that he'd served on a minesweeper in the Pacific. Raphael Samuel, Preface to Raphael Samuel, Ewan MacColl and Stuart Cosgrove, eds, *Theatres of the Left 1880–1935* (London: Routledge & Kegan Paul, 1985), p. x.

32. Andy Croft, 'The Boys Round the Corner: the Story of Fore Publications' in Andy Croft, ed., *A Weapon in the Struggle: The Cultural History of the Communist Party of Great Britain* (London: Pluto, 1998), pp. 142–63.

33. James Miller, 'Capitalism, Writing, and the War', *Our Time*, 2.13 (July 1943), pp. 27–9.

34. Miller, 'Capitalism', p. 27.

35. Miller, 'Capitalism', p. 28.

36. Miller, 'Capitalism', p. 29.

37. Miller, 'Capitalism', p. 29.

## Chapter 5, 'A Richer, Fuller Life'

1. Joan Littlewood, *Joan's Book: The Autobiography of Joan Littlewood* (London: Methuen, 1994), p. 157.

2. Littlewood later described the new name as 'a precaution'. *Joan's Book*, p. 157. Betsy Miller also considered the new name to be part of the story of Jimmie's desertion. Betsy Miller, interview by Charles Parker, 29 January 1969. Charles Parker Archive, Birmingham Central Library, CPA MS 4000/5/1/3/6/D.

3. Hugh MacDiarmid had been proclaiming a Scottish Literary Renaissance since 1923. He saw the Scots language as a vital medium for modern literary creation much eroded by the spread of standard English, and the Renaissance as a force for stimulating Scottish cultural confidence and entrenching national pride. He argued that the Scots language, also called Lallans or the Doric, provided the resources for a modern literature that could emulate the work of the Makars, or medieval court poets. Kenneth Buthlay, *Hugh MacDiarmid* (Edinburgh and London: Oliver & Boyd, 1964); Alan Riach, ed., *Hugh MacDiarmid: Selected Prose* (London: Carcanet, 1992); Angus Calder, Glen Murray and Alan Riach, eds, *Hugh MacDiarmid: The Raucle Tongue: Hitherto Uncollected Prose, Volume III* (Manchester: Carcanet, 1998).

4. Barbara Niven painted MacDiarmid's portrait in 1935. She and her husband Ern Brooks spent the summer of 1938 with MacDiarmid at his Whalsay home. Hugh MacDiarmid, *New Selected Letters*, ed. Dorian Grieve, Owen Dudley Edwards and Alan Riach (Manchester: Carcanet, 2001), p. 554.

5. The text is reprinted in Valentina Bold, ed., *Smeddum: A Lewis Grassic Gibbon Anthology* (Edinburgh: Canongate, 2001), pp. 3–168, at p. 136.

6. Eóghan would usually be translated as Evan, not Ewan, suggesting that MacColl got the name from *The Scottish Scene*. For MacColla, see Derick S. Thompson, *The Companion to Gaelic Scotland* (Oxford: Blackwell, 1983), p. 162.

7. Evan MacColl, *The Mountain Minstrel; or Clarsach namm Beann* (Glasgow: Maclachlan and Stewart, 1836). A Gaelic version was republished in 1937, out of Glasgow, by the Evan MacColl Memorial Committee. Both editions are in the British Library.

8. Littlewood, *Joan's Book*, p. 146.

9. Rosalie Williams, interview by author, 1 October 2003, Manchester.

10. Howard Goorney, *The Theatre Workshop Story* (London: Methuen: 1981), p. 40; interview by author, 9 April 2003, Bath.

11. Littlewood, *Joan's Book*, pp. 155–6; Ewan MacColl, *Journeyman* (London: Sidgwick & Jackson, 1990), pp. 243–4. For CEMA, see Andy Croft, 'Betrayed Spring: The Labour Government and British Literary Culture' in Jim Fyrth, ed., *Labour's Promised Land? Culture and Society in Labour Britain 1945–51* (London: Lawrence & Wishart, 1995), pp. 199–209.

12. Littlewood, *Joan's Book*, p. 156.

13. It was considered unwise to allow Littlewood to produce plays for ENSA, though acceptable for her to work as an actress. D. L. R. Osborn to Major Turner, 9 March 1944. National Archives, KV/2/2175/36.

14. Croft, 'Betrayed', pp. 209–11.

15. Joan Littlewood, *Omnibus*, BBC, 19 April 1994. See also Nadine Holdsworth, 'They'd Have Pissed on My Grave: the Arts Council and Theatre Workshop', *New Theatre Quarterly*, 57 (February 1999), pp. 3–17.

16. Goorney, *Theatre Workshop Story*, p. 40.

17. Littlewood, *Joan's Book*, p. 162.

18. Littlewood, *Joan's Book*, p. 159.

19. Littlewood, *Joan's Book*, p. 244.

20. Littlewood, *Joan's Book*, p. 166.

21. Stuart Cosgrove, 'From Shock Troupe to Group Theatre' in Raphael Samuel, Ewan MacColl and Stuart Cosgrove, eds, *Theatres of the Left 1880–1935* (London: Routledge, 1985), p. 269.

22. The manifesto is held in Box 8.1 of the Merseyside Left/Unity Theatre Archive, Liverpool.

23. Quotation from Theatre Workshop promotional handbill [1945] in Theatre Royal Archive, Stratford East, London (pre-1953 box). My summary is drawn from the following sources: W. Davidson, 'Theatre With a Method: Enterprise and Co-operation', *Our Time* (July 1946), pp. 258–9; an earlier draft version of this article is in the Merseyside Left/Unity Theatre Archive, Box 8.1; an unsourced article by Margot Lawrence, labelled '1945' in the Theatre Royal Archive; June Johns, 'The Uncommercial Actors', *Illustrated*, week ending 12 April 1947; 'Theatre Workshop', unsigned article by Hugh MacDiarmid, *The Voice of Scotland* (June 1946), reprinted in *The Raucle Tongue III*, pp. 95–101.

24. Noreen Branson, *History of the Communist Party of Great Britain 1941–51* (London: Lawrence & Wishart, 1997), p. 97.

25. *Sailors' Wives*, broadcast 3 September 1941; Littlewood also worked on *Women at War* in October 1944. Both programmes fed into *Johnny Noble*. BBC WAC/Littlewood, Joan/Artist File, 1933–1962.

26. The staging of *Johnny Noble* is discussed in *From Kendal to Berlin: The Diary of Theatre Workshop*, broadcast on the North of England Home Service on 5 August 1947. I'm very grateful to Nadine Holdsworth for letting me see her copy of the script.

27. The script is reprinted in Howard Goorney and Ewan MacColl, eds, *Agit-prop to Theatre Workshop* (Manchester: Manchester University Press, 1986), pp. 35–73.

28. Script in Ewan MacColl and Peggy Seeger Archive, Ruskin College, Oxford.

29. Theatre Workshop promotional handbill [1945], Theatre Royal Archive; see also Goorney, *Theatre Workshop Story*, p. 46.

30. Goorney, *Theatre Workshop Story*, p. 200.

31. Theatre Workshop handbill, 'The Press Verdict on Current Productions' [*Johnny Noble* and *The Flying Doctor*], Merseyside Left/Unity Theatre Archive, Box 8.1; write-ups in *Penrith Observer*, 4 September 1945, *Lake District Herald*, 8 September 1945, and the *Wigan Examiner*, 15 September 1945.

32. Davidson, 'Theatre with a Method', p. 259; Littlewood, *Joan's Book*, pp. 176–7; MacColl, *Journeyman*, p. 247.

33. Littlewood, *Joan's Book*, pp. 185, 182; Goorney, *Theatre Workshop Story*, p. 200.

34. Quoted in Goorney, *Theatre Workshop Story*, p. 48.

35. MacColl, *Journeyman*, p. 246.

36. Ian McKay, 'Mr Butlin Makes Even Hollywood Look Shabby', *News Chronicle*, 23 May 1946, p. 3.

37. A shorter version of the play was premiered at the Newcastle People's Theatre on 18 February 1946. By April, it had reached its full length of two hours. It was published in 1948 as *Uranium 235: A Documentary Play in Eleven Episodes* (Glasgow: William MacLellan, nd). A revised version was published in 1986 in Goorney and MacColl, eds, *Agit-prop*, pp. 73–131.

38. MacColl, *Journeyman*, p. 251; Goorney, *Theatre Workshop Story*, pp. 52–3; Goorney, interview by author, 9 April 2003, Bath.

39. Ian McKay, 'Red Bearded Playwright's Drama of the Atom', *News Chronicle*, 25 May 1946, p. 3.

40. Sophie Raikes, *Ormesby Hall* (National Trust, nd), pp. 42–7.

41. June Johns, 'The Uncommercial Actors', *Illustrated*, week ending 12 April 1947, p. 20.

42. Margot Lawrence's magazine article on Theatre Workshop, unsourced clipping in Theatre Royal Archive.

43. 'News of Theatre Workshop', circular letter, 7 June 1946. Merseyside Left/Unity Theatre Archive, Liverpool.

44. Promotional Theatre Workshop handbill for 'Summer School 13–27ᵗʰ July [1946] at Ormesby, Middlesbrough'. Merseyside Left/Unity Theatre Archive, Liverpool, Box 8.1.

45. Littlewood, *Joan's Book*, pp. 209, 215; Goorney, *Theatre Workshop Story*, p. 56.

46. Littlewood, *Joan's Book*, p. 208.

47. Goorney, *Theatre Workshop Story*, p. 55.

48. Rosalie Williams, interview by author, 1 October 2003, Manchester.

49. Littlewood, *Joan's Book*, p. 213.

50. Howard Goorney, interview by author, 9 April 2003, Bath.

51. Valerie Preston-Dunlop, *Rudolf Laban: An Extraordinary Life* (London: Dance Books, 1998), pp. 223–5, 229–30, 238; John Hodgson, *Mastering Movement: The Life and Work of Rudolf Laban* (London: Methuen, 2001), pp. 4–8.

52. MacColl, *Journeyman*, p. 254.

53. Jean Newlove/MacColl, interview by author, 22 July 2003, London; Littlewood, *Joan's Book*, pp. 215, 220.

54. MacColl, *Journeyman*, p. 254.

55. Karen O'Brien, *Kirsty MacColl: The One and Only* (London: André Deutsch, 2004), p. 4.

56. O'Brien, *Kirsty MacColl*, p. 4.

57. Jean Newlove/MacColl, interview by author, 22 July 2003, London.

58. Goorney, *Theatre Workshop*, p. 205.

59. In 1946 MacLellan planned to publish an anthology of MacColl's writings as *The Plays of Ewan MacColl*, but the project fell through. *Uranium 235* was published by MacLellan in 1948. For the proposed collection, see the programme for the 1946 Queen's Theatre, Glasgow production of *Uranium 235*, deposited in the Scottish Theatre Archive at Glasgow University, STA FM, Box 8/20–24.

60. Hugh MacDiarmid, 'Theatre Workshop', *The Voice of Scotland* (June 1946). Reprinted in Calder, Murray and Riach, eds, *The Raucle Tongue*, pp. 95–101, at p. 97.

61. MacColl, *Journeyman*, p. 258.

62. Littlewood, *Joan's Book*, p. 220.

63. Programme in Scottish Theatre Archive, FM, Box 8/20–4.

64. 'Successful Experiment in Stagecraft', *Glasgow Herald*, 15 October 1946; 'Johnnie Noble', *The Scotsman*, 1 October 1946.

65. 'Drama Picasso', unsourced clipping in Theatre Royal Archive; 'Modern Morality Play at Glasgow Queen's', *Glasgow Herald*, 22 October 1946.

66. Two key collections were Maurice Lindsay, ed., *Modern Scottish Poetry: An Anthology of the Scottish Renaissance* (London: Faber & Faber, 1946) and Hugh MacDiarmid, ed., *The Golden Treasury of Scottish Poetry* (London: Macmillan, 1940).

67. Christopher Harvie, *Scotland and Nationalism: Scottish Society and Politics 1707 to the Present*, 3rd edn. (London and New York: Routledge, 1994), p. 30.

68. MacColl was first described as 'a young Scots writer' in a Theatre Workshop promotional handbill released from Kendal in 1945 (Theatre Royal Archive).

In an untitled and unsigned article in *Forward*, 19 October 1946, he's described as 'a Glasgow dramatist', as in a number of articles about Theatre Workshop written during their Scottish tour. By the time *Uranium 235* is published in 1948, it's Auchterarder.

69. MacDiarmid, 'Theatre Workshop' in *Raucle Tongue*, p. 101; Littlewood, *Joan's Book*, p. 389.
70. Goorney, *Theatre Workshop Story*, p. 201.
71. Littlewood, *Joan's Book*, pp. 226–7.
72. Littlewood, *Joan's Book*, p. 228.
73. Script in MacColl/Seeger Archive and National Library of Scotland, ACC 10893/223.
74. Littlewood, *Joan's Book*, p. 226.
75. Littlewood, *Joan's Book*, p. 229.
76. Jean Newlove/MacColl, interview by author, 9 August 2004, London.
77. A letter written by Littlewood to the BBC on 29 December gives the address. BBC WAC R/Cont 1/Miller, James/Copyright File 1 1937–62.
78. MacColl, *Journeyman*, p. 38.
79. Littlewood to BBC, 27 January 1947. BBC WAC/R Cont 1/James Miller/ Copyright File 1/1937–62.
80. Joan Littlewood to Howard Goorney, 12 February 1947.
81. Littlewood, *Joan's Book*, p. 231.
82. Tom Driberg, *Reynolds News*, 12 January 1947.
83. Littlewood, *Joan's Book*, pp. 217, 238; Goorney, *Theatre Workshop Story*, pp. 142–3; Rosalie Williams, interview by author, 1 October 2003, Manchester.
84. Goorney, *Theatre Workshop Story*, p. 143.
85. Rosalie Williams, interview by author, 1 October 2003, Manchester; Goorney, *Theatre Workshop Story*, p. 143.
86. Littlewood, *Joan's Book*, p. 263.
87. Littlewood, *Joan's Book*, pp. 248–9; Howard Goorney, interview by author, 9 April 2003, Bath; Jean Newlove/MacColl, interview by author, 9 August 2004, London.
88. Angus Calder, *The People's War: Britain 1939–1945* (1969; London: Pimlico, 2000), p. 337.
89. According to Littlewood, they hired a Manchester-based Jungian who combed through his novel and plays for insights into their author's psychological constitution. Littlewood, *Joan's Book*, p. 232.
90. Joan Littlewood to Howard Goorney, 12 February 1947. Howard Goorney's private collection.
91. Littlewood to Goorney, 13 February 1947. Howard Goorney's private collection.
92. Littlewood to Goorney, 13 February 1947.
93. Littlewood to Goorney, 28 February 1947. Howard Goorney's private collection.
94. Littlewood to Goorney, 28 February 1947.
95. Jean Newlove/MacColl, interview by author, 9 August 2004, London.
96. James Henry Miller, Military Records, Army Personnel Centre; Betsy maintained that Ewan had 'played it up a treat' to get himself out of

Northfield. Betsy Miller, interview by Charles Parker, 29 January 1969. CPA MS/4005/1/3/5/C.

97. 'Apart from those who were genuinely too neurotic to be useful,' writes Angus Calder of those discharged from the military on medical grounds, 'there were those who, as it were, came to an agreement with the military authorities that a relationship disagreeable to both parties should now be honourably terminated.' Calder, *People's War*, p. 337.

98. Jean Newlove/MacColl, interview by author, 9 August 2004, London.

99. James Henry Miller, Military Records, Army Personnel Centre.

100. Gerry Raffles to Joan Littlewood, 11 March 1947. Reprinted in Littlewood, *Joan's Book*, p. 261.

101. Gerry Raffles to Joan Littlewood, 5 March 1947. Reprinted in Littlewood, *Joan's Book*, p. 259.

102. Gerry Raffles to Joan Littlewood, 13 March 1947. Reprinted in Littlewood, *Joan's Book*, p. 264.

103. Gerry Raffles to Joan Littlewood, 4 March 1947. I'm grateful to Nadine Holdsworth for passing on information about this letter. The account in *Joan's Book* excludes these details.

104. Goorney, *Theatre Workshop Story*, p. 59. For Chico Marx, see Simon Louvish, *Monkey Business: The Lives and Legends of the Marx Brothers* (London: Faber & Faber, 1999), pp. 358, 371–2.

105. Broadcast at prime time on 5 August. The residency began on 4 August.

106. 'Last Night's Manchester Shows', *Manchester Evening News*, 5 August 1947.

107. Goorney, *Theatre Workshop Story*, p. 62.

108. The Arts Council was funded by the Treasury rather than the Ministry of Education and therefore suffered from the Treasury's 1947 capital expenditure cuts. Croft, 'Betrayed Spring', p. 211.

109. 'British Theatre Conference', *Theatre Today* (1947), p. 1; Croft, 'Betrayed Spring', p. 210.

110. Goorney, *Theatre Workshop Story*, p. 96.

111. Littlewood, *Joan's Book*, p. 290.

112. Goorney, *Theatre Workshop Story*, p. 67.

113. Littlewood, *Joan's Book*, pp. 371, 385, 765.

114. Littlewood, *Joan's Book*, pp. 302, 304–8.

115. MacColl submitted *Rogues' Gallery* on 30 March 1948; it was rejected on 28 April. Littlewood sent in *The Other Animals* on 26 April; it was rejected on 16 June. BBC WAC/R Cont 1/James Miller/Scriptwriter File/1948–62.

116. A radio adaptation of MacColl's *Johnny Noble* had been broadcast on BBC North Region Home Service, 30 January 1947.

117. BBC WAC/ N/18/3,389/1/ Jimmy Miller/Personal File/1936–62.

118. Trevor Hill, interview with Olive Shapley [nd], tape in MacColl/Seeger Archive.

119. Hugh MacDiarmid, foreword to *Uranium 235* by Ewan MacColl (Glasgow: MacLellan, nd [1948]), p. 6.

120. Ewan MacColl to Molly [?] at BBC Third Programme, 30 March 1948. BBC WAC/ R Cont 1/James Miller/Scriptwriter/1948–62.

121. Reprinted in Goorney and MacColl, eds, *Agit-prop*, pp. 131–99.

122. Littlewood, *Joan's Book*, p. 323.
123. Jean Newlove/MacColl, interview by author, 9 August 2004, London.
124. *Daily Telegraph*, 6 July 1948; Theatre Workshop handbill, 'The Critics and *The Other Animals*', Manchester Central Library Theatre Collection, TH 792 0924273.
125. *Manchester Guardian*, 6 July 1948.
126. Goorney, *Theatre Workshop Story*, p. 66.
127. Equity Membership Records, e-mail to author, 15 September 2004.
128. Goorney, *Theatre Workshop Story*, p. 143; Littlewood, *Joan's Book*, pp. 328–33. For Umeni Lidu see Appendix Three in Littlewood, *Joan's Book*, pp. 767–9.
129. Littlewood, *Joan's Book*, pp. 356–8.
130. Reviews are sampled in Winifred Bannister, 'New Scottish Drama', *Con Brio* (Festival edn, 1949), p. 14.
131. Letter cited in Hugh MacDiarmid, 'Some Recent Scottish Books', *The National Weekly*, 3 October 1948. Reprinted in *Raucle Tongue*, p. 173.
132. Bannister, 'New Scottish Drama', p. 14. The play was then staged in London by Unity Theatre in 1950. See Colin Chambers, *The Story of Unity Theatre* (London: Lawrence & Wishart, 1989), p. 314.
133. Littlewood, *Joan's Book*, p. 359; Goorney, *Theatre Workshop Story*, p. 146; Jean Newlove/MacColl, interview by author, 22 July 2003 and 9 August 2004, London.
134. Goorney, *Theatre Worksop Story*, pp. 146–8.
135. Littlewood, *Joan's Book*, pp. 777–9. See also pp. 364, 366, 370.
136. Goorney, *Theatre Workshop Story*, pp. 47, 148.
137. Goorney, *Theatre Workshop Story*, p. 202.
138. Script in MacColl/Seeger Archive, Oxford. The play was revived on the continent. A German version, *Das Kumme Gewerbe*, opened at Landestheater Sachsen-Anhalt in autumn 1949; the play was staged again in 1954/5 and again in 1976. Programmes are held in the MacColl/Seeger Archive.
139. *Manchester Guardian*, 27 July 1949.
140. Valerie Preston-Dunlop, *Rudolph Laban: An Extraordinary Life* (London: Dance Books, 1998), pp. 251–2.
141. Jean Newlove/MacColl, interviews by author, 22 July 2003, 9 August 2004, London.
142. *Theatre Newsletter*, 4.79 (10 September 1949).
143. Unsigned editorial, 'The City of Dreadful Knights', *The Voice of Scotland* (December 1947), reprinted in *Raucle Tongue*, pp. 110–12.
144. *Theatre Newsletter*, 4.79 (10 September 1949), p. 4.
145. *Glasgow Herald*, 6 September 1949; *Evening Dispatch*, 6 September 1949; *The Scotsman*, 25 August 1949.
146. Winifred Bannister, 'New Scottish Drama', *Con Brio* (Festival edn, 1949), p. 13.
147. MacColl had first met Henderson the previous year, but they became firm friends during the 1949 festival. 'Ewan MacColl on Hamish', *Tocher*, 43 (1991), pp. 13–14.
148. Ewan MacColl to Hamish Henderson, 10 February 1950. MacColl/Seeger Archive.

## Chapter 6, 'Towards a People's Culture'

1.  Theatre Workshop programme for *Johnny Noble* and *The Flying Doctor* [1951], Ewan MacColl and Peggy Seeger Archive, Ruskin College, Oxford; Theatre Workshop manifesto (1945), Box 8.1, Merseyside Left/Unity Theatre Archive, Liverpool.
2.  Goorney, *The Theatre Workshop Story* (London: Methuen, 1981), pp. 203–5; handbill for *Landscape with Chimneys* tour in MacColl/Seeger Archive.
3.  Goorney, *Theatre Workshop Story*, p. 203.
4.  Goorney, *Theatre Workshop Story*, pp. 75–8; Ewan MacColl, *Journeyman* (London: Sidgwick & Jackson, 1990), pp. 258–60.
5.  Joan Littlewood, *Joan's Book: The Autobiography of Joan Littlewood* (London: Methuen, 1994), p. 403.
6.  Littlewood's late 1930s radio adaptation of Gogol's story 'The Overcoat' was revived, rehearsed and performed on one tour. Goorney, *Theatre Workshop Story*, p. 82; Littlewood, *Joan's Book*, p. 405. The script is held in the Joan Littlewood collection, Harry Ransom Humanities Research Center, University of Texas in Austin.
7.  MacColl, *Journeyman*, p. 261.
8.  Noreen Branson, *History of the Communist Party of Great Britain, 1941–1951* (London: Lawrence & Wishart, 1997), pp. 212–13; John Callaghan, *Cold War, Crisis and Conflict 1951–1968* (London: Lawrence & Wishart, 2003), pp. 141–2.
9.  Goorney, *Theatre Workshop Story*, pp. 82, 189; Littlewood, *Joan's Book*, pp. 204–5.
10. Handbill in MacColl/Seeger Archive.
11. See James Hinton, 'Self-help and Socialism: The Squatters' Movement of 1946', *History Workshop Journal* 25 (Spring 1988), pp. 100–27 and Paul Burnham, 'The Squatters of 1946: A Local Study in a National Context', *Socialist History* 25 (2004), pp. 20–46.
12. In later life MacColl would become uneasy with the song's mass popularity, often appearing to forget its title, and claiming he'd rattled it off in a few minutes to cover a scene change. Later recorded by The Dubliners, The Spinners, Rod Stewart and The Pogues, on one occasion it was sung at Old Trafford football ground by 68,000 football supporters in a failed bid to get themselves in the record books. *English Dance and Song* (Summer 2005), p. 6. MacColl forgot the title at his Royal Festival Hall seventieth birthday concert on 21 January 1985. The story of the song covering a scene change is given in MacColl's autobiography, *Journeyman*, p. 276.
13. Branson, *Communist Party*, p. 206.
14. Report by C. D. Heriot, 28 December 1950. Lord Chamberlain Collection. I'm grateful to Nadine Holdsworth for bringing the report to my attention.
15. Local press coverage of these tours was predictably scant. One exception was the *Western Mail and South Wales News*, which carried a series of sympathetic articles. See 9 January 1951, p. 4; 9 October 1951, p. 4; and 16 October 1951, p. 6. I'm grateful to Nadine Holdsworth for sharing these references.

16. Quoted in Goorney, *Theatre Workshop Story*, p. 189 and Littlewood, *Joan's Book*, p. 404.

17. BBC WAC Artist/Miller, Jimmie/, Personal File 1936–62, N18/3,389/1.

18. E. David Gregory, 'Lomax in London: Alan Lomax, the BBC and the Folk-Song Revival in England, 1950–8', *Folk Music Journal*, 8.2 (2002), pp. 136–69, at pp. 139–40.

19. MacColl, *Journeyman*, p. 269.

20. Ronald D. Cohen, General Introduction to Cohen, ed., *Alan Lomax: Selected Writings 1934–1997* (New York and London: Routledge, 2003), p. ix.

21. *American Ballads and Folksongs* (1934) and *Negro Folk Songs as Sung by Leadbelly* (1936) were co-published with his father John Avery Lomax; *Our Singing Country: A Second Volume of American Ballads and Folk Songs* (1941) was a collaboration with his father and Ruth Crawford Seeger. For Lomax's early career, see Ed Kahn, '1934–1950: The Early Collecting years' in Cohen, ed., *Alan Lomax: Selected Writings*, pp. 1–7, Ronald D. Cohen, *Rainbow Quest: The Folk Music Revival and American Society 1940–1970* (Amherst and Boston: University of Massachusetts Press, 2002) and Judith Tick, *Ruth Crawford Seeger: A Composer's Search for American Music* (New York and Oxford: Oxford University Press, 1997).

22. *The Martins and the Coys: A Contemporary Folk Tale* was recorded for the BBC in New York in March 1944 and produced by D. G. Bridson. For the making of the programme, see Ed Cray, *Ramblin' Man: The Life and Times of Woody Guthrie* (New York and London: W. W. Norton, 2004), p. 275. In interviews, MacColl would often recall hearing the original broadcast. See Robin Denselow, *When the Music's Over: The Story of Political Pop* (London: Faber & Faber, 1989), p. 22 and Ewan MacColl interview with Charles Parker, 26 June 1972, transcript in Charles Parker Archive, Birmingham Central Library, file CPA 1/7/4. The programme was commercially issued as *The Martins and the Coys* (CD, 1819, Rounder, 2000).

23. For the significance of Waldemar Hille, ed., *The People's Songbook* (New York: Boni and Gaer, 1948), see Michael Brocken, *The British Folk Revival 1944–2002* (Aldershot: Ashgate, 2003), pp. 32–3.

24. Kahn, '1934–50', pp. 5–7.

25. Gregory, 'Lomax in London', p. 138.

26. Gregory, 'Lomax in London', p. 137.

27. Littlewood, *Joan's Book*, p. 434.

28. Liner-notes to *The Alan Lomax Collection Sampler* (CD, 1700, Rounder, 1997), p. 62. MacColl recalls the session in *Journeyman*, p. 269.

29. MacColl had undertaken music research for 'Bonny Teesdale', a regional social history programme scripted by Littlewood and starring Wilfred Pickles, broadcast on Children's Hour, North of England Home Service, 3 April 1949. MacColl then wrote and presented a spin-off programme, 'Tracking Down Songs in Teesdale', also for Northern Children's Hour, broadcast on 5 June 1949. The quotation is from the latter programme. Both scripts are in the BBC Written Archive. MacColl discusses the programme on track 12 of Ewan MacColl and Peggy Seeger: *Folk on Two* (CD, Mash 002, Cooking Vinyl, 1996).

30. And quoted in Mrs Gaskell's Manchester novel *Mary Barton* (1848) a century earlier. *The Columbia World Music Library of Folk and Primitive Music, Volume 3: England* (LP, Columbia KL 206, 1951), reissued as *World Library of Folk and Primitive Music 1, England* (CD, 1741, Rounder 1998).

31. MaccColl's second song was 'The Chevalier's Muster Roll'. *The Columbia World Music Library of Folk and Primitive Music, Volume 6: Scotland* (LP, KL 209, Columbia, 1951), reissued as *World Library of Folk and Primitive Music 3, Scotland* (CD, 1743, Rounder, 1998). For the series, see Gregory, 'Lomax in London', pp. 143–5.

32. MaccColl to D. G. Bridson, 21 May 1952. BBC WAC/Miller, James/ Scriptwriter File/1948–62.

33. Hugh MacDiarmid, 'MacDiarmid replies to Mackenzie', *Scottish Journal* (October 1952). Reprinted in Angus Calder, Glen Murray and Alan Riach, eds, *Hugh MacDiarmid: The Raucle Tongue, Hitherto Uncollected Prose, Volume III* (Manchester: Carcanet, 1998), pp. 308–9.

34. Hugh MacDiarmid to Alex McCrindle, 5 October 1951, reprinted in Alan Bold, ed., *The Letters of Hugh MacDiarmid* (London: Hamish Hamilton, 1984), pp. 647–9.

35. Broadcast on the BBC Third Programme, 6 February 1951, and repeated on 10 February. Also for the Third Programme, 'The Lallan Makars: An Account of some Scottish Poets by Ewan MaccColl' explored the work of some of MaccColl's new friends and acquaintances including Sydney Goodsir Smith, Douglas Young and Robert Garioch, who were presented as MacDiarmid's heirs. The programme was eventually broadcast almost a year after recording, BBC Third Programme, 23 June 1952.

36. Martin Milligan was the organiser (and kept the Communist Party's cultural secretary abreast of developments); Glasgow-based activists Janey and Norman Buchan did much of the spadework; the committee also reflected the broader labour movement – the Workers' Music Association, the Musicians' Union, Labour Party, Co-operative and trade union branches. Martin Milligan's correspondence about the festival, including letters to cultural committee secretary Sam Aaronovitch, are held in the Gallacher Memorial Library, Glasgow Caledonian University; Janey Buchan, interview by author, 3 August 2004, Glasgow.

37. Ewan MaccColl, 'Garderloo! Garderloo', manuscript in Hamish Henderson's papers, National Library of Scotland, M 272/9; 'This is no' my ain hoose', reprinted in Peggy Seeger, ed., *The Essential Ewan MaccColl Songbook* (New York and London: Oak, 2001), p. 305. Communist festival organiser Martin Milligan reported on the conference in 'Edinburgh People's Festival', *Communist Review* (March 1952), pp. 85–9, at p. 87.

38. Hamish Henderson, 'The Edinburgh People's Festival, 1951–4' in Andy Croft, ed., *A Weapon in the Struggle: The Cultural History of the Communist Party of Great Britain* (London and New York: Pluto, 1998), pp. 163–71; Osmond Robb, 'People's Festival', *Daily Worker*, 22 August 1951; Osmond Robb, 'They Did It Without Dollars', *Daily Worker*, 31 August 1951.

39. Proceedings were recorded by Alan Lomax and recently issued on CD as *1951 Edinburgh People's Festival Ceilidh* (CD, 1161–1786–2, Rounder, 2005).

40. Honor Arundel, 'I Go to a Sing Song', *Daily Worker*, 3 September 1951, p. 3.

41. Goorney, *Theatre Workshop Story*, p. 83.

42. Littlewood, *Joan's Book*, p. 425; Oscar Lewenstein, *Kicking Against the Pricks* (London: Nick Hern, 1994), p. 83; Alan Strachan, *Secret Dreams: The Biography of Michael Redgrave* (London: Weidenfeld & Nicolson, 2004), p. 284.

43. Goorney, *Theatre Workshop Story*, p. 83.

44. Strachan, *Secret Dreams*, p. 284.

45. *Daily Mirror* review sourced from Strachan, *Secret Dreams*, p. 284; *Daily Mail* on handbill for the follow-on production of *Uranium 235* at the Dolphin Theatre, Brighton (Theatre Workshop Archive); Harold Hobson in *The Times*, 19 June 1952, p. 3. See also *The Stage*, 26 June 1952.

46. Noted in a retrospective article by Gerald Fay, 'The Littlewood Touch', *Guardian*, 10 May 1961.

47. Littlewood, *Joan's Book*, pp. 426–7.

48. His moonlighting was written up by Derrick Stewart-Baxter, 'Preachin' the Blues', *Jazz Journal*, 5.8 (August 1952), pp. 4–5.

49. Joan Littlewood to D. G. Bridson, nd [June 1952]. BBC WAC/Joan Littlewood/Artist File, 1933–62.

50. Goorney, *Theatre Workshop Story*, pp. 83–4.

51. Littlewood, *Joan's Book*, p. 427.

52. Ewan MacColl, *The Travellers*. Script in MacColl/Seeger Archive.

53. 'The truthfulness and historical exactitude of the artistic image', wrote social realist henchman A. A. Zhdanov, 'must be linked with the task of ideological transformation, of the education of the working people in the spirit of socialism.' A. A. Zhdanov's, *On Literature, Music and Philosophy* (London: Lawrence & Wishart, 1950), p. 15.

54. National Archives, KV/2/2176/26.

55. Quotation from unsigned editorial note to *Arena: A Magazine of Modern Literature, Special Issue*, 2.8 (June–July 1951), p. 2. Also Sam Aaronovitch, 'The American Threat to British Culture', *Arena: A Magazine of Modern Literature, Special Issue*, 2.8 (June–July 1951), pp. 3–23. This issue printed contributions to a conference held by the Communist Party's National Cultural Committee in April 1951. For the National Cultural Committee, see Callaghan, *Cold War*, pp. 87–95; Branson, *Communist Party*, pp. 169–72. *The British Road to Socialism: Programme Adopted by the Executive Committee of the Communist Party, January 1951* (London: Communist Party, 1951).

56. For the CP and the Korean War, see Callaghan, *Cold War*, p. 142 and Willie Thompson, *The Good Old Cause: British Communism 1920–1991* (London: Pluto, 1992), p. 88.

57. For the Communist Party's take on Stalin's mass purge of 'Titoites', see Callaghan, *Cold War*, p. 53.

58. Ewan MacColl, *The Travellers*, p. 89. Script in MacColl/Seeger Archive.

59. For those Nazi party members redeployed as civil servants in the new West Germany, see Callaghan, *Cold War*, p. 56.

60. Joan Littlewood to D. G. Bridson, 10 April 1951. BBC WAC/Littlewood, Joan/Artist File, 1933–62.

61. *Daily Worker*, 21 August, 27 August, 1 September and 9 September 1952.

62. *The Travellers* was revived at the Theatre Royal, Stratford East between 24 November and 8 December 1953. Donald Douglas, 'It's Worth a Medal', *Daily Worker* (undated clipping in MacColl/Seeger Archive); see also 'The Story of the Greatest Peace Play Since Journey's End', *Forward*, 7 November 1953.

63. *Hell is What You Make It* was staged in Prague in 1949; *Rogues' Gallery* had been staged in East Germany in 1950 and would enjoy further East German revivals in the mid-1950s and mid-1970s. Programmes in MacColl/Seeger Archive, 'Theatre Programmes: plays by Ewan MacColl' file. *Operation Olive Branch* and *Uranium 235* had been published in Berlin in 1948 and 1949 respectively; Ewan MacColl, *Unternehmen Oelzweig*, trans. Anne Maria Weber (Berlin: Verlag Bruno Henschel und Sohn, 1948) and *Uranium 235*, trans. Rolf Italiander (Berlin: Verlag Bruno Henschel und Sohn, 1949).

64. Details about *Soviet Art* are given in a letter intercepted by MI5 in November 1952. National Archives, KV/2/2176/26. Theatre programmes in MacColl/Seeger Archive. It was also published as *Pociaq Mozna Zatrzymac*, trans. Maria Szietynska (Warsaw: Czytelnik Spoldzielnia Wydawnicza, 1956).

65. According to Hamish Henderson, *The Travellers* 'played straight into the hands of the right wing minority' of the festival committee. Hamish Henderson, 'The Edinburgh People's Festival, 1951–4', in Croft, ed., *Weapon*, pp. 163–71, at p. 169. See also Hamish Henderson to Hugh MacDiarmid, 27 April 1953 and Hamish Henderson to the *Scotsman*, 12 May 1962 in Alec Finlay, ed., *The Armstrong Nose: Selected Letters of Hamish Henderon* (Edinburgh: Polygon, 1996), pp. 63, 111.

66. Martin Milligan to Sam Aaronovitch, 3 January 1953. Gallacher Memorial Library, Glasgow. See also Norman Buchan, 'On Hamish', *Tocher*, 43 (1991), p. 20.

67. 'Third Edinburgh People's Festival Programme' in Gallacher Memorial Library, Glasgow.

68. Ewan MacColl and Gabriel, 'The People Make Their Own Fun', *Daily Worker*, 4 September 1953.

69. Jean Newlove/MacColl, interview by author, 9 August 2004, London; Littlewood, *Joan's Book*, pp. 432–5; Goorney, *Theatre Workshop Story*, pp. 85–6.

70. It was here that Harry Corbett started to reveal his true potential with a memorably downcast Andrew Aguecheek. Littlewood, *Joan's Book*, pp. 430–1; the company's appearance at George Watson's Boys' College, Edinburgh was written up in the *Scotsman*, 13 December 1952.

71. Translated by Lallans poet Thurso Berwick (the pseudonym of Morris Blythman). Handbill in Theatre Workshop Archive, Theatre Royal, Stratford

East, pre-1953 box. 'Lively Classics', *Scotsman*, 9 December 1952; 'Theatre Workshop', *Glasgow Herald*, 9 December 1952.

72. MacColl to Sam Aaronovitch, 9 October 1952. This letter was intercepted by MI5 and added to MacColl's file. KV/2/2176/25.

73. *Glasgow Herald*, 9 December 1952; handbill for *The Imaginary Invalid*.

74. Gerry Raffles, interview footage on Joan Littlewood, *Omnibus*, BBC, 19 April 1994. Littlewood recalled that the initial rent was £20 per week (*Joan's Book*, p. 440). Correspondence in the Theatre Workshop Archive suggests that the company were paying £40 per week by the summer of 1953.

75. MacColl, *Journeyman*, pp. 266–9; Goorney, *Theatre Workshop Story*, pp. 87–90.

76. Jean Newlove/MacColl, interview by author, 9 August 2004, London.

77. Goorney, *Theatre Workshop Story*, p. 99.

78. Goorney, *Theatre Workshop Story*, p. 205. Programmes and handbills in Theatre Workshop Archive, Stratford East.

79. Jean Newlove/MacColl, interviews by author, 22 July 2003 and 9 August 2004, London.

80. Programme in Theatre Workshop Archive, Stratford East.

81. MacColl, *Journeyman*, p. 268.

82. Andrew Means, 'The World of Ewan MacColl', *Melody Maker*, 11 November 1972, pp. 69–70, at p. 69. Exactly how the recordings came about remains a mystery, though MacColl's new friendships with Peter Kennedy (whose father was the more progressive EFDSS director and who straddled the worlds of the EFDSS and the BBC) and the ever-supple A. L. Lloyd (one foot in the EFDSS, the other in the Communist Party) are likely to have played a part.

83. Transportation song 'Van Dieman's Land' and 'Lord Randall' on one record, and the long ballads 'Sir Patrick Spens' and 'Eppie Morrie' on the second. HMV B10259 and HMV B10260.

84. Review by FH, *Folk Music Journal*, VII, 1 (December 1952), p. 54 and A. L. Lloyd, 'Recent Recordings', *English Dance and Song*, XVII, 2 (October–November 1952), pp. 52–3.

85. MacColl, *Journeyman*, p. 279.

86. The history of the WMA was told by Eric Winter, 'Achievement: the story of twenty-one years', *Sing*, 3.6 (February–March 1957), pp. 82–3. See also Brocken, *British Folk Revival*, pp. 49–55.

87. John Hasted, *Alternative Memoirs* (Itchenor: Greengate Press, 1992), p. 100.

88. MacColl, *Journeyman*, p. 279; Jean Newlove/MacColl, interview by author, 22 July 2003, London.

89. A Topic Records discography is printed in Michael Brocken, *The British Folk Revival*, pp. 146–216.

90. Of the fifteen records they issued between September 1952 and June 1953, ten were MacColl titles; *WMA Bulletin* (April 1953).

91. *Daily Worker*, 7 March 1953. Sourced from Callaghan, *Cold War*, p. 54. Ewan MacColl and Al Jeffrey, 'The Ballad of Stalin'/the Soviet Choir and Orchestra, 'Sovietland' (TRC 54, Topic, 1953). *The Railway King*, scripted

by MacColl and produced by Denis Mitchell, broadcast on NEHS, 29 May 1951 (and repeated on the National Home Service on 4 January 1953)

92. Ewan MacColl, 'Ballad of Stalin', *Sing* 1.5 (January–February 1955), p. 92; reprinted in Seeger, ed., *Essential Ewan MacColl Songbook*, p. 388.

93. Federico García Lorca, *Lament for the Death of a Bullfighter*, trans. A. L. Lloyd (London: Heinemann, 1937); MacColl, *Journeyman*, p. 247.

94. Littlewood, *Joan's Book*, pp. 316–17, 307.

95. The project grew out of *Johnny Miner* (1947), a radio feature dramatising the life of the pit communities for which Lloyd was commissioned to collect songs. E. David Gregory, 'Starting Over: A. L. Lloyd and the Search for a New Folk Music, 1945–49', *Canadian Journal for Traditional Music*, 27.1 (1999–2000); the programme was broadcast on the BBC Home Service, 23 December 1947 and adapted for the London stage by the WMA opera group in the spring of 1948, playing at the Rudolf Steiner Hall for a five-night run. See James Forsyth's untitled review, *Our Time* (April 1948), p. 185. After turning up fifteen suitable pieces, Lloyd persuaded the National Coal Board to help with a more thorough search. Adverts were placed in the NCB magazine *Coal*; Lloyd appealed from the screens of pit community cinema newsreels for colliers to send in songs. See Leslie Shepard, 'A. L. Lloyd – A Personal View' in Ian Russell, ed., *Singer, Song and Scholar* (Sheffield: Sheffield Academic Press, 1986), pp. 125–32.

96. Ewan MacColl interview, Barrie Gavin's Channel Four film *Bert* (1984).

97. 'Fourpence a Day', 'The Gresford Disaster' and MacColl's own song, 'The Plodder Seam'.

98. A. L. Lloyd, Introduction to Lloyd, ed., *Come All Ye Bold Miners: Ballads and Songs of the Coalfield* (London: Lawrence & Wishart, 1952), p. 17.

99. Lloyd, *Come All Ye Bold Miners*, p. 17.

100. Ewan MacColl to D. G. Bridson, 29 March 1952. BBC WAC/Miller, Jimmie/Scriptwriter, 1948–62. Lomax's broadcasts from this period included 'Adventure in Folksong', BBC Home Service, 13, 20, and 27 February 1951; 'Patterns in American Folk Song', BBC Third Programme, 15, 20 and 30 August 1951 and 'The Art of the Negro', BBC Third Programme, 3, 31 October and 28 November 1951. See Gregory, 'Lomax in London', pp. 139–43.

101. In the year prior to the London move, he dashed off comic songs about Blackpool, Skegness, Cleethorpes, Filey and Morecambe Bay for a series on British holiday resorts. 'Northern Seaside resorts', broadcast on North of England Home Service through June, July and August 1952. BBC WAC/ Miller, James H./Copyright file 1, 1937–62.

102. George Thomson, *Marxism and Poetry* (London: Lawrence & Wishart, 1945), p. 19. MacColl quoted Thomson's book at his 'Towards People's Theatre' lecture of 1952, and frequently afterwards.

103. 'Come All Ye Bold People: A Programme About Ballads Compiled by Ewan MacColl', recorded 28 December 1952. Broadcast 7 September 1953 on the BBC Third Programme.

104. MacColl speaking on 'Folk Song Forum: What is a Folksong?', Northern Ireland Home Service, 5 May 1955. Scipt in MacColl/Seeger Archive.

105. Broadcast BBC Third Programme, 31 December 1952.

106. MacColl on Folksong Forum, 5 May 1955.
107. Secret Report, 18 November 1952. National Archives KV2/2/2176.
108. Original broadcast dates were 10 March, 17 March, 24 March, 31 March, 7 April and 14 April 1953. Scripts in MacColl/Seeger Archive.
109. According to MacColl's much-embellished version of events, Ballads and Blues had a 'shattering effect' on an 'enormous public' and 'provided the impetus needed to launch the revival'. 'And So We Sang', Ewan MacColl, interview by Fred Woods, Folk Review, 2.3 (June 1973), pp. 4–7, at p. 7; MacColl, Journeyman, p. 275. In fact the programmes drew only a third of the listeners that Burl Ives had recently attracted in the same slot. BBC Listener Research Report for Ballads and Blues: The Singing Sailormen, BBC WAC N2/4; Ewan MacColl, 'Ballads and Blues', Radio Times, 6 March 1953.
110. BBC Listener Research Report for Ballads and Blues: The Singing Sailorman, BBC WAC N2/4.
111. BBC Listener Research Report for Ballads and Blues: Bad Lads and Hard Cases, BBC WAC N2/4.
112. Osmond Robb, Daily Worker, 21, 25, 26, 27, 31 August 1953.
113. The project was a coup for the Salfordian MacColl – Hamish Henderson felt this was his turf. Ewan MacColl, ed., Scotland Sings (London: Workers' Music Association, 1953). A streamlined version was published as Personal Choice (London: Workers' Music Association, London, 1954), reprinted by Hargail Music Press, New York, in 1962.
114. Review by Derrick Stewart-Baxter, Jazz Journal, 6.11 (November 1953), p. 22.
115. Ewan MacColl, interview with Fred Woods, 'And So We Sang', Folk Review, 2.8 (June 1973), pp. 4–7, at p. 6; MacColl, Journeyman, p. 361.
116. MacColl, Journeyman, p. 272. MacColl did similar work alone. In 1952, for example, he performed at the Fire Brigade's Union conference; in February 1955 he arranged the choral music for the Albert Hall celebration of the Daily Worker's twenty-fifth birthday. 'The Firefighter's Song', reprinted in The Essential Ewan MacColl Songbook, ed. Peggy Seeger (New York and London: Oak, 2001), p. 78; Daily Worker, 15 February 1955.
117. 'His Song is of a Hero', Daily Worker, 23 November 1953. Bert Baker, 'The Third Cultural Conference', World News, 10 October 1953, pp. 33, 40; WMA Bulletin (April 1953); Doris Lessing, Walking in the Shade (London: HarperCollins, 1997), p. 108; Doris Lessing to Ben Harker, 2 April 2003; 'Something to Sing About: Ten Years of People's Poland' concert, 18 July 1954, Cambridge Theatre, London, advertised in the Royal Festival Hall Ballads and Blues concert programme.
118. TLP1, Sailors' Songs and Shanties. Later reissued as The Singing Sailor, TRL3. The first LP issued by the WMA, the record was reviewed in Folk Music Journal, VII, 4 (December 1955), p. 260. It was followed by a series of LPs for the more developed US folk music market. See Gregory, 'Lomax in London', p. 154 and Cohen, Rainbow Quest, p. 109. The most significant early MacColl/Lloyd recordings were for the American Riverside label; their series The English and Scottish Popular Ballads comprised five double albums, 82 songs in total. Volume 1, RLP 12–621/2 was issued in 1956.

MacColl and Lloyd would continue to record together for the best part of a decade. Highlights include Ewan MacColl and A. L. Lloyd, *Blow Boys Blow* (LP, TLP 1026, Tradition, nd; reissued as CD, TCD 1924); their last joint release for Topic was *English and Scottish Folk Ballads* (LP, 12T103, Topic, 1964).

119. They also attracted the attention of the authorities. By the third festival in Berlin, 1951, Labour politicians were warning of 'Communist controlled youth organisations' campaigning 'for peace on Soviet terms'. Branson, *Communist Party*, pp. 226–30, at p. 227.

120. Ewan MacColl, interview by Charles Parker, 26 June 1972. Transcript in Charles Parker Archive, Birmingham, file CPA 1/7/4.

121. National Archives, KV/2/2175/15 and KV/2/2176/17 respectively.

122. John Hasted, 'A Warsaw Notebook'; John Hasted, Hylda Sims and Eric Winter, 'Did you hear about the Festival?' in *Sing*, 2.4 (October–November 1955), pp. 61, 54, 55, 58.

123. Script in MacColl/ Seeger Archive.

124. *You're Only Young Once* script in MacColl/Seeger Archive; the song 'See you in Warsaw' was printed in *Sing*, 2.3 (August–September 1955), p. 46.

125. Jean Newlove/MacColl, interview by author, 9 August 2004, London.

126. MacColl, *Journeyman*, p. 276.

127. MacColl, *Journeyman*, pp. 356–63.

128. 'None of these songs can be considered as poetry,' MacColl wrote in a letter to Communist Party Cultural Commissar Sam Aaronovitch; 'the idea was to produce contemporary folk-song material in the traditional style.' This letter was intercepted by Special Branch. MacColl to Aaronovitch, 'December 2 1953' [actually 1952], National Archives, KV/2/2176/24.

129. 'The Dove', *Sing*, 1.3 (September–October 1954), p. 56 and 'Fare Thee Well, Westminster', *Sing*, 2.1 (May Day supplement, 1955), p. 16. Roughly produced and with a circulation of less than a thousand, *Sing* printed nine of MacColl's new songs in its first year alone. The magazine was founded in 1954 by members of the London Youth Choir, had loose ties to the World Federation of Democratic Youth and the WMA, and supported organisations such as the British–Roumanian Friendship Association. Above all, it aimed to stimulate the type of songs MacColl was now writing. 'Song has a powerful role to play in the struggle of the British people for peace and socialism,' ran one editorial; songs were 'to inspire unity' and shed light on contemporary events; such songs were also to connect the present with the past, 'reminding people of the tradition from which our present day songs arise by drawing on earlier songs for example and inspiration.' Unsigned editorial, *Sing*, 2.1 (May Day 1955), p. 12. Other printed songs called for Americans to be sent home, and celebrated the Edinburgh People's Festival and the *Daily Worker*. Norman Buchan, 'Send them Hame [sic]', *Sing*, 1.5 (January–February 1955), p. 85; Norman Buchan, 'The People's Festival', *Sing*, 1.2 (July–August, 1954), p. 32; John Hasted, 'Ballad of the Daily Worker', *Sing*, 1.6 (nd [1955]), p. 121.

130. Reprinted in Seeger, ed., *Essential Ewan MacColl Songbook*, p. 284; recorded on Ewan MacColl, *Chorus from the Gallows* (LP, 12T16, Topic, 1960), reissued on CD as TSCD02. Clinton Heylin, *Dylan: Behind the Shades* (London: Viking, 1991), p. 65.

131. Reprinted in Seeger, ed., *Essential Ewan MacColl Songbook*, p. 284; recorded on Phil Ochs, *I Ain't Marching Anymore* (LP, EKL-287, Elektra, 1965).

132. Unsigned article, 'The Ballads and Brooms', plugging a new season of Ballads and Blues concerts, starting at St Pancras Town Hall. The line-up for the first event featured MacColl and Lloyd, a skiffle band, and Michael Gorman's ceilidh band. *Sing*, 1.5 (January–February 1955), p. 101.

133. Derrick Stewart-Baxter, 'Preachin' The Blues', *Jazz Journal*, 6.7 (July 1953), pp. 17–18. Backed by the new Theatre Royal Supporters' Club, the 1953 Sunday evening concerts provided much-needed revenue and were revived the following winter. Goorney, *Theatre Workshop Story*, p. 92; Littlewood, *Joan's Book*, p. 461; handbill in Theatre Workshop Archive, Stratford East; programme in Theatre Workshop Archive, Stratford East. The hastily organised tour of cavernous and half-empty halls was a financial disaster, even if the critics were unanimously upbeat about the show. *WMA Bulletin* (February 1954), *WMA Bulletin* (March 1954). Paper cuttings in MacColl/Seeger archive, Ballads and Blues file.

134. Unsigned, 'Folksongs Tonight Won't All be Blues', *Daily Worker*, 5 July 1954; Ewan MacColl, 'On the Trail of a Song', *Challenge*, 3 July 1954.

135. Programme for Ballads and Blues, Royal Festival Hall, 5 July 1954. Working Class Movement Library, Salford.

136. Unsigned review, 'Ballads and Blues at the Festival Hall', *Sing*, 1.3 (September–October 1954), pp. 40–3.

137. *WMA Bulletin* (September 1954).

138. Programme for Ballads and Blues, Royal Festival Hall, 5 July 1954; B. Nicholls, 'A Jazzman's Diary', *Jazz Journal*, 7.8 (August 1954), p. 11.

139. Unsigned review, 'Ballads and Blues at the Festival Hall', *Sing*, 1.3 (September–October 1954), pp. 40–3, at p. 43.

140. Mike Dewe, *The Skiffle Craze* (Aberystwyth: Planet, 1998), p. 6.

141. Ewan MacColl, interview by Charles Parker, 26 June 1972, transcript in Charles Parker Archive, Birmingham, File CPA 1/7/4.

142. Dewe, *Skiffle Craze*, pp. 24–5; Hasted, *Alternative Memoirs*, pp. 121, 144.

143. Hasted, *Alternative Memoirs*, pp. 134–5; Shirley Collins, *America Over the Water* (London: SAF, 2004), p. 16.

144. Robin Denselow, *When the Music's Over: The Story of Political Pop* (London: Faber & Faber, 1989), p. 24.

145. Colin Harper, *Dazzling Stranger: Bert Jansch and the British Folk and Blues Revival* (London: Bloomsbury, 2000), p. 22.

146. Graham Boatfield, 'Skiffle Artificial', *Jazz Journal*, 9.4 (April 1956), p. 2.

147. MacColl, *Journeyman*, p. 274.

148. Alan Lomax, 'Skiffle: Where is it Going?', *Melody Maker*, 7 September 1957, p. 5.

## Chapter 7, 'Croydon, Soho, Moscow, Paris'

1. *Sixteen Tons/The Swan-Necked Valve* (Single, TRC 97, Topic, nd [1956]). Unfavourably reviewed by JA, 'Discussion: New Topics', *Sing*, 3.1 (April–May 56), p. 10.

2. These included *Great American Ballads* (LP, CLP 1192, HMV, nd), *Hard Case/Dirty Old Town* (Single, F10787 Decca, nd) and *American Song Train* (LP, NPL 1813, Nixa, nd).

3. In time Shirley would become Lomax's girlfriend, and move into his unconventional domestic set-up, joining his ten-year-old daughter, ex-wife and her boyfriend. Shirley Collins, *America Over the Water* (London: SAF, 2004), pp. 21–2.

4. Judith Tick, *Ruth Crawford Seeger: A Composer's Search For American Music* (New York and Oxford: Oxford University Press, 1997); Ann M. Pescatello, *Charles Seeger: A Life in American Music* (Pittsburgh and London: University of Pittsburgh Press, 1992).

5. Tick, *Ruth Crawford Seeger*, pp. 236, 259.

6. Tick, *Ruth Crawford Seeger*, p. 306.

7. Peggy Seeger interview with Michael O'Rourke and Mary Orr, in 'Part One: The Making of a Folksinger', *Parsley, Sage and Politics: The Lives and Music of Peggy Seeger and Ewan MacColl*, US National Public Radio (1985).

8. He'd enjoyed one bout of critical acclaim in the early 1940s performing alongside Josh White, Lee Hays and Woody Guthrie in The Almanac Singers. Ten years later he was a commercial success with the more anodyne Weavers, who signed to Decca, sold over a million copies of their first single, Leadbelly's 'Goodnight, Irene', and commanded huge fees for nightclub, radio and television work. David King Dunaway, *How Can I Keep From Singing: Pete Seeger* (London: Harrap, 1985), pp. 144–5; Ronald D. Cohen, *Rainbow Quest: The Folk Music Revival and American Society 1940–1970* (Amherst and Boston: University of Massachusetts Press, 2002), pp. 67–71 and Bryan K. Garman, *A Race of Singers: Whitman's Working Class Hero From Guthrie to Springstein* (Chapel Hill and London: University of North Carolina Press, 2000), pp. 136–40.

9. Pete was called to appear before the House Un-American Activities Committee. Courageously, he refused to follow the usual course of exercising his right to silence – for Seeger, this created the impression of something to hide. Instead he asserted his right to free speech, knowingly facing a lengthy legal battle and the likelihood of a substantial prison sentence for Contempt of Congress. King Dunaway, *Pete Seeger*, p. 179.

10. Tick, *Ruth Crawford Seeger*, pp. 292, 347.

11. 'Hard Case/Dirty Old Town' (Single, F10789, Decca, nd); *Alan Lomax and the Ramblers* (7 inch EP, DFE6367, Decca, nd); *Alan Lomax and the Ramblers* (LP, DS 3212/1–2, Decca, nd).

12. In 1953 he collaborated with young producer David Attenborough on *Song Hunter: Alan Lomax*, an eight-part BBC television series that beamed exotic musical cultures from Britain and beyond into the nation's front rooms. MacColl made a brief appearance. *Song Hunter: Alan Lomax*, BBC TV. Part one was broadcast on 25 June 1953. Previewed in *Radio Times*, 9 June, 1953, p. 15. See E. David Gregory, 'Lomax in London', *Folk Music Journal*, 8.2 (2002), pp. 136–71. Lomax's earlier appearance on the small screen had caught the ever-watchful eye of Special Branch. Lomax, who came to Britain partly to evade the red-necked, paranoiac excesses of McCarthyism, found

himself implicated in the more reserved British version. His file, PF 151, 441, was quietly filling out. Lomax's file is cross-referenced in MacColl's MI5 dossier, KV 2/2176, files 15 and 21, National Archives.

13. The first instalment of *The Ramblers*, a six-part TV series, was broadcast on Granada TV Network on 18 June 1956 at 10.30 pm. Scripts (incomplete) in MacColl/Seeger archive.

14. *The Ramblers*, 18 June 1956, script in MacColl/Seeger archive.

15. *The Ramblers*, 18 June 1956, script in MacColl/Seeger archive.

16. In the second programme MacColl observed, 'These old ballads all end up in a way that seems rather abrupt to us. Their composers just gave the facts and quit.' *The Ramblers*, 22 June 1956, script in MacColl/Seeger archive. The group's spin-off songbook earned the opprobrium of one Cecil Sharp House traditionalist for 'left-wing sympathies' and attempting 'to insert American attitudes into British songs'. RJM, review of *The Skiffle Album*. *English Dance and Song*, XXII, 2 (November–December 1957), p. 69.

17. Seeger, ed., *Peggy Seeger Songbook*, p. 48.

18. Seeger made recordings of American Folksongs for future BBC use on 15 August 1956; two days later she worked with MacColl on the North of England Home Service programme, 'People Talking – in Prison'. BBC WAC/ Artist File/R Cont 1/Peggy Seeger, 1956–62.

19. Peggy Seeger, 'Self-Portrait', *Sing*, 4.6 (October 1958), pp. 67–8.

20. The advent of 12-inch LPs worked wonders for the commercial viability of specialist music: production costs weren't much greater than for EPs, but the finished article retailed for six times as much, greatly increasing small companies' turnover. Pete Heywood, 'Bill Leader: Fifty Years in the Recording Industry Part One', *Living Tradition*, 68 (May–June 2006), pp. 26–30, at p. 28. Kenneth Goldstein's Riverside label, for example, scheduled to issue eight LPs per year with the WMA acting as the agents. Much of the work came MacColl's way. Ewan MacColl to Hamish Henderson, 1 May 1956. ACC 10528/National Library of Scotland. In 1956 Topic appointed Bill Leader as their new recording manager, acquired their own recording machine, moved into bigger premises and launched a new series of folk records, hoping to break into a wider distribution network. *WMA Bulletin* (September 1956); EW, 'Discussion: Topic Folk Song Label', *Sing*, 5.4 (October–November 1956), p. 51.

21. Early Seeger releases included *Freight Train/Cumberland Gap* (Single, TRC 107, Topic, nd), *Pretty Little Baby/Child of God* (Single, TRC 108, Topic, nd) and *Eleven American Ballads and Songs* (10-inch LP, 10T9, Topic, 1957). Jack Elliott recorded titles including *Talking Miner Blues/Pretty Boy Floyd* (Single; TRC 98, Topic, nd) and *Woody Guthrie's Blues* (8-inch EP, 8T5, Topic, nd).

22. Ewan MacColl, *Journeyman: An Autobiography* (London: Sidgwick & Jackson, 1990), p. 379.

23. Peggy Seeger, interview by author, 14 October 2004, Sheffield.

24. Peggy Seeger, interview by author, 14 October 2004, Sheffield.

25. Behan's *The Quare Fellow* opened at Stratford East that May, and transferred to the West End in July.

26. Clive Barker, interview by author, 10 August 2004, Sidcup.

27. Peggy Seeger, interview by author, 16 November 2003, York.
28. MacColl appeared alongside future television stars Bill Owen (Mack the Knife/Compo in *Last of the Summer Wine*) and Warren Mitchell (Crookfinger Jake/Alf Garnett in *Till Death Us Do Part*) in a production that divided the critics between a sinister exercise in 'Marxist science' and 'a wild red bloom on the stagnant boards of our musical theatre'. Unsigned review, *Punch*, 27 February 1956; Robert Muller, 'Soho – Made in Germany', *Picture Post*, 3 March 1956, p. 29. The show is now recognisably part of the Royal Court watershed in the new wave of British theatre.
29. MacColl to Hamish Henderson, 1 May 1956, file ACC 10528, National Library of Scotland, Edinburgh.
30. Peggy Seeger, interview by author, 14 October 2004, Sheffield.
31. Ewan MacColl to Peggy Seeger, 21 December [1958].
32. MacColl, *Journeyman*, p. 280.
33. Peggy Seeger, interview by author, 14 October 2004, Sheffield.
34. Irwin Silber, 'Peggy Seeger – The Voice of America in Folksong', *Sing Out!*, 12 (Summer 1962), pp. 4–8, at p. 6.
35. MacColl, *Journeyman*, p. 208.
36. MacColl interview on Part Five, *Parsley, Sage and Politics* (1985).
37. Seeger, ed., *The Essential Ewan MacColl Songbook* (New York and London: Oak, 2001), p. 28
38. Seeger, ed., *MacColl Songbook*, p. 28.
39. Report on Ewan MacColl 'from a reliable source', 31 March 1954. National Archives, KV/2/2176/20.
40. Staged by the Australian WEA players in Sydney in July 1956. Press cuttings from *Tribune*, 25 July 1956 and *Sunday*, 23 July 1956 in MacColl/Seeger archive.
41. Script in MacColl/Seeger Archive; Goorney, *Theatre Workshop Story*, pp. 104, 153.
42. Clive Barker, interview by the author, Sidcup, 10 August 2004. Minutes for Theatre Workshop company meeting, 31 March 1955. Reprinted in Goorney, *Theatre Workshop Story*, pp. 217–21, at p. 217.
43. Joan Littlewood, *Joan's Book: The Autobiography of Joan Littlewood* (London: Methuen, 1994), pp. 178–80. The play was staged as *Rummelplatz* in 1961.
44. Clive Barker, interview by author, 10 August 2004, Sidcup.
45. Clive Barker, interview by author, 10 August 2004, Sidcup.
46. Goorney, *Theatre Workshop Story*, pp. 93, 199, 215.
47. Oscar Lewenstein, *Kicking Against the Pricks: A Theatre Producer Looks Back* (London: Nick Hern, 1994), pp. 24–5.
48. Jean Newlove/MacColl, interviews by author, 22 July 2003 and 9 August 2004, London.
49. Stan Wasser, 'Soviet takes to Jazz', *Melody Maker*, 17 August 1957, p. 5.
50. Stan Wasser, 'Soviet takes to Jazz', *Melody Maker*, 17 August 1957, p. 5.
51. 'Talking Moscow' (no author listed), *Sing*, 4.4/5 (December 1957), p. 59.
52. Ewan MacColl to Hamish Henderson, 10 January 1957, file ACC 10528, National Library of Scotland, Edinburgh. Shirley Collins, *America*, pp. 18–19; Colin Harper, *Dazzling Stranger: Bert Jansch and the British Folk*

*and Blues Revival* (London: Bloomsbury, 2000), p. 26; unsigned, 'Moscow to Hear Scott and Reece', *Melody Maker*, 9 March 1957, p. 16.

53. Ewan MacColl to Peggy Seeger, 14 October 1957.
54. Peggy Seeger, interview by author, 14 October 2004, Sheffield.
55. Ewan MacColl to Peggy Seeger, 7 November [1957].
56. Ewan MacColl to Peggy Seeger, 14 October 1957.
57. Ewan MacColl to Peggy Seeger, 14 October 1957.
58. Arthur Scargill to Ben Harker, 4 April 2003.
59. John Callaghan, *Cold War, Crisis and Conflict: The CPGB 1951–68* (London: Lawrence & Wishart, 2003), p. 113.
60. Callaghan, *Cold War*, pp. 62–4.
61. James Eaden and David Renton, *The Communist Party in Britain Since 1920* (Basingstoke and New York: Palgrave Macmillan, 2002), pp. 118–22.
62. Andy Croft, *Comrade Heart: A Life of Randall Swingler* (Manchester: Manchester University Press, 2003), p. 227.
63. *For Soviet Britain: The Programme of the Communist Party Adopted on 2 February 1935* (London: CPGB, 1935), p. 19.
64. On the face of it, the party's new Music Group publication *Music and Life* seemed a welcome development, but it was too eclectic in its scope and too tentative in its approach to folk music for MacColl's tastes. *Music and Life* was launched by the Communist Party Music Group in April 1956. Copies are held in file CP/Cent/Cult/16/02 of the People's History Museum, Labour History Archive and Study Centre, Manchester. MacColl is conspicuously absent from the journal's pages.
65. MacColl performed at two Young Communist League 'Festivals of Socialism', the first at St Pancras Town Hall (24–26 May 1958) and the second at Holborn Assembly Rooms on (30 November 1958). Handbills can be found in file CP/YCL/17/2 at the Labour History Archive and Study Centre, Manchester. MacColl would never be categorically drawn on his departure from the Communist Party during interviews. Due to the party's concern that membership records might fall into the hands of the authorities, details were not kept centrally, but only locally, and then often on a year-by-year basis. It therefore hasn't been possible to pinpoint the exact date when MacColl withdrew from the CP; he certainly made no public statement at the time. On the basis of the sometimes conflicting recollections of friends, family and Communist Party members, we can be reasonably sure that he allowed his card to lapse in the early 1960s, possibly when he moved to Beckenham. The matter is further discussed in Chapter 9; it may be finally cleared up in 2015 when MacColl's post-1955 MI5 file is reviewed for declassification.
66. Ewan MacColl [and Peggy Seeger], *Shuttle and Cage: Industrial Folk-Ballads* (10-inch EP, 10T13, Topic, 1957); *WMA Bulletin* (November 1957); *WMA Bulletin* (January 1958).
67. The record's sequel, *Second Shift: Industrial Folk Ballad* (10-inch EP, 10T25, Topic, 1958) was issued the following year. The two discs were later released as a single LP, *Steam Whistle Ballads: Industrial Songs Old and New* (LP, 12T104, Topic, 1964).

68. Jeff Smith, 'The Hootenanny Takes Hold', *Melody Maker*, 18 January 1958, p. 5.
69. Graham Boatfield, 'An Eye Upon the Skiffle', *Jazz Journal*, 10.8 (August 1957), pp. 5–6.
70. Notably Vivian de Sola Pinto and Allen Edwin Rodway's anthology *The Common Muse: An Anthology of Popular British Ballad Poetry from the Fifteenth to the Twentieth Century* (London: Chatto & Windus, 1957); Ralph Vaughan Williams and A. L. Lloyd, eds, *The Penguin Book of English Folk Songs* (Harmondsworth: Penguin, 1959) also played an important role in shaping the song repertoire of revival singers over the next decade.
71. *A Ballad Hunter Look at Britain*. Broadcast on the Home Service in November and December 1957. See Gregory, 'Lomax in London', *Folk Music Journal*, 8.2 (2002), pp. 156–9. Lomax also managed to persuade the corporation to back his ambitious *Sing Christmas and the Turn of the Year*, a live Christmas Day broadcast which explored the folk roots of Christmas carols, linked up to live festivities in different BBC regions (MacColl was master of ceremonies in Castleton, Derbyshire). Broadcast on the BBC Home Service on 25 December 1957 at 11 am. Script is in the BBC Written Archives, Caversham; reissued as *Sing Christmas and the Turn of the Year: The Live Christmas Day 1957 Broadcast on BBC Radio* (CD, 1850, Rounder, 2000). Folk music broke into the TV listings once more that summer with *The Ballad Story*, a cornball Rediffusion series of half-hour programmes in which MacColl featured. Directed by Roger Jenkins, the series was broadcast in May, June and July 1957 and featured singers and musicians including MacColl, Peggy Seeger, A. L. Lloyd, Isla Cameron, Jimmie MacGregor, Jeannie Robertson and Seumus Ennis. An incomplete selection of scripts is held in the MacColl/Seeger archive.
72. Unsigned, 'The English Folk Music Festival: Was it Worth While?', *English Dance and Song*, XXII, 3 (January 1958), pp. 104–5, at p. 104.
73. Not for the first time, Tom Driberg used his public profile to support MacColl. Driberg's *New Statesman and Nation* column of 19 April 1958 appealed for the BBC to commission a new series of *Ballads and Blues* radio programmes, a proposition that was seriously debated within the corporation, but eventually shelved in June 1958 on the grounds of cost. BBC Written Archives, Caversham, 'Ballads and Blues' file.
74. Income and expenditure sheet for Ballads and Blues Concert series in Broadcasts/Radio/Ballads and Blues file, MacColl/Seeger Archive, Ruskin College.
75. Handbill for 'Ballads and Blues 1957', Charles Parker Archive, Birmingham, CPA 1/8/10; concert schedules in Broadcasts/Radio/Ballads and Blues file, MacColl/Seeger Archive.
76. Handbill in Charles Parker Archive, CPA 1/8/10.
77. Parallel developments were afoot in Bradford, under the influence of WMA member and Communist Alex Eaton. Dates are difficult to pin down, but the Topic Folk Club in Bradford was certainly among the first to be formed outside London. See Pete Heywood, 'Bill Leader: 50 Years in the Recording Industry', *Living Tradition*, 68 (May–June 2006), pp. 26–30.

78. Eric Winter, 'The Flowers of Manchester', *Manchester Guardian*, 3 March 1958.
79. Ewan MacColl to Peggy Seeger, 12 December 1957.
80. Jeff Smith, 'The Hootenanny takes Hold', *Melody Maker*, 18 January 1958; Malcolm Nixon, 'Hoots Are a Great Success', *WMA Bulletin* (January 1958).
81. Pat Mackenzie, interview by author, 14 September 2003, Salford.
82. Ewan MacColl to Peggy Seeger, 12 December 1957.
83. Malcolm Nixon, 'Hoots are a Great Success', *WMA Bulletin* (January 1958).
84. Karl Dallas, interview by author, 22 October 2003, Bradford.
85. Eric Winter, 'The Flowers of Manchester', *Manchester Guardian*, 3 March 1958.
86. Ewan MacColl to Peggy Seeger, nd [1958].
87. MacColl, interview by Charles Parker, 26 June 1972, transcript in Charles Parker Archive, CPA 1/ 7/4.
88. Ewan MacColl MI5 file, KV2/2176, file 21, National Archives, Kew.
89. BBC /WAC/Scriptwriter/ Miller, James/1948–1962.
90. Between 1953 and 1957 he wrote just one script for the BBC, almost certainly commissioned before the blacklisting took hold. *The Spinner of Bolton: The Story of Samuel Compton*, broadcast on the North of England Home Service on 3 December 1953. Script in BBC Written Archives. Throughout these years he appeared as a singer in *Coaldust Minstrel*, A. L. Lloyd's radio play about County Durham pit village bard Tommy Armstrong, and took on minor acting roles. *Coaldust Minstrel* was broadcast on the North of England Home Service on 19 March 1953. Script in BBC Written Archives. MacColl's acting roles included appearances in *Tenant of Wildfell Hall*, broadcast on the North of England Home Service, 3 March 1954, and *The Story of Rolls Royce*, broadcast on the North of England Home Service on 15 June 1954. He continued to develop his working relationship with innovative documentary radio and filmmaker Denis Mitchell, notably through *People Talking in Prison*, originally a Home Service radio programme about life in Strangeways, reworked by Mitchell as *In Prison*, the first film to be made inside a British jail. Broadcast on the BBC Home Service on 26 June 1957; Mitchell's *Night in the City* was pre-recorded for future NEHS use on 10 October 1954. It was worked up into a film of the same title, broadcast in the BBC 'Eye to Eye' series on 14 June 1957. MacColl wrote and performed music for both versions. BBC WAC/ Copyright/ Jimmie Miller/1937–62. Copies of excerpts from both films are in the MacColl/Seeger archive. MacColl wrote 'The Lag's Song' for the film version, a fragile and contemplative piece that once again worked through traumatic memories of his own imprisonment ten years before. Reprinted in Peggy Seeger, ed., *Essential Ewan MacColl Songbook*, p. 288.
91. Parker included a short CV in his letter to 'Mr. Stephens', 27 February 1961, CPA 1/3/1/1. Additional biographical data from Paul Long, 'British radio and the politics of culture in post-war Britain: Charles Parker', *Radio Journal*, 2.3 (2004), pp. 131–52 and Trevor Fisher, *Aspects of a Pioneer* (Birmingham: Charles Parker Archive, 1986).

92. Quoted in Long, 'British Radio', p. 139.
93. MacColl, *Journeyman*, p. 311.
94. Parker to Mac [Stewart McAllister of British Transport Films], 24 October 1958. CPA 2/64/3/1.
95. Ewan MacColl to Peggy Seeger, nd [1958].
96. See Long, 'British Radio', p. 35 and Ronald D. Cohen, *Rainbow Quest: The Folk Music Revival and American Society 1940–70* (Amherst and Boston: University of Massachusetts Press, 2002), p. 33. The programme was released on record (10-inch, DL-5054, Decca, 1943). Later reissued by Folkways, MacColl bought the disc at Parker's recommendation (MacColl to Parker, 17 July [1957], CPA 2/64/1/6).
97. Parker wrote to the programme's producer Norman Corwin on 19 October 1959. CPA 2/64/3/1.
98. Parker to Johnny Dankworth, 17 March 1959, CPA 2/64/3/1; Parker to Denis Mitchell, 16 July 1957. CPA 2/64/1/6.
99. Parker to Denis Mitchell, 16 July 1957, CPA 2/64/1/6. For Free Cinema, see Christophe Dupin's booklet to *Free Cinema*, British Film Institute, BFI DVD717, 2006.
100. Parker to Ewan MacColl, 12 July 1957. CPA 2/64/1/6.
101. 'John Axon', BBC Memo from Charles Parker to Midland Region Programme Executive, 11 September 1957. BBC WAC/R Cont 1/Jimmy Miller/Copyright File/1937–62. There's no correspondence in the BBC Archives or Charles Parker's papers about the lifting of the BBC blacklist. It's possible that MacColl's post-1955 MI5 file, to be considered for declassification in 2015, will shed further light on this.
102. *Ministry of Transport and Civil Aviation Report* (London, 1957).
103. Gladys Axon to Charles Parker, 13 July 1957. CPA 2/64/1/6.
104. Parker first wrote to Gladys Axon on 12 July 1957; she gave her consent in early August. Correspondence in CPA 2/64/1/6.
105. Parker saw Axon's story as 'the perfect vehicle for a type of show I have been wanting to have a go at for some time'. Parker to MacColl, 12 July 1957. CPA 2/64/1/6.
106. Parker to C. H. Phoenix, nd [late summer 1957]. CPA 2/64/1/6.
107. Seán Street, 'Programme-makers on Parker: occupational reflections on the radio production legacy of Charles Parker', *Radio Journal*, 2.3 (2004), pp. 187–94. The term 'actuality', which MacColl and Parker used, derived from pioneering 1920s and 1930s filmmaker John Grierson, who famously defined documentary as 'the creative use of actuality'. See Kevin Macdonald and Mark Cousins, eds, *Imagining Reality: The Faber Book of Documentary* (London and Boston: Faber & Faber, 1996), p. 93.
108. Parker to MacColl, 18 July 1957; 'John Axon', BBC Memo, Parker to Midland Region Programme Executive, 11 September 1957. CPA 2/64/1/6.
109. The Ministry of Transport and Civil Aviation report was eventually published in October. Parker to MacColl, 30 September 1957. CPA 2/64/1/6.
110. Parker to C. H. Phoenix, nd [late summer 1957]. CPA 2/64/1/6.
111. Parker's original conception was for 'a 30 minute musical radio ballad of a somewhat unusual form, possibly involving a very small amount of actuality'.

Parker, 'John Axon' memo to Midland Region Programme Executive, 11 September 1957. BBC WAC/R Cont 1/Jimmy Miller/Copyright. This document can also be found in CPA 2/64/1/6.

112. Ewan MacColl, 'The Radio Ballads', unpublished typescript of a long essay held in the MacColl/Seeger archive. There are two versions of this essay, one dated August 1981, the other undated.

113. Ewan MacColl to Peggy Seeger, 12 December 1957.

114. BBC WAC/Peggy Seeger/Artist file/1956–62.

115. Script in BBC Written Archives, Caversham and MacColl/Seeger archive. Recording details in BBC WAC/R Cont 1/Peggy Seeger/Artist/1956–62.

116. MacColl, *Journeyman*, p. 314.

117. The programme was issued as a record in 1965 (LP, DA139, Argo, 1965) and as a CD in 1999 (CD, TSCD801, Topic, 1999).

118. Charles Parker, 'The Ballad of John Axon', *Radio Times*, 27 June 1958.

119. MacColl, *Journeyman*, p. 312.

120. MacColl, 'The Radio Ballads', *Sing Out!* (April–May 1967), p. 7.

121. MacColl, 'The Radio Ballads', p. 7.

122. The first use of the term I've found is in Parker's 'John Axon memo' of 11 September 1957. CPA 2/64/1/6.

123. Adrian Clancy, 'Last Moments of a Hero: This BBC Ballad of Death is Shocking, Weird', *Daily Mail* (Northern edn), 2 July 1958; Adrian Clancy, 'Tribute to GC Hero "horrific – and fine"', *Daily Mail* (Northern edn), 4 July 1958.

124. Unsigned inset next to Clancy's article, 2 July 1958.

125. Charles Parker, 'The Ballad of John Axon', *Radio Times*, 27 June 1958. Toned down for publication, Parker's feelings about American cultural imperialism are more explicit in the draft version of the article, written on 12 June 1958. 'Our popular songs are the product of another people, or sad copies of them', he wrote, 'our heroes are imported; we even sing in a language not our own.' BBC WAC/R44/839/1/John Axon publicity file.

126. Robert Robinson, 'The Up Line', *Sunday Times*, 6 July 1958; Audience Research Department Report in CPA 2/6/4/2/1.

127. Memo from Sound Publicity Officer, 13 June 1958, *Ballad of John Axon* publicity file, BBC WAC/R44/839/1.

128. Robinson, 'The Up Line'; 'Human and Exciting', unsigned review in *Daily Worker*, 8 July 1958; Paul Ferris, 'Noise with a Purpose', *Sunday Observer*, 6 July 1958.

129. Tom Driberg, *New Statesman and Nation*, 12 July 1958.

130. Correspondence about the film in CPA 2/64/3/1; Dai Vaughan, *Portrait of an Invisible Man: The Working Life of Stewart McAllister, Film Editor* (London: BFI, 1983), p. 188.

131. Correspondence in CPA 2/64/3/1.

132. Charles Parker to Head of Features and Assistants, dated the 16th [probably July 1958], BBC WAC/James Miller/Scriptwriter 1948–62, file 1.

133. Laurence Gilliam to Parker, 23 July 1958. BBC WAC/James Miller/Scriptwriter 1948–62, file 1.

134. Gilliam to Parker, memo 18 July 1958. CPA 2/64/1/6.

135. Joan Ruddock, ed., *CND Scrapbook* (London: Optima, 1987), p. 7.

136. Seeger, ed., *The Peggy Seeger Songbook* (London and New York: Oak, 1998), p. 45; Peggy Seeger, interview by author, 14 October 2004, Sheffield; Pete Seeger, 'From Aldermaston to London: They Walked and Sang for Peace, *Sing Out!*, 10.4 (December 1960–January 1961), pp. 14–15.
137. The 1959 march reversed the route of the previous year and culminated in a 25,000-strong rally in Trafalgar Square. Co-written with Denise Keir, MacColl's adaptation of the American labour song 'Buddy Won't You Roll Down the Line?' – now 'Brother Won't you Join In the Line?' – became a favourite on the fifty-seven-mile march. Pete Seeger, 'Aldermaston to London', p. 15. That June Peggy Seeger was back in Trafalgar Square performing with Paul Robeson at the rally of the March for Life against Nuclear Death. *WMA Bulletin* (August 1959); Peggy Seeger, e-mail to author 27 November 2004. Songsheets were issued by *Sing* and guerrilla songleaders appointed; Karl Dallas set up a Nuclear Disarmament Choir based at the Partisan Café on Carlisle Street, Soho; Topic Records rushed out *Songs Against the Bomb: The London Youth Choir* featuring songs by Dallas, MacColl, Seeger and others in time for the 1960 march. Songsheet in Working Class Movement Library, Salford, Ewan MacColl box; *Songs Against the Bomb* (LP, 12001, Topic, 1959).
138. *Absolute Beginners* (1959), Colin MacInnes' panoramic novel of contemporary London, satirised Ballads and Blues as an organisation that 'seeks to prove that all folk music is an art of protest' related to 'the achievements of the USSR, ie, Mississippi jail songs are in praise of sputniks'. Colin MacInnes, *Absolute Beginners* (1959; London: Allison & Busby, 2001), p. 124.
139. Charles Parker Archive, CPA 2/68. 'Hootenanny' files.
140. Eventually sidelined for regional only broadcast (both the National Home Service and Light Programme found the recordings too raw), 'Hootenanny' was broadcast in the BBC Midland Home Service in six half-hour weekly programmes beginning on 19 February 1959.
141. Parker, 'Hootenanny', *Radio Times*, 6 February 1959.
142. Charles Parker to Head of Planning at Light Programme, 23 September 1958. Charles Parker Archive, CPA 2/68.
143. Wizz Jones, interview by author, 19 November 2004, York.
144. Peggy Seeger, ed., *Peggy Seeger Songbook*, p. 11.
145. Correspondence in BBC/WAC/Peggy Seeger/Artist File/1956–62.
146. Hugh MacDiarmid to Valda Grieve, 15 July 1958. In Dorian Grieve, Owen Dudley Edwards and Alan Riach, eds, *Hugh MacDiarmid: New Selected Letters* (Manchester: Carcanet 2001), p. 237.
147. Ewan MacColl to Peggy Seeger, nd [1958].
148. Ewan MacColl to Peggy Seeger, nd [1958].
149. Jean Newlove/MacColl, interview by author, 9 August 2004, London.
150. Promotional programme in CPA 1/8/10.
151. Colin Irwin, *A Carthy Chronicle*, p. 12. This biographical booklet is part of *The Carthy Chronicles* (CD box set, FRQCD-60, Free Reed, 2001).
152. Jean Newlove/MacColl, interview by author, 9 August 2004, London.

153. Peggy Seeger, interviews by author, 14 October 2004, Sheffield and 28 November 2005, Salford. Also Karen O'Brien, *Kirsty MacColl: The One and Only* (London: André Deutsch, 2004).

154. Jean Newlove/MacColl, interview by author, 9 August 2004, London.

155. This option is discussed as a last resort in letters MacColl wrote to Seeger in late 1958.

156. Colin Harper, *Dazzling Stranger: Bert Jansch and the British Folk and Blues Revival* (London: Bloomsbury, 2000), pp. 96–7.

157. Peggy Seeger, interview by author, 14 October 2004, Sheffield.

158. *WMA Bulletin* (June 1959).

159. MacColl's friends and associates including Karl Dallas and Bill Leader debated the relationship between folk music, the folk and the Labour Movement. Fred and Betty Dallas, 'Traditional Music and the Labour Movement', *WMA Bulletin* (April 1959); Fred Dallas, 'The Folk Music Revival' and Bill Leader, 'For the Record', *WMA Bulletin* (February 1958).

160. The Ballads and Blues' considerable profile was in part dependent on the managerial and organisational talents of Malcolm Nixon, who was now sure that the folk scene was to break into the broader culture, and planning accordingly. Claiming a membership of 1,600 members, he was efficiently running the association and his agency from his office premises in Finsbury, negotiating with the Denmark Street music publishers, and running a sideline co-hosting prestigious concerts with the National Jazz Federation, including Chris Barber and Muddy Waters' St Pancras Town Hall Concert that October. Ballads and Blues Promotional Programme, August–December 1958. CPA 2/68/2. Newly relaxed visa and passport regulations meant that more American musicians were making the trip to the growing British scene: Nixon would soon be involved in co-ordinating tours for The Weavers and Pete Seeger. Karl Dallas, 'The Weavers and it's Big Business', *Melody Maker*, 19 September 1959 and Karl Dallas, 'Pete Seeger – the Folk Legend – Comes to Life', *Melody Maker*, 3 October 1959. Karl Dallas used his *Melody Maker* column to register the fact that Nixon had 'turned' the Hootenannys into 'a real weekly moneyspinner, packing audiences of 200 and over week after week into larger and still larger premises'. Dallas, 'The Weavers', *Melody Maker*, 19 September 1959.

161. In January 1959 Peter Grant, Reg Hall and Mervyn Plunkett established *Ethnic*, a journal committed to supporting folk traditions in a manner free from the 'overwhelmingly genteel and precious' emphasis of the EFDSS or *Sing* magazine, the WMA and 'Hootenanny inc'. Unsigned, 'Policy', *Ethnic: A Quarterly Survey of English Folk Music, Dance and Drama*, 1.3 (Summer 1959). Copies in Vaughan Williams Memorial Library, London.

162. Vic Gammon, interview by author, 2 April 2003, Leeds.

163. Fred Dallas, *WMA Bulletin* (December 1959).

164. 'Wonder Boy' was published in the *WMA Bulletin* (June 1959). Both songs are reprinted in Peggy Seeger, ed., *Ewan MacColl Songbook*, pp. 44, 242.

165. First published as a joint-composition in *Sing*, 5.1 (November 1959), p. 18. Reprinted in Seeger, ed., *Peggy Seeger Songbook*, p. 50.

166. Ewan MacColl and Dominic Behan, *Streets of Song: Childhood Memories of City Streets from Glasgow, Salford and Dublin* (LP, 12T41, Topic, 1959);

previously released for the American market as *The Singing Streets* (LP, FW 8501, Folkways, 1958).

167. Riverside LPs rlp 12–632 and rlp 12–612 respectively. Neither is dated.
168. Ewan MacColl, *Songs of Robert Burns* (LP, FW 8758, Folkways, 1959).
169. The offending record was Ewan MacColl and Peggy Seeger, *Classic Scots Ballads* (LP, TLP 1015, Tradition, nd [1959]), reissued on CD thirty-three years later (CD, TCD 1051 Tradition/Rykodisc, 1997). Seeger's new liner-notes registered some concern with their 'fairly sensitive assaults on the songs'.
170. Significant MacColl and Seeger records from the period include *British Ballads of Crime and Criminals: Bad Lads and Hard Cases* (LP, Riverside RLP 12–632, nd), *Still I Love Him* (with Isla Cameron and Ralph Rinzler; 10-inch EP; 10 T50, Topic, 1958). Guitarist Jimmy MacGregor and harmonica player John Cole contributed to *Barrack Room Ballads* (10-inch LP, 10 T26, Topic, 1958), later reissued as *Bundook Ballads* (LP, 12 T130, Topic, 1965). With A. L. Lloyd, Steve Benbow and John Cole, MacColl recorded *Bold Sportsman All: Gamblers and Sporting Blades* (10-inch EP, TOP71, Topic, 1958), issued in America as *British Songs of Sporting and Gambling: Champions and Sporting Blades* (LP, RLP12–652, Riverside, nd).
171. *Hazard at Quebec* was broadcast on the BBC Home Service, 23 September 1959; *My People and Your People*, also on the Home Service, went out on 22 July 1959. Both scripts are held in the BBC Written Archives, Caversham. MacColl also worked on *Bold Nelson's Praise*, produced by Charles Parker and broadcast on the Home Service, 21 October 1959. MacColl and Seeger also submitted to Bridson a proposal for an ambitious six-part historical survey of British Folk Song. Here MacColl hoped to elucidate his materialist theories of class structure, literacy and the politics of folk music. Despite a hearty recommendation from Bridson, the programme was never commissioned. D. G. Bridson, memo to CTP, 'British Folk Song Series by Ewan MacColl and Peggy Seeger', 24 July 1959; MacColl's typewritten proposal is labelled 'Programmes for Geoffrey', BBC WAC/R Cont 1/James Miller/Artist File, 1935–62.
172. Parker to Mr Hobson, 27 October 1958; Parker's expense forms for three days in the Potteries CPA 1/7/4; Charles Parker, draft typescript of 'Article for Radio Times for Song of a Road', 15 October 1959, CPA 2/74/2/1; Charles Parker to Head of Midland Radio Production, 27 November 1958, BBC WAC/MS/155.
173. Parker, draft typescript for 'Article for Radio Times', 15 October 1959, CPA 2/74/2/1.
174. *Song of a Road* was first broadcast on the BBC Home Service, 5 November 1959. Forty years later it was released on CD. *Song of a Road* (CD, TSCD 802, Topic, 1999).
175. Parker to Assistant Head of Midland Radio Production, 19 October 1959. BBC WAC MS/155.
176. Ewan MacColl, unpublished typescript, 'The Radio Ballads', undated version. MacColl/Seeger Archive.
177. *Song of a Road* script in BBC Written Archives, Caversham.

178. Charles Parker, 'Singing of a Motorway', *Granta*, 69.1236 (14 May 1964), pp. 2–4, at p. 3.
179. Script, cue 183.
180. Peggy Seeger describes this in Seeger, ed., *Ewan MacColl Songbook*, p. 119, MacColl in 'The Radio Ballad', unpublished typescript, undated version and Parker in 'Singing of a Motorway'.
181. Parker, 'Singing of a Motorway', p. 4.
182. Script, cues 84–8.
183. Script, cues 173–88.
184. MacColl, 'The Radio Ballads', unpublished typescript, undated version, MacColl/Seeger archive.
185. Good reviews included Paul Ferris, 'Legend in Concrete', *Observer*, 8 November 1959 and Alex Walker's column in the *Birmingham Post*, 6 November 1959. The anonymous *Daily Telegraph* critic complained that the programme 'seemed to call for a new spirit of dedication on the part of the listener' (9 November 1959), while Robert Robinson of the *Sunday Times* charged the Radio Ballad with 'supplying a romance not inherent in the events' (8 November 1959).
186. MacColl, *Journeyman*, p. 316.
187. MacColl, *Journeyman*, pp. 316–17; 'The Radio Ballads', unpublished typescript, undated version, MacColl/Seeger Archive.
188. The offending review was David Paul's 'Spoken Word' column in *The Listener*, 12 November 1959. Parker fired off an angry response the same day; the editor of *The Listener* then complained to Parker's boss (Parker's letter was 'extremely long ... highly personal and somewhat violent' in tone). Parker was reprimanded. Correspondence in BBC WAC MS/155/1 and CPA 2/74/2/4.
189. Parker to *Radio Times* art editor, 26 November 1959, BBC WAC MS/155/1.
190. Parker, 'Singing of a Motorway', p. 4.

## Chapter 8, 'The Bard of Beckenham'

1. Ronald D. Cohen, *Rainbow Quest: The Folk Music Revival and American Society, 1940–70* (Amherst and Boston: University of Massachusetts Press, 2002), pp. 102–3.
2. Bob Dylan, *Chronicles: Volume One* (New York and London: Simon & Schuster, 2004), p. 69.
3. Dylan, *Chronicles*, p. 72.
4. Peter D. Goldsmith, *Making People's Music: Moe Asch and Folkways Records* (Washington and London: Smithsonian Institute Press, 1998), p. 301.
5. Cohen, *Rainbow*, p. 110.
6. Cohen, *Rainbow*, p. 152
7. Cohen, *Rainbow*, p. 115.
8. Cohen, *Rainbow*, pp. 161, 128.

9. MacColl and Seeger kept a record of songs performed at all concerts from 1960 onwards. These are held in the MacColl/Seeger Archive, Ruskin College, Oxford.

10. Robert Shelton, untitled review in *New York Times*, 5 December 1960.

11. MacColl to Parker, 1 January 1960. Charles Parker Archive, Birmingham Central Library, CPA 2/78/1/2.

12. *Ewan MacColl and Peggy Seeger Songbook* (New York: Oak, 1963), pp. 59, 54: Charles Parker memo to Head of Midland Radio Production, 19 November 1960. BBC Written Archives, Caversham, M5/153. MacColl worked on a freelance basis for the National Coal Board Film Unit on scores of films including Alun Falconer dir., *New Power in their Hands* (1959) and Robert Vas dir., *Two Choirs and a Valley* (1965).

13. '"Singing English": A Discussion Programme on the Making of the Radio Ballads between Ewan MacColl, Peggy Seeger and Charles Parker', Midland Home Service, 16 January 1962.

14. MacColl to Parker, 1 January 1960, CPA 2/78/1/2.

15. Memo from Head of Central Programme Operations to Charles Parker, 27 October 1959, BBC WAC/M5/155.

16. Parker to AHMRP, 19 October 1959, BBC WAC/ M5/155.

17. Charles Parker, 'Reflections on production techniques used in *Singing the Fishing*', 14 June [1960]. CPA 2/78/2/1.

18. Parker to MacColl, 22 June 1961. CPA 82/2/1.

19. Parker from Critics Group tape transcript, tape 23, 20 October 1964, CPA 1/8/9/1; MacColl to Parker, 17 February 1960, CPA 2/78/1/2.

20. Peggy Seeger explains the process of composition in Seeger, ed., *The Essential Ewan MacColl Songbook* (New York and London: Oak, 2001), pp. 15–16.

21. Bruce Turner to Parker [nd], CPA 2/78/1/2.

22. Parker, memo to AHMRP, 25 April 1960, BBC WAC/M5/153.

23. Charles Parker, '"Singing the Fishing" – Equipment', 24 June 1960, BBC WAC/M5/153.

24. MacColl to Parker, 17 September 1959, CPA 2/74/1/1.

25. Parker to MacColl, 16 June 1960, CPA 2/78/1/2.

26. Parker to AHMRP, 22 June 1960, CPA 2/78/2/1.

27. Parker to MacColl, 24 June 1960, CPA 2/78/1/2.

28. BBC Audience Research Report for the Home Service broadcast, MacColl/Seeger Archive; report for repeat on the Third Programme (6 November 1960) in CPA 2/78/2/1. Paul Ferris, 'Herring Tales', *Observer*, 21 August 1960; unsigned reviews in *Daily Worker*, 19 August 1960 and *The Listener*, 25 August 1960.

29. Music Bookings to Midland Programme Executive, 14 October 1960. BBC WAC/Peggy Seeger/Artist File/1956–62.

30. Music Bookings to Midland Programme Executive, 14 October 1960. BBC WAC/Peggy Seeger/Artist File/1956–62.

31. Parker, Memo, 3 September 1959. CPA 2/74/1/1.

32. Ewan MacColl, *Journeyman* (London: Sidgwick & Jackson, 1990), p. 327.

33. MacColl, *Journeyman*, p. 327.

34. Ken Hunt, 'Killen Time', *Folk Roots*, 97 (July 1991), pp. 29–31.
35. MacColl, *Journeyman*, p. 328.
36. Peggy Seeger, interview by author, 14 October 2004, Sheffield.
37. MacColl, *Journeyman*, p. 329; Peggy Seeger to Charles Parker, 16 May 1972, MacColl/Seeger Archive.
38. *The Times*, unsigned, 'Change in style of documentaries', 2 August 1961.
39. Unsigned obituary of Parker, *Time Out*, 18 December 1980; Paul Ferris, 'Unorthodox Innovator', *Observer*, 14 December 1980.
40. MacColl, *Jouneyman*, p. 329.
41. *The Big Hewer* (CD, TSCD 804, Topic, 1999).
42. MacColl, *Singing English*.
43. *The Times*, unsigned, 'Poetic Documentary with Worker Heroes', 27 January 1962.
44. Peggy Seeger, interview by author, 28 November 2005, Salford.
45. Peggy Seeger, interview by author, 28 November 2005, Salford.
46. Peggy Seeger and Ewan MacColl, foreword to Seeger and MacColl, eds, *Songs for the Sixties* (London: Workers' Music Association, 1961), p. 2.
47. Preface to Seeger and MacColl, eds, *The Singing Island* (London: Belwin-Mills, 1960), p. 1. Other projects included MacColl, ed., *Personal Choice: Scottish Folksongs and Ballads* (New York: Hargail, 1962), the *Ewan MacColl/Peggy Seeger Songbook* (New York: Oak, 1963) and MacColl, ed., *Folk Songs and Ballads of Scotland* (New York: Oak, 1965).
48. Unsigned review, *English Dance and Song* (New Year 1961), p. 24.
49. Betsy Miller and Ewan MacColl, *A Garland of Scots Folksong* (LP, FL116, Folklyric, 1962).
50. Eric Winter, 'Focus on Folk', *Melody Maker*, 7 July 1962; also John Makepeace, 'MacColl and his Mother', *Sing*, 6.10 (June 1962), p. 110.
51. Liner notes to *The Best of Ewan MacColl* (LP 13004, Prestige, nd).
52. MacColl made a three-LP series of unaccompanied ballads, *The English and Scottish Popular Ballads (Child Ballads)* for Folkways. Volume 1 (FG 3509) appeared in 1961; volumes 2 (FG 3510) and 3 (FG 3511) came out in 1964. Peggy joined him for *Bothy Ballads of Scotland* (LP, FW 8759, Folkways, 1961).
53. *Broadside Ballads London: (1600–1700)* (LP, FW 3043, Folkways 1962) and *Broadside Ballads Volume 2 (London: 1600–1700): Female Frollicks and Politicke* (LP, FW 3044, Folkways, 1962).
54. *Songs of Two Rebellions: The Jacobite Wars of 1715 and 1745 in Scotland*, (LP FW 8756, Folkways 1960); reissued in slightly different form as *The Jacobite Rebellions: Songs of the Jacobite Wars of 1715 and 1745* (LP, 12T76, Topic, 1962).
55. MacColl, interview by Charles Parker, 1 July 1966. CPA MS 4000 5/4/1/11c.
56. These ideas were developed in an interview for *Ready, Steady, Stop*, an exploration of contemporary pop music by Geoffrey Reeves and Stuart Hall broadcast on the BBC Midland Home Service in the summer of 1967. MacColl was interviewed on 9 September 1965. Transcript in CPA 2/121.
57. MacColl in *Singing English*.

58. Charles Parker, unpublished typescript, 'Some Aspects of Traditional Song', MacColl/Seeger Archive.

59. Special Correspondent, interview with MacColl, 'Living Oral Tradition in Popular Art', *The Times*, 28 September 1961.

60. *Ewan MacColl/Peggy Seeger Songbook* (New York: Oak, 1963).

61. Volume 1 (FW 08732) was released on Folkways in 1960, volume 2 (FW 08734) in 1962.

62. Seeger and MacColl, foreword to *Songs for the Sixties*, p. 2; liner-notes for *British Folksong Revival* (LP, FW 8728, 1962).

63. MacColl, liner-notes to *The Best of Ewan MacColl* (LP 13004, Prestige, nd).

64. These ideas were also elucidated by Charles Parker in *Not Known in Denmark Street: An Appraisal of Some Songwriters of the Current Folk Revival in Britain*, a BBC radio programme featuring MacColl, Seeger, Matt McGinn and others broadcast on the Third Programme, 5 August 1962.

65. *Melody Maker*, 30 December 1961.

66. *Melody Maker*, 12 October 1963; Colin Harper, *Dazzling Stranger: Bert Jansch and the British Folk and Blues Revival* (London: Bloomsbury, 2000), p. 73.

67. *Melody Maker*, 6 January 1962, 13 February 1965.

68. *Melody Maker*, 17 March 1962.

69. *Melody Maker*, 30 March 1963.

70. *Melody Maker*, 8 October 1960, 19 August 1961; Tony Russell, obituary of Gill Cooke, *Guardian*, 7 February 2006; Harper, *Dazzling*, p. 115.

71. *Melody Maker*, 23 April 1960.

72. MacColl, 'Why I am Opening a New Club', *Sing*, 5.4 (August 1961), p. 65.

73. *Melody Maker*, 22 October 1960.

74. Harper, *Dazzling*, pp. 137–9; *Melody Maker*, 22 October 1960, 6 May 1961, 28 July 1962, 6 April 1963, 5 October 1963, 11 January 1964.

75. MacColl, 'Why I am Opening a New Club', *Sing*, 5.4 (August 1961), p. 65.

76. *Melody Maker*, 30 January 1960, 19 March 1960.

77. *Melody Maker*, 1 October 1960.

78. Peggy Seeger, interview by author, 14 October 2004, Sheffield.

79. *Melody Maker*, 1 October 1960.

80. Recorded on *New Briton Gazette Volume 2* (LP FW 08734, Folkways, 1962) and printed in Seeger, ed., *Essential Ewan MacColl Songbook*, pp. 244–5.

81. Karl Dallas, 'The Roots of Tradition', pp. 83–134, at p. 90 in Dave Laing, Karl Dallas, Robin Denselow and Robert Shelton, *The Electric Muse: The Story of Folk into Rock* (London: Methuen, 1975); Peggy Seeger, interview by author, 16 November 2003, York; and Harper, *Dazzling*, pp. 41, 164–5, 183.

82. Harper, *Dazzling*, p. 71.

83. Dunnet formally resigned from his duties in 1986. Bruce Dunnet to Ewan MacColl and Peggy Seeger, 31 May 1986, MacColl/Seeger Archive.

84. *Melody Maker*, 24 June 1961.

85. 'Ewan MacColl Hits Out', *Melody Maker*, 10 June 1961; Ewan MacColl, 'Why I am Opening a New Club', *Sing*, 5.4 (August 1961), p. 65. All quotations are from the latter source.

86. MacColl's liner-notes to Peggy Seeger and Ewan MacColl, *Two Way Trip: American, Scots and English Folksongs* (LP, FW 8755, Folkways, 1961).

87. The Singers' Club team parodied themselves in their submissions to the *Melody Maker* listings, cracking jokes about 'acolytes and disciples' and tablets from Sinai. See 16 December 1961.

88. Eric Winter, 'EFDSS Could Lead the Way', *Melody Maker*, 29 July 1961.

89. 'Going American?', interview with Ewan MacColl and Peggy Seeger. *English Dance and Song* (New Year 1961), pp. 19–20, at p. 20.

90. MacColl, liner-notes to *Two Way Trip* (1961).

91. *Melody Maker*, 18 November 1961.

92. *Melody Maker*, 10 March, 1 December and 10 November 1962 respectively; the Stewarts appeared the weeks of 3 February 1962, 7 April 1962, and 20 October 1962.

93. Peter Wood, 'Louis Killen, Pioneer', *Living Tradition*, 47 (March–April 2002), pp. 28–31; Ken Hunt, 'Killen Time', *Folk Roots*, 97 (July 1991), pp. 29–31. Killen's Singers' Club appearance included the weeks of 8 July 1961, 20 January and 12 May 1962.

94. *The Collier's Rant* (7-inch EP, TOP 74, Topic, 1962) and *Northumbrian Garland* (7-inch EP, TOP 75, Topic, 1962); reviewed in *Melody Maker*, 10 November 1962.

95. Colin Irwin, biographical booklet to *The Carthy Chronicles* (CD box set, FRQCD-60, Free Reed, 2001), p. 15.

96. Ken Hunt, 'Killen Time'; Bob Blair, interview by author, 3 August 2004, Glasgow; Sandra Kerr, interview by author, 16 August 2006, Gateshead.

97. Irwin Silber, Foreword to the *Ewan MacColl/Peggy Seeger Songbook* (New York: Oak, 1963), pp. 7–8, at p. 8.

98. Peggy Seeger, interview by author, 14 October 2004, Sheffield.

99. *Melody Maker* listing, 18 November 1961.

100. Eric Winter, 'Unaccompanied Singers', *Sing*, 6.4 (December 1961), p. 12.

101. Wizz Jones, interview by author, 19 November 2004, York.

102. *Melody Maker*, 21 October 1961.

103. *Melody Maker*, 19 May 1962 and 19 November 1962.

104. Programme books, MacColl/Seeger Archive.

105. MacColl/Seeger Archive.

106. Pete Seeger, 'Statement to Court', *Sing Out!*, 11.3 (Summer 1961), pp. 10–11; David King Dunaway, *How Can I Keep From Singing: Pete Seeger* (London: Harrap, 1985), pp. 206–10; unsigned, 'Seeger on Trial', *Sing*, 5.4 (August 1961), p. 63.

107. King Dunaway, *Pete Seeger*, pp. 206–10.

108. King Dunaway, *Pete Seeger*, p. 209; unsigned, 'Seeger on Trial', *Sing*, 5.4 (August 1961), p. 63.

109. *Melody Maker*, 17 June 1961.

110. Eric Winter, 'The Hard Cost of Speaking His Mind', *Melody Maker*, 21 October 1961; also unsigned cutting, *Daily Californian* [labelled 'October 1961'] in MacColl/Seeger Archive.

111. Peggy Seeger, interview by author, 14 October 2004, Sheffield.
112. Ken Hunt, 'Sandals and Spooks', *New Humanist* (July–August 2006), pp. 26–7, at p. 26.
113. Peggy Seeger in Irwin Silber, 'Peggy Seeger – the voice of America in Folksong', *Sing Out!*, 12 (Summer 1964), pp. 4–8, at p. 7.
114. Winter, 'The Hard Cost of Speaking His Mind'; also unsigned cutting, *Daily Californian* [labelled 'October 1961'] in MacColl/Seeger Archive.
115. MacColl, *Journeyman*, p. 363.
116. *Edmonton Times*, 10 October 1961; *Saskatoon Star*, 7 October 1961; *Salt Lake Tribune*, 31 October 1961.
117. Peggy Seeger, interview by author, 14 October 2004, Sheffield.
118. Frank Coppieters, 'Arnold Wesker's Centre 42: A Cultural Revolution Betrayed', *Theatre Quarterly*, V, 18 (June–August 1975), pp. 37–55; David Watt, '"The Maker and the Tool": Charles Parker, Documentary Performance, and the Search for a Popular Culture', *New Theatre Quarterly*, 19, 1 (February 2003), pp. 41–66.
119. *Centre 42: First Stage in a Cultural Revolution* (London, 1961). MacColl/Seeger Archive.
120. Clive Barker, 'Report and Recommendations on the Policy of Centre 42', 26 August 1961. CPA 1/8/7/1.
121. 'Living Oral Tradition and Popular Art', *The Times*, 28 September 1961; the 1960 song is reprinted in Seeger, ed., *Essential Ewan MacColl Songbook*, pp. 86–7; unsigned article in *The Garment Worker* (December 1960).
122. Coppieters, 'Arnold Wesker's Centre 42', p. 42; Clive Barker, interview by author, 10 August 2004, Sidcup.
123. See Watt, 'The Maker and the Tool'.
124. Harper, *Dazzling*, pp. 101–3.
125. Michael Kustow, *Tribune*, 11 January 1963, pp. 6–7, at p. 7.
126. Clive Barker, interview by author, 10 August 2004, Sidcup.
127. Ken Hunt, liner-notes to *Classic Anne Briggs: The Complete Topic Recordings* (CD, FECD 78, Fellside, 1990).
128. Christopher Logue, 'The Poet at the Canteen Table', *Sunday Times*, 27 January 1963, p. 22.
129. Roy Bailey, interview by Dai Jeffries, *Folk on Tap*, 107 (April–June 2006), pp. 17–19, at p. 17, p. 18.
130. Peggy Seeger, interview by author, 28 November 2005, Salford.
131. A. L. Lloyd, 'The Folk Song Revival and the Communist Party', *Music & Life*, 18 (14/1962), pp. 18–19, at p. 18.
132. Katherine Thompson [sic], 'An International Symposium of Workers' Songs', *Music & Life*, 13 (2/1961), p. 16.
133. A. L. Lloyd, 'The English Folk Song Revival', *Sing Out!*, 12.2 (April–May 1962), pp. 34–7, at p. 36.
134. A. L. Lloyd, 'Industrial Folklore' proposal, mailed to MacColl on 7 August 1961. MacColl/Seeger Archive, Historical and Critical Material file.
135. MacColl on transcript of tape 18, Critics Group meeting [nd, summer 1964?]. CPA 1/8/9/1.

136. The songs MacColl and Lomax collected from Harry Cox can be heard on MS/4000/5/1/1C in the Charles Parker Archive. Some are included on *Harry Cox: The Bonny Labouring Boy* (CD, TSCD512D, Topic, 2000).

137. The ethics of song-collecting and copyright were discussed by A. L. Lloyd in 'Who Owns What in Folk Song?', *English Dance and Song* (New Year 1961), pp. 15–18. MacColl talks about his song-collecting in the transcript to tape 18, Critics Group meeting [nd, summer 1964?], CPA 1/8/9/1. A series of contracts drawn up by MacColl and Seeger for use when song-collecting are deposited in the MacColl/Seeger Archive, Miscellaneous Documents file.

138. *Now is the Time for Fishing: Songs and Stories from Sam Larner* (LP, FG 3507, Folkways, 1961).

139. *Melody Maker*, 19 August 1961.

140. *The Elliotts of Birtley: A Musical Portrait of a Durham Mining Family* (LP FG 3665, Folkways, 1962). The two records were reviewed together in *English Dance and Song* (September 1962), p. 96 and by Robert Shelton, 'The Versatile MacColl', *New York Times*, 16 September 1962.

141. Sourced from Ian Watson, *Song and Democratic Culture in Britain* (London: Croom Helm, 1983), p. 37.

142. *Melody Maker,* 16 June 1962.

143. A. L. Lloyd, 'The Folk Song Revival and the Communist Party', *Music & Life*, 18 (4/1962), pp. 18–19, at p. 19.

144. Broadcast on the BBC Home Service on 13 February 1963.

145. MacColl, *Journeyman*, pp. 331–2.

146. The Beatles first made the front cover of *Melody Maker* on 23 March 1963 and had their first number one hit on 2 May; script in MacColl/Seeger Archive.

147. Charles Parker, 'On the Edge' (1970), reprinted as sleeve-notes for *On the Edge* (CD, TSDCD 806, Topic, 1999).

148. Unsigned [Parker and/or MacColl] 'Some Notes on the Radio Ballads', nd. MacColl/Seeger Archive; Parker, 'On the Edge' (1970).

149. Charles Parker to IOMR, 30 January 1963. CPA 2/92/2/1.

150. Ewan MacColl, unpublished typescript, 'The Radio Ballads' (August 1981), p. 21.

151. Peggy Seeger, interview by author, 14 October 2004, Sheffield.

152. Broadcast on the BBC Home Service, 27 March 1962; *Melody Maker,* 4 March 1961.

153. *The Body Blow* (CD, TSCD805, Topic, 1999). Script in MacColl/Seeger Archive.

154. Peter Wilsher, 'Sound Pictures and a Radio Ballad', *Sunday Times*, 7 July 1963; Paul Ferris, 'Ballad with a Punch', *Observer*, 7 July 1963.

155. *The Fight Game* (CD, TSCD 807,Topic, 1999). Script in MacColl/Seeger Archive. The songs are reprinted in Seeger, ed., *Essential Ewan MacColl Songbook*, pp. 163–83.

156. Parker to Miss Penty, 17 May 1963. BBC WAC/Peggy Seeger/Artist File, 1963–67.

157. *Fight Game* balance sheet, CPA 2/94/2/1.

158. Sourced from Karen O'Brien, *Kirsty MacColl: The One and Only* (London: André Deutsch, 2004), p. 21. Hamish MacColl, telephone conversation with author, 12 November 2006.

159. 'Sing in the New', broadcast on Granada Television, 31 December 1962. MacColl and Seeger were joined by Lou Killen, Bob Davenport, Colin Ross and Enoch Kent. Script in MacColl/Seeger Archive.

160. Liam Mac Con Iomaire, 'Where I come for they all sing like that: Seosamh Ó hÉanaí: his life and singing tradition' and Fred McCormick, 'I never had a steady job: Joe Heaney: A life in song': both excellent essays are reprinted as liner-notes for *Joe Heaney/Seosamh Ó hÉanaí: The Road from Connemara: songs and stories told and sung to Ewan MacColl and Peggy Seeger* (CD, TSCD 518D, Topic, 2000). The CD is based on MacColl and Seeger's five-hour interview with Heaney from 1964. Full transcripts can be read on www.mustrad.org.uk.

161. Sourced from *Road from Connemara* booklet, p. 13.

162. *Road from Connemara*, p. 13.

163. 'Broomfield Hill', 'Earl o' Errol's wife' and 'Eppie Morrie'. Programme books, MacColl/Seeger Archive.

164. Cohen, *Rainbow Quest*, pp. 234–8; Robert Shelton, *No Direction Home: The Life and Music of Bob Dylan* (London: Penguin, 1986), pp. 301–4.

165. Shelton, *No Direction Home*, p. 254.

166. Clinton Heylin, *Dylan: Behind the Shades, The Biography* (London: Viking 1991), pp. 64–5.

167. There's some dispute among Dylan scholars what the second song was, though it's agreed that he only sang two.

168. Shelton, *No Direction Home*, p. 253; Heylin, *Behind the Shades*, p. 253; Harper, *Dazzling*, pp. 109–11.

169. 'Bob Dylan Talks to Max Jones', *Melody Maker*, 23 May 1964. Sandra Kerr and Peggy Seeger both remember Dylan's performance as underwhelming; John Faulkner remembers everyone being impressed.

170. MacColl, unpublished typescript, 'The Radio Ballads' (August 1981), p. 23. MacColl/Seeger Archive.

171. Ewan MacColl and Peggy Seeger, Introduction to MacColl and Seeger, eds, *Travellers' Songs from England and Scotland* (London: Routledge & Kegan Paul, 1977), p. 15.

172. Peggy Seeger, interview by author, 28 November 2005, Salford.

173. Charles Parker, 'The Travelling People', *BBC Midland Sound Broadcasting News*, 6 April 1964. CPA 2/97/2/1.

174. Parker to *Radio Times* art editor, 4 March 1964, CPA 2/97/2/1.

175. *The Travelling People* (CD, TSCD808, Topic, 1999). Script in MacColl/ Seeger archive.

176. Songs reprinted in Seeger, ed., *Essential Ewan MacColl Songbook*, pp. 201–16.

177. Liner-notes to *My Father's the King of the Gypsies: Music of English and Welsh Travellers and Gypsies* (CD, TSCD 661, Topic, 1998), p. 20.

178. Seeger, ed., *Essential Ewan MacColl Songbook*, pp. 204–5.

179. Parker to APH, 12 December 1963, CPA 2/97/1/1.

180. Broadcast on 17 April 1964. Parker to APH, 19 November 1963. CPA 2/97/1/1.
181. Parker to APH, 29 November 1963. By this date the team knew the series was over. CPA 2/97/1/1.
182. The British Film Institute's experimental documentary *Momma Don't Allow*, for example, was made for £425 in 1956 (or about £590 in 1963 prices). Many of the radio ballads cost three times as much.
183. Parker, 'Notes on the Production of the Travelling People – December 1963', CPA 2/97/1/1; *Fight Game* cost sheet, CPA 2/64/2/1; Parker to Ewan MacColl and Peggy Seeger, 3 October 1960 (on budget for *Big Hewer*), CPA 2/82/1/1.
184. These other radio ballads are discussed by Ian Campbell, who worked on music: Ian Campbell, 'The Missing Radio Ballads', www.mustrad.org.uk, accessed 13 November 2004; precise listening figures are not available, but the BBC Audience Research Reports for the Radio Ballads consistently indicate that the audiences were less than 0.1 per cent of the population, or well under one million people.
185. Parker, 'Notes on the Production of the Travelling People, December 1963', CPA 2/97/1/1.
186. MacColl, unpublished typescript, 'The Radio Ballads' (August 1981), p. 24.
187. MacColl 'The Radio Ballads', p. 25.
188. 'It is becoming increasingly apparent to me', Parker wrote with characteristic self-deprecation, 'that, as in so much else, I have some very dubious and romantic ideas about the relationships between, lyrics, music and actuality.' Charles Parker, 'The Fight Game: Critique of Production Method', CPA 2/94/1/6. See also his articles 'The Radio Ballad', *New Society*, 14 November 1963, pp. 25–7, and 'Singing of a Motorway', *Granta*, 14 May 1964.
189. Issued on the Argo Label: *The Ballad of John Axon* (LP, DA 139, Argo, 1965); *Singing the Fishing* (LP, DA 142, Argo, 1966); *The Big Hewer* (LP, DA 140, Argo, 1967); *The Fight Game* (LP, DA 141, Argo, 1967); *The Travelling People* (LP, DA 133, Argo, 1968); and *On the Edge* (LP, DA 136, Argo, 1970).
190. Memo from Controller, Programme Organisation, 10 February 1961. BBC WAC/M5/153/1.
191. Coverage in the national press included Anne Karpf, 'The Voice of the People', *Guardian*, 27 May 1999, Robert Hanks, 'Nostalgia Revisited', *Independent* (Friday Review), 18 June 1999 and David Jays, 'Old Labour', *New Statesman*, 7 June 1999.

*Chapter 9, 'Let a Hundred Flowers Blossom'*

1. Steve Benbow, 'Focus on Folk', *Melody Maker*, 11 January 1964.
2. Programme books, Ewan MacColl/Peggy Seeger Archive, Ruskin College, Oxford.
3. Peggy Seeger, interview by author, 28 November 2005, Salford.
4. Stuart Birch, 'The Day the Tinkers Serenaded the '"folk" folk at Home', *Belfast Telegraph*, 16 November 1969.

5. Peggy Seeger, interview by author, 28 November 2005, Salford.

6. Peggy Seeger, interview by author, 28 November 2005, Salford.

7. Reviewed in *Melody Maker*, 28 November 1964.

8. Donald Dorcey, 'Good show – but what an audience', *Evening Press* (Dublin), 21 November 1964.

9. As at the Grey Cock Folk Club, Birmingham, 6 July 1969. Charles Parker Archive, Birmingham Central Library, MS/4000/5/3/5/4/2C. (The disc is catalogued as 'June 1969'.)

10. Peggy Seeger, interview by author, 28 November 2005, Salford.

11. *Melody Maker*, 30 May 1964.

12. *Melody Maker*, 24 August 1964.

13. *Melody Maker*, 11 April 1964.

14. *Melody Maker*, 14 September 1964, 8 February 1964, 12 June 1965, 20 February 1965 respectively.

15. Ewan MacColl, interview by Charles Parker, 1 July 1966. Charles Parker Archive, MS/40000/5/4/1/11C.

16. Karl Dallas, 'Focus on MacColl', *Melody Maker*, 18 September 1965.

17. Ewan MacColl, 'Topical Songs and Folksinging, 1965', *Sing Out!*, 15.4 (September 1965), pp. 12–13, at p. 13.

18. Dallas, 'Focus on MacColl', *Melody Maker*, 18 September 1965.

19. Transcript of 'Ewan MacColl: Tape Number 7' [1964/5], Charles Parker Archive, CPA 1/8/9/2.

20. Ewan MacColl, 'Topical Songs and Folksinging, 1965', *Sing Out!*, 15.4 (September 1965), pp. 12–13, at p. 13.

21. Karl Dallas, 'Now Singing is Back on the Map', *Daily Worker*, 28 September 1963.

22. Karl Dallas, interview by author, 22 October 2003, Bradford.

23. Alex Campbell, 'The Folkies, Popnicks and the Entertainer', *Folk Music*, 1.2 [nd], pp. 2, 4,5, 20, at p. 2.

24. 'Ewan MacColl Replies to Alex Campbell', *Folk Music*, 1.4 [nd], pp. 20–1.

25. Jack Speedwell, 'Politics, S** and the Folk Revival', *Folk Music*, 1.5 [nd], pp. 16–17, at p. 16.

26. Jack Speedwell, 'Love and the Critics', *Folk Music*, 1.6 [nd], pp. 16–21, at p. 16.

27. Jack Speedwell, 'His Confessions', *Folk Music*, 1.9 [nd], pp. 21–24, at p. 21.

28. Jack Speedwell, 'Speedwell on MacColl', *Folk Music*, 1.11 [nd], pp. 12–3, at p. 13.

29. Ewan MacColl, 'Topical Songs and Folksinging, 1965', *Sing Out!*, 15.4 (September 1965), pp. 12–13, at p. 13.

30. Karl Dallas, 'Focus on MacColl', *Melody Maker*, 18 September 1965.

31. Dallas, 'Focus on MacColl', *Melody Maker*, 18 September 1965.

32. Jack Speedwell, 'His Confessions', *Folk Music*, 1.9 [nd], p. 24.

33. Sandra Kerr, interview by author, 16 August 2006, Gateshead.

34. Karl Dallas, interview by author, 22 October 2003, Bradford.

35. Ewan MacColl, *Journeyman* (London: Sidgwick & Jackson, 1990), p. 338.

36. Louis Killen, 'Pop or Trad', *English Dance and Song*, XXVI, 5 (October 1964), p. 111; *Melody Maker*, 11 September, 18 September 1965.

37. Paperwork for 'Conference, Tuesday 29 June, Beckenham' [nd], CPA 1/8/9/7; *Melody Maker*, 30 May 1964.

38. Peggy Seeger, interview by author, 28 November 2005, Salford.

39. Eric Winter, 'Unaccompanied Singers', *Sing*, 6.4 (December 1961).

40. MacColl, *Journeyman*, p. 305.

41. They gave talks to the 'East and South Shropshire Youth Committees' over the weekend of 25/26 March 1961, paperwork in CPA 1/3/1/1; between 28 December 1964 and 4 January 1965 they ran classes at a residential course at the College of St Matthias, Fishponds, Bristol. MacColl/Seeger Archive, Teaching Materials file.

42. Notably Louis Killen. Ken Hunt, 'Killen Time', *Folk Roots*, 97 (July 1991), pp. 29–31.

43. Jim Carroll, interview by the author, 14 September 2003, Salford.

44. MacColl, *Jouneyman*, p. 305; also 'a self-aid group' in interview with Karl Dallas, 'MacColl: A True Critic', *Melody Maker*, 22 February 1975.

45. Sandra Kerr, interview by author, 16 August 2006, Gateshead.

46. Frankie Armstrong with Jenny Pearson, *As Far as the Eye Can Sing: an Autobiography* (London: Women's Press, 1992), p. 34.

47. 'John Faulkner in interview with Tony Jasper', *Folk Review*, 5.12 (October 1976), pp. 16–20, at p. 17; John Faulkner interviewed by Tim May, unedited videocassette in MacColl/Seeger Archive.

48. Des Geraghty, *Luke Kelly: A Memoir* (Dublin: Basement Press, 1994), p. 74.

49. Precisely who owned the tapes later became a contentious issue. They were bought by the Critics Group and a selection was transcribed by Parker's BBC secretary. They are held, catalogued and digitised, in the Charles Parker Archive, Birmingham Central Library.

50. Quotations from episode one of *The Song Carriers*, broadcast on the Midland Home Service, 28 January 1965. Script in CPA2/104. I'm grateful to Bob Blair for enabling me to hear the original recordings.

51. *The Song Carriers*, episode one; also transcript of 'Tape 5' [labelled April 1964], CPA 1/8/9/1.

52. Transcript of 'Tape 5' [labelled April 1964], CPA 1/8/9/1.

53. Transcript of 'Tape 5' [labelled April 1964], CPA 1/8/9/1.

54. Typescript of 'Folk Music and Style' [misdated 'Keele 1961?'], a talk given by MacColl at the Keele Folk Music Festival in 1965. Teaching materials file, MacColl/Seeger Archive.

55. *The Song Carriers*, episode one.

56. These ideas appear in *The Song Carriers*, 'Folk Music and Style' typescript and an undated transcript entitled 'Folk Music: the Music of the People', both held in the Teaching Materials file, MacColl/Seeger Archive.

57. Transcript of 'Tape 5' [labelled April 1964], CPA 1/8/9/1. These ideas are recalled by Frankie Armstrong, *As Far As*, p. 33.

58. Transcript of 'Tape 5' [labelled April 1964], CPA 1/8/9/1.

59. Transcript of 'Tape 5' CPA 1/8/9/1; 'Folk Music and Style' typescript.

60. Transcript of 'Tape 5', CPA 1/8/9/1.

61. 'Reading List and Bibliography for members of the Critics Group of Folksong Studies, London 1964'. MacColl/Seeger Archive.
62. Armstrong, *As Far As*, p. 35.
63. Back in the late 1940s he and Laban had planned to write a book developing these ideas. Though the book never materialised, MacColl had drawn upon Laban's schema ever since, especially when selecting audio footage for the radio ballads – MacColl believed that workers intuitively employed a wider range of efforts than their employers. Transcript of Critics Group meeting, 29 November 1966, 'Research Project on Relationship Between Speech and Sound'. MacColl/Seeger Archive.
64. Sandra Kerr, interview by author, 16 August 2006, Gateshead.
65. Charles Parker, 'MacColl, against the tyranny of the nice guy', *Folk Music*, 1.11 [nd], pp. 2–7, at p. 4.
66. Constantin Stanislavski, *An Actor Prepares* (1937; London: Methuen, 1980), pp. 54–72. These ideas were extensively explored in Critics Group meetings at the end of 1966. CPA MS 4000/5/4/2/88C.
67. The word 'if', claimed Stanislavski, could function as 'a lever to lift us out of everyday life onto the plane of imagination'. Stanislavski, *An Actor Prepares*, p. 54.
68. Meeting on 31 January 1968, CPA MS/4000/5/4/2/171/c and 172C.
69. Stanislavski, *An Actor Prepares*, p. 163.
70. Sandra Kerr, interview by author, 16 August 2006, Gateshead.
71. Jim Carroll, interview by author, 14 September 2003, Salford.
72. Peggy Seeger, interview by author, 28 November 2005, Salford.
73. *The Luke Kelly Story*, dir. Sinéad O'Brien (RTE, 1999); Gordon McCulloch, telephone conversation with author, 10 December 2006.
74. *The Luke Kelly Story*.
75. Transcript of tape 24 (20 October 1964), CPA 1/8/9/1.
76. CPA MS4000/5/4/2/171C, 172C. Meeting on 31 January 1968.
77. Sandra Kerr, interview by author, 16 August 2006, Gateshead.
78. As on 23 June 1964. Transcript of Tape 15. CPA 1/8/9/1, or on 24 June 1969, transcript in MacColl/Seeger Archive.
79. Armstrong, *As Far As*, p. 33.
80. Jim Carroll, interview by author, 14 September 2003, Salford.
81. *Melody Maker*, 31 July 1965; 'Notes Taken at Critics Group Business Meeting July 1970', CPA 1/8/9/2.
82. *Melody Maker*, 14 September 1963.
83. The club moved back to the Pindar of Wakefield in October 1965, over to the nearby New Merlin's Cave pub, Margery Street in January 1965, down to the John Snow in Soho in March 1966, then back up to the Union Tavern on Lloyd Baker Street that November. Singers' Club handbills, CPA 1/8/10 and MacColl/Seeger Archive.
84. *Melody Maker*, 30 November 1963, 8 February 1964.
85. Programme books, MacColl/Seeger Archive.
86. Singers' Clubs programmes, CPA 1/4/1/5; CPA 1/8/10.
87. Singers' Club programmes, CPA 1/8/10; undated circular from Mel [?], CPA 1/8/9/7.
88. *Singers' Club News*, 5 (July 1966). CPA 1/8/10.

89. Bob Davenport's views were also expressed in the *Melody Maker*, 11 December 1965.

90. MacColl, *Journeyman*, p. 293.

91. Pat Mackenzie, interview by author, 14 September 2003, Salford.

92. Christy Moore, *One Voice: My Life in Song* (London: Hodder & Stoughton, 2000), p. 84.

93. Hugh MacDiarmid to the *Scotsman*, 7 April 1964. Folksong's relevance to progressive culture was hotly debated by Hamish Henderson, academic David Craig and Hugh MacDiarmid in the pages of the *Scotsman* through the spring of 1964. The whole acrimonious correspondence is republished in Alec Finlay, ed., *The Armstong Nose: Selected Letters of Hamish Henderson* (Edinburgh: Polygon, 2006), pp. 116–41.

94. 'Theatre Workshop' promotional article for *Oh! What a Lovely War* (1963) in Theatre Workshop Company File, Theatre Museum, Covent Garden.

95. MacColl quoted in Howard Goorney, *The Theatre Workshop Story* (London: Methuen, 1981), pp. 127–8.

96. Broadcast in late 1964 and early 1965. Scripts can be found in the Clive Barker Archive, Rose Bruford College, Sidcup. A post-mortem conference was held on 14 March 1965. Transcript in MacColl/Seeger Archive.

97. Though the corporation's decision not to screen the film provoked the inevitable mutterings of political censorship, BBC Controller Richard Cawston's blunt assessment – 'shapeless, pretentious and, to be frank, boring' – wasn't so far off the mark. Lance Pettitt, 'Philp Donnellan, Ireland and Dissident Documentary', *Historical Journal of Film, Radio and Television*, 20.3 (2000), pp. 351–65, at p. 358.

98. Episodes 1–10 were broadcast weekly between 28 January and 18 March 1965; episodes 11–14 went out between 14 May and 6 June. Scripts in CPA 2/104.

99. *The Song Carriers*, episode 13, broadcast BBC Midland Home Service, 28 May 1965.

100. Charles Parker memo of 14/1/65. Correspondence in CPA 2/104.

101. Ewan MacColl, *Ours the Fruit*, p. 63. Manuscript in MacColl/Seeger Archive.

102. Staged at Theatre Royal, Drury Lane on Sunday 5 July. Programme in CPA 1/7/4.

103. Unsigned, 'Co-ops Tell Their History in Song', *Daily Worker*, 6 July 1964.

104. Transcript of Critics Group meeting 'Tape 10' [June 1964], CPA 1/8/9/1.

105. Transcript of Critics Group meeting 'Tape 10' [June 1964], CPA 1/8/9/1.

106. Ewan MacColl, 'Folk Theatre', *Folk Music*, 1.11 [nd], pp. 8–10, at p. 8.

107. MacColl, 'Folk Theatre', p. 10.

108. MacColl, 'Folk Theatre', p. 10.

109. Ewan MacColl, 'St. George and the Dragon: A Modern Pace-Egging Play for Easter'. Manuscript in MacColl/Seeger Archive.

110. *Melody Maker*, 26 June 1965, 31 July 1965.

111. *Singers' Club News*, 2 (November 1965); *Melody Maker*, 23 October 1965.

112. Sandra Kerr, interview by author, 16 August 2006, Gateshead.

113. MacColl's potted history of the *Festival of Fools* first appeared in *Singers' Club News*, 3 (November 1965); it was reprinted in the programmes to all subsequent shows. Production scripts and programmes are held in the MacColl/Seeger Archive.

114. Programme to the 1967/8 *Festival of Fools*, MacColl/Seeger Archive.

115. Pre-production correspondence in MacColl/Seeger Archive.

116. John Faulkner, interview by Tim May, unedited videocassette in MacColl/ Seeger Archive.

117. Pat Mackenzie, interview by author, 14 September 2003, Salford.

118. V. J. Arthey and J. Warshaw, 'Press Release, December 1965'. MacColl/ Seeger Archive.

119. Script in MacColl/Seeger Archive.

120. Stanley Karnow, *Vietnam: A History* (1983; London: Penguin, 1984), pp. 413–15, at p. 415.

121. Karnow, *Vietnam*, p. 431.

122. MacColl, 'Execution Song', reprinted in Peggy Seeger, ed., *The Essential Ewan MacColl Songbook* (New York and London: Oak, 2001), p. 317.

123. Reprinted in Seeger, ed., *Ewan MacColl Songbook*, p. 90.

124. Reprinted in *Peggy Seeger Songbook* (London and New York: Oak, 1998), p. 66.

125. *Melody Maker*, 8 January 1966.

126. MacColl quoted in Goorney, *Theatre Workshop Story*, p. 128.

127. First meeting held on 13 July 1966. Minutes in MacColl/Seeger Archive.

128. *Singers' Club News*, 7 (January 1967). CPA 1/8/10; 'Folksingers for Freedom in Vietnam', Newsletter 1 (Easter 1967). MacColl/Seeger Archive.

129. MacColl, Critics Group meeting, 14 November 1967. CPA MS4000/5/ 4/2/166C. MacColl, Seeger and the Critics Group gave a concert at the Horseshoe on Tottenham Court Road 'in support of the movement for National Liberation in Vietnam' on 26 April 1967. *Singers' Club News*, 8 (May–September 1967) in CPA 1/8/10. MacColl appeared at a St Pancras Town Hall benefit on 4 February 1967; he and Seeger also played a benefit at the 2,000-seat Birmingham Town Hall on 30 June 1967. An audio recording was made of the concert, CPA MS/4000/5/3/1/10C.

130. Reprinted in Seeger, ed., *Essential Ewan MacColl Songbook*, pp. 70–1.

131. The song was reprinted on both sides of the Atlantic at this time: *Sing*, 10.3 (September 1968) and *Sing Out!* (December 1967/January 1968).

132. Written for the *Festival of Fools* 1967/8; reprinted in Seeger, ed., *Essential Ewan MacColl Songbook*, p. 312.

133. *Wounded Night*, 8-inch single, benefit record for Medical Aid for Indochina [nd or catalogue number]. Correspondence about the disc in MacColl/Seeger Archive, General Correspondence file, 1973.

134. *Cuu Quoc Weekly* to MacColl and Seeger, 14 July 1968.

135. 'Notes taken at a Business Meeting of the Critics Group in late July 1970', CPA 1/8/9/2.

136. Frank Zappa's acknowledgement from *The Lost Episodes* is reproduced on the CD reissue of MacColl and Lloyd's *Blow Boys Blow* LP (1967) (CD, TCD1024, Tradition, 1996); Marc Eliot, *Phil Ochs: Death of a Rebel* (London: Omnibus, 1990), pp. 230, 289; the Jagger story was told by

MacColl to Karl Dallas. Karl Dallas, interview by author, 22 October 2003, Bradford.

137. Stanislavski, *An Actor Prepares*, p. 56.
138. Karen O'Brien, *Kirsty MacColl: The One and Only One* (London: André Deutsch, 2004), p. 111.
139. Sandra Kerr, interview by author, 16 August 2006, Gateshead.
140. Reprinted in Seeger, ed., *Essential Ewan MacColl Songbook*, pp. 73, 75.
141. Reprinted in *Peggy Seeger Songbook*, pp. 75, 82, 84.
142. Unsigned editorial, *New City Songster*, volume 1 [nd].
143. Peggy Seeger to Waldemar Hille, 11 September 1971.
144. MacColl's Communist Party membership is also discussed in Chapter 7.
145. The ructions were painstakingly chronicled in Edward Crankshaw, *The New Cold War: Moscow v. Pekin* (London: Penguin, 1963).
146. Mao Tse Tung, *Quotations from Chairman Mao Tse-Tung* (Peking: Foreign Language Press, 1966), p. 279.
147. 'Talks at the Yenan Forum on Art and Literature', *Selected Works of Mao Tse Tung*, IV (Bombay, 1956), p. 66.
148. Crankshaw, *New Cold War*, p. 84.
149. Mao, *Quotations*, p. 74.
150. Mao, *Quotations*, p. 61.
151. The Communist Party's scrutiny of Birch can be traced through correspondence and paper cuttings kept in the Communist Party's records in the Labour History Archive and Study Centre, Manchester (CP/Ind/Dut/19/9 and CP/Ind/Goll/04, file 6); Birch is also the subject of a biography by Will Podmore, *Reg Birch: Engineer, Trade Unionist, Communist* (London: Bellman, 2004). William Ash tells his own story in *A Red Square: The Autobiography of an Unconventional Revolutionary* (London: Howard Baker, 1978). MacColl and Seeger subscribed to the monthly broadsheet published by the China Policy Study Group from May 1965 until December 1974. George Thomson's book *From Marx to Mao-Tse-Tung: A Study in Revolutionary Dialectics* (London: China Policy Study Group, 1972) became a handbook for British Maoists.
152. Also Mao's 'little red book', *Quotations for Chairman Mao Tse-Tung* (Peking: Foreign Language Press, 1967) and *Mao Tse-Tung on Literature and Art* (Peking: Foreign Language Press, 1967).
153. *Peking Review*, 2 (9 January 1970).
154. *Peking Review*, 21 (22 May 1970). Jim Carroll remembers MacColl being incensed by the critique. Interview with author, 14 September 2003, Salford.
155. 'The Economic Background to *The Marxist*', *Hammer or Anvil* (July–August 1967), pp. 12–15, at p. 18. LHASC CP/Ind/Dutt/17/9.
156. MacColl made the claim in interview by Michael O'Rourke and Mary Orr, Portland, Oregon (November 1984) and London (January–February 1985), transcript in MacColl/Seeger Archive. In fact he didn't write a single article and couldn't stomach the interminable editorial meetings. He did lend his services as singer, appearing at a couple of fundraising concerts. Mike Faulkner, telephone interview by author, 21 October 2006. Copies of the journal are held in the MacColl/Seeger Archive. MacColl, Seeger and three

Critics gave a London benefit concert on 26 May 1967. 'Club Calendar – Spring/Summer 1967', CPA 1/8/9/3.

157.  Peggy Seeger, e-mail to author, 21 March 2003.

158.  Birch's new party was launched in July 1968. Reg Birch to MacColl and Seeger, 10 October 1968. MacColl/Seeger Archive, General Correspondence 1968 file.

159.  *The Manchester Angel* (LP 12T147, Topic, 1966).

160.  Eric Winter, 'Specialist Label with a Rich Harvest', *Sing*, 10.3 (September 1968), p. 20.

161.  Alan Holmes to MacColl and Seeger, 6 August 1969. MacColl/Seeger Archive, General Correspondence file.

162.  *The Amorous Muse* (LP, ZFB 66, Argo, 1966); *The Wanton Muse* (LP, ZFB 67, Argo, 1968); *The Angry Muse* (LP, ZFB 65, 1968).

163.  *The Paper Stage: Some Broadside Ballads of Plays by Elizabethan Dramatists* (LP, ZDA 98, Argo, 1968 and LP, ZDA 99 Argo, 1968).

164.  Ewan MacColl and Peggy Seeger, *The Long Harvest* (LPs, ZDA 66–76, 1967–8).

165.  'Ewan MacColl and Peggy Seeger talk to Madeau Stewart about Folk-Music and Recording', *Audio Record Review* (September 1968), pp. 636–7.

166.  *Melody Maker*, 2 December 1967; also 7 October 1967, 2 March 1968, 15 June 1968.

167.  Ewan MacColl, interview by Michael O'Rourke and Mary Orr, Portland, Oregon (November 1984) and London (January–February 1985), transcript in MacColl/Seeger Archive.

168.  Reprinted in Seeger, ed., *Essential Ewan MacColl Songbook*, p. 30.

169.  *Voices: An Anthology of Sounds, Music, Song and Speech Presented in Association with Penguin Education* (5 LPs, DA 91–95, Argo, 1968); *Poetry and Song* (14 LPs, ZDA 50–63, Argo, 1966–7).

170.  There was talk of the Critics Group also producing an LP based on John Gay's eighteenth-century *Beggar's Opera*, but the project failed to materialise. Discussed in Critics Group meeting, 13 February 1968, CPA MS/4000/5/4/2/173C.

171.  *Sweet Thames Flow Softly* (LP, ZFB 61, Argo, 1966); *A Merry Progress to London* (LP, ZFB 60, Argo, 1967); *As We Were A' Sailing* (LP, ZDA 137, Argo, 1970); *Ye Mariners All* (LP, ZDA 138, Argo, 1971); *Waterloo–Peterloo* (LP, ZFB 68, Argo, 1968); *The Female Frolic* (LP, ZFB 64, Argo, 1968).

172.  More sympathetic reviews appeared in smaller magazines such as *Club Folk*, 2.4 (July–August 1969), p. 20 and *Chapbook*, 4.3 [nd], pp. 22–3.

173.  Unsigned, 'Criticising the Critics', *Folk Music Ballads and Songs* [nd], pp. 17–18, at p. 18.

174.  Karl Dallas, interview by author, 22 October 2003, Bradford.

175.  Ian Campbell, 'Illusion and Reality', *Sing*, 10.1 (June 1967), pp. 10–11, at p. 10.

176.  Critics Group meeting, 31 March 1969, CPA MS 4000/5/4/2/216c.

177.  Karl Dallas, 'It's fine, hard stuff but not all copyright', *Morning Star*, 5 June 1967.

178.  John Craig to Ewan MacColl and Peggy Seeger, 27 August 1968; Charles Ringrose to Peggy Seeger, 27 December 1967; Workers' Music Association

to Ewan MacColl, 2 March 1970. MacColl/Seeger Archive, General Correspondence file.

179. Peggy Seeger, interview by author, 28 November 2005, Salford.
180. MacColl responded in the *Festival of Fools*, as discussed below.
181. Karl Dallas, 'Those Revivalists Who Won't Get Their Feet Wet', *Morning Star*, 20 September 1967; Karl Dallas, 'What Folk Means Today', *Melody Maker*, 30 December 1967. Following quotations from the *Morning Star* version.
182. Peggy Seeger, interview by author, 28 November 2005, Salford.
183. Karl Dallas to Ewan MacColl, 12 February 1969. MacColl/Seeger Archive, General Correspondence file.
184. Ewan MacColl, script for 1967/8 *Festival of Fools* includes a long sketch ridiculing Western media distortions of Chinese affairs; the sketch was repeated in the 1971/2 shows. Both scripts in MacColl/Seeger Archive.
185. Peggy can be heard selling *The Marxist* at the Critics Group meeting, 16 February 1971, CPA MS 4000/5/4/2/250; Mike Rosen also remembers the *China Policy Study Group Broadsheet* being circulated (interview by author, 1 March 2006). The 1968/9 *Festival of Fools* is highly critical of the Soviet Union. Frankie Armstrong recalls the trip to Albania in *As Far As*, pp. 42–3.
186. Bob Pegg, *Folk Britannia*, dir. Mike Connolly, BBC 4, 3 February 2006, 10 February 2006.
187. Mao, *Quotations*, p. 259; Charles Parker took MacColl to task for 'thunderous authoritarianism' after one outburst. Parker refers to the policy of 'no answers', whereby those criticised have to accept the criticism, and also talks of 'the mass line concept we are struggling to master'. Parker to MacColl, 30 November 1966. CPA 1/8/9/4.
188. Armstrong, *As Far As*, p. 40; Sandra Kerr, interview by author, 16 August 2006, Gateshead.
189. Armstrong, *As Far As*, p. 70.
190. Gordon McCulloch, telephone conversation with author, 10 December 2006.
191. Mike Rosen, 'Response to PSN10', *Political Song News*, 11 (March 1991), pp. 7, 12, at p. 7.
192. Programme Books, MacColl/Seeger Archive; Stuart Birch, 'The Day the Tinkers Serenaded the '"folk" folk at Home', *Belfast Telegraph*, 16 November 1969.
193. Robin Denselow, *When the Music's Over: The Story of Political Pop* (London: Faber & Faber, 1989), pp. 28–9.
194. *The World of Ewan MacColl and Peggy Seeger* (LP, ZRG 3274, Argo, 1970).
195. Script in MacColl/Seeger Archive.
196. 'Cut Price Hero', 'Tall and Proud', 'The New Boys'. Reprinted in Seeger, ed., *Essential Ewan MacColl Songbook*, pp. 219, 320, 254.
197. 'Holiday Song', reprinted in Seeger, ed., *Essential Ewan MacColl Songbook*, p. 345.
198. Audio recording of show. CPA MS4000/5/3/5/5/44C and D.
199. Robin Denselow, 'Festival of Fools', *Guardian*, 29 December 1967.

200. Clive Barker, interview by author, 10 August 2004, Sidcup.
201. *Peggy Seeger Songbook*, p. 196.
202. *Peggy Seeger Songbook*, p. 196.
203. Hamish MacColl, telephone conversation with author, 12 November 2006.
204. Sandra Kerr, interview by author, 16 August 2006, Gateshead.
205. Ewan MacColl in conversation with Charles Parker, 10 February 1971. CPA MS4000/5/4/1/16C.
206. On the tape, MacColl jokes how he plans always to keep a tape recorder at his side, so that any deathbed insights might benefit the group. MacColl in conversation with Charles Parker, 10 February 1971.
207. All quotations from CPA, MS 4000/5/4/1/16C.
208. Critics Group meeting, 16 February 1971. CPA, MS 4000/5/4/2/250.
209. Critics Group meeting, 16 February 1971.
210. Armstrong, *As Far As*, p. 70.
211. Bob Blair, interview by author, 3 August 2004, Glasgow.
212. *The World of Ewan MacColl and Peggy Seeger, Volume Two: Songs from the Radio Ballads* (LP, SPA-A-216, Argo, 1972); Philip Donnellan prod., *Before the Mast*, broadcast on BBC 2, 4 December 1971.
213. John Goldshmidt dir., *A Kind of Exile*, broadcast on ATV on 20 July 1971. Recording of film in MacColl/Seeger Archive.
214. Nancy Banks-Smith, *Guardian*, 22 July 1971; Peter Black, *Daily Mail*, 21 July 1971; unsigned reviews in the *Telegraph*, 25 July 1971 and *The Sunday Times*, 26 July 1971.
215. 'Minutes of Theatre Group Meeting, 11 May 1971', CPA 1/8/9/6.
216. Critics Group meeting, 16 February 1971, CPA MS 4000/5/4/2/250.
217. Mike Rosen, interview by author, 1 March 2006, London.
218. Sandra Kerr, interview by author, 16 August 2006, Gateshead.
219. Peggy Seeger, circular to group members [nd], CPA 2/125.
220. The 1971/2 show was filmed. An edited version was released in 1973. Publicity material in MacColl/Seeger Archive.
221. Peegy Seeger, interview by author, 28 November 2005, Salford.
222. Peegy Seeger, interview by author, 28 November 2005.
223. Sandra Kerr, interview by author, 16 August 2006, Gateshead.
224. Mike Rosen, interview by author, 1 March 2006, London.
225. Ewan MacColl in conversation with Charles Parker, 10 February 1971. CPA MS4000/5/4/1/16C.
226. Peegy Seeger, interview by author, 28 November 2005, Salford.
227. Reprinted in *Peggy Seeger Songbook*, p. 110.
228. Sandra Kerr, interview by author, 16 August 2006, Gateshead.
229. Dissolution papers were circulated as a result of that meeting. CPA 1/8/9/4.
230. Sandra Kerr, interview by author, 16 August 2006, Gateshead.
231. Peegy Seeger, interview by author, 28 November 2005, Salford.
232. Sandra Kerr, interview by author, 16 August 2006, Gateshead.
233. Mike Rosen, interview by author, 1 March 2006, London.

*Chapter 10, 'Sanctuary'*

1. Peggy Seeger to Charles Parker, 16 May 1972. Charles Parker file, Ewan MacColl/Peggy Seeger Archive, Ruskin College, Oxford.
2. John Faulkner, interview by Tony Jasper, *Folk Review*, 5.12 (October 1976), pp. 16–20; songbooks included *Garland* (October 1974). I'm grateful to Pam Bishop for generously sharing her resources on Combine.
3. Quotation from Jack Warshaw, 'Some Recent Stirrings of the Folk Process in Britain', *Sing Out!*, 24 (1975), pp. 16–20, at p. 16; Dave Marshall, 'Dónal Maguire', *Living Tradition*, 46 (January–February 2002), pp. 15–17; for early 1970s political theatre, see Alan Filewood and David Watt, *Workers' Playtime: Theatre and the Labour Movement Since 1970* (Sydney: Currency Press, 2001), pp. 38–83.
4. Ewan MacColl, interview by Michael O'Rourke and Mary Orr, Portland, November 1984 and London, January–February 1985. Transcript in MacColl/Seeger Archive.
5. Sandra Kerr, interview by author, 16 August 2006, Gateshead.
6. Karl Dallas, 'MacColl – a True Critic', *Melody Maker*, 22 February 1975.
7. Michael Rosen, interview by author, 1 March 2006, London.
8. Peggy Seeger to Charles Parker, 16 May 1972. Charles Parker file, MacColl/Seeger Archive.
9. Calum MacColl, interview by author, 9 March 2006. London.
10. Neill MacColl, interview by author, 27 February 2006. London.
11. Unsigned, 'Echoes of "Broadcasting in the Seventies": BBC's Intention to Sack Italia Prize Winner', *ABS, Journal of the Association of Broadcasting Staff*, 28 (October 1972), pp. 54–60.
12. Produced by Philip Donnellan, three television 'radio ballads' were broadcast on BBC television between 1972 and 1974. *Singing the Fishing* went out on 3 July 1972, *The Fight Game* on 16 June 1973 and *The Big Hewer* on 9 May 1974.
13. Gillian Reynolds, 'The Ides of Long March', *Guardian*, 17 November 1972.
14. Peggy Seeger to Charles Parker, 17 November 1972. Charles Parker file, MacColl/Seeger Archive.
15. Peggy Seeger to Charles Parker, 16 May 1972. Charles Parker file, MacColl/Seeger Archive.
16. Peggy Seeger to Charles Parker, 17 November 1972. Charles Parker file, MacColl/Seeger Archive.
17. Charles Parker to Peggy Seeger, 24 May 1972. Charles Parker file, MacColl/Seeger Archive.
18. Charles Parker to *The Times*, 18 November 1972; the letter was printed on 20 November; Parker also wrote to the *Guardian* on 18 November; that letter was also printed on 20 November.
19. Carol Dix, 'Parker's Double Line', *Guardian*, 6 July 1973.
20. Charles Parker to Peggy Seeger, 8 July 1973. Charles Parker file, MacColl/Seeger Archive. MacColl quotes the letter in *Journeyman* (London: Sidgwick & Jackson, 1990), p. 335.

21. Ewan MacColl to *English Dance and Song*, 43.3 (1981), p. 21. He was responding to Roy Palmer's obituary of Parker, *English Dance and Song*, 43.2 (1981), p. 28.

22. Ewan MacColl, interview with Michael O'Rourke and Mary Orr, *Parsley Sage and Politics*, Part 5 (1985).

23. Ewan MacColl and Peggy Seeger, interview by Fred Woods, 1973. The transcripts for these interviews, sections of which were serialised in the magazine *Folk Review* between May and August 1973, are held in the MacColl/Seeger Archive.

24. Unsigned, 'Roberta Flack Wins Two Grammies for her Record', *New York Times*, 5 March 1973.

25. BMI certificates in MacColl/Seeger Archive.

26. Peggy Seeger, interview by author, 28 November 2005, Salford.

27. Neill MacColl, interview by author, 27 February 2006, London.

28. Peggy Seeger, interview by author, 28 November 2005, Salford.

29. Calum MacColl, interview by author, 9 March 2006, London.

30. *The Peggy Seeger Songbook: Forty Years of Songmaking* (New York and London: Oak, 1998), p. 116.

31. *Peggy Seeger Songbook*, p. 146.

32. Neill MacColl, interview by author, 27 February 2006, London; e-mail to author, 15 February 2007.

33. Peggy Seeger to Alan Lomax, 7 December 1976, MacColl/Seeger Archive. Unless otherwise indicated, all correspondence is from the chronologically sequenced General Correspondence files in the MacColl/Seeger Archive.

34. Peggy Seeger, interview by author, 14 October 2004, Sheffield; Coral McKendrick, 'Another Seeger Singer', *Winnipeg Free Press*, 18 July 1979.

35. Correspondence and contracts in BBC Written Archives, Caversham, Ewan MacColl/Personal File M31/1,894/1, Midland Region 1963–74.

36. *The Ideas of Karl Marx* (New York and London: Educational Audovisual, 1973). Copy in MacColl/Seeger Archive.

37. Ewan MacColl to Donald Alexander, [nd]. Television file, MacColl/Seeger Archive.

38. Ewan MacColl to Neill [nd]. MacColl/Seeger Archive.

39. Ewan MacColl to Donald Alexander, 19 July 1977. MacColl/Seeger Archive.

40. The film was made by Document Productions Ltd; MacColl and Seeger signed the contract on 13 October 1969 and were paid £650 (£7,200 in 2006 prices); Equity to Ewan MacColl, 20 April 1970, MacColl/Seeger Archive.

41. Boris Ford to Ewan MacColl and Peggy Seeger, 16 September 1969; Peggy Seeger to Boris Ford, 2 October 1969; Boris Ford to Ewan MacColl and Peggy Seeger, 14 September 1971. MacColl/Seeger Archive.

42. Karl Dallas, ' MacColl – a True Critic', *Melody Maker*, 22 February 1975; Ewan MacColl to Trevor Fisher, 4 September 1975; Roger Brooks to Ewan MacColl, 8 December 1975. MacColl/Seeger Archive.

43. MacColl spent two days in The University of Birmingham Drama Department in November 1975 – Robert Leach to Ewan MacColl, 16 November 1975; in September 1971 he'd been contracted to prepare Open University broadcasts

on 'Renaissance and Reformation' and 'Popular Poetry and Ballads of the Sixteenth Century'. The programmes were recorded on 9 October 1971. BBC WAC/James Miller/Artist File, 1968–72.

44. Vic Gammon, interview by author, 2 April 2004, Leeds.

45. *The Times*, 1 April 1986. The degree was awarded on 18 July, *University of Exeter Gazette* (October 1986); there's a photograph of the ceremony in *Journeyman*. Calum MacColl, interview by author, 9 March 2006, London.

46. Peggy Seeger to John Ashworth, 17 September 1987. MacColl/Seeger Archive.

47. Peggy Seeger, ed., *Essential Ewan MacColl Songbook* (New York and London: Oak, 2001), pp. 150–1; the song appears on Peggy Seeger and Ewan MacColl, *Folkways Record of Contemporary Songs* (LP, FW 8736, Folkways, 1973).

48. Ewan MacColl and Peggy Seeger, transcript of interview by Fred Woods, 1973. The project had a long gestation but came to nothing. It was a development of MacColl's earlier ideas about the next radio ballad; Philip Donnellan mentions a possible film along these lines in a letter to Peggy Seeger written on 29 March 1983. MacColl/Seeger Archive.

49. Ben Bright to Ewan MacColl and Peggy Seeger, 3 January 1974. Radio Scripts file, MacColl/Seeger Archive.

50. *History Workshop Journal* was launched in 1976. Raphael Samuel to Ewan MacColl, 14 August 1977, 29 November 1978. MacColl/Seeger Archive.

51. A. L. Lloyd, *Folk Song in England* (London: Lawrence & Wishart, 1967).

52. Andrew Means, 'The World of Ewan MacColl', *Melody Maker*, 11 November 1972.

53. Peggy Seeger to Oliver Boyd Publishers, 8 December 1973.

54. Peter Kennedy, ed., *Folksongs of Britain and Ireland* (London and New York: Oak, 1975).

55. Ewan MacColl and Peggy Seeger, introduction to *Travellers' Songs from England and Scotland* (London: Routledge & Kegan Paul, 1977), p. 15.

56. *Travellers' Songs*, p. 2.

57. Hamish Henderson, 'Songs of Travelling People', 7 *Days*, 10 February 1978, p. 16; Douglas Dunn, 'What the Tinks Sing', *The Listener*, 8 December 1977, pp. 757–8.

58. Sheila Stewart tells the family's story in *An Ancient Oral Culture* (Scone, 2000).

59. Records include *The Travelling Stewarts* (LP, 12T179, Topic, 1968).

60. Ewan MacColl and Peggy Seeger, eds, *Till Doomsday in the Afternoon* (Manchester: Manchester University Press, 1986), p. ix.

61. The book was rejected by publishers including Routledge & Kegan Paul, Oxford University Press, the University of Texas Press and Croom Helm. Correspondence in *Till Doomsday in the Afternoon*, Correspondence and Notes File, MacColl/Seeger Archive.

62. 'I think you have made a very good job of it,' Sheila Stewart wrote, 'especially as regards the songs.' Sheila Stewart to Peggy Seeger and Ewan MacColl,

1 April 1986. MacColl and Seeger, *Till Doomsday*, p. ix; unsigned review in *Traveller Education* (1987), p. 14.

63. MacColl and Seeger, *Till Doomsday*, p. 32.

64. *Till Doomsday*, p. 35.

65. *Till Doomsday*, p. 33.

66. Peggy Seeger in Philip Donnellan prod., *Stories and Songs of a Scottish Family*, broadcast on BBC2 Television on 24 September 1980. There's a copy of the film in the MacColl/Seeger Archive. Other reviews included Norman Buchan, 'Ewan MacColl Repays a Debt', *Chartist*, 110 (June–August 1986), pp. 34–5; Anne Smith, 'A Mater's Mak'-ye'-Ups', *Times Literary Supplement*, 30 May 1986, p. 22 and Alastair Clark, 'Tales of a Dying Tradition', *Scotsman*, 26 April 1986, p. 10.

67. Ewan MacColl in Philip Donnellan prod., *Stories and Songs of a Scottish Family*. There's a copy of the film in the MacColl/Seeger Archive.

68. MacColl in *Stories and Songs*.

69. Unsigned editorial [Peggy Seeger], *New City Songster*, 6 (May 1971) [no page numbers] and *New City Songster*, 19 (March 1984), p. 1.

70. Peggy Seeger, interview by Fred Woods, 1973. Transcript in MacColl/Seeger Archive.

71. Trevor Fisher's pamphlet, *We're Only In It For The Money* (1972) was widely circulated through the folk scene and presented a critical diagnosis of the revival that reflected the views of Midlands-based early 1970s political folk pressure group, the Parkhouse Convention.

72. Doc Rowe, 'The Knave of Clubs', *Parkhouse Convention Bulletin* [nd]; the article was a reprint from the *Hackney People's Press*, 10 (April 1974).

73. Leon Rosselson, 'Stand Up, Stand Up For--?', *Sing Out!*, 24.4 (1975), pp. 10, 11, 14, at p. 10.

74. Andrew Means, 'The World of Ewan MacColl', *Melody Maker*, 11 November 1972, pp. 69–70, at p. 69.

75. Ewan MacColl and Peggy Seeger, interview by Charles Parker, 26 June 1972. Transcript in Charles Parker Archive, Birmingham Central Library, CPA 1/7/4.

76. Fisher, *We're Only In It*, pp. 6, 11.

77. Programme books in MacColl/Seeger Archive. Concert reviews: CAR, 'Hothouse of Folk', *Croydon Advertiser*, 1 June 1973; Peter Godfrey, 'Good Old Fashioned Folk Music', *Liverpool Daily Post*, 5 December 1974; Karl Dallas, 'Ewan MacColl', *Melody Maker*, 8 February 1975.

78. Concert promotional leaflet; unsigned, 'AMWU to sponsor famed folk singers' Australian tour', *Amalgamated News*, 2.14 (September 1976); Dorothy Goodwin, 'Magic MacColls', *Weekend News* (Perth), 16 October 1976; unsigned, 'Singing to improve the quality of life', *West Australian*, 18 October 1976; Warren Owens, 'Cultural Spree for Metal Workers', *Sydney Sunday Herald*, 10 October 1976.

79. Jim Carroll, editorial, *The Lark: The Singers' Club Newsletter* (January 1980).

80. Mark Turner to David Fairbanks, 14 June 1975. Singers' Club file, MacColl/Seeger Archive.

81. Programmes in Singers' Club file, MacColl/Seeger Archive.

82. Peggy Seeger to Alan Lomax, 7 December 1976.
83. Unsigned, 'The Workers' Music: Interview with Folk Singers Ewan MacColl and Peggy Seeger', *Militant*, 28 July 1976.
84. Peggy Seeger, interview by author, 28 November 2005, Salford.
85. *Memorandum and Articles of Association of Blackthorne Records Limited, 18 August 1976.* MacColl/Seeger Archive.
86. Peggy Seeger, interview by author, 28 November 2006, Salford.
87. Blackthorne products were distributed under licence by Folkways in America and Larrikin in Australia.
88. Blackthorne Records Limited, Balance Sheets and Accounts 1977–89, Blackthorne File, MacColl/Seeger Archive.
89. 'Parliamentary Polka'/'Song of Choice', 7-inch single (BR20535, Blackthorne, 1977); 'My Son'/'Housewife's Alphabet' (7-inch single, BR 20525, Blackthorne, 1977); Peggy Seeger, *Penelope Isn't Waiting Anymore* (LP, BR 1050, Blackthorne, 1976) and *Different Therefore Equal* (LP, BR 1061, Blackthorne, 1979); Peggy Seeger and Ewan MacColl, *Saturday Night at the Bull and Mouth* (LP, BR 1055, Blackthorne, 1977); Peggy Seeger and Ewan MacColl, *Cold Snap* (LP, BR 1057, Blackthorne, 1977), and *Hot Blast* (LP, BR 1039, Blackthorne, 1978). All of the albums were also issued in the US on Folkways, except *Penelope Isn't Waiting*, which was released on Rounder records as Rounder 4011.
90. Reprinted in Seeger, ed., *Essential Ewan MacColl Songbook*, p. 88.
91. Reprinted in Seeger, ed., *Essential Ewan MacColl Songbook*, p. 255.
92. Reprinted in Seeger, ed., *Essential Ewan MacColl Songbook*, p. 51.
93. Reprinted in Seeger, ed., *Essential Ewan MacColl Songbook*, p. 104; Ewan MacColl and Peggy Seeger, *Kilroy Was Here* (LP, BR 1063, Blackthorne, 1980).
94. Reprinted in Seeger, ed., *Essential Ewan MacColl Songbook*, p. 102.
95. Calum MacColl, interview by author, 9 March 2006, London.
96. 'Folk music is not only entertainment,' she wrote in 1980, 'it is a record of a way of life ... The accompanist is secondary and if he cannot confine himself to that he should stick to dance music.' Peggy Seeger, 'Some Notes on Accompaniment', *The Lark: The Singers' Club Newsletter*, 3 (Summer 1980), no page numbers. Quotation from this article.
97. Neill MacColl, interview by author, 27 February 2006, London.
98. Calum MacColl, interview by author, 9 March 2006, London.
99. Neill MacColl, interview by author, 27 February 2006, London.
100. Neill MacColl, interview by author, 27 February 2006, London.
101. Calum MacColl, interview by author, 9 March 2006, London.
102. Gordon McCulloch, 'MacColl Out of Touch?', *Folk News*, 12/79; this review also appeared in *Melody Maker*, undated clip in MacColl/Seeger Reviews File, MacColl/Seeger Archive.
103. Peter Godfrey, 'Good Old-Fashioned Folk Music', *Liverpool Daily Post*, 5 December 1974; Michael Grosvenor Myer, review of *Saturday Night at the Bull and Mouth*, in *Folk Review* (January 1978), p. 14.
104. Programme Books, MacColl/Seeger Archive; Ewan MacColl's passport, issued 15/4/75, MacColl/Seeger Archive.
105. Peggy Seeger, interview by author, 28 November 2005, Salford.

## Chapter 11, 'Endgame'

1. Hamish MacColl, telephone conversation with author, 12 November 2006.
2. Peggy Seeger, interview by author, 28 November 2005, Salford.
3. Ewan MacColl and Peggy Seeger, liner-notes to *Blood and Roses*, Volume 5 (LP, ESB 83, Blackthorne, 1986); Donny O'Rourke, 'Full Circle of a Folk Hero', *Glasgow Herald*, 15 December 1987.
4. Volume 11, *Ballads Resident and Migrant* (provisional catalogue number ZDA 76) and Volume 12, *Second Crop* (provisional catalogue number ZDA 77).
5. MacColl and Seeger, liner-notes to *Blood and Roses*, Volume 5 (LP, ESB 83, Blackthorne, 1986).
6. Volume 1 (ESB 79) came out in 1979, Volume 2 (ESB 80) in 1981, Volume 3 (ESB 81) in 1982. Volumes 4 (ESB 82) and 5 (ESB 83) were issued in 1986. Reviews included Karl Dallas, 'A Continuing Colossus' in *Acoustic Music* (July 1980), p. 23, and Dave Lloyd, 'The Folk From the Blackthorne Outlet' in *Morning Star*, 18 December 1979.
7. Ewan MacColl and Peggy Seeger, *Kilroy was Here* (LP, BR 1063, Blackthorne, 1980). Claire Bradley, 'Blasting the Androids', *Militant*, 19 December 1980; Dave Harbord, untitled review, *Morning Star*, 12 November 1980.
8. Reprinted in Peggy Seeger, ed., *The Essential Ewan MacColl Songbook: Sixty Years of Songmaking* (London and New York: Oak, 2001) pp. 110, 362.
9. Reprinted in Seeger, ed., *Essential Ewan MacColl Songbook*, pp. 104, 102.
10. Reprinted in Seeger, ed., *Essential Ewan MacColl Songbook*, pp. 262, 258, 268, 266.
11. Bob Campbell, 'A Chip off the Old Block', *Sunday Times*, 2 August 1981.
12. John Miller, 'Kirsty's Hot Hit', *Daily Record*, 15 July 1981.
13. Karen O'Brien, *Kirsty MacColl: The One and Only* (London: André Deutsch, 2004), p. 11.
14. Sourced from O'Brien, *Kirsty MacColl*, p. 66.
15. O'Brien, *Kirsty MacColl*, p. 28.
16. The single flopped the first time, but would be a number two hit for Tracey Ullman in September 1983.
17. O'Brien, *Kirsty MacColl*, p. 64.
18. Hamish MacColl, telephone conversation with author, 12 November 2006.
19. For example, MacColl sent a copy of his *Good Soldier Schweik* to PhD student William Walker on 4 December 1973; Ewan MacColl, letter to Mary Simpson, 4 October 1978. Unless otherwise indicated, all letters are from the General Correspondence files of the Ewan MacColl and Peggy Seeger Archive, Ruskin College, Oxford.
20. Jon Myers to Ewan MacColl, 29 December 1976; Raphael Samuel to Ewan MacColl, 14 August 1977 and 29 November 1978. Sections of the book were first published in *History Workshop Journal*, 4 (1977). Raphael

Samuel, Ewan MacColl and Stewart Cosgrove, eds, *Theatres of the Left 1880–1935: Workers' Theatre Movements in Britain and America* (London: Routledge & Kegan and Paul, 1985).

21. Howard Goorney, *The Theatre Workshop Story* (London: Methuen, 1981), p. x. Littlewood's last show for Theatre Workshop was in 1973; the name 'Theatre Workshop' was used until 1978.

22. Howard Goorney to Ewan MacColl, 26 October 1977 and 31 January 1978.

23. Howard Goorney and Ewan MacColl, eds, *Agit-prop to Theatre Workshop* (Manchester: Manchester University Press, 1986).

24. Elizabeth MacLellan, *The Moon Belongs to Everyone: Making Theatre With 7:84* (London: Methuen, 1990); John McGrath, 'Better a Bad Night in Bootle', *Theatre Quarterly*, V, 19 (September–November 1975), pp. 29–55; John McGrath, *A Good Night Out: Popular Theatre: Audience, Class and Form* (London: Methuen, 1981).

25. Linda MacKenney, 'Popular Theatre in Scotland' in *Clydebuilt Souvenir Programme*, MacColl/Seeger Archive. Also John McGrath, *The Bone Won't Break* (London: Methuen, 1990), pp. 77–91.

26. The other plays were George Munro's *Gold in His Boots* (1947), Ena Lamont Stewart's *Men Should Weep* (1947) and Joe Corrie's *In Time of Strife* (1927).

27. Four years earlier Gaughan had contributed to a Ewan MacColl tribute LP. Dave Burland, Tony Capstick, Dick Gaughan, *Songs of Ewan MacColl* (LP, CRO215, Black Crow, 1978).

28. Dick Gaughan, 'Ewan MacColl (1915–1989)', www.dickalba.demom.cou.uk/chain/ewan_mc.html. Accessed 2 April 2003.

29. Cordelia Oliver, 'Johnny Noble', *Guardian*, 10 April 1982; Allen Wright, 'Johnny Noble', *Scotsman*, 9 April 1982; Mary Brennan, 'Johnny Noble', *Glasgow Herald*, 8 April 1982. The show toured East Kilbride, Paisley, Perth, Ayr and Cumbernauld between 19 and 24 April, and was revived for the Edinburgh Fringe Festival in August. P. H. Scott, 'Johnny Noble', *Scotsman*, 27 August 1982.

30. Clive Barker to Ewan MacColl, 15 December 1984; John McGrath to Ewan MacColl, 5 March 1986.

31. Ewan MacColl and Peggy Seeger to Tim Mason, 8 May 1988.

32. Programme books, MacColl/Seeger Archive.

33. Ewan MacColl, *Journeyman: An Autobiography* (London: Sidgwick & Jackson, 1990), p. 380.

34. Peggy Seeger to George Deacon, 20 September 1983.

35. Ewan MacColl to John [McGrath], 27 October 1982. National Library of Scotland, 10893/231.

36. John McGrath to Ewan MacColl, 27 September 1983. McGrath had passed the script to Theatre Royal, where he was currently working. Danny Boyle to Ewan MacColl [nd].

37. Script to *The Shipmaster* (the play's alternative title), MacColl/Seeger Archive.

38. Ewan MacColl, '*Shore Saints and Sea Devils*: Learning a New Language', production programme, no page numbers; MacColl later described the play

as 'a closely worked metaphor for the passing of *laissez-faire* capitalism'. MacColl, *Journeyman*, p. 380.

39. The first episode of the five-part series was broadcast on BBC 2 on 7 November 1982; MacColl avidly watched the series.

40. Calum MacColl pointed this out to his father, who was taken aback by the thought. Calum MacColl, interview by author, 9 March 2006, London.

41. *The Shipmaster*, cue 1417.

42. Robin Thornber, 'Shore Saints and Sea Devils', *Guardian*, 11 November 1983.

43. Alan Hulme, 'Shore Saints and Sea Devils', *Manchester Evening News*, 10 November 1983.

44. Joan Littlewood to Ewan MacColl [nd]. Joan Littlewood Correspondence, MacColl/Seeger Archive.

45. Seeger was arrested on 15 November 1983, Mikki Doyle, 'Singing for a New Tomorrow', *Morning Star*, 7 February 1984; unsigned, 'Tuneful Defence is Rejected', *Guardian*, 9 February 1984.

46. 'Tomorrow' was the song. Reprinted in *The Peggy Seeger Songbook: Forty Years of Songmaking* (New York and London: Oak, 1998), p. 178.

47. Peggy Seeger to Don Lange, 2 March 1984.

48. 'Pay-Up Song', reprinted in *Peggy Seeger Songbook*, p. 136.

49. The track was released with MacColl's 'We Are The Engineers' on a single produced by the Amalgamated Union of Engineering. 50,000 copies of the record were issued. 7-inch single, AUEW1, nd [1976].

50. 'Folk with Feeling' interview with Peggy Seeger, *Spare Rib* (July 1976), pp. 41–2. The magazine was launched in 1972.

51. Angela Phillips and Jill Nichols, 'Different Therefore Equal', *Guardian*, 19 June 1979.

52. Unsigned, 'My Wife the Writer', *Folk News* (April 1978), p. 12.

53. *Peggy Seeger Songbook*, p. 144.

54. 'Emily' and 'Winnie and Sam', reprinted in *Peggy Seeger Songbook*, pp. 134 and 156 respectively.

55. Peggy Seeger, interview by author, 14 October 2004, Sheffield.

56. Ewan MacColl, 'Greenham Woman'. Poems file, MacColl/Seeger Archive.

57. Ewan MacColl, interview in Dave Boulton prod., *Daddy, What Did You Do in the Strike?*, broadcast on Granada Television, 15 December 1985.

58. 'Only Doing Their Job', reprinted in Seeger, ed., *Essential Ewan MacColl Songbook*, p. 290.

59. 'Holy Joe of Scabsville'. Seeger wrote the tune. Reprinted in Seeger, ed., *Essential Ewan MacColl Songbook*, p. 94.

60. 'The Media', reprinted in Seeger, ed., *Essential Ewan MacColl Songbook*, p. 346.

61. The only song he wrote about women's experience left the miner's wife at home waiting to bathe her husband's picket-line wounds. MacColl's 'On the Picket Line' is reprinted in Seeger, ed., *Essential Ewan MacColl Songbook*, p. 92; 'Daddy, What Did You Do in the Strike?', reprinted in Seeger, ed., *Essential Ewan MacColl Songbook*, p. 96; Seeger's 'Women's Union' (1986), *Peggy Seeger Songbook*, p. 205.

62. Ewan MacColl and Peggy Seeger, *Daddy, What Did You Do in the Strike?* (Cassette, BS1, Blackthorne, 1984).
63. Concert appearances included Sunderland on 13 June 1984, Newcastle on 30 June 1984, and Hounslow Miners' Support Group on 22 July 1984, where £1,000 was raised. Programme Books, MacColl/Seeger Archive.
64. Alex Callinicos and Mike Simons, *The Great Strike* (London: Socialist Worker), p. 197; unsigned, 'Thatcher sees pit victory within grasp', *Guardian*, 22 January 1985.
65. Neill MacColl, interview by author, 27 February 2006, London.
66. David Boulton, 'Song and Struggle', *Listener*, 9 November 1989, pp. 4–5, at p. 4.
67. Ewan MacColl, interview in Dave Boulton prod., *Daddy, What Did You Do in the Strike?*
68. Byron Rogers, 'Meet the Liver Boys', *Sunday Times*, 22 December 1985.
69. Richard Last, 'Simplistic Left Romantic', *Daily Telegraph*, 16 December 1985.
70. Robin Denselow, *When the Music's Over: The Story of Political Pop* (London: Faber & Faber, 1989), p. 226. Alan Sked and Chris Cook, *Post-War Britain: A Political History*, 4th edn (1979; London: Penguin, 1993), p. 458.
71. 'The Artist: Maker or Tool?', symposium programme, MacColl/Seeger Archive. Raymond Ross, 'Celebrating Ewan MacColl', *Glasgow Herald*, 4 March 1986.
72. Clips from the concerts were broadcast by BBC Radio 2 on 15 March 1986 and later issued on Ewan MacColl and Peggy Seeger, *Folk on 2* (CD, Mash CD002, BBC Radio2/Cooking Vinyl, 1996). The CD also features recordings made at MacColl and Seeger's English Folk Dance and Song Society Gold Badge award concert, recorded at Cecil Sharp House on 27 October 1987.
73. Philip Donnellan prod., *The Other Music: The Folk Song Revival 1945–1981*, BBC television, 1981. MacColl was interviewed for the programme.
74. Dave Harker, *One for the Money: Politics and Popular Song* (London: Hutchinson, 1980) and *Fakesong: The Manufacture of British Folksong from 1700 to the Present Day* (Milton Keynes: Open University Press, 1985). Subsequent critiques include Georgina Boyes, *The Imagined Village: Culture, Ideology and the English Folk Revival* (Manchester and New York: Manchester University Press, 1993) and Michael Brocken, *The British Folk Revival 1944–2002* (Aldershot: Ashgate, 2003).
75. 'Dave Harker talks of the revival as a Stalinist plot,' Karl Dallas later told me. 'Would that it had been. It would have been much more effective if we'd had the party behind us.' Interview by author, 22 October 2003, Bradford. MacColl alludes to Harker's 'shrill exposé of the folk revival' in *Journeyman*, p. 310.
76. Concert Programme, MacColl/Seeger Archive.
77. Neill MacColl, interview by author, 27 February 2006, London.
78. Dan James of Tower Hamlets TUC to MacColl and Seeger, 12 February 1986.

79. Billy Bragg, interview with Mike Harding. Mike Harding Show, Radio Two, 8 June 2005.
80. The Pogues, 'Dirty Old Town' (7-inch single, Stiff BUY243, Stiff Records, 1985). The track failed to reach the top fifty. It was included on their album *Rum, Sodomy and the Lash* (LP, SEEZ58, Stiff Records, 1985).
81. Denselow, *Music's Over*, p. 19.
82. Bragg recalls the occasion in O'Brien, *Kirsty MacColl*, p. 131.
83. Peggy Seeger, interview by author, 28 November 2005, Salford.
84. Denselow, *Music's Over*, p. 187.
85. Denselow, *Music's Over*, p. 191.
86. Ewan MacColl, 'The Ballad of Sharpeville', reprinted in Seeger, ed., *Essential Ewan MacColl Songbook*, p. 220; Peggy Seeger, 'I Support the Boycott', reprinted in *Peggy Seeger Songbook*, p. 64; Ewan MacColl, 'Black and White', reprinted in Seeger, ed., *Essential Ewan MacColl Songbook*, p. 236.
87. Ewan MacColl, 'White Wind, Black Tide', reprinted in Seeger, ed., *Essential Ewan MacColl Songbook*, p. 228.
88. Peggy Seeger, 'Festival of Fools Newsletter 9', nd [early January 1972].
89. Ewan MacColl, 'The Great Conspiracy', reprinted in Seeger, ed., *Essential Ewan MacColl Songbook*, p. 224.
90. Ewan MacColl, 'Ten Young Women and One Young Man', reprinted in Seeger, ed., *Essential Ewan MacColl Songbook*, p. 226.
91. Peggy Seeger to Hamish Henderson, 27 June 1986; Peggy Seeger, 'No More', reprinted in *Peggy Seeger Songbook*, p. 202.
92. Ewan MacColl and Peggy Seeger, *White Wind, Black Tide* (Cassette, BSC 2, Blackthorne, 1986); Tarin Brokenshire to Peggy Seeger, 24 March 1987.
93. MacColl in EFDSS Gold Badge Award Concert, Cecil Sharp House, 27 October 1987. Ewan MacColl and Peggy Seeger, *Folk on 2* (CD, Mash CD002, BBC Radio 2/Cooking Vinyl, 1996).
94. Ewan MacColl, 'The Joy of Living', in Seeger, ed., *Essential Ewan MacColl Songbook*, p. 372. First recorded on Peggy Seeger and Ewan MacColl, *Items of News* (LP, BR 1067, Blackthorne, 1986).
95. The song was first performed at a benefit for West London TUC on 14 September 1986.
96. Programme Books; 'Ewan MacColl', *Kvatch*, 6 (1987), pp. 16–19, at p. 18.
97. Minutes from Singers' Club meeting, 7 March 1986. MacColl/Seeger Archive.
98. Peggy Seeger and Ewan MacColl to Singers' Club Committee, 20 March 1987; minutes for meetings of 20 December 1987, 10 April 1988, 25 June 1989. MacColl/Seeger Archive.
99. Peggy Seeger to Jack Mitchell, 26 May 1987, 10 October 1987.
100. Peggy Seeger to D. R. Riley, 25 February 1987.
101. Calum MacColl, interview by author, 9 March 2006, London.
102. Barry Roderick to Ewan MacColl and Peggy Seeger, 11 November 1984. They gave four concerts in Juneau, Alaska in April 1987.
103. MacColl, *Journeyman*, pp. 3, 382.
104. Peggy Seeger, Introduction to *Journeyman*, p. 2.

105. Scott Alarik, 'Ewan MacColl: Finding the Common Thread', *Sing Out!*, 33.2 (Winter 1988), pp. 2–6, at p. 2.
106. Peggy Seeger, interview by author, 16 November 2003, York.
107. MacColl, *Journeyman*, pp. 171–5; Seeger, 'Ewan MacColl: the Songmaker' in Seeger, ed., *Essential Ewan MacColl Songbook*, p. 12.
108. MacColl, *Journeyman*, pp. 381, 148; also pp. 157–8, 75.
109. MacColl, *Journeyman*, p. 297.
110. Dianna Coles to Peggy Seeger, 19 January 1990.
111. MacColl, *Journeyman*, pp. 311–36. The chapter is a rewrite of MacColl's 'The Radio Ballads', *Sing Out!*, 17.2 (April–May 1967), pp. 6–15 to which MacColl added a passage from a second unpublished essay, also called 'The Radio Ballads', written in August 1981. The latter is held in the MacColl/ Seeger Archive and can also be read on www.pegseeger.com.
112. MacColl, *Journeyman*, p. 341.
113. MacColl, *Journeyman*, p. 309.
114. MacColl, *Journeyman*, pp. 343–55.
115. Peggy Seeger, Introduction to *Journeyman*, p. 2.
116. Calum MacColl, interview by author, 9 March 2006, London.
117. MacColl and Seeger gave a concert at Cecil Sharp House on 17 October 1987. Vic Gammon's award citation was reprinted in *English Dance and Song*, 49.3 (Christmas 1987), p. 7. The concert was later broadcast on BBC Radio 2 on 11 November 1987, and then issued on Ewan MacColl and Peggy Seeger, *Folk on 2* (CD, Mash CD002, BBC Radio2/Cooking Vinyl, 1996).
118. Peter Heathfield to Ewan MacColl and Peggy Seeger, 16 February 1987.
119. Neill MacColl, interview by author, 27 February 2006, London.
120. Recorded on Peggy Seeger and Ewan MacColl, *Items of News* (LP, BR 1067, Blackthorne, 1986). The song is reprinted in Seeger, ed., *Essential Ewan MacColl Songbook*, p. 98.
121. Calum MacColl, interview by author, 9 March 2006, London.
122. Peggy Seeger, Introduction to *Journeyman*, p. 5.
123. Seeger describes this period in interview with Ken Hunt, 'Peggy 'n' All', *fRoots*, 266/7 (August–September 2005), pp. 50–3.
124. Neill MacColl, interview by author, 27 February 2006, London.
125. Calum MacColl, interview by author, 9 March 2006, London.
126. Peggy Seeger in *Peggy Seeger Songbook*, p. 196.
127. Peggy Seeger, 'Ewan MacColl: The Songmaker' in Seeger, ed., *Essential Ewan MacColl Songbook*, p. 21.
128. MacColl, *Journeyman*, p. 381.
129. MacColl, *Journeyman*, pp. 388–9.
130. MacColl, *Journeyman*, pp. 356–77.
131. Willie Thompson, *The Good Old Cause: British Communism 1920–1991* (London: Pluto, 1992), pp. 197–9.
132. MacColl, *Journeyman*, p. 385.
133. MacColl, *Journeyman*, p. 386.
134. MacColl, *Journeyman*, p. 385.
135. Home video of MacColl, October 1989, sourced from Tim May prod., *The Ballad of Ewan MacColl*, BBC Television, 1990.

136. Peggy Seeger, interview by author, 28 November 2005, Salford.
137. Peggy Seeger, 'Ewan MacColl: The Songmaker' in Seeger, ed., *Essential Ewan MacColl Songbook*, p. 19.
138. Recorded shortly before MacColl's death, the final Ewan MacColl and Peggy Seeger album was issued in 1990: *Naming of Names: Topical Songs* (LP, CD, Cassette, Cook 036, Cooking Vinyl, 1990).
139. Peggy Seeger, e-mail to the author, 13 December 2006.
140. Raphael Samuel, 'Ewan MacColl 1915–1989', *History Workshop Journal*, 29 (Spring 1990), pp. 216–22, at p. 222.
141. Calum MacColl, interview by author, 9 March 2006, London.
142. *The Late Show*, BBC 2, 23 October 1989.
143. Unsigned, '"The People's Singer" MacColl dies aged 74', *Independent*, 24 October 1989; Unsigned, 'Ewan MacColl Dies', *New York Times*, 24 October 1989; Raphael Samuel, 'Ewan MacColl', *Independent*, 30 October 1989; Michael Grosvenor Myer, 'Breathing New Life into Folk Song and Theatre', *Guardian*, 24 October 1989; Norman Buchan, 'Ewan', *Morning Star*, 28 October 1989; unsigned, 'Ewan MacColl', *Daily Telegraph*, 24 October 1989; unsigned, 'Ewan MacColl', *The Times*, 24 October 1989.
144. Cited in unsigned, 'Ewan MacColl', *Folknick* (January–February 1990), p. 7.
145. Fintan O'Toole, 'Ewan MacColl, hero of many parts', *Irish Times*, 28 October 1989.
146. Correspondence in 'Memorials' file, MacColl/Seeger Archive.

# Index

Compiled by Sue Carlton

In sub-entries EM refers to Ewan MacColl